A Lover of God

SUNY series in Islam

Seyyed Hossein Nasr, editor

A Lover of God

The Ecstatic Sufi Nūrī

DORA ZSOM

SUNY
PRESS

Cover: "Dancing Dervishes." Folio from a Divan of Hafiz, ca. 1480. Painting attributed to Bihzad. Metropolitan Museum of Art. Rogers Fund, 1917

Published by State University of New York Press, Albany

Printed in the United States of America

For information, contact State University of New York Press, Albany, NY
www.sunypress.edu

Library of Congress Cataloging-in-Publication Data

Name: Zsom, Dora, author.
Title: A lover of god : The ecstatic Sufi Nūrī / Dora Zsom.
Description: Albany : State University of New York Press, [2024] | Series: SUNY series in Islam | Includes bibliographical references and index.
Identifiers: ISBN 9781438498430 (hardcover : alk. paper) | ISBN 9781438498447 (ebook) | ISBN 9781438498423 (pbk. : alk. paper)
Further information is available at the Library of Congress.

I dedicate this book to my teacher,
Tamás Iványi.

Contents

Acknowledgments		ix
Introduction		1
Chapter 1	Kalābādhī: Doctrine of the Sufis *(Kitāb al-taʿarruf)*	19
Chapter 2	Sarrāj: Book of Flashes *(Kitāb al-lumaʿ)*	49
Chapter 3	Sulamī: Generations of the Sufis *(Ṭabaqāt al-ṣūfiyya)*	81
Chapter 4	Sulamī: Realities of Interpretation *(Ḥaqā'iq al-tafsīr)*	101
Chapter 5	Kharkūshī: Revision of the Secrets *(Tahdhīb al-asrār)*	131
Chapter 6	Abū Nuʿaym: Ornament of God's Friends *(Ḥilyat al-awliyā')*	153
Chapter 7	Qushayrī: Treatise *(al-Risāla al-qushayriyya)*	165
Chapter 8	Sīrjānī: Black and White in the Words of Wisdom *(Kitāb al-bayāḍ wa-l-sawād)*	185
Chapter 9	Correspondence between Nūrī and Junayd Preserved in the Cairo Genizah	203

Chapter 10 Stations of the Hearts *(Maqāmāt al-qulūb)* 219

Chapter 11 Conclusions 243

Appendix A Arabic Texts 253

Appendix B Comparative Table of the Material Related to Nūrī 281

Appendix C Technical Terms 291

Notes 295

Bibliography 341

Index 349

Acknowledgments

I would like to express my gratitude for the support of my colleagues at the Department of Arabic, Eötvös Loránd University, Budapest. I am especially grateful to Professor István Ormos for reading an earlier draft of this book. I also thankfully acknowledge the work of the anonymous readers of this manuscript, whose remarks and suggestions helped me improve the text. Finally, I wish to recognize my enduring indebtedness to Professor Sarah Stroumsa, who first encouraged me to conduct research in the field of Sufism.

Introduction

Aim and Scope of the Study

Sufism is frequently described as having two main branches: moderate (or "sober"), and ecstatic (or "drunken"), which on the surface seem to be mutually exclusive categories. The original Arabic term meaning "drunkenness" or "intoxication" *(sukr)* is often rendered as "ecstasy" *(wajd)* in English scholarly usage, and "intoxicated Sufis" are usually referred to as "ecstatics." This usage is justified, and based on the Sufi conception of drunkenness, which sees an intrinsic connection between intoxication and ecstasy, as the most famous Sufi theoretician Qushayrī put it: "Drunkenness is exclusive to those who experience ecstasy."[1] The sober-drunken dichotomy as distinguishing between two rival groups was formulated originally by Hujwīrī (d. ca. 1074) and was adopted both by Sufi and Western authors.[2] However, in the first Sufi manuals these terms describe states of mind, or forms of behavior rather than opposing mystical trends. Sobriety and intoxication are alternate states that complement and mutually support each other, while ecstasy is a possible but not a necessary manifestation of spiritual drunkenness. Intoxicated ecstasy, which is a distinctive feature of Sufism, may induce bizarre forms of behavior unacceptable for the broader religious community. In fact, ever since the formative period of Sufism, one of its distinguishing marks from mainstream religiosity was its unconventionality finding expression in the activity of such eccentric figures as Ḥallāj and Abū Yazīd al-Bisṭāmī, who promptly gained the attention of the masses and scandalized the religious authorities. The history of Sufism abounds in such extraordinary personalities, some of them (temporarily, at least) expurgated from

Sufi tradition, while others integrated into it. One of these nonconformist mystics is Abū l-Ḥusayn al-Nūrī (d. 907/8), famous for his quasi-blasphemous utterances and shocking public behavior.

This study attempts to reveal how such a deviant figure is integrated into Sufi tradition, how his ecstatic utterances and eccentric behavior fit into the broader religious framework, and how complex the spirituality attributed to him is. The examination of Nūrī's relationship with his moderate companions, especially Junayd, reveals much about the group dynamics of early Sufi communities. However, the focus of the research is not Nūrī's historical personality but his divergent representations shaped by the distinct intentions of the authors who give accounts of him. The study seeks to add nuance to the oversimplified view of Nūrī that is often projected in his scholarly treatments.

Sufi compilations often mention Nūrī as a counterpart of his contemporary and friend, Junayd (d. 910), the emblematic figure of moderate, or "sober" Sufism. Despite a certain tension between them, which is obvious in most of the sources that contain traditions associated with both of them, it is evident that their relationship was friendly, even intimate; they frequently exchanged letters, engaged in discussions that were conducted occasionally in a heated tone, and they criticized and even reproved each other. They were more or less the same age; they followed divergent trends of mysticism, and their interaction does not betray a clear hierarchical relationship. Regardless of the fact that their approach to mysticism was markedly different—Nūrī being often enraptured by a passionate love of God, often succumbing to temptation and displaying outward signs of ecstasy, while Junayd constantly kept his moderate posture—they sought the company of each other, and Nūrī especially seemed to be drawn to Junayd. He asked for the latter's advice in various letters (some of which survive) and requested access to his mystical knowledge. Although no relation of master and disciple existed between them (both Junayd and Nūrī were the disciples of Sarī al-Saqaṭī), various sources attest that Nūrī subjected himself to Junayd's guidance—although such presentation of their relationship by the compilers of Sufi manuals, and biographical lexicons might have an apologetic objective, namely, to demonstrate that ecstatic, intoxicated Sufism is subordinate to moderate, sober Sufism. In any case, both of them belonged to the so-called mystical school of Baghdad—a term of Western scholarship distinguishing Baghdadi Sufis primarily from the mystics of Khorasan (especially Nishapur).[3] The Baghdadi Sufis, however, never applied such a term to themselves, and it is questionable whether they perceived themselves as belonging to the same "school." Muslim biographers may group together Sufis by geographical region and thus talk about the "sheikhs of Iraq" without necessarily considering them as following one particular trend, as members of an intellectual school certainly do.[4] According to Abdel Kader, the peculiar themes of the school of Baghdad are *shaṭaḥāt* (ecstatic utterances), *ʿibāda* (worship of God), and *lisān* (tongue),[5] and these are indeed characteristic of Nūrī's sayings as well. Nevertheless, some of Nūrī's ideas (and especially his behavior) are so different, even totally opposite to those of Junayd, that it is difficult to conceive them as representatives of the same school of thought. Although the early sources do not mention disciples of Nūrī by name, Abū Nuʿaym's *Ornament of God's Friends* references his close companions; and Hujwīrī enlists the "Nūrīs," the followers of Nūrī among the ten accepted sects of Sufism.[6] According to Hujwīrī, the Nūrīs are characterized by attaching great importance to favoring others over oneself *(īthār)*, by regarding mysticism *(taṣawwuf)* as superior to poverty *(faqr)*, and companionship *(ṣuḥba)* as superior to seeking isolation *(ʿuzla)*. Moreover, Hūjwīrī states that concerning norms of conduct, Nūrī has much in common with Junayd, which might seem surprising given their totally contradictory behavior, for example, with regard to exhibiting or hiding ecstasy.

The two divergent branches of Baghdadi mystics, sober and intoxicated Sufis, are exemplified in Western scholarship mainly by Junayd and Ḥallāj (d. 922) respectively; both Junayd and Ḥallāj have received much scholarly interest, while the figure of Nūrī has remained vague and undefined. That is all the more regrettable since the type of intoxicated or ecstatic mysticism Nūrī represents is markedly different from the spirituality of Ḥallāj, the archetypal intoxicated Sufi figure. A meticulous study of Nūrī's teachings and personality may cast light on the nature and inner dynamics of the so-called mystical school of Baghdad.

In Western scholarship, Nūrī is best known for his poems and short, gnomic sayings; for his brave and unselfish conduct in facing the death sentence because of the accusations of Ghulām Khalīl; and for his extraordinary (and legendary) end when he bled to death from wounds caused by his ecstatic wandering in a freshly cut field of reeds while repeating a line from a love poem. Scholars usually introduce him as one of God's "lovers," who takes pleasure in suffering and unrequited love that tempts him even to apparently blameworthy acts,[7] or as an ecstatic Sufi par excellence known for his altered states of mind.[8] In general, it can be said that the representation of Nūrī is too simplistic in Western scholarship, each researcher selecting and expounding upon those narratives that narrowly serve the authors' theses. In most cases, they simply ignore the surprisingly great number of moderate, even theoretical sayings that are recorded under his name in the Sufi collections, and concentrate instead on the eccentric facets of his spirituality. Naturally, this tendency is understandable in the case of scholarly works that do not discuss Nūrī as their main subject but treat him only tangentially.

Besides the studies that discuss Nūrī briefly or incidentally, mention must be made of two scholarly works that deal extensively with Nūrī's legacy: those written by Paul Nwyia and Richard Gramlich. Nwyia based his discussion almost entirely on a treatise attributed to Nūrī, entitled *The Stations of the Hearts (Maqāmāt al-qulūb)*, which is preserved in four manuscripts in Istanbul (two of them were copied in the nineteenth century, and two of them were undated).[9] Nwyia, who published the treatise, never called into question Nūrī's authorship, although the fact that no part of the treatise is quoted in the early sources, and no reference can be found in these sources to a similar treatise (or any other kind of treatise) attributed to Nūrī, evidently casts doubt on the authenticity of the text. Nwyia did not study Nūrī's sayings scattered in early Sufi compilations, nor did he compare that corpus with the *Stations of the Hearts*, in order to see whether its terms and ideas in general are in line with the sayings. It must be remarked that Nūrī's one and only saying about the mystical parts of the heart *(qalb)*, quoted in one of the early sources, is incompatible with the structure of the heart described in the *Stations of the Hearts*.[10] On the other hand, the exposition in the *Stations of the Hearts* shows an obvious similarity to al-Ḥakīm al-Tirmīdhī's (d. ca. 932) treatise on the structure and parts of the heart.[11] It might be suggested that an anonymous treatise modeled partly on al-Ḥakīm al-Tirmīdhī's work was attributed to Nūrī due to an association between Nūrī and the heart *(qalb)*, which recurs in his epithets. Junayd calls him "commander of the hearts" *(amīr al-qulūb)*, while Sīrjānī refers to him as "the support of the hearts" *(sanad al-qulūb)*.[12] On the other hand, the term *nūr* (meaning "light"), evoking the name of Nūrī (meaning "luminous"), occurs in the treatise with great frequency, which might contribute to its attribution to him.

Nūrī's biography was reconstructed in detail by Gramlich on the basis of dozens of sources ranging from the tenth to the seventeenth century.[13] It is beyond question that Gramlich's contribution is enormous, for he gathered information from an extraordinarily wide range of sources both in Arabic and in Persian. However, when combining the information scattered in the numerous sources to one coherent account of Nūrī's life, Gramlich did not wish to offer a diachronic perspective of the material, marking the distinctions between the sources dating from different periods; apparently, he regarded the latest sources to be just as authentic as the earliest ones. Neither did he take interest in questions of genre or the wider context of the literary works, such as their overt or disguised purpose, which usually affects the mode and the content of the representation to a certain extent. He gave virtually no attention to the inconsistency of the narratives, which is most obvious in the case of Nūrī's death, which according to one narrative occurred in a reedbed, while according to another took place in the Shūnīzīyya mosque; the circumstances of his death are even more varied than its actual location.

Gramlich also collected and interpreted Nūrī's sayings, poems, and anecdotes about him that are scattered in the various sources. The lack of a diachronic perspective is characteristic of Gramlich's presentation of Nūrī's ideas as well; he sketches Nūrī's portrait and outlines his teachings, taking into account the totality of the sources, without making a distinction between earlier and later ones or paying attention to the context of the works in which the traditions are found. Consequently, he presents a picture that results from a combination of sources very distant both in genre and in time: a picture that would never arise from one specific source and that in fact never existed as such in any given historical period.

Naturally, another way of approaching Nūrī's figure can be offered, and that is my intention here. It might be of interest to study the sources one by one, comparing the material contained in them in order to determine the difference between the distinct personalities of Nūrī that emerges. The divergence of the sources manifests itself not only in the discrepancy of the material they comprise but also in the different ways of presenting the limited number of traditions shared among them and the key Sufi technical terms they employ.

Obviously, one cannot expect that as a result of such study the true historical figure of Nūrī could be revealed, or that the authentic corpus of his teachings and literary production could be determined; authenticity was not among the foremost concerns of authors and compilers of the early sources themselves, who were apparently more devoted to the content than obsessed with the form.

The purpose of this study, thus, is disclosing and understanding the complex spirituality attributed to such a mystical character as Nūrī, rather than unearthing a historical figure hidden beneath multiple layers of legendary traditions. As we do not think that the sources are reconcilable, we wish to examine in the first place the discrepancies between the portrayals in the different sources. Evidently, a source betrays as much about itself as it communicates about its subject, and this peculiarity should be considered when studying the content it offers. For this reason, the chapter division of this book is based on the sources it explores, and each chapter discusses all the material the given source contains about Nūrī, rejecting a selective method focusing on some information and ignoring others. An evident advantage of studying the sources one by one as opposed to opting for a chapter division based on subject matter is that the context of the traditions is preserved in this manner, which obviously contributes to the in-depth analysis of said traditions. A more comprehensive and deeper understanding of the deliberately ambiguous mystical traditions is the first priority of this study, and such an endeavor necessitates being aware of both the broad and the immediate contexts each compiler creates.

The examination of Nūrī's image as created in the various sources negates the superficial approach that supposes that an ecstatic mystic par excellence like Nūrī would display only (or mostly) drunken or extreme forms of behavior. While Nūrī's position in the drunken-sober, extreme-conservative, or ecstatic-moderate dichotomy is beyond question, since both his contemporaries and the later authors classify him among the drunken ecstatics, many of the traditions related to him do not show any distinctively "drunken" feature. It is among the objectives of this study to consider Nūrī's literary legacy from the aspect of the drunken-sober pair of qualities as well. What proportion of the traditions related to him displays the characteristics of drunken mysticism in fact? Does his extreme manifestations outnumber his perfectly sober or moderate sayings and acts? And how do we differentiate between drunken and sober qualities? For the answer to the latter question, we must turn to the Sufis: both to Nūrī's contemporaries and to later authors. Sometimes they explicitly identify some of Nūrī's acts or words as "drunken" or "ecstatic." For example, Junayd describes Nūrī as one of the ecstatics *(arbāb al-mawājīd),* and states that he is "not sober";[14] Sarrāj introduces Nūrī as "one of the ecstatics" *(wājidūn)*[15]—but mostly the distinction must be made on the basis of the authors' general discussions on intoxication and sobriety. For the sake of this study, the following peculiarities are regarded as "drunken": displaying ecstasy either verbally or nonverbally (as opposed to hiding enrapture); extraordinary sayings (*shaṭaḥāt*); use of controversial vocabulary (e.g., *ʿishq,* "passionate love"); inclination to participate in mystical concerts or recitals *(samāʿ)* inducing ecstasy. As will be shown in the study, the line between drunken and sober is not always clear, and even the same saying or event may be communicated in different ways depending on the source.

Finally, it must be said that the terms "drunken," "ecstatic," and "extreme" on the one hand, and "sober," "conservative" and "moderate" on the other, are used synonymously in this study since the use of these terms has become a convention in modern scholarship, as Mojaddedi has already pointed out.[16]

The Sources Studied

Not all the sources that mention Nūrī have been consulted; Persian, or non-Sufi works were not studied. The choice of the sources was conditioned primarily by their originality, that is, the uniqueness of the material related to Nūrī they contain. Thus, preference was given to the early sources, including the most representative and better-known works written in the formative period of Sufism.

But the study includes a recently published source on the eleventh century as well since it contains much new material. Early sources that did not collect traditions attributed to Nūrī save one or two sayings (like Makkī's *Qūt al-qulūb,* for example), are not included in this study.[17] From the eleventh century, sources mostly repeat what had already been collected, sometimes adding details here and there to make the traditions more comprehensible, or to put them in a required context; they also provide miraculous narratives and pious topoi; as a result, the proportion of sayings in Nūrī's name versus narratives about him shifts in favor of the latter. In general, the overlap between later and earlier sources is considerable; therefore, later sources have remained outside the confines of this study. Nevertheless, two later texts of somehow disputable authenticity are included, a treatise and a letter; neither of them has been translated into English before, and one of them has not been published until now, even in Arabic. The reason for their inclusion is their incongruity with the rest of the sources containing detached, scattered traditions that are purported to have been transmitted orally in the beginning. As opposed to these short sayings, poems, and anecdotes, the two longer texts are considered writings of Nūrī himself, and consequently their structure and style differs completely from the former texts. Our expectation is that in light of the divergent sources, a complex image emerges that tells us a lot about what each author and generation thought to be attributable to such an extraordinary personality as Nūrī, regarded mostly as a representative of the extreme, passionate trend of Sufism.

Sufi Manuals and Biographies

The study covers seven of the earliest works in which traditions attributed to Nūrī appear. These are the following: *Doctrine of the Sufis (Kitāb al-taʿarruf li-madhhab ahl al-taṣawwuf)* by Abū Bakr al-Kalābādhī (d. 990/995); *Book of Flashes (Kitāb al-lumaʿ fī l-taṣawwuf)* by Abū Naṣr al-Sarrāj (d. 988);[18] *Generations of the Sufis (Ṭabaqāt al-ṣūfiyya)* by Abū ʿAbd al-Raḥmān al-Sulamī (d. 1021);[19] *Revision of the Secrets (Tahdhīb al-asrār)* by ʿAbd al-Malik al-Kharkūshī (d. 1015/1016);[20] *Ornament of God's Friends (Ḥilyat al-awliyā')* by Abū Nuʿaym al-Iṣfahānī (d. 1038); *Treatise (al-Risāla al-qushayriyya)* by Abū l-Qāsim al-Qushayrī (d. 1072);[21] and *Black and White in the Words of Wisdom (Kitāb al-bayāḍ wa-l-sawād min khaṣā'iṣ ḥikam al-ʿibād fī naʿt al-murīd wa-l-murād)* by Abū l-Ḥasan al-Sīrjānī (d. ca. 1077).[22] Although exact dates of composition are not available for most of the sources, all of them were surely composed within a hundred-year period, between the late tenth and late eleventh centuries.

These sources altogether contain more than a hundred traditions attributed to Nūrī, a quarter of which are poems and the rest being short sayings and anecdotes.[23] Not one of the traditions is quoted in all the seven compilations, or even in six of them. More than half of the traditions are quoted in one of the studied sources only. This obviously raises the question of the authenticity of the traditions and the accuracy of the picture that emerges from each of the compilations, let alone the verity of Nūrī's portrayal as sketched by combining all the information contained in the sources. Traditions collected in the earliest sources are not necessarily more authentic than those quoted in works compiled some decades later; and the fact that a saying is quoted and attributed to Nūrī in various sources does not in itself prove that it is more original than another found in a single source only.

The textual overlap between the sources is not significant in the case of the six earliest works; the number of shared traditions in any two of these is usually three to four, but it may be only one, or even none.[24] On the other hand, Sīrjānī's *Black and White in the Words of Wisdom* contains numerous traditions shared between it and the six earlier sources.

A Sufi Commentary on the Quran

Besides the manuals and the biographical lexicons, the discussion includes Sulamī's *Realities of Interpretation (Ḥaqā'iq al-tafsīr),* one of the earliest mystical commentaries of the Quran.[25] In theory, the genre of a commentary differs substantially from that of the collections of sayings, but in practice a marked overlap may be observed between the two sources. Early Sufi commentaries include plenty of maxims and short sayings similar or identical with those collected in the biographical lexicons and theoretical works on

Sufism. It may be supposed that such maxims were linked with the Quranic passages posteriorly, without having direct relation to the verses they "comment" upon. It might be interesting to investigate the proportion of this kind of secondary material within the full corpus in comparison with genuine comments intended as such from the outset. Although the connection between the Quranic text and the comments (genuine or secondary) cannot be always determined with certainty, proportions can evidently be perceived. The *Realities of Interpretation* contains some thirty sayings of Nūrī, six of which are attested to also in the manuals and biographies discussed above—but none of them in Sulamī's *Generations of the Sufis*. The rest of the traditions transmitted in Nūrī's name appears to represent in equal measure actual comments on the one hand and sayings constructed as such posteriorly on the other: roughly half of the traditions are mystical interpretations of Quranic verses closely connected with the passages, and half of them seem to be completely independent from the sacred text originally.

MS Taylor-Schechter Arabic 41.1

In addition to these compilations, the study extends to a hitherto unpublished manuscript from the Cairo Genizah, now preserved in the Cambridge University Library (Taylor-Schechter Arabic 41.1). The manuscript is a remnant of a Sufi anthology containing, among other texts, a correspondence between Nūrī and Junayd on the subject of tribulation *(balā')*. Reference to this specific correspondence can be found in Sarrāj's *Book of Flashes*, but in all likelihood it did not survive save in the fragment preserved in the Cairo Genizah. The manuscript is undated but was most probably copied between the eleventh and the thirteenth centuries. Unfortunately, it is fragmentary and in some places barely legible. Despite that, the seven folios of the text (containing about twenty-five lines per folio) constitute a relatively large portion of Nūrī's oeuvre, assuming of course that we accept the authenticity of the correspondence preserved in the manuscript. Doubts regarding the authenticity of the traditions attributed to Nūrī can be rightly entertained even in case of his sayings and poems collected in the earlier sources, however, and for that reason it does not seem to be reasonable to exclude this unique, medieval manuscript from the study.

Stations of the Hearts

The *Stations of the Hearts (Maqāmāt al-qulūb)* is a brief treatise attributed to Nūrī, which describes the inner structure of the heart conceptualized as concentric spheres corresponding to spiritual domains of ever-increasing mystical levels. The treatise expounds on several allegories of the heart, among them the "house," the "seven (concentric) fortresses" besieged by the Satan, the "ten gardens," and the "three seas." The colorful imagery of the descriptions differs substantially both from the concise style of Nūrī's sayings and the intimate (and frequently passionate) tone of his poems.[26]

Some Methodological Observations, the Use of Sufi Commentaries

Although two of the sources, Kalābādhī's *Doctrine of the Sufis* and Qushayrī's *Treatise,* have already been translated into English by Arthur John Arberry and Alexander D. Knysh, respectively, their terminology is neither entirely compatible with each other's nor with the terminology proposed in this book, and consequently a new translation was necessary for the purpose of this study. Naturally, the scholarly translations of Arberry and Knysh were consulted throughout the work, and the same holds true of the available Muslim commentaries on the sources. I have made every effort to translate the Arabic texts as close to their literal meaning and their peculiar way of expression as possible. I deliberately refused to follow both a phenomenological approach (replacing the original Sufi technical terms with etic terms drawn especially from Christian religious language) and the temptation of conforming to the requirements of belles lettres, which was especially strong in the case of Nūrī's poetical production. Obviously, I am aware that other approaches would have been possible, and I do not deny the legitimacy of phenomenological studies, let alone that of literary translations. In any case, for an artistic translation of the poems the reader is directed to Arthur John Arberry's work. The purpose of this study, however, is a deep intellectual understanding of the traditions attributed to Nūrī, and that requires the preservation of the original phraseology of the texts insofar as possible, even if it results in translations that are not pleasing from an artistic point of view. For that reason, Sufi terms are translated systematically, aiming at preserving the original or common meaning of the words that in Sufi usage became endowed with special significance, without, however, losing their ordinary sense. Sufis frequently play with double meanings of the words employed in the texts. The effort to preserve the original phraseology involves translating words derived from the same root with English equivalents likewise derived from the same root, even if it produces odd constructions or repetition that might not satisfy Western literary tastes. Naturally, practical considerations may overrule theoretical principles established as general rules, and therefore, where such a solution was impossible for any reason, the original Arabic term is always indicated. On the other hand, for the sake of legibility, I found it necessary to omit formulas of blessing that accompany the name of God and that of the Prophet Muhammad.

As for the interpretation of the texts, I follow the example of Carl W. Ernst, who composed his masterpiece on Sufi ecstatic expressions relying on the commentaries of Sufi mystics rather than on his own conjectures, "since I do not, for the purposes of this study, claim any sort of esoteric knowledge"[27]—as he put it. Therefore, the explication of the texts related to Nūrī takes into consideration the Muslim commentaries when these were accessible. Commentaries necessarily come later than the text they comment on; this is an inherent and inevitable characteristic of the genre. Naturally, they reflect the Sufi milieu and the intellectual conventions, tendencies of their specific era to a great extent. However, not all material the commentaries contain is obviously contemporary with their compilers. On the contrary, Muslim authors tended to collect and divulge the knowledge accumulated in the course of the preceding centuries, and a given commentary in most cases can be considered as the last phase in an uninterrupted chain of interpretational tradition. For this reason, commentaries written in the fourteenth, fifteenth, or even nineteenth centuries are far from being irrelevant for the interpretation of traditions recorded in the tenth to eleventh centuries, especially if earlier commentaries are not available.

Kalābādhī's *Doctrine of the Sufis* is discussed in light of ʿAlā al-Dīn ʿAlī ibn Ismāʿīl al-Qūnawī's (d. 1329) commentary entitled *Ḥusn al-taṣarruf fī sharḥ kitāb al-taʿarruf li-madhhab ahl al-taṣawwuf.*

The manuscript copy I studied is preserved in the Österreichische Nationalbibliothek (MS Cod.N.F.289), and according to its colophon it was copied in 1831.[28] The commentary clearly shows that Qūnawī was an original thinker whose comments are not limited to the mere elucidation of the subject treated and to the clarification of the saying under question; his commentary also extends to a comprehensive analysis of the concepts mentioned that often surpasses the scope of the saying he comments on. It is not an exaggeration to say that his comments are frequently short essays that might be read independently of the text commented upon. For the interpretation of Qushayrī's *Treatise* I availed myself of the commentary entitled *Aḥkām al-dalāla ʿalā taḥrīr al-risāla,* written in 1488 by Zakariyyā al-Anṣārī, and I used also the *Natāʾij al-afkār al-qudsiyya fī bayān maʿānī sharḥ al-Risāla al-qushayriyya,* which is a supercommentary on that of Zakariyyā al-Anṣārī, written in 1854 by Muṣṭafā Muḥammad al-ʿArūsī.[29] These are less ingenious than Qūnawī's commentary and in most cases do not extend beyond basic explications. Despite that, they were very useful for interpreting the text, which in the case of mystical literature is never obvious. Commentaries are not available for the remainder of the sources studied here; therefore I always discuss the traditions they contain in close connection with both their immediate and broader contexts. In the case of theoretical manuals like Sarrāj's *Book of Flashes* or Qushayrī's *Treatise,* traditions are interpreted focusing on the main concepts they are related to. If the compilation's author covered these concepts in his work, then they are explained in light of the compiler's exposition. I always translated or summarized the remarks of the compilers on the sayings or poems they quoted; such remarks or comments were, however, extremely infrequent. Pure biographical works, like Sulamī's *Generations of the Sufis,* or Abū Nuʿaym's *Ornament of God's Friends* do not include theoretical discussions, let alone reviews of Sufi vocabulary and ideas. Therefore, I discussed the traditions in light of the interpretative context created by the compiler through his peculiar way of arranging these traditions: for example, presenting some of them as belonging together, forming a continuous narrative; or, on the contrary, detaching texts that might well be interrelated. I give special attention to the Sufi technical terms occurring in each collection, and the frequency of the specific terms and their peculiar usages are indicated. This might help us to understand how mystical expression changed and developed toward standardization in the early period of Sufism. That kind of survey is limited to the earliest compilations that do not significantly overlap textually; Sīrjānī's manual, however, which is based mainly on the previous sources, is not studied from this point of view. The genre of Sulamī's commentary on the Quran, Nūrī's and Junayd's correspondence preserved in the Cairo Genizah, and the *Stations of the Hearts* attributed to Nūrī differ substantially from his short sayings collected in the biographical lexicons and manuals, and this divergence is reflected in their terminology as well.

Each chapter of the book is dedicated to a separate source in which traditions related to Nūrī are gathered. In order to distinguish between the text of the traditions attributed to Nūrī and their discussion, the translations of the source texts related to Nūrī are block quotations.

Social, Religious, and Historical Context

It has already been noted that the historical authenticity of the Sufi sources is problematic since this aspect was completely irrelevant for the authors (or editors or composers). As Mojaddedi, Avery, and others have already argued, the purpose of the traditions is not to record historical facts but to transmit a knowledge revealing something from the mystical reality.[30] The biographies of Sufi masters were not conceived as accurate documentation but as models for imitation and inspiration, or at least as archetypes of divergent approaches in the Sufi path. Despite that, some elements of the contemporary historical reality of tenth-century Iraq may show up in the narratives.

Nūrī's activity coincided with the decline of the Abbasid caliphate and an age of turmoil both in the empire and in Baghdad. From the end of the ninth century, the Abbasid military power suffered gradual deterioration as a consequence of the introduction of foreign troops, and the decentralization of the empire began due to the practice of farming out the provinces to military commanders who developed into almost independent provincial governors. Baghdad lost its position as an administrative center in 836, when the caliph moved the capital to Samarra. During this period, Baghdad was besieged and raided; many of its quarters were destroyed. In 892, the caliph Muʿtamid restored the central position of the city, renewed official buildings, and built new palaces. Abbasid society was characterized by extensive economic and commercial activity that led to the unprecedented luxury of the upper classes and by a certain religious and moral laxity (indulgence in alcohol and sexual practices related both to female slaves and effeminate young boys), which provoked criticism in the forms of both the revolutionary violence of religious sects and in the ascetical, mystical doctrines of the Sufis. The rising religious movements (Shīʿites, Qarmaṭians, Ismāʿīlites, etc.) acted as centrifugal forces promoting the disintegration of the empire. Social injustice and deprivation led to uprisings with religious overtones, like the sanguineous rebellion of the Zanj slaves that lasted fourteen years (870–883). The caliphs imposed their religious views on the subjects by instituting the inquisition *(miḥna)*.[31] The caliph Ma'mūn was the first to establish the inquisition in 833, in order to enforce the doctrines of the rationalistic Muʿtazila movement that he promulgated as the official religious ideology of the state. The religious persecution lasted more than a decade (from 833 until 848 or 852).[32] Among its famous victims was the founder of the strictest traditionalist school of law, the Baghdadi Aḥmad ibn Ḥanbal, who was imprisoned for years and flogged several times. He refrained from teaching publicly until the inquisition was finally abolished. Less than half a century later, one of his followers, the Ḥanbalī Ghulām Khalīl, turned the caliphal regent al-Muwaffaq against the mystics of Baghdad, who now became the target of an inquisitorial process (877/878), called as such (i.e., *miḥna)* by the Sufis.[33] Nūrī was among those denounced, and although he was released eventually, according to some reports he fled to Raqqa in Syria and spent a period there in self-imposed exile, during which he lost not only his followers but also his physical health.[34] This was not unprecedented at all: in the formative period of Sufism, many mystics had to face similar consequences of their teaching and public activity. Sufism, which "on the surface violated the dogmatic creedal formulations of the religious establishment"[35] provoked hostile responses, possibly as a result of both the religious and the political tensions that characterized the historical period.[36]

While historical events are not mentioned normally in Sufi teachings, sayings, and edifying anecdotes, some peculiarities of the Abbasid society, even episodes of historical relevance surface in the traditions related to Nūrī. Naturally, the most important among these is the inquisition provoked by the denunciations of Ghulām Khalīl, and the consequences of the trial that show certain similarities to Aḥmad ibn Ḥanbal's withdrawal of public activity.[37] Nūrī's relation to the caliphs is a recurring and ambiguous theme: the central religious authority is distressing and threatening, but no injustices are committed in the end. Moreover, in some instances the caliph (or its representative) seems to support Nūrī either in words or by financial means. The outcome of the interrogations is invariably the same: formal recognition of Nūrī's orthodoxy. The caliph may also endorse Baghdadi Sufis financially by ordering Nūrī to distribute it among them.[38] It should be repeated that the historicity of such reports cannot be verified, as the question of historical authenticity was absolutely irrelevant for the transmitters of the Sufi traditions and teachings. Some traditions reveal homosexual inclinations not alien to the manners of Abbasid society: Nūrī's relation to young men seems to be more than mere sympathy. Besides the (sometimes implicit) content of such reports, some explicit expressions that describe the events as "courting,"[39] or refer to a young man who "conquered the heart"[40] of Nūrī, evidence such inclinations.

Besides these fragmentary details that reflect the everyday reality of Abbasid society, some small pieces of information relevant to Nūrī's living conditions may also be gathered from the sources. These pieces of information should not be regarded necessarily as facts but rather as a kind of spiritual authenticity rather than historical verity. According to a report preserved by Qushayrī, Nūrī had a shop in the market of Baghdad. At the beginning of his mystical vocation, he used to hide his piety from his family. For twenty years, he left his house in the morning, spent the forenoon in the mosque, then went to the market and opened his shop. During all this time he was fasting: his family thought he was eating at the market, while everyone else thought he was eating at home.[41] He also owned an estate: a "piece of land," which he sold and threw its price to the canal (the same story is reported about the contemporary Shiblī, as well).[42] Finally, he had a maidservant, who served also Abū Ḥamza and Junayd, and apparently belonged to the Sufi community in some way.[43]

CHAPTER 1

Kalābādhī

Doctrine of the Sufis *(Kitāb al-taʿarruf)*

Introduction

Kalābādhī's (d. 990/995) *Kitāb al-taʿarruf li-madhhab ahl al-taṣawwuf (Doctrine of the Sufis)*[1] is one of the earliest sources in which Nūrī's ideas were preserved. Kalābādhī's compilation is a manual that summarizes and explains the basic tenets of Sufism in a polemical vein. At the time of its composition Sufi ideas were attacked as heretical. The author, Abū Bakr al-Kalābādhī, was a Ḥanafī jurist who also composed a commentary on Prophetic traditions (entitled *Baḥr al-fawā'id fī maʿānī l-akhbār*) that survived in various manuscripts.[2] According to Massignon, he was a disciple of Abū l-Qāsim Fāris al-Dīnawarī (d. 957), a follower of Ḥallāj,[3] and indeed Kalābādhī quotes Fāris several times in his Sufi manual: he introduces the quotes with the remark "I heard Fāris say," which evidences the direct relationship between them.[4] Kalābādhī might not have been a Sufi master himself (there is no evidence that he had any disciples) but obviously had firsthand knowledge of Sufism. He wished to defend Sufism against the charges of heterodoxy, presumably against those suspicions that were aroused due to Ḥallāj's controversial activity. Kalābādhī cites Ḥallāj extensively, albeit without mentioning his name; moreover, in Arberry's view, he did "missionary propaganda on his behalf" by making his views circulate.[5]

The *Doctrine of the Sufis* is a general introduction to the mystical sciences, which places this peculiar branch of Islam within the frame of the orthodox religious system. It explains the basic tenets of Sufism, their technical vocabulary, the stations of the mystical way, and the spiritual states the wayfarer experiences. As for its structure, it is basically a collection of sayings by Sufi masters arranged by topic. Kalābādhī rarely interprets the traditions gathered, for mostly they are to be understood from the context in light of the collected sayings themselves. Many poems are inserted in the text that reinforce and illustrate the exposition of each topic in a poetical and hence more intuitive way than the prose text.

It is not the aim of the *Doctrine of the Sufis* to introduce the individual Sufis and characterize their special approach to mysticism, placing them in specific lines of thought by presenting a summary of their teachings. Kalābādhī wished to create a coherent exposition of each topic he discussed without seeking to gather a "representative selection" of the individual Sufis' ideas. Consequently, the traditions related to Nūrī are scattered throughout the work, and their selection is conditioned by their relevance to the subject topics of the manual rather than by the purpose of portraying his personality and advancing his teachings. Kalābādhī quoted about twenty traditions related to Nūrī, which means that the information regarding him is quite scarce: it does not exceed nine sayings, two anecdotes, and ten poems. The sayings are short and enigmatic, and the poems are usually even more obscure. The interpretation of the texts draws on the commentary written by ʿAlā al-Dīn ʿAlī ibn Ismāʿīl al-Qūnawī (d. 1329), entitled *Ḥusn al-taṣarruf fī sharḥ kitāb al-taʿarruf li-madhhab ahl al-taṣawwuf.* Before Qūnawī, Ismāʿīl al-Mustamlī composed a commentary on the *Doctrine of the Sufis* in Persian, probably before the year 1310. However, since Persian sources are not included in this monograph, his commentary was not consulted.[6] For the detailed justification of using Sufi commentaries composed centuries after Nūrī's death in general, and the commentary of Qūnawī in particular, see the introduction to this monograph.[7]

Sufism

The *Doctrine of the Sufis,* similarly to other such manuals, starts with a discussion on the meaning of Sufism. The definitions the individual masters offer are never theoretical, advancing a theological doctrine; on the contrary, they always emphasize practical aspects of the mystical way.[8] Their dictions are normally very concise, focusing on a single feature of the spiritual quest. The definitions are by no means aimed to be mutually exclusive; each approach is considered valid and commensurate with the other. From among Nūrī's sayings on Sufism, Kalābādhī choses to include here a statement about divesting oneself from the needs and desires of the carnal soul.

> Abū l-Ḥusayn al-Nūrī was asked: "What is Sufism?" He replied: "To renounce what belongs to the carnal soul (*nafs*)."[9]

Nafs is a basic term of Sufism. Its common meaning is double: on the one hand, it means "soul," but it also functions as a reflexive pronoun denoting the self. The constant struggle against the *nafs* is one of the fundamental tenets of Sufism shared by all of its branches. *Nafs* embodies the lower instincts of man, including sensual appetites but also negative character traits like malice, envy, conceitedness, wrath, impatience, and more subtle vices like indulging in (selfish) acts of piety or hypocrisy. *Nafs* is frequently associated with wild animals (snake, fox), or untamed domestic animals (dog, horse, camel), seductive women, and the like. The untrained *nafs* is the unrestrained, egocentric aspect of man. Sufi discipline aims to train and dominate the lower self. Purifying the self consists in gradually reducing the selfish actions of the *nafs*, diminishing one's lower character traits and developing instead those qualities that enable man to draw closer to God. The ultimate goal is to eliminate one's own character traits and to "clothe oneself" with the divine attributes. The *nafs* is dominated and tamed with physical exercises, like fasting or night vigils, and by spiritual discipline, like acts of humility and self-degradation. The carnal soul *(nafs)* is the counterpart of the spirit *(rūḥ)*; while the former is the source of the blameworthy character traits, the latter is associated with praiseworthy qualities, and it is the seat of love *(maḥabba)*.[10] Qūnawī's comment on Nūrī's saying takes the idea of renouncing the desires of the *nafs* much further, stating that the *nafs* must be ultimately eliminated: "If your self *(nafs)* does not die, your heart will not live."[11] The reason is that *nafs* is treacherous and tends to deceive man, giving the false impression of being obedient while following its own inclinations. Therefore, man should be suspicious of himself and should strive for eliminating every trace belonging to the carnal self.

Another saying of Nūrī is also relevant with regard to the definition of Sufism:

> What characterizes the poor (*faqīr*) is calmness when he has nothing, and spending freely, preferring others [to himself] when he has something.[12]

The saying is quoted in several collections as the characterization of the Sufi, evidencing that *faqīr* ("poor") and *ṣūfī* ("Sufi") became interchangeable terms early on.[13] According to the Sufi approach, poverty—or the lack of goods and means—is not a goal in itself but rather a quality that helps man to experience his dependence on God. Poverty is not limited to renouncing material properties but includes abandoning everything that connects man to the world or even to himself. The aim is to reach perfect "need of God" *(iftiqār ilā Allāh)*, dependence upon God. Material poverty is a phase of the spiritual quest that ultimately must be superseded. A person who achieved his ambition to be free from the desire of possession may even own properties since that does not affect his intrinsic independence of ownership. This idea is also expressed by Qūnawī, according to whom poverty liberates man from the burden of possessions, which might divert him from concentrating on God. "By choosing what subsists *(al-bāqī)* he may give away what passes away *(al-fānī)*."[14] Qūnawī plays with the opposite meanings of "subsists" and "passes away," which is a frequent literary technique, especially in Arabic poetry, and much employed in mystical language. His statement is paradoxical; it advises against striving for lasting, enduring aims and encourages the pursuit of that which vanishes. "Subsisting" and "passing away" have opposite connotations in common usage, unlike their technical meanings in Sufi terminology. Striving for what (apparently) subsists would seem commonsensical, yet it is rejected by mystical thinking. Persisting things are valueless in the face of annihilation, which is the only way that leads to the Eternal. Qūnawī cites a parallel of Nūrī's saying that emphasizes the dangers of ownership: "What characterizes the poor is calmness when he has nothing, and worrying when he has something."[15] The inclination of the carnal soul toward welfare and comfort may divert man from God and may attract him to worldly delights. According to Qūnawī, that is the reason of the Prophet's saying: "I do not have fears for you because of poverty, but I do fear that the world may offer itself to you as it has offered itself to those before you, and destroy you as it has destroyed them."[16] Therefore, poverty—or lack in the mystical sense—means that the "poor," or the needy are in need of God solely, and that kind of poorness or neediness is absolutely positive.

Both of Nūrī's definitions on Sufism emphasize renunciation, and both mention common Sufi ideas, without reference to anything peculiar to ecstatic or intoxicated Sufism. However, a third definition of Sufism quoted in Nūrī's name (see below) treats a more controversial issue: the relation of Sufis to disclosing mystical knowledge and experience.

Overt Expression of Mystical Experience

Hiding mystical knowledge is not an inherent necessity of Sufism, although the spiritual masters unanimously agree that novices should be introduced to the mystical ideas gradually, which means that the masters should withhold information from them. Secrecy never has a purpose in itself but is conditioned by the spiritual level of the audience. The early Sufi masters discussed overt communication of both knowledge and experience mostly from two points of view: (1) public instruction of the (uninitiated) people; and (2) public display of ecstatic states whether verbally or nonverbally. Their considerations in both respects were motivated by inner demands of the Sufi communities related to the quest of spiritual perfection. However, the situation changed radically after the execution of the ecstatic mystic Ḥallāj (in 922), which apparently shocked the Sufi communities and forced them to adopt a more precautious position, limiting the publicity of controversial ideas and practices. Sufis, including Nūrī, were attacked by representatives of the religious authority well before Ḥallāj's execution, but the latter event proved to be a milestone in the development of Sufism. Later Sufi manuals, for example Suhrawardī's (d. 1168) *Ādāb al-murīdīn (Rules for the Novice)*, expressly prohibit divulging mystical knowledge to the uninitiated.[17]

Nūrī, being an ecstatic mystic, did not refrain from displaying enraptured behavior in public, or even uttering scandalous sentences that bewildered the audience. Kalābādhī, however, decided not to include these in his *Doctrine of the Sufis*. Nonetheless, he quotes Nūrī repeatedly regarding exhibiting spiritual states or expressing mystical experience verbally. It may be supposed that an ecstatic mystic is more disposed to disclose mystical states unwillingly and unconsciously than his sober counterparts; on the other hand, he is less likely to give theoretical lectures on mystical concepts. The sober Junayd, for example, is frequently depicted as lecturing to people, but at the same time, he rebukes the ecstatic Sufi Shiblī for making manifest *(ẓāhir)*for the public mystical ideas that should be hidden.[18] The traditions quoted in Nūrī's name regarding the overt expression of mystical experiences are not entirely consistent. Some warn against indulgence in speech without proper understanding; others stress that the appropriate verbalization of a genuine experience is impossible; one of his sayings highlights the communication of mystical attainment as the essence of Sufism, while another condemns Sufis talking to men as "empty."

> Nūrī was asked about Sufism, and he said: "It is promulgating a station (*nashr maqām*) and connection with an essence (*ittiṣāl bi-qiwām*)." The inquirer said: "And what are their characteristics?" He said: "They bring happiness to others and avoid harming them."[19]

This definition of Sufism is quoted in the chapter "On Sufism and Being at Ease *(istirsāl)* with God," which enumerates sayings on absolute presence with God that obliterate all existing beings and any form of consciousness except for consciousness focusing on God. In fact, Sufis are described as "children in the lap of God,"[20] enjoying unconscious moments of complete absorption in God. This condition is regarded as transitory, a kind of blackout in which the world ceases to exist: consequently, communication becomes utterly impossible and senseless. In such a context, Nūrī's words emphasizing precisely the "promulgation" *(nashr)* of the wayfarer's spiritual attainment may seem surprising. The public character of promulgation may be connected to the nature of intoxicated states in which ecstatic mystics indiscriminately disclose secrets in a state of rapture.

Although Kalābādhī usually quotes the traditions without interpreting them, in this case he comments upon the saying and, moreover, changes the apparent meaning of Nūrī's words to almost their opposite meaning. To begin with, Kalābādhī contrasts Nūrī's view with a statement by Abū ʿAbd Allāh al-Nibājī: "[The symptoms of] Sufism are like [that of] the disease called *birsām:* at the beginning [it makes the sick person] talk senselessly in delirium, but when it develops, it makes him mute."[21] According to Kalābādhī, Nibājī's words mean that at the beginning of the mystical journey one may talk about his stations and states, but when God reveals Himself to the wayfarer, he becomes perplexed and refrains from speech. Consequently, he who talks openly about his mystical experience is in fact an untrained beginner still far away from God. In this sense, Nibājī's saying might be regarded as a critique of Nūrī's position. However, as Kalābādhī immediately shows, the contradiction of the two views concerning speaking and silence is illusory. He explains that Nūrī's saying about "promulgating a station" *(nashr maqām)* should be understood in a restrictive sense, meaning that "if he expresses himself [at all], he talks about his own state, not about the state of others with the tongue of learning *(bi-lisān al-ʿilm),*"[22] that is, according to what he has learned about mystical states in theory. This explication is rather distanced from the literal meaning of the original statement since the explanation implies that Sufis normally do not disclose their states, although Nūrī's view ("Sufism [. . .] is promulgating a station") seems to declare exactly the opposite. Kalābādhī's comment on the second part of Nūrī's definition mentioning "connection with an essence" restricts the legitimacy of communication to one's own spiritual experience: "His state *(ḥāl)* transports him through his own state away from the state of others"[23]—thus making it impossible for him to talk about these states. In summary, Kalābādhī clearly intends to incorporate into the moderate Sufi tradition a seemingly controversial view that singles out the unrestricted exhibition of mystical experience as the essence of Sufism.

Apparently, the fourteenth-century commentator, Qūnawī was well aware of Kalābādhī's intention and the inconsistency between the demands of divulging or, contrarily, hiding mystical experiences: "You may think that this [saying of Nūrī] is in contradiction with what has been said before [about Sufism as compared to the illness *birsām*], namely, that Sufism in an advanced level requires the mystic to keep silent."[24] Similarly to Kalābādhī, he dissolves the contradiction by limiting the validity of both requirements to specific and distinct cases. He associates the opposing acts of exhibiting and hiding with the pair of concepts subsistence *(baqā')* and self-annihilation *(fanā')*. The Sufi, who annihilates himself completely in God, loses both consciousness of the world and command over his acts; moreover, his complete absorption in God brings about silence. He does not communicate his individual mystical experience since he does not perceive either his own individual existence or that of the world. For the latter reason he keeps silent about mystical experience in general, as well. But, when he regains consciousness, he returns to the world without detaching himself from God's presence: "He masters his state in order to realize the true reality of annihilation without being absent from the things that happen. His face is turned towards God and he awaits God's order regarding all his affairs."[25] He is again endowed with the possibility of free will and choice, and he is conscious of the surrounding world. He is in the station of *baqā'* ("persistence, subsistence"—the opposite and the complementary of the station of *fanā')*. "The Real does not veil him who subsists *(bāqī)* from the creatures [. . .] but him who experiences annihilation *(fānī)* is veiled from the creatures by the Real. Therefore, 'promulgating his station' *(nashr al-maqām)* [concurrently] with connection with the Real Provider *(al-ḥaqq al-qawwām)* is appropriate to him who is in the station of *baqā'*."[26] These words paraphrase Nūrī's saying, adding definite articles here and there (*al-maqām, al-qawwām)* that modify the meaning of Nūrī's original words substantially.[27] The intention of Qūnawī, similarly to Kalābādhī, is the reconciliation of two apparently divergent approaches to Sufism, introducing a technical distinction that blunts the edge of Nūrī's words.

Returning to Kalābādhī, he closes the whole discussion with citing one of Nūrī's poems that conforms to his interpretation respecting both the exclusive and the incommunicable nature of the mystical experience, in this case, regarding *ḥāl* (state) instead of *maqām* (station).

> You discouraged me from the description of a state
>   (*ḥāl*) by means of the state itself
> For how could one who does not speak, describe?
> Do not give credence to anyone who pretends a state
> Until the state [itself] interprets its owner.[28]

If we consider the immediate context, supposing that Kalābādhī selects the poems in order to illustrate his exposition, we may conclude that the poems' meaning is in intimate connection with the former passages explaining that the Sufi may communicate about mystical experience only in exceptional cases. Since Sufism is practice *(ʿamal)* in the first place, as opposed to learning *(ʿilm)*, discourse about spiritual qualities is at the best secondary to realizing them in practice. Therefore, a real Sufi does not speak about his spiritual states but manifests them with his behavior. Acts, not words, authenticate the attainments of the mystic.

According to Qūnawī's explication,[29] the poet addresses God, who prevents the wayfarer from describing his state by the very nature of the mystical experience, which distracts him from the wish of communication. Moreover, a state cannot be in fact expressed verbally, since it is an inner quality *(ṣifa bāṭina)*, with which only the person experiencing it is fully familiar. However, his state does not remain completely occulted. Its outward signs appear on the person, giving evidence of the inner quality he encounters and making manifest his state without any verbal communication.

In the light of the literal meaning of the previous tradition cited in Nūrī's name, the poem seems to reinforce the supposition that in Nūrī's view, Sufism is exhibiting mystical experience without talking about it. On the other hand, we have seen that both Kalābādhī and Qūnawī understood Nūrī's definition of Sufism ("promulgating a station") as referring to verbal communication, but they harmonized it with the moderate Sufi position approving of silence and refraining from speech. Another tradition Kalābādhī included in the chapter on "Discoursing to Men" may elucidate further Nūrī's view:

> Nūrī was asked: "When does a man become entitled to discourse to the people?" He said: "When he received understanding from God, then it is right that he makes God's servants understand. But when he did not receive understanding from God, [nevertheless he gives a talk to men] then the affliction caused by him will be upon his whole land, and over all his servants."[30]

The subject matter of this tradition is lecturing the people, giving them a public talk *(kalām)* in order to teach them. In this respect, it differs to some extent from Nūrī's previous utterances, for his definition of Sufism pointed out "promulgating *(nashr)* a station," which besides verbal expression might entail nonverbal exhibition, as well (although both Kālābādhī and Qūnawī understood it as referring to speech). Conversely, Nūrī's poem on "describing a state" evidently concerns verbal communication, although not necessarily a formalized discourse, a public lecture given to men. It may well be any spontaneous expression of a personal experience. Such communication is either condemned or regarded as impossible in the poem. However, "discoursing to the people" is another genre. Nūrī's position in this respect is permissive, with the restriction that the lecture must be ultimately inspired by God. Nūrī's approach to public lectures, or preaching, is contrasted with that of Junayd in the following anecdote quoted in the same chapter:

> We were at Junayd when Nūrī passed by and greeted him. Junayd returned his greeting: "And on you be peace, commander of the hearts. Talk [to us]!" Nūrī said: "Abū l-Qāsim [al-Junayd]! You deceived them, and they sat you on the pulpit; I gave them sincere advice, and they cast me on the dunghill." Junayd said: "I have never seen my heart more grieved than at that moment." Then, another Friday he [Nūrī] came to us, and said: "If you see a Sufi giving a talk to men, know that he is empty."[31]

This story reveals a certain tension between Nūrī and his contemporary, Junayd, the sober mystic par excellence. Junayd addresses

Nūrī with the honorific title "commander of the hearts" *(amīr al-qulūb)*, to which Nūrī reacts unexpectedly with a short and severe rebuke, dressing down Junayd in front of his disciples. Junayd, however, does not take offense; on the contrary, he accepts Nūrī's reprimand. The story ends with Nūrī's sharp condemnation of public speech. His harsh remark that disapproves of discoursing indiscriminately is in contrast with his formerly discussed opinion according to which a person inspired by God is entitled to talk in public. The contradiction may be resolved by postulating that in his view, an inspired person may give moral lessons or may preach to the people; however, a Sufi, even if illuminated by God, may not.

The story contains several obscure points that the commentator, Qūnawī, elucidates. He quotes a parallel and more complete version of the story, in which Junayd asks Nūrī after the latter's reproachful remark: "How did I deceive them, and how did you advise them?" Nūrī replies: "Your deceit was that you positioned yourself between God and the creatures [by talking to them], and my sincere advice was that I entrusted them to their Lord [by refraining to talk to them]."[32] Qūnawī takes Junayd's side in the conflict; he asserts that Junayd is superior to Nūrī with regard to his spiritual rank, and he interprets his actions as the manifestations of his elevated spirituality and humility. He explains the word "empty" *(fārigh)* in Nūrī's last remark ("If you see a Sufi giving a talk to men, know that he is empty") as meaning "not concerned with God; since he who is concerned with God has no empty time and capacity *(lā yatafarragh)* to discourse to people."[33] He distances himself from Nūrī's position by observing that it contradicts the activity of the prophets, who were obviously concerned with God, yet they did speak to the people.

The overall picture that emerges from the different traditions attributed to Nūrī about exhibiting and expressing mystical experience is complex: it evidently permits, even praises, the overt display of spiritual states but discourages talking about them, since instead of words, "the state itself [should] interpret its owner,"[34] as he formulates in the last line of his poem. A Sufi shall not discourse to people, although public talk about God is permitted for inspired people in general (except the Sufis). Nonetheless, if "promulgating a station" means talking about it (as both Kalābādhī and Qūnawī understands), rather than merely displaying it, the position of Nūrī would end up somehow contradictory. On the one hand he would permit (even praise) discussions about mystical experience under certain circumstances; on the other, he would condemn Sufis engaging in public discourse.

Ways to God: Contemplation versus Intellect

Nūrī's attitude of reserve toward discourse may stem from the Sufis' common dismissal of rationalistic approach to God. Intellect *(ʿaql)* is widely criticized in Sufi texts since mystics hold inspired knowledge *(maʿrifa)* in much higher esteem than learning *(ʿilm)* and intelligence.

> Someone asked Nūrī: "What is the guide to God?" He replied: "God." The other asked: "Then what is the intellect (*ʿaql*)?" He replied: "The intellect is incompetent, and what is incompetent can guide only to something likewise incompetent."[35]

By citing this tradition, Kalābādhī positions Nūrī among the representatives of mainstream Sufism, for he includes his saying immediately after a tradition establishing that Nūrī's view coincides with the universally accepted Sufi teaching: "The consensus *(ijmāʿ)* [of the Sufis] is that the proof of God is God alone, and they hold that intellect *(ʿaql)* is defined by him who uses his intellectual faculty *(ʿāqil)* requiring a proof; for it is created, and what is created can prove only something likewise created."[36]

Qūnawī's comments on the passage elucidate perfectly the difference among the approach of the Sufis and other religious groups in Muslim society.[37] According to the Muʿtazilites[38] God can be known by means of the intellect; according to the *ahl al-sunna* (Sunnites), by means of proof texts *(dalīl)*;[39] according to the Sufis, by means of God. Furthermore, Sufis hold that inspired knowledge can be obtained without intellectual cognition, and vice versa. For example, birds can possess inspired knowledge concerning God,[40] as evidenced by the story of the hoopoe (Quran 27:20–26), who informed King Solomon about the Queen of Sheba and the sun worshippers, saying: "I found her and her people prostrating themselves to the Sun, not to God; the Satan made them believe that their acts were appropriate" (Quran 27:24). The story shows that although the hoopoe lacks rational faculties, nevertheless he is not devoid of inspired knowledge about God. Moreover, Qūnawī adds that all nonrational things share that kind of inspired knowledge since according to the Quran (17:44) "there is not a thing which does not glorify Him." On the other hand, continues Qūnawī, a person's rational mind can be highly developed irrespective of his absolute lack of inspired knowledge. The most obvious evidence of this are those rational thinkers among the nonbelievers *(kafara)*, whose innate intelligence *('aql gharīzī)* is more perfect than the intelligence of many believers. A valid proof in itself is not sufficient for acquiring inspired knowledge since the effectiveness of a proof depends on God's will. God may make some people receptive to a certain proof while causing others to be insensitive to it, as the Quran (6:111) testifies: "Even if We made the angles to descend unto them, and even if the dead spoke to them, and even if We gathered before their eyes everything, they would not be the ones to believe, unless God wanted [them to believe]." According to Qūnawī, this and similar verses of the Quran clearly show that the real proof and guide that leads to inspired knowledge is God.[41] If intelligence or rational proof were sufficient for obtaining inspired knowledge, all rational thinkers would possess it. Qūnawī corroborates his view with a *ḥadīth* according to which the Prophet admitted that he was incapable of praising and extolling God properly because divine bounty and attributes are incomprehensible to human beings. Since Muḥammad, the perfect man, confessed that his intelligence could not grasp God, it is evident that ordinary men, whose mental faculties are necessarily below than that of the Prophet, are even more lacking in this respect. Qūnawī adds, that this inability is the reason for religious dissent: intelligence cannot conceive divine realities, neither the attributes nor the substance.

Contemplation and Witnessing God

Nūrī, and Sufis in general, reject the possibility that God could be known through the rational faculty. Instead, he singles out contemplation and witnessing *(mushāhada* and *shuhūd*, the terms are interchangeable in his usage) as the way of establishing connection with God. The idea of contemplation takes a prominent part in

Nūrī's conception of Sufism, and Kalābādhī quotes several of his poems and sayings related to it.

> Connection (*ittiṣāl*) is unveiling the hearts and contemplating the inner hearts.[42]

Two points should be stressed here. First, Sufi texts usually do not refer to the ultimate end of the mystical quest as "becoming one" *(ittiḥād)* or *unio mystica* with God, but as "connection," or "arrival at God" *(ittiṣāl, wuṣūl).*[43] Second, contemplation is not an intellectual procedure, but a spiritual perception of the unveiled secrets of the inner hearts. Nūrī's concise saying employs Sufi technical terms that must be explained here in some detail.

Heart *(qalb)* and Inner Heart *(sirr)*

The word *sirr* means, in ordinary use, "secret; heart, inner centre." In Sufi terminology it denotes the inner heart, the most hidden and subtle part of the outerheart *(qalb).* The inner heart is "the place where God can be witnessed" *(maḥall al-mushāhada),* that is, experienced directly.[44] The outer heart, on the other hand, is where inspired knowledge can be obtained *(maḥall al-maʿārif).* The human being has access to his inner heart, but the very center of the inner heart *(sirr al-sirr)* is accessible only to God. Thus, one's innermost reality is completely concealed from him since it is essentially divine, not human—although it forms part of human nature. The word *sirr* is used also to denote the intimate content of mystical states, which is a secret shared confidentially between God and the individual, that should not be divulged and cannot be disclosed by others. The following saying expresses the concept of *sirr* vividly, playing with the double meaning of the word: "Our secrets/inner hearts *(asrār)* are virgins that cannot be deflowered by anyone's delusive imagination."[45]

Unveiling *(mukāshafa)*

Kalābādhī explains the phrase "unveiling the hearts" with a *ḥadīth* according to which Ḥāritha said to the Prophet: "[I became truly a believer] as if I saw the Lord's throne set upright."[46] Unveiling is an act of God by which He removes the veils concealing Him so that He could be "seen," or perceived directly. Such perception entails the evanescence of accidental qualities and apparent existents. Qūnawī expounds upon Ḥāritha's saying as follows: Ḥāritha turned away from this world so definitively that "its nuggets of gold and its clods of earth became the same for him," and thus he attained connection with the other world: true realities *(ḥaqā'iq)* were unveiled to him *(inkashafa)*, as if he was seeing the throne of God directly without perceiving anything other than God in the world.[47]

Witnessing and Contemplation *(shuhūd or mushāhada)*

Seeing, witnessing, and contemplation appear to be interchangeable notions in Nūrī's phraseology. Both *shuhūd* and *mushāhada* mean "seeing with one's own eyes, sensory perception, witnessing," while in the mystical context they refer to mental reflection, insight, contemplation. Both Nūrī and his commentators frequently play with multiple meanings of the terms. Kalābādhī comments upon the expression "contemplating the inner hearts," referring to a *ḥadīth* according to which the Prophet commanded: "Serve God as if you were seeing Him!"[48] Qūnawī explains that "seeing God" is superior to "seeing the throne," and therefore witnessing *(mushāhada)* is superior to unveiling *(mukāshafa)*, just as the innermost heart is superior to the heart itself. In connection with Nūrī's saying, Kalābādhī relates a story about Ibn ʿUmar, who was so immersed in devotion while circumambulating the Kaʿba that he did not notice when a person greeted him. He excused himself for not returning his greeting by saying: "We were seeing God at that place." Qūnawī explains Kalābādhī's comment: Ibn ʿUmar was outwardly occupied with performing his religious duty, which is an aspect of servitude; however, deep down he was overwhelmed by true reality *(ḥaqīqa)*, that is, contemplating lordship *(mushāhadat al-rubūbiyya)* since "the law *(sharīʿa)* is that you serve Him, and true reality is that you see Him *(tashhaduhu)*."

Connection *(ittiṣāl)*

Sufis normally do not employ the term "becoming one" with God *(ittiḥād)* but talk about "connection" *(ittiṣāl)* or "arrival" *(wuṣūl)* realized through the act of "approaching" God *(taqarrub)*, or sometimes by the personal and direct experience of "tasting"

God *(dhawq)*. Qūnawī, for example, comments on Nūrī's maxim distinguishing several degrees of "arrival" at God. The inferior degree is "arriving at pure certainty in the way of tasting *(dhawq)* and ecstasy *(wijdān)*."[49] A subsequent degree is that of finding God through acts: the person becomes annihilated with regard to his own acts and the acts of others by becoming God's agent, renouncing his own choice and free will. The next degree is arriving at God by theophany through divine attributes *(tajallin bi-ṭarīq al-ṣifāt)*, when God reveals his attributes and unveils His splendor *(jalāl)* and benevolence *(jamāl)*. The highest degree is reserved for the chosen elite of those brought closest to God *(muqarrabūn)*, and through theophany God's substance is revealed *(tajallī al-dhāt)*. The mystic is elevated to the station of self-annihilation; he does not witness himself at all, and his interior *(bāṭin)* is embraced by the lights of certainty.[50]

Summing up, the meaning of Nūrī's saying is that the human being can find connection with God by means of contemplating his inner heart, the place where God can be witnessed. By such concentration he may attain to the perception of certainty: certainty is witnessing.[51] Qūnawī explains certainty as inner confidence obtained through divine unveilings. Ultimate certainty is realized by means of detaching oneself from the world through attaching oneself to God.[52] The notion of certainty *(yaqīn)* is often connected to the concept of "reunion" or "being together" with God *(jamʿ)*.

According to an unnamed Sufi master who Qūnawī quotes, knowing certainty *(ʿilm al-yaqīn)* is separation [from God] *(tafriqa)*, the essence of certainty *(ʿayn al-yaqīn)* is reunion [with God] *(jamʿ)*, and the reality of certainty *(ḥaqq al-yaqīn)* is reunion of the reunion *(jam al-jam)*.[53] According to Qushayrī, separation from God means to see *(shuhūd)* other beings belonging to God; reunion with God means to see other beings through God; while the reunion of the reunion is complete abolition *(istihlāk)* and the annihilation of perceiving anything but God. He who realizes his own existence and the existence of the creation but sees *(shāhada)* everything as existing through God, is in the state of reunion. But when he is drawn away from seeing *(shuhūd)* the creation, detached from his self and captivated by the power of reality in such a way that he is unable to perceive anything at all, then he is in the state of reunion of reunion.[54]

My reunion [with You] (*jam*ʿ) while I became
annihilated (*fī fanā'ī*) showed me [falsely] that I was
drawing near
Way off the mark! Drawing near (*taqarrub*) can result
only from You, in accord with You
I have no patience [to restrain myself] from You, but
none of my tricks works on You
You are unavoidable, You are inevitable for me
Some people drew near to You through hope, and You
granted them contact (*waṣṣaltahum*)
But what do I have, being far from You? Everything is
destroyed.[55]

A mystical state, even if it originates from God, may deceive the seeker, giving him the impression of false certainty and thus, in fact, distancing him from God.[56] Therefore, the implications of a state are not obvious. Nūrī complains of such delusion in the first lines of the poem.

Kalābādhī interprets the verses as the description of an illusion generated by a mystical state making one believe that passing away from everything but God *(fanā')*, and reunion with Him *(jam*ʿ*)*, actually mean closeness to Him. However, as Kalābādhī explains, self-annihilation and reunion are human attributes, not divine ones, while closeness to God can be reached only by God's initiative and through His involvement, not through the seeker excersising their will and qualities.

It might be added to Kalābādhī's explication that spiritual states that occur in pairs are peculiar to the human being and are transitory. Passing away *(fanā')* is balanced with subsistence *(baqā')*; reunion *(jam*ʿ*)* is followed and preceded by separation and detachment *(tafriqa)*. *Jam*ʿ describes a state similar to that of the union of lovers, which ends necessarily with their separation. Their being together is transient, imperfect. The ultimate end of the mystical way, however, is permanent connection *(ittiṣāl)*, that is, everlasting contact with God, which is often conceptualized as "closeness" *(qurb)*, and not as "becoming one with" the divine *(ittiḥād)*. Closeness to God may be attained by assuming His attributes, "clothing oneself in God's attributes" as Sufis express the idea, and by eliminating the personality's own character traits or suppressing the self *(nafs)*. However, self-annihilation does not guarantee the success of the seeker's quest since intimate closeness to God cannot be initiated by man through exerting his human faculties but must originate in the will of God.

The tone of the poem is passionate, thus revealing a facet of Nūrī's personality that has not been exposed yet. While Kalābādhī does not comment upon the tone, Qūnawī finds it necessary to justify it: the lack of patience is due to the overwhelming ardent love of the mystic fervidly seeking intimacy with God. In order to achieve his aim, the lover may even resort to tricks; but these are ineffective since connection to God is not subject to causality *(al-wuṣūl [. . .] ghayr maʿlūl)* and cannot be conceived as a relation of cause and effect.[57] The same applies to those who "drew close through hope"; they did not attain to God's nearness owing to their acts but solely due to God's grace, or as Qūnawī puts it: "Attaining to Your closeness does not necessarily follow from drawing close to You."[58]

Nūrī bemoans the false sense of nearness and expresses his despair in the following poem, as well:

> Oh, You, whom I witness [as being] with me, therefore
> I regard to be close[59]
> Though the quest for Him is so heavy
> When I force myself to divert from Him, witnessing
> (*shuhūd*) turns me back to Him
> The wonders of which never pass away (*tanfā*).[60]

The false impression of nearness is created by witnessing, contemplating God *(mushāhada)*, which evidently warns about the possibility of self-deception in one's mystical experience. Nūrī laments the false illusion of God's closeness, the impassable distance between God and the human being, causing him to occasionally lose hope in ever getting closer to God. In such moments, he desists from his endeavor and tries to force himself to abandon God. The same act of contemplation *(shuhūd)*, however, encourages him again, and his despair abates.[61]

Connection with God through contemplation is attained only if the wayfarer submerges in absence *(ghayb)*. Seeking perfect consciousness of God entails losing consciousness of the world, of oneself, even of the act of contemplation.

I witnessed [Him] perceiving, not witnessing [anything else]
It is enough for a witness to perceive without [anything else] being caused to be witnessed
I became absent, absenting myself to the absence of His absence (*ghayb*)
Therefore, the appearance of His absence manifested itself, not being deprived [from me].[62]

The term absence *(ghayb)* in its ultimate meaning refers to the hidden, unknown world of God, to God's inner life. In the human level it refers to the withdrawal of the mystic from the world, including his self (his inner world), as a means of approaching God.[63] The withdrawal of the mystic is imperfect absence compared with God's absolute, perfect absence, or hidden world. When the consciousness of contemplation, of absenting oneself from the world and concentrating solely on God disappears, when self-consciousness fades away, the mystic reaches through his absence from worldly affairs and spiritual concerns the perfect absence of God, God's ultimate intimacy.[64]

The mystic's absence from the world does not require physical withdrawal; perhaps it is not even perceived by the people surrounding him:

I veiled myself from the world with veils of concerns regarding Him
Confusing me through the rank of Him whose rank is far above my rank
Neither the word realizes that I am absent from it (*ghā'ib*)
Nor do I realize the matters that go on
When I dedicate myself entirely to His allegiance
I do not ever care about the world.[65]

The poet veils himself from the vicissitudes of the world, the course of everyday life. And he becomes absent spiritually, not physically, without the world realizing his absence. Everyday matters and incidents vanish for him, but he is unaware of their disappearance because he is concerned with God and not with the process of his spiritual distancing from the world.[66] In such a state, the difference between opposite qualities vanishes, and divine presence manifests itself in all aspects of life:

> Contentment (*riḍā*) is bitterness swallowed regardless of satisfaction
> Every time that turbid water is found sweet
> An effect that causes some [of the divine] presence to be witnessed
> Since only a lean camel grazes every sort [of pasturage].[67]

Witnessing equals presence before God, and the human being's presence with God is in the proportion of his absence from creation.[68] Nūrī's poem describes the Sufi idea of contentment *(riḍā)* with God, with divine decrees, with both good and evil circumstances, and even finding delight ("sweetness") in pain or bitterness of faith. As Atif Khalil has demonstrated, early Sufism distinguishes between divine and human contentment, and lays the emphasis on the latter (i.e., man's contentment with God). Being content with pleasing circumstances is not appreciated as a virtue but as a natural response. Spiritual wayfarers, however, struggle to exhibit sincere contentment in twists of fate, suffering, and pain. The higher levels of contentment involve finding pleasure in suffering, not as a consequence of masochistic inclinations but as a result of complete surrender to God's decree and renunciation of will, which produces a sense of overwhelming tranquillity. The pleasure does not lie in the pain itself but "in something which outweighs the pain." Mystics that attain the highest level of spiritual perfection become immersed in the contemplation of God, being unaware of the joys and pains of the world.[69]

The metaphor of the lean camel in Nūrī's poem alludes to an excessive preoccupation with the creatures by employing a comparison: the person who occupies himself with every kind of concern is likened to a camel that grazes in every kind of grass. Such a camel is lean (having unappeasable hunger), just as a person busy with mundane affairs is weak and deficient, while those who attained contentment are strong and firm.[70]

A significant part of the traditions related to Nūrī that Kalābādhī chose to include in the *Doctrine of the Sufis* treats contemplation as a means of approaching God. These traditions are in line with the sober Sufi tendency, no trace of intoxicated mysticism can be discerned in them, and nothing peculiar to ecstatic Sufism can be distinguished. However, inclination toward intoxication and ecstasy appears in the traditions related to *dhikr.*

Dhikr and Ecstasy

Dhikr means "remembering, recollection" but also "mentioning," especially mentioning, or uttering God's name repeatedly while trying to realize perfect concentration on the divine. Such *dhikr*-ceremony may be performed individually or in public, and the mystic may repeat God's names (or short phrases on which he concentrates) mutely, in his heart, or aloud, with his tongue. However, the special meaning of *dhikr* as a peculiar Sufi ceremony is not attested in the earliest sources, and in most early traditions the word simply means either remembering, recollecting (bringing to consciousness), or uttering. In the *Doctrine of the Sufis* Kalābādhī correlates recollection with contemplation. He quotes Junayd: "Whoever says: 'God', without witnessing [him], is a liar."[71] Since "the heart is for witnessing, and the tongue is for expressing what is witnessed, and whoever expresses [something] without witnessing it, is a false witness."[72] Contemplation thus leads to recollection, but perfect recollection of God entails losing consciousness and experiencing ecstasy *(wajd).*

> My love (*ḥubb*) is so immoderate that I want to
> recollect Him night and day
> But, how strange! During ecstasy recollection
> disappears (*ghaybat al-dhikr*)
> And even more strangely, ecstasy sometimes
> disappears
> Nay, recollection itself disappears, whether being far
> or near.[73]

The poem expresses the paradox of losing consciousness in ecstasy while awaking oneself to the consciousness of God by recollection.

Kalābādhī introduces the chapter on *dhikr* in the *Doctrine of the Sufis* establishing that "the true essence of recalling *(dhikr)* is forgetting everything but God."[74] He illustrates this statement with a quotation from the Quran: "Recall *(udhkur)* your Lord when you forget!" (Quran 18:24). According to Kalābādhī's interpretation—which disregards the original context of the passage—the direct object of the verb "to forget" is everything except God, including the act of remembering Him. By means of this implicit addition to the original verse, Kalābādhī is capable of offering a Quranic support for this clearly mystical idea.[75] The traditions Kalābādhī chooses to include in the chapter emphasize the role of annihilation *(fanā')*, forgetting and absence. He explains that in the most elevated level of recollection the wayfarer sees, or rather witnesses *(shuhūd)* whom he recollects, and passes away from the act of recollection *(fanā')* since the attributes of whom he recollects annihilate both his attributes and his self-consciousness.[76] Nūrī's poem expresses a similar idea employing the term *ghayba* (absence, translated here with the verb "to disappear")—the term has already been discussed. Nūrī singles out love as the motive of constant recollection, which is in line with the approach of the famous Baghdadi mystic Qāsim Sumnūn, nicknamed "the Lover," who was closely related to the circle of Nūrī.[77] According to a tradition preserved in Sarrāj's *Book of Flashes*, "Sumnūn was asked about love *(maḥabba)* and said: 'The purity of love *(ṣafā' al-wudd)* implies constant recollection *(dawām al-dhikr)*, since him who loves something recalls it all the time.' "[78] Kalābādhī, however, avoids including traditions mentioning love in the chapter on *dhikr*, apart from the poem of Nūrī and another by Ibn ʿAṭā'.[79] Kalābādhī passes in silence over the phenomenon of "immoderate love" *(farṭ al-ḥubb)* Nūrī articulates, although excessive love *(ʿishq)* is an important and controversial issue of early Sufism. Neither his chapter on love in the *Doctrine of the Sufis* contains references to *ʿishq*, most probably since the concept was much debated and refused by several religious authorities. On the other hand, the definition of *ʿishq* quoted in the name of Abū ʿAlī al-Daqqāq in Qushayrī's *Treatise* corresponds exactly to the "immoderate love" mentioned by Nūrī: "*ʿIshq* is exceeding the limit in love *(mujāwazat al-ḥadd fī l-maḥabba)*."[80] Qushayrī, following

Daqqāq, refuses such excesses, and Kalābādhī's disregard suggests the same.[81]

The last line of Nūrī's poem may need further explication. According to Qūnawī's interpretation, recollection passes away both in the states of nearness and farness. In nearness it evanesces due to the excessive awe that the presence of God inspires while the mystic is absorbed in the contemplation of the divine attributes. In farness *dhikr* ceases because the Sufi is intimidated by the veils with which God shrouds Himself from him, and by the fact that he is deprived of connection *(waṣl)* to God.[82]

Nūrī describes *ḍikr* as "return" to God through focusing exclusively on the divine:

> Repentance [tawba, literally: "returning"] means that you return from recollecting (*dhikr*) anything except God.[83]

The chapter on repentance *(tawba)* in the *Doctrine of the Sufis* begins with several traditions about the plain meaning of the word, that is, regretting one's sins and asking for God's forgiveness.[84] However, even these sayings operate with the (etymologically) literal meaning of the word, expressing that "returning" involves more than leaving behind wrong deeds. The mystical sense of *tawba,* the repentance of the elite, implies returning to God from any other being, concept or preoccupation.[85]

Nūrī's poem that has been discussed above indicates that *dhikr* may lead to ecstasy *(wajd);* but while *dhikr* is an internal act initiated and performed by the human being, ecstasy is an external impact that descends *(wārid)* upon him and causes apparent or latent physical agitation:

> Ecstasy is a flame that appears in the inner hearts, turns [you] away from longing, and when it comes upon (*wārid*) you, your members become stirred either by joy or grief.[86]

A parallel version preserved in one of the manuscripts reads, "Ecstasy is a flame that originates in the inner heart *(sirr)* and turns [you] away from the outer heart *(qalb)*,"[87] which makes the meaning of the saying more evident. Ecstasy diverts the mystic from outer, superficial, or secondary realities and turns him toward the inner, hidden, primordial, and secret essence. Ecstasy is an oncoming event *(wārid)* kindled in the inner heart: in the "place where God can be witnessed" *(maḥall al-mushāhada)* or experienced directly.[88] This suggests that according to Nūrī ecstasy is inspired by God and equals direct experience of the divine manifesting itself in physical ways, as well. Kalābādhī possibly also indicates God as the source of ecstasy since he identifies *wajd* with *ḥāl,* or the various transient spiritual states that overcome the mystic. However, he differentiates between strong and weak ecstasy; the former is hidden (controlled and mastered by the person experiencing it), while the latter is manifest, exhibited. He cites Nūrī's saying as an illustration of weak ecstasy, thus positioning it as an acceptable but imperfect mystical manifestation. Qūnawī seems to maintain an even more reserved attitude toward Nūrī's approach: he asserts that although ecstasy is kindled in the inner heart, it does not originate there, and it does not necessarily proceed from God. It may originate from inner excitement "oncoming upon the lover's inner heart from his sense of hearing, seeing or insight"[89]—referring possibly to the imaginative faculty. In that case, his passion is kindled by his own fantasy, as if his longing originated from futility.[90]

Kalābādhī relates a story in which Nūrī acts to a certain extent similarly to later Sufis attending the *dhikr*-ceremony: he keeps repeating God's name in an ecstatic state. His rapture is particularly lengthy (unlike common *dhikr*-ceremonies); it continues for days. The fact however, that he does not neglect his religious duties (prayers) confuses the observer, for he thinks Nūrī is "sober" and has not lost the sense of discrimination. The event is referred to Junayd, who explains that God takes control over the ecstatic and preserves him from committing omissions or defaults.

> Junayd was told that Abū l-Ḥusayn al-Nūrī has been standing in the Shūnīzīyya mosque for days, without eating, drinking or sleeping, and he kept saying "God, God." However, he recited the [obligatory] prayers at their fixed times. Someone who heard this said that he was sober (*ṣāḥin*). But Junayd said: "No, he is not. Ecstatics (*arbāb al-mawājīd*) are preserved before God during their ecstasies."[91]

The counterpart of sobriety is intoxication, which Kalābādhī defines as "the absence of discrimination *(tamyīz)* between things, without being absent from the things themselves"[92]—the Sufi retains consciousness of the world but does not distinguish among its constituents and does not differentiate between good and bad—a quality and its opposite. Intoxication is not identical with ecstasy, for sober mystics (like Junayd) may likewise experience ecstasy without manifesting it in any way.[93] Kalābādhī defines annihilation *(fanā')* as "losing the capacity of discrimination while annihilating from the things."[94] The first half of the definition corresponds to that of intoxication cited above, while the second half contrasts with it. Kalābādhī explains that God overpowers the Sufi in the state of annihilation, takes charge of his actions, and ensures the performance of his duties. Some of the Sufis hold that annihilation is not permanent; he who experiences it eventually returns to his original attributes or personality. However, the "greatest Sufis," as Kalābādhī puts it, mentioning explicitly both Junayd and Nūrī, are convinced that annihilation of the self is a divine gift that cannot be earned but granted, and if a person reverted to his original attributes, the divine gift would be annulled. Therefore, the Sufi is not "returned" to his own attributes but to those of God, and by acquiring God's attributes, he persists in the spiritual station of subsistence *(baqā')*. Thus, ultimate annihilation *(fanā')* is subsistence in God. Kalābādhī quotes the story of Nūrī's intoxicated ecstasy in order to prove how the Sufi annihilated (and subsisting) in God nevertheless performs his religious duties, obligatory prayers despite his passing away in intoxicated ecstasy. He retains his human qualities and is not converted into a spiritual being or an angel.[95]

Nūrī's ecstatic behavior is not dismissed or overlooked in the *Doctrine of the Sufis*. Ecstasy in the traditions related to Nūrī is connected with passions and outward manifestations: it is compared to "flame," it agitates the body, it causes overwhelming emotions like joy or grief, but it is also associated with "immoderate love" and drunkenness. These intense sensations, however, do not lead to antinomian behavior; what is more, they are justified by the sober Sufi par excellence, Junayd. Kalābādhī emphasizes the uncontroversial aspects of Nūrī's ecstasy while ignoring those that might have problematic results, like his confession of immoderate love. He creates contexts in which Nūrī's words and behavior are perfectly acceptable, even exemplary (e.g., when he relates the story of Nūrī's intoxicated, ecstatic *dhikr* in the mosque as an example of the mystic who carries out his religious duties even in unconscious states). Furthermore, he explicitly raises Nūrī to the rank of Junayd when he refers to both of them as "the greatest Sufis" precisely in the context of losing self-consciousness.

Addressing God

While most of the traditions quoted until now described God or a sensation related to Him, Nūrī's following poems address God directly. They reveal a sense of intimacy, gratitude, and contentedness but also betray the fear of losing God's intimate closeness.

> I fear You without being afraid of the treats of fate
> I'm frail, but You are a friend so intimate, surpassing every mate
> You [alone] donate to the inner hearts their hidden secrets
> You [alone] comprehend what is concealed to consciousness
> But I exalt You [because I exalt You more] than to exalt anything else as You, of weightless weight.[96]

Kalābādhī includes Nūrī's poem in the chapter on fearing God *(taqwā)*. He explains that a God-fearing person in fact fears the world and seeks refuge in God's sweet proximity.[97] He quotes the poem in this context, and he passes over the expression "intimate friend" *(ilf,* the word has the meaning "lover," as well). Although Kalābādhī ignores the term, its importance is confirmed by Qūnawī's comments, who interprets the poem as the lover's sensation of intimacy *(uns)* with God.[98]

The line mentioning "the hidden secrets of the inner hearts" is a reference to the *sirr al-sirr*, the very center of the inner heart, accessible exclusively to God. The center of the inner heart is a divine component in the human being, intrinsically connected to God, which human consciousness cannot access.

The sense of intimacy, gratitude, and contentment is also expressed in the following poem:

> I express my gratitude (*shukr*) not because I want to
> repay Your grace
> But merely for the sake of saying 'Thank God' once
> again
> I recall (*adhkur*) the days I spent with You, how nice
> they were
> Since the last duty of a grateful man is to recall [the
> benevolence].[99]

The poem articulates the impossibility of compensation between a human being of restricted conditions and the infinite God. An interesting comment by Qūnawī correlates the poem with a passage of the Quran: "If you recollect me, I will recollect you; give thanks to me and do not be ungrateful!" (Quran 2:152). This suggestion is not arbitrary: the phraseology of the Quran, combining *shukr* (gratefulness, thanks) and *dhikr* (recalling, recollection) is obviously reflected in the wording of the poem.[100] Thus, the plain sense of the poem is expressing gratitude merely in order to join the choir of those who praise God, while according to Qūnawī's understanding one should voice his gratefulness in order to obey God's order. Either way, the poem is perfectly compatible with the tenets of Islam.

The last poem is about spiritual struggle *(jihād)*. It addresses God in a tone of despair, confessing frustration and desperateness. The sensation of failure does not completely overshadow hope, although the last words express the poet's fear of alienation and detachment from God. The plaintive tone of the poem endows it with a sense of confidence and intimacy.

> I say: I have almost reached the limit today
> But what I say I've almost reached is far away
> I fail in every struggle (*jihād*) of mine
> And it's a struggle that I am unable to keep on
> struggling
> My hope is that You bring about contentment (*riḍā*)
> Otherwise, in the hereafter I'll be destined to be
> distanced.[101]

Kalābādhī includes the poem in the chapter on struggle and endeavor, which argues that personal actions should not be regarded as means necessarily leading to God, for God's closeness cannot be earned by deeds; rather, it is granted as a divine gift. In this context the frustrated voice of the poet calling for consolation is perceived as the formulation of complete reliance on God.[102]

Conclusions

Nūrī's ecstatic behavior and some of his utterances ("immoderate love," "intimate friend") that might be regarded as controversial or extreme evidence that he indeed belonged to the group of intoxicated ecstatics *(arbāb al-mawājīd,* as Junayd called them), but this aspect of his teachings and personality is not emphasized by Kalābādhī. On the contrary, the context in which he quotes Nūrī's words usually divests them of any contentious meaning, or at least eclipses them, obscuring them by highlighting and drawing attention to that part of the content that is acceptable to the Muslim community. Kalābādhī expressly places Nūrī among the "greatest Sufis" along with Junayd, however, he also reduces him to a lower mystical rank by pointing out his outwardly manifested ecstasy as weak, or imperfect in comparison with perfect or controlled and concealed ecstasy.

Nūrī's contemporary and friend, Junayd, is mentioned in two of the traditions. In the story about Nūrī's intoxicated ecstasy while performing *dhikr* for days, he attests to the state of Nūrī, namely, that he is not "sober" *(ṣāḥin)* but drunken—in the mystical sense of the word that, however, does not divert him from his religious duties. This tradition might be regarded apologetic, defending Nūrī, an intoxicated Sufi par excellence, from the suspicions of religious laxity. The other tradition that mentions Junayd shows a certain tension between the two of them. While Junayd addresses his fellow with a honorific title ("Peace be on you, commander of the hearts!"), the other reacts by rebuking him (in the presence of Junayd's disciples), saying that he misled the people, who, in turn choose him as their leader: "They sat him on the pulpit," as Nūrī says. Apparently, Junayd does not refute the accusation, nor does he counterattack. He accepts Nūrī's reproach silently, a fact that shows his modesty and might indicate how intimate the relationship between both Sufi masters was; or it might have an apologetic aim, again defending Nūrī, even placing him (and ecstatic Sufis in general) above the more moderate Junayd. The story ends with Nūrī's warning to Junayd's disciples against discoursing to men.

Disclosing mystical knowledge or experiences is a theme that recurs in the traditions related to Nūrī (it appears in two sayings, one poem and one story). His view on the issue is complex, depending on the circumstances. The saying about "promulgating a station" is very difficult to interpret, its literal meaning seems to contradict the context that Kalābādhī produces when composing the chapter. According to Kalābādhī's interpretation, Nūrī holds that Sufis should not talk about mystical experiences in general but could communicate their own specific experience verbally. A poem by Nūrī seems to contradict this interpretation since it unequivocally proclaims that instead of words, acts should reveal spiritual attainment. However, Nūrī does not deny that on certain occasions it is right to instruct the people. When asked about discoursing to men, he replies that a person (not necessarily Sufi) whose knowledge and understanding originates in God is entitled to enlighten others. This answer can be contrasted with his disappointed remark to Junayd ("I gave them sincere advice, and they cast me on the dunghill"), and his admonition to the disciples ("If you see a Sufi giving a talk to men, know that he is empty").[103]

The central theme of Nūrī's sayings and poems is witnessing God: almost a quarter of the traditions that are preserved in the *Doctrine of the Sufis* treats that subject. The terminology of the traditions is not rigid; the terms "seeing, witnessing" *(shuhūd)*, and "contemplation" *(mushāhada)*—including the respective verbal forms, of course—refer more or less to the same phenomenon. Contemplation is associated with absence *(ghayb, ghayba)*, annihilation *(fanā')*, recollection *(dhikr)*, and ecstasy *(wajd)*. With regard to "absence," another thing we can say about Nūrī's terminology is that he uses the verbal noun *ghayb* in the technical sense, referring to God's hidden world, while the other verbal noun, *ghayba* has a more general meaning in his usage, employed as a common verbal noun of the verb *ghāba*, meaning "to disappear," retaining, however, the verb's mystical connotation.[104] Nearness and farness are also frequent topics of the traditions.

It is interesting to examine the Sufi technical terms that occur in the traditions. Although Nūrī was an early Sufi, key terms of full-fledged Sufi mysticism are abundant in his poems and sayings, which suggests that the terminology of Sufism must have become rather established by the end of the ninth century. If one might call into question the authenticity of the sayings and suppose that their present forms reflect the Sufi phraseology of the editor, that is, Kalābādhī, then obviously the same conclusion applies to the end of the tenth century. The recurring technical terms are the following (in order of frequency of the occurrences): absence *(ghayb, ghayba, ghāba, ghā'ib, etc.)*, contemplation, witnessing *(mushāhada, shuhūd, shahida, etc.)*, recollection *(dhikr)*, ecstasy *(wajd)*, nearness *(qurb, qarīb, taqarrub, etc.)*, farness *(buʿd, baʿīd, etc.)*, inner heart / secret *(sirr)*, connection *(ittiṣāl)*, annihilation *(fanā')*, self / carnal soul *(nafs)*, heart *(qalb)*, and contentment *(riḍā)*.[105]

CHAPTER 2

Sarrāj

Book of Flashes *(Kitāb al-lumaʿ)*

Introduction

The *Book of Flashes (Kitāb al-lumaʿ fī l-taṣawwuf)* was one of the earliest Sufi works to be passed down to us.[1] Its author, Abū Naṣr ʿAbd Allāh ibn ʿAlī al-Sarrāj (d. 988), was a native of Ṭūs in Khorasan; his compilation, however, exposes mainly the teachings of Iraqi Sufis, to whom he was personally related in several ways. He was a pupil of Jaʿfar al-Khuldī (d. 959), one of the more intimate disciples of Junayd;[2] furthermore, according to the *Kashf al-maḥjūb* by Hujwīrī, he was the overseer of the Sufis associated with the Shūnīziyya mosque in Baghdad.[3] His compilation, the *Book of Flashes*, has the clear objective of demonstrating that Sufism is in accord with Muslim religious law. It discusses the theoretical background of Sufism, its relation to the Islamic sciences, its origins and peculiarities. It enlists and explains the mystical stations and states, presents the characteristics of mystical exegesis, the Sufis' relation to the Quran, the Prophet, his Sunna, and his Companions. It elaborates on the Sufis' norms of behavior *(ādāb)* with respect to devotional practices (prayer, ablutions, fasting, pilgrimage, etc.), social interactions (relation of master and disciples, friendship, family life, traveling, etc.), and bodily needs (dress, eating, sickness, etc.). It offers a collection of mystical poems, supplications and epistles; a list of the Sufi technical terms and their definitions;

a collection of ecstatic utterances with their explications. Finally, it dedicates several chapters to the audition ceremony *(samāʿ)*, the concept of ecstasy, and erroneous views *(ghalaṭ)* held by some sects *(ṭā'ifa, firqa)*. It does not contain a separate part dedicated to the mystics' biographies, although it does deal in some chapters with the more controversial figures among them. The author explains in the introduction that he composed the book at the request of a person seeking to understand the nature of Sufi teachings: whether they are commendable, valueless, or possibly heretical. The anonymous request might be a pretext or a mere literary convention, but it clearly defines the purpose and the content of the book: to present and to explain both the tolerated and the "suspicious" Sufi teachings. Consequently, some of the most notable sections of the work discuss extensively contentious mystical concepts, practices, and heterodox ideas that should be refused and avoided.

Sayings and poems attributed to Nūrī are scattered throughout the *Book of Flashes,* especially in the chapters dedicated to the Sufis' *ādāb* and to their technical terms. Nūrī is among those few mystics to whom Sarrāj dedicated separate chapters due to their controversial activity. However, the section on Nūrī is missing from the edition prepared by Nicholson, which preserves only its title *(bāb fī dhikr Abī l-Ḥusayn al-Nūrī wa mā . . .)*,[4] and was published later by Arberry under the title *Pages from the Kitāb al-Lumaʿ of Abū Naṣr al-Sarrāj being the Lacuna in the Edition of R. A. Nicholson* from a manuscript preserved in Bankipur Library.[5] The fact that Sarrāj deals with Nūrī in a separate chapter indicates the importance he attributes to him as one of the unconventional dissenting mystics whose teachings Sarrāj wished to interpret and to defend. He characterizes Nūrī as follows: "He was one of the ecstatics *(wājidūn)* and of those who spoke with subtle allusions *(ahl al-ishārāt al-laṭīfa)*. He has various sayings and a lot of poems."[6]

Since no commentary on the *Book of Flashes* exists, Nūrī's words are interpreted here according to the context in which Sarrāj quotes them, that is, against the background of the main subject and the basic concepts of the chapter in which they occur. Where Sarrāj comments upon a certain saying, his remarks are summarized or translated. The *Book of Flashes* contains about thirty texts related to Nūrī, although the exact number depends on how we count since Sarrāj sometimes divides originally continuous texts into smaller units that he includes in different chapters according to subject matters. About half of the texts are short sayings, most of them not exceeding a single sentence. Some traditions are elaborate and markedly theoretical answers given to actual questions and can be regarded as short discourses on well-defined topics. Sarrāj relates several anecdotes about Nūrī, and he quotes five poems bearing his name. Three of these are love poems that hardly differ from secular love poetry. The most interesting part of Sarrāj's collection is his long report on the accusations Nūrī had to face because of his *shaṭaḥāt* (or quasi-blasphemous) ecstatic utterances.

The traditions included in the *Book of Flashes* display an obvious duality: most of them are perfectly compatible with moderate or sober Sufism, while the rest show the overtly ecstatic or intoxicated tendencies. Despite being underrepresented quantitatively, the latter type seems to be more characteristic of Nūrī. It has to be noted also that in the separate section Sarrāj dedicated to Nūrī, his confrontation with the religious authorities takes the most prominent role and is treated most extensively.

Sufism and Ecstasy

The importance of ecstasy in Nūrī's approach to mysticism may be discerned in his explication of the word "Sufi," which associates Sufism and ecstasy, although not exclusively, since the saying has a double meaning and is open for interpretation as well. The explanation appears in the chapter collecting various answers to the question concerning the Sufis' self-denomination:

> They received this name since they wrap themselves in the manifest [guise] of the servants of God, [hiding themselves] from the people, and since they dedicate themselves to the Real [God] according to the grades of the ecstatics (*wājidūn*).[7]

The origin of the word "Sufi" was a controversial issue with divergent answers offering different possible etymologies, which deduced the word either from the noun *ṣafā* (purity), or *ṣuffa* (bench, referring to "the people of the bench," some destitute companions of the

Prophet Muḥammad), or *ṣūf* (wool). These proposals, however, did not mutually exclude each other, rather they intended to emphasize different aspects of Sufism. Nūrī's saying is evidently related to the possibility of deriving "Sufi" from the word "wool." He refers to the outward appearance of the Sufis, who "wrap themselves" in the clothing of the humble servants of God, that is, to the woollen garment worn by mystics. The second part of the saying has double sense: *wājid* may refer to those who experience *wajd* (ecstasy), or to "those who encounter God" (which is one of the meanings of the word).[8] Since it is not plausible that Nūrī would confine the validity of the term "Sufi" to the ecstatic mystics, he probably plays with the double sense of the word alluding to the intimate and esoteric aspect of encountering, meeting God (as opposed to the manifest aspect of wearing wool), but at the same time, he emphasizes the ecstatic nature of such encounter.

When Nūrī was asked who in fact counts as a Sufi, he singled out an even more controversial feature than ecstasy, namely, the *samāʿ* ceremony:

> Abū l-Ḥusayn Aḥmad ibn Muḥammad al-Nūrī was asked: "Who is a Sufi?" He said: "He who listens to audition (*samāʿ*), but prefers [its underlying] reasons (*asbāb*)."[9]

Samāʿ, whose literal meaning is "hearing," is a spiritual practice consisting of listening to the recitation of poems accompanied by music.[10] The listeners may get into a state of emotional agitation, which they might express with bodily movements including dancing or whirling. Ecstatic rapture caused by the *samāʿ* might lead to immoderate or scandalous actions like rending one's garment or indulging in sensual pleasures. This might also mislead simple people, making them believe that Sufism is essentially listening to music and poems while dancing or letting oneself be drawn into ecstatic behavior.[11] The poems recited on these occasions might pertain to the genre of secular love and wine poetry that should be interpreted allegorically, as referring to divine love and mystical intoxication. Such poems, however, always convey their plain meaning, too, and therefore can be attractive for those with a predilection for such pleasures. When Nūrī draws attention to the underlying reasons of the ceremony, he emphasizes the true purpose of the mystical practice and warns against merely enjoying the superficial pleasure caused by music and poetry. Ecstasy caused by *samā'* is essentially an inner quality, which might have external manifestations as well. However, these are secondary with respect to realization of the "underlying reasons."

Love and Ecstasy

An example of love poems inducing ecstasy may be the poem Nūrī recited on the occasion of a scholarly discussion of a theological issue:

> It was related that Abū l-Ḥusayn al-Nūrī and a group of sheiks were invited, so they joined together and entered into discussion about a theological problem (*mas'ala fī l-ʿilm*). Abū l-Ḥusayn al-Nūrī, however, kept silence. After a while, he raised his head and recited to them these lines:
>
> How many times a wailing dove
> Cooed in the rising heat of the forenoon trees
> My weeping might soften her heart
> Her weeping might cover me as wings
> If she complains, I do not understand her
> And when I complain, she understands me not
> But I recognize her by [her] ardent love (*al-jawā*)
> And by [my] ardent love she recognizes me, too
>
> There was not one of them who did not show ecstasy (*tawājada*) when Nūrī recited these lines.[12]

The poem does not use Sufi terms and does not differ essentially from a secular love poem, which it might have been originally. Secular love poems were widely interpreted by Sufis as allegories of divine love, and such poems are frequently attributed to Sufi masters. Sometimes it is not easy to distinguish between a secular and a mystical composition: a mystical poem does not necessarily contain Sufi terms, and the authorship is always questionable.[13]

In a mystical context, the poem can be explained as an allegory of the spirit longing for its primordial closeness to God. The dove symbolizes the spirit[14] that separated from God and descended to the human body but yearns to return to its place of origin. The dove coos in the middle of the day, desperate in her love and longing—although the passion of love torments the lovers conventionally during the night or at dawn. The emphasis on the rising heat of daytime is an allusion to the intensity of the emotion: it overpowers the spirit even when worldly concerns are most likely to overshadow the nostalgia for the primordial state. The human being weeps similarly to the spirit, desirous of reunion with his beloved; emotion and nostalgia join man and spirit together. However, mundane love is distinct from spiritual longing, and therefore the spirit cannot understand human desire, just as man cannot comprehend the rapture of the spirit. Despite that, the strong emotion both the human being and the spirit experience, the sensation of ardent love they share, establishes a connection between mundane and divine love, and reveals an intrinsic correspondence between the two types of passion and desire.

Sarrāj quotes the poem and narrates the context of its recitation in the chapter on how true mystics show ecstasy *(tawājud al-mashāyikh al-ṣādiqīn)*. Sarrāj distinguishes between genuine and false display of ecstasy. He does not simply differentiate between *wajd* and *tawājud*, experiencing ecstasy and exhibiting ecstasy but adds that some of those who exhibit ecstasy might be in fact mere imitators of the true ecstatics. According to his explication, ecstasy has several external and manifest signs: shivering, heavy breathing, weeping, fainting, losing consciousness, shouting, moaning.[15] A person experiencing ecstasy does not necessarily exhibit all, or even any, of these signs: "Don't you see that some of them lose composure and begin to move, and their heavy breathing becomes perceptible; and others, who are more composed while experiencing ecstasy, will not display anything similar."[16] Therefore, the categories of *wajd* and *tawājud* do not mutually exclude each other; they partially overlap. Sarrāj frequently classifies in triads the mystical phenomena according to their level of perfection. Similarly, he enumerates three types of people who experience ecstasy *(wājid)*: (1) those for whom ecstasy is an almost permanent companion but whose selfish necessities, obligations of human nature, and natural dispositions divert them from their state and disturb their mystical moment *(waqt)*; (2) those whose ecstasy is roughly permanent but are occasionally overcome by something similar to their ecstasy due to the calamities that the audition session *(samāʿ)* may cause (they find pleasure and stimulation in it, but it alters their ecstasy); and (3) those who are in a state of permanent ecstasy (since ecstasy has annihilated them), and they do not perceive anything, not even their ecstatic state. Sarrāj expounds also on those who exhibit ecstasy *(tawājud)*, distinguishing the following three types: (1) valueless pretenders and imitators (2) those who after having given up mundane attachments diverting them from their spiritual quest summon mystical states with some difficulty. Showing ecstasy is appropriate in their case, although not optimal, since it is caused by their celebration of their renunciation of worldly affairs. Sarrāj remarks that his position concerning the soundness of such behavior might be refused or criticized, and therefore he proves his view by a *ḥadīth*, according to which the Prophet Muḥammad said: "When you meet these tormented people, weep, or if you don't weep, show weeping!"[17] Just as showing weeping is commendable if one is unable to weep truly, showing ecstasy is appropriate if one is incapable of experiencing real ecstasy. (3) The third group is that of the "sons of the mystical states, the masters of the hearts, and those who fully realize their will"—that is, accomplished mystics. In Sarrāj's view, if such persons are unable to control their bodily members and to hide their mystical experience, they show their ecstasy and relieve themselves from what they cannot tolerate. Exhibiting ecstasy is considered a debility on their part: they are "the weak ones from among the people of true realities."

Ghazālī also quotes the poem and the story and in his *Iḥyā ʿulūm al-dīn*, and interprets it as a manifestation of the dichotomy between the heart and the intellect.[18] Rational discourses do not impress the listener's heart, save in exceptional cases. Poems, however, give expression to the states of the heart, and are accessible to everyone. The situation in which Nūrī recited the poem was that of a learned discussion, which did not affect the heart's equilibrium. The love poem, by contrast, had an immediate effect on everybody who heard it, "and this ecstasy did not overcome them because of the learning in which they were engaged, although their learning was real and serious."[19]

Nūrī's refusal of the intellectual approach to God is evidenced by a long and theoretic discourse on this topic:

> Abū l-Ḥusayn al-Nūrī was asked: "How did you get to know God?" He replied: "By God." Thereupon, he was asked: "Then, what is the role of intellect?" He replied: "The intellect is incompetent, can guide only to something likewise incompetent. When God created the intellect, He said to it: 'Who am I?' And it kept silent. So He smeared its eyes with the light of divine unity (*waḥdāniyya*), thence it said: 'You are God.' So, the intellect was not capable of knowing God, only by God." Then he was asked about the first obligation God imposed upon His servants: what was it? He replied: "Knowledge (*maʿrifa*), in accordance with His saying: 'I created the jinn and the men so that they may serve Me.' [Quran 51:56] And Ibn ʿAbbās said:[20] 'So that they may know [Me].' "[21]
>
> Nūrī was told: "How can it be that the intellect cannot grasp Him, despite He cannot be known only through intellect?" He replied: "How could the finite grasp the infinite? Or how could the flawed grasp the flawless and the unblemished? Or how could be described by 'how' Him who made how-ness, and how could be described by 'where' Him who made where-ness, and named it 'where'? Who made the first to be first, and the last to be last, and named them first and last? Were He not made the first first, and the last last, firstness and lastness would not be known! Then he said: What is pre-eternity in fact, unless it is infinity? There is no separation between them, just like firstness is lastness, and lastness is firstness. And similarly, manifestness and hiddenness [are the same], but sometimes He makes you lose it and sometimes He makes you witness it, in order to renew pleasure and to show [your] servanthood to God (*ʿubūdiyya*). He who gets to know Him through creation, does not get to know Him by direct contact (*mubāshara*), since creation is in accordance with His word:'Be!', and direct contact is revealing a great measure of holiness."[22]

Probably Sarrāj divided the text, which appears to be originally continuous, into two parts, and included them in different chapters of his book: in the chapter on the difference between the believer *(mu'min)* and the knower *(ʿārif)* on the one hand, and in the chapter on inspired knowledge *(maʿrifa)* on the other. The second part can be found a few pages earlier in the book than the first part.[23] According to Sarrāj's explication, by "direct contact" *(mubāshara)* Nūrī means "certainty's direct contact and the heart's contemplation of the truths of faith through absence *(ghayb)*."[24] Sarrāj interprets Nūrī's text as a discourse on God's eternity and omnipotence, His radical distinctness from the human being. God is not subject either to time or to change; the nearest thing for Him is equal to the farthest, and the farthest to the nearest. Distinction between closeness and farness, alternation between contentment and displeasure are attributes of the creatures, not the attributes of the Real; therefore, such categories are in fact irrelevant with respect to God.

The text may be regarded as the theoretical background of Nūrī's unexpected action of reciting a love poem in the midst of a theological discussion. Reciting a secular love poem under such conditions might be compared to a modern performance or an artistic expression aimed at provoking the immediate reaction of the public. Nūrī's action is provocative and effective; it represents the counterpart of the speculative answers given to the questions inquiring about intellect. Both traditions affirm the priority of intuition over rationality.

The following love poem quoted in Nūrī's name in the chapter on the inner heart *(sirr)* again may be interpreted either as a secular love poem or as a mystical one:

By my life! I've never entrusted my secret and her
  secret (*sirr*)
to other than ourselves, lest secrets (*sarā'ir*) become
  divulged
And my eye has never looked at her secret
lest watching eyes witness our intimate conversation
  (*najwā*)
But I've made imagination an envoy between us
and it accomplishes what our innermosts (*ḍamā'ir*) conceal.[25]

A version of the poem is quoted among other compositions on secular love in the *Rawḍat al-qulūb* by Shayzarī (twelfth century) in a chapter on things avoided by the fine people *(ẓurafā')* and dignitaries.[26] In that context it treats a well-known aspect of mundane love, that is, jealousy, and the unwanted consequences of other people's awareness of the lovers' passion. However, in the context of Islamic mysticism the poem obtains a different signification, all the more so, since the three lines quoted here employ many Sufi technical terms (in the *Rawḍat al-qulūb* the poem has a fourth line as well).[27] The central topic of the poem is *sirr,* with emphasis on its meaning "secret" when the composition is interpreted as a secular poem, and with accent on its meaning "inner heart," if it is read as a mystical text. The feminine pronominal suffix ("her secret") might indicate that it was originally a secular love poem, indeed; but we can also posit that it is used conventionally and refers to God from the outset.[28] The poem depicts a lover who avoids revealing his passion for his beloved before the people and therefore refrains from speaking about their intimate relations. He guards both his tongue and his eyes, lest his gaze betray his affection for the beloved. Sarrāj quotes the poem along with other poems and sayings stressing the aspect of secrecy and intimacy: like the line from Yūsuf b. al-Ḥusayn: "The hearts *(qulūb)* of the people are the tombs of the secrets/inner hearts."[29] The pun cannot be translated to English: on the one hand, the saying alludes to the concept that the heart is not identical with its innermost content, which is inaccessible to the human being; on the other hand it defines the hearts as permanent, impenetrable repositories of secrets. In order to appreciate the full meaning of the saying it is necessary to combine both semantic contents.

Another example of Nūrī's love poetry invested with mystical meaning is the following composition. Unlike the previous one, it is primarily a mystical poem intended as such by its composer, who availed himself of the literary devices of the pre-Islamic *qaṣīda.*

Let me weep with you over the signs of hearts (*ishārāt al-qulūb*)
from which nothing remained save erased marks
Let me weep with you over hearts from which
the generous clouds showered seas of wisdom so many times

Let me weep with you over souls the witness of
which
lost his way in what is behind space and before time
Let me weep with you over the tongue of the Real
(*lisān al-ḥaqq*), which
vanished for long, and its remembrance faded from
[our] imagination
Let me weep with you over clarity to which
yield the ears of intelligent speakers whose speech is
clear
Verily, let me weep with you over a community which
used to keep its riding beasts in the recesses of
taciturnity[30]
Everyone is gone, there is no eye [=man], nor trace [left]
as ʿĀd has gone, and the first [peoples] have been
lost, like Iram.[31]

According to Sarrāj's laconic explication, the poem describes the mystic's feeling when he loses his mystical state. It might be added that a state, since it is normally considered as originating from God, is regarded as a divine gift, the loss of which inevitably generates a sense of desolation. The structure and the theme of the poem correspond to the conventional nostalgic opening *(nasīb)* of the pre-Islamic *qaṣīda*. The poet laments to his companion the evanesced signs of a heart similar to the ancient Arab poet who stopped his camel at a former site of encampment for which he had so many feelings of nostalgia and loving reminiscences—he asked his travel companion to halt in order to recall the days past.[32] The Sufi poem articulates mystical content using the classical structure and theme; it transforms the ancient form into an allegory expressing longing for divine love. The lines are replete with Sufi terms and concepts, most of which are related to communication (sign, tongue, clarification, speech, taciturnity). The terms *bayān* (clarity) and *lisān* (tongue) appear in the poem as an interconnected pair of concepts and refer especially to God's communication. *Bayān* denotes God's declaration and clear statement to the people (cf. Quran 3:138) and is paired with *lisān al-ḥaqq*, the "tongue of the Real," or the divine way of expression, which is unattainable to the human being. Taciturnity—or, more specifically, refraining from excessive, unnecessary speech *(qillat al-kalām)*—is one of the virtues

Sufis have praised for a long time, together with scarcity of food and sleep *(qillat al-ṭaʿām, qillat al-manām).* The last line describes evanescence with an allusion to the extinction of ancient, mythical tribes of ʿĀd and Iram mentioned in various verses of the Quran.[33]

The poem is frequently attributed to Ḥallāj, and is purportedly one of the poems he recited the night before being executed.[34] Sarrāj divided the poem into two parts: he quoted the first six lines in the chapter on *sirr*, but included the last line in the chapter discussing Sufi vocabulary, in the entry on the term *ʿayn* (meaning literally "eye" or "source," and metaphorically "self, substance"). He attributes also the last line to Nūrī, and since the poem is attested in longer versions that include the last line, it is reasonable to reunite the parts here. The disintegration of complete textual units into short, separate parts, even at the expense of the text's meaning, is characteristic of Sarrāj's composition method.

Hearing a love poem, especially in the emotionally agitated atmosphere of the *samāʿ* ceremony may induce permanent and unending unconsciousness, that is, totally uncontrollable ecstasy:

> It was related about Abū l-Ḥusayn al-Nūrī that he went to an audition-session (*samāʿ*), where he heard the following verse:
>
> Because of my love (*widād*) for you, I always take
> lodgings at a resting place
> at which hearts become perplexed when they take a
> rest
>
> He stood up, showed his ecstasy (*tawājada*) and wandered about in rapture aimlessly. He walked into a thicket of reeds that had been already [cut and] carried away, so the stumps of the reeds that remained there were sharp as swords. He started to walk over the stumps with his feet bleeding, and repeated this verse until next morning. His legs and feet swelled up. He lived a couple of days more and he died.[35]

Should such a death be regarded as the ultimate end and the perfect realization of an ecstatic mystic's life? Not according to Sarrāj, who includes the story in the chapter on how "intermediate level Sufi masters" *(al-mutawassiṭūn al-ʿārifūn)*[36] behave during *samāʿ* sessions, as opposed to the masters who reached the perfection of mystical knowledge and whose outer appearance is not altered by emotions and rapture caused by the *samāʿ*.[37] Such a distinction clearly places Nūrī among the imperfect mystics.[38]

But what is indeed love for Nūrī? He defines it in a metaphorical saying that evokes the most intimate moment of the bridal night:

> Abū l-Ḥusayn al-Nūrī was asked about love (*maḥabba*), and he said: "It means to tear the veils (*hatk al-astār*) and to uncover the secrets (*kashf al-asrār*)."[39]

The secular layer of the meaning alludes both to the groom's act of uncovering the bride's face for the first time during the wedding ceremony and to the consummation of the marriage as the final act of the wedding performance. Employing such a sensual metaphor for the description of love between the human being and God is utterly bold and may arouse suspicion and provoke rejection. Sarrāj does not blunt the message of the saying by denying the underlying semantic realm connected with the sexual act but does distance himself to a certain extent from the saying by classifying it in the middle category of his customary triads of mystical perfection. He demonstrates the legitimacy of the concept of love *(maḥabba)* in mysticism by enumerating several Quranic passages speaking about the love of God toward humankind and vice versa.[40] Furthermore, Sarrāj explains that love is not a station that could be attained by one's own efforts but a state originated by God. His opinion is not unanimously shared by the Sufis, for others hold that love is a station the wayfarer should strive for.[41] However, if love is a state, that is, a divine gift, it follows that its legitimacy is beyond question. The sayings by which Sarrāj describes the lowest state of love include notions like "finding sweetness in intimate conversation with God"; "doing one's outmost, and the beloved does what he wants."[42] A more elevated degree of love is that of the righteous *(ṣādiq)* and the accomplished mystic *(mutaḥaqqaq)*, whose heart beholds God's majesty, wealth, power, and knowledge. Sarrāj exemplifies that kind of love citing

Nūrī's saying, among others that mention erasure of one's will and attributes, or finding pleasure in tasting God's closeness and intimate conversation with Him. The utmost degree of love is that of the upright *(ṣiddīq)*, and of the *ʿārif*, who possess inspired knowledge concerning the unconditioned, preeternal love of God, and in turn loves God unconditionally. Such a love is no longer attached to the personality of the mystic: "Love having no turbidity in it at all means that love is abolished from the heart and the bodily members, until the love is not in them, but the matters are through God and [possessed] by Him *(bi-llāh wa-li-llāh):* such a person is God's lover *(al-muḥibb li-llāh).*"[43] Junayd's explication clarifies the essential meaning of such love: "The attributes of the Beloved take the place of the attributes of the lover."[44]

The traditions discussed so far employ the term *maḥabba,* an unquestionably acceptable word for describing either divine or human love—its legitimacy is granted by the Quranic occurrences of the term in this context. Nūrī, however, did not refrain from using the highly controversial term *ʿishq* (passionate love) to describe the relation between him and God. His utterances in this respect were regarded as blasphemous: Nūrī was arrested, and his case was investigated by the religious authorities.

Blasphemous Sayings

> Abū Naṣr [al-Sarrāj] said: It has reached me that in the days of Muwaffaq, Abū l-Ḥusayn Aḥmad ibn Muḥammad al-Nūrī was accused by Ghulām al-Khalīl. He denounced him to Muwaffaq, who was the commander of the believers at that time: "There is a heretic in Baghdad whose blood is permitted to be shed, and if the commander of the believers kills him, his blood is on me!" So the caliph ordered to capture him. He was brought before the caliph, and Ghulām al-Khalīl testified against him: "I have heard him to say: 'I am in [passionate] love (*ʿishq*) with God and God is in [passionate] love with me!'" Nūrī said: "I have heard God to say: 'He loves them (*yuḥibbuhum*) and they love Him', [Quran 5:53] and to be in love is not more than to love, but the love (*ʿishq*) of

the former is unfulfilled, while the love (*maḥabba*) of the latter is requited." Muwaffaq burst out crying because of the gentleness of his speech.

They also testified against him that he heard the call of a muezzin and said: "A stab and a lethal poison!" But when he heard a dog barking, he said: "I wait intent upon obedience to You!" He was questioned about this, and he said: "As for the muezzin: I blame him because he utters the name of God heedlessly and takes the reward for it. Were it not for the meagre vanities of this world he takes as a reward, he would not remember (*dhakara*) God! That is why I said to him: A stab and a lethal poison. God—may His remembrance (*dhikr*) be exalted—has said: 'There is not a thing but glorifies and praises Him, but you do not understand their glorification.' [Quran 17:44] Therefore the dog, and everything remember (*yadhkurūna*) God without [any trace of] hypocrisy, not for the sake of reputation and without expecting any compensation. That is why I have said what I have said."

Nūrī was taken to the caliph again, and they testified against him that he said: "Yesterday I was at home with God." He was asked about this, and he said: "He told the truth, and I am with God right now as well. When I am at home, I am with God; and when I am in the desert, I am with God, too. He who is with God in this world, will be with God in the world to come. Has not God said: 'We created man, and We know what his soul whispers to him, for We are nearer to him than his jugular vein'? [Quran 50:16] Hearing that, the caliph put his hand over him, and said: "Speak as you wish!" And Nūrī spoke and he told things that were never heard before. The caliph burst out crying and everybody cried with him, and they said: "These know God better than anyone else.[45]

Sarrāj relates these stories in his entry on Nūrī, entitled "Chapter on Abū l-Ḥusayn al-Nūrī and what was testified against him about blasphemy *(kufr)* before the caliph, and other issues." The *Book of Flashes* does not contain biographical entries, but it does dedicate separate chapters to some of the leading figures of ecstatic Sufism (Abū Yazīd al-Bisṭāmī, Shiblī, Abū Ḥamza, etc.), whose activity was controversial enough to raise the suspicion of the religious authorities. With a clear apologetic intention, Sarrāj devotes a separate part of his book to the explication of ecstatic utterances, which appear to be blasphemous despite their inherent truth. The chapter on Nūrī is included in this part, identifying Nūrī obviously as associated with the group of controversial ecstatic mystics. As opposed to the sayings of Abū Yazīd, Shiblī, and other mystics, Sarrāj does not comment upon the words of Nūrī quoted in this chapter—most probably since he finds the explications provided by Nūrī himself sufficiently self-explanatory: just as the caliph was convinced of Nūrī's innocence, the reader should acknowledge his blamelessness.

According to Sarrāj's account, the trial took place before the "caliph" Muwaffaq (d. 891), who was in fact the brother of the caliph Muʿtamid. According to the report of Dhahabī (d. 1348), however, the event took place in AH 264 (AD 877/878), before the caliph Muʿtamid.[46] It is not evident whether the accusations were presented at the same occasion or in several instances. It seems reasonable to suppose that several elements, like being denounced to the religious authorities, the inquisition of Ghulām Khalīl, and some scandalous utterances of Nūrī became loosely associated, and in Sarrāj's account they are presented as a coherent narration, while in other sources the same incident is narrated with different details. And some elements (like Nūrī's words about the muezzin and dog) are not related to the legal case at all.[47]

It has to be noted that Sarrāj also recounts quite a banal motive that led to the vexation of the Sufis by Ghulām Khalīl. According to that, one of the mystics of Baghdad, Sumnūn, was a very attractive and charming man whose teachings focused on divine love. His spiritual disposition was so conspicuous that he was nicknamed "the Lover" *(al-Muḥibb)*. One of his female followers fell in love with him, and when he became aware of that, he sent her away. She complained about her passion to Junayd, saying: "What is your opinion about a man who was my path towards God; but God went away and the man remained?"[48] The consolation Junayd offered could not relieve her, and she offered herself to Sumnūn in marriage. When Sumnūn rejected her, she went to Ghulām Khalīl, whose hostility to the Sufis was blatant, and accused the mystics of meeting her every night with the purpose of having forbidden relations with her. In turn, Ghulām Khalīl testified against the Sufis, and they were sentenced to decapitation. The death sentence was not carried out, however, since God saved the mystics.[49]

Nūrī's bold expressions may be regarded as the manifestation of his complete sincerity in his relation to God. Sincerity for Nūrī means to disregard people's consent:

> Nūrī—I think—was asked about sincerity (*ikhlāṣ*) and he said: "To desist from [seeking] the creatures' approval."[50]

Such a demand might lead to controversial actions, or even to the formation of heretical groups similar to which Sarrāj characterizes among the communities holding erroneous views. One of these is a group of Baghdadi Sufis who hold that perfect sincerity requires complete disregard for creatures—which is precisely the expectation formulated by Nūrī. However, as Sarrāj explains, this requirement cannot be fulfilled by mere mechanical imitation, without having traversed the stations of the spiritual path leading to complete absorption in God. Those who err in this regard wish to skip the stations of self-discipline and cross the limits set by religious law.[51]

Miracles

The spiritual power of the Sufi masters resides in their special connection to God, which endows them with quasi-magical potential. Their followers perceive mystical, or possibly magical, power radiating from them constantly, which is regarded as a permanent effusion or outflow of their spirituality. The manifestations of the mystics' special power are the miracles *(karāmāt)* attributed to them. The *Book of Flashes* includes a chapter on miracles, which contains two completely contradictory stories regarding Nūrī's attitude to miracles. One of the stories depicts Nūrī as a self-willed and capricious person demanding God to perform a seemingly senseless miracle.[52] The story starts abruptly, its antecedent is not clear:

> Nūrī said: "I fancied a miracle (*karāma*) like these. So I took a reed from the boys, stood between two boats and said: '[I swear] by Your might, I will drown myself in the water, unless You bring out from the water a fish of three raṭl weight for me! And a fish of three raṭl came out for me.'" The story reached Junayd, and he said: "He would have deserved that a viper come out for him in order to bite him."[53]

It seems as if Nūrī wanted to impress these boys by demonstrating his extraordinary relationship with God, who would do whatever pleased him. In the view of the sober mystic Junayd, such liberties with God are unacceptable. Sarrāj remarks concerning Junayd's rebuke that Nūrī's request entails temptation *(fitna)*, and the snake's bite would have been purification and atonement for his sin. Sarrāj's choice of including this story in his book corresponds to his view of Nūrī as an imperfect mystic, whose special connection to God is, however, undeniable (after all, God performed the miracle Nūrī asked for). On the other hand, he counterpoints Nūrī's questionable behavior relating another story, in which he behaves in a perfectly modest and flawless manner.

> "It has been mentioned concerning Nūrī that one night he came to the Tigris, and he said: "I found that one of its banks has joined the other bank. But I said: '[I swear] by Your might, I won't cross it, but only on boat.'"[54]

Although both stories occur in the same chapter, and the parallelism between them can be observed even in their phraseology (the oath formula used in them), Sarrāj does not juxtapose them, neither does he comment on their obvious contradictions. His view on the stories may be inferred from the context created by the traditions he includes in the chapter. The sayings that set the tone of the chapter express the mystics' reservation about supernatural power granted to them by God. Sarrāj quotes several stories in which the mystic, who is capable of performing supernatural acts, declines to access his special power. A truly advanced Sufi master abandons the performance of miracles: for example, Abū Yazīd al-Bisṭāmī is granted inspired knowledge after he refuses to pay attention to the miraculous deeds God shows him.[55] In light of that, it is possible Sarrāj wished to portray Nūrī as an unstable personality to whom miracles are granted but who is not always capable of controlling his special power.[56]

Moderateness and Soberness

Most of the traditions discussed until now reveal unconventional aspects of Nūrī's mysticism, or are at least related to these. He is portrayed as an ecstatic, intoxicated mystic unable to control either his rapture or his supernatural capacities. His ardent love drives him to risk his life in unconscious delirium or through blasphemous utterances made in public. He approaches God through love, denies the relevance of the intellectual faculty, and expresses his ideas by poems of either mystical or secular love. Roughly a third of the traditions included in the *Book of Flashes* are connected to this facet of Nūrī's personality. As for the rest, they are wholly compatible with sober mysticism and do not manifest any trace of extremism. Most of these traditions treat cognition, concentration, immersion in contemplation, and absence. Cognition for Nūrī is not an intellectual process but rather the action of the heart; visual observation and mental perception are repeatedly contrasted in the sayings. Certain knowledge is attained through contemplation and not by intellectual speculation:

> Certainty is witnessing (*mushāhada*).[57]

Such mental perception may be compared to eyewitnessing:

> The unveilings (*mukāshafāt*) of the eyes happen through vision, while the unveilings of the hearts (*qulūb*) happen through connection (*ittiṣāl*).[58]

According to Sarrāj, unveiling is "the clarity *(bayān)* of what is hidden from understanding, but is unveiled for the servant, as if he saw it with his eyes."[59] Unveiling is closely connected to contemplation *(mushāhada)*; the two terms are frequently paired and sometimes interchangeable. The concept, which Nūrī's words articulate, is expressed by others with the idea of the heart's contemplation of God *(mushāhadat al-qulūb)*.[60] The eye's act of seeing, and the heart's act of contemplating are paralleled and even interconnected, as the following saying of ʿAmr b. ʿUthmān al-Makkī (d. 909) shows: "Contemplation is the combination of the hearts' action of seeing and the eyes' action of witnessing, since the hearts' action of seeing happens when revealing certainty, while imagination is intensified. That is expressed by the Prophet's words to ʿAbd Allah b. ʿUmar: 'Worship God as if you saw Him!' "[61] Nūrī also emphasizes the contrast between sensual and mental perception in the following saying:

> Everything the eyes see is attributed to learning (*ʿilm*), and everything the hearts learn about is attributed to certainty (*yaqīn*).[62]

ʿIlm, translated here as "learning," usually refers to both secular and religious sciences that can be obtained through one's own efforts, as opposed to inspired knowledge *(maʿrifa)* granted by God. The heart's act of "learning" is in fact preparing itself to accept God's inspiration.

According to Sarrāj, the heart's cognition of God is through theophany *(tajallin)*, which he defines as follows: "Theophany is when the Real turns toward the hearts turning to Him, and His lights illuminates these hearts."[63] In the chapter on theophany he includes a saying of Nūrī, which describes the effect of divine illumination or the lack of it:

> Good deeds are good and proper when He reveals Himself, but are bad and repulsive when He hides Himself.[64]

God deliberately hides or reveals Himself, which fundamentally alters the quality of things, just as the presence or the absence of light radically influences the perception of the same object. Another saying of Nūrī in the same chapter points out the paradoxical role creation plays in a person's awareness of God: although it reveals divine attributes and purpose, and proves the existence of the Creator, it may camouflage the real reason for the existing phenomena.

> He revealed Himself to the creatures through creation, and hid Himself from the creatures through creation.[65]

Creation, or the infinite multiplicity of existing beings, distracts the human being from God, unless he detaches himself mentally from the surrounding world and ceases to see the existents as separate entities from God but perceives everything through Him:

> I think, Nūrī was the one who said: Reunion (*jam ʿ*) with the Real is separation (*tafriqa*) from everything else, and separation from everything else is reunion with Him.[66]

Reunion *(jam ʿ)* and separation *(tafriqa)* are terms that normally occur in pairs.[67] They describe alternate, transitory states that complement each other. Sarrāj explains that if a person mentally "reunites" his perception of the world and attains to perfect concentration, ". . . he says "God" and nothing else"—he perceives God exclusively, while in the state of separation he perceives both this world and the world to come. Sarrāj justifies the legitimacy of the concept by a Quranic precedent in which apparently God himself perceives and communicates as if being first in the state of reunion and immediately after it in the state of separation: "God bears witness that there is no god but Him . . ." (Quran 3:18), that is, detects divine existence solely; but the passage continues, "and the angels and the men of learning . . ." (Ibid.) enumerating separate entities. Sarrāj gives preference to reunion over separation, since he views the former as fundamental *(aṣl)*, and the latter as derivative *(far ʿ)*, but he also emphasizes that reunion without separation is heresy *(zandaqa)*, and separation without reunion invalidates one's actions *(ta ʿṭīl)*—by which he distances himself from heterodox ideas.

Reunion with God supposes mental distance from the world, not physical seclusion. The mystic does not necessarily differ outwardly from the common believers; his communion with God does not require any extravagant actions:

> Both the common people and the elite wear the shirt of servanthood (*ʿubūdiyya*), but the Real attracted (*jadhaba*)

> those who were more sublime among them, and He erased (*maḥā*) them from themselves with regard to their movements, and established them at Himself.[68]

Common worshippers and the mystics are equal in their position of servanthood to God, but the mystics are distinguished as the elite due to God's concern for them, which shows itself in "attraction" *(jadhb)* and "erasure" *(maḥw)*. Sarrāj gives the definition of erasure as follows: "The passing away of a thing in such a manner that no trace of it remains."[69] Sarrāj's interpretation of Nūrī's saying begins with a quotation from the Quran that employs the same terms as Nūrī: "God erases what He wants and establishes what He wants" (Quran 13:39). It has to be noted that there is a certain tension between the passage of the Quran and Nūrī's words, since according to the latter God erases and establishes "the more sublime" from among His servants, while the Quran does not make such distinction. Sarrāj does not relate to this difference but explains that "establishing" corresponds to attraction *(jadhb)*, which is in fact reunion *(jamᶜ)*, that is, God's act of gathering his servants to Himself. Erasing them from themselves signifies that God erases their self-image of being agents of their movements and actions and establishes Himself as the ultimate agent.

"Erasure" is similar to *fanā'* (annihilation) to a certain extent, since the result of both actions is vanishing from worldly affairs and concerns, even from one's own self. A basic difference between the two terms could be that the active agent of the act of erasure is always God, while annihilation can be a reflective act as well: the human being may annihilate himself in God; but he cannot erase himself. Furthermore, although the originator of *fanā'* is God, it requires the active participation of man as well. That is not the case with *maḥw*, which is exclusively a divine act, similar to *jadhb* (God's action of attracting a person to Himself), independently of his action or inaction.

Nūrī's following poem may illustrate the difference between erasure and annihilation: the latter action is initiated now by the human being, now by God.

> Don't you see that He captivated me?
> He chased me away from my abode (*waṭan*)

When I absent myself, He appears (*badā*)
And if He appears, He makes me absent (*ghayyabanī*)
He says: You don't see what you see (*tashhad*)
Unless you see Me![70]

The poem is quoted in the entry on the mystical term *waṭan* (abode), which Sarrāj defines as follows: "The abode of the servant is the point where his state ultimately leads him, where he abides steadily. They say he abides at a certain state or at a certain station."[71] *Watanāt* is sometimes counterposed with *khaṭarāt:* the first term indicates permanent, lasting conditions while the second points to fugacious, transient moments.[72] The verb translated here as "chased me away" *(sharradanī)* alludes to a technical term, which Sarrāj explains in the next entry. According to that, "*Shurūd* [running away, roaming, straying] means to release the attributes *(ṣifāt)* from the positions of the realities and from insisting on obligations."[73] The term apparently refers to an unstable state in which man's normal dispositions are suspended, and his customary feelings and conditions melt away.

The second line, detached from the poem, appears also in the entry on presence *(ḥuḍūr),* which is defined by Sarrāj as follows: "Presence means the presence of the heart *(qalb),* when through pure certainty it is absent from seeing itself. It is as if it was present with itself, although it is absent from itself."[74] Presence is counterpointed by absence: "It means the absence of the heart from contemplating *(mushāhada)* the creation through its presence with the Real and His contemplation, without the manifest alteration of the servant['s appearance]."[75]

The poem employs the literary device of the paradox, which is characteristic of mystical language, since it manifests the imperfection of logic, rational reasoning, and human way of expression (speech). Nūrī alludes to that in the following story:

> As for the state of the greatest and most accomplished Sufis, it corresponds to what Abū l-Ḥusayn al-Nūrī said to a person who visited him:
> "Where are you from?"
> "From Baghdad."
> "Whom do you associate with there?"

> "Abū Ḥamza."
>
> "If you go back, say to Abū Ḥamza: The closest closeness in the sense to which we allude is the farthest farness."[76]

A fuller version of Nūrī's words appears in the chapter on nearness, along with an even more elaborate variant in Qushayrī's *Treatise,* where the relevance of Nūrī's saying is indicated, namely, that Abū l-Ḥamza was famous for speaking about the closeness to God using the allusive language associated with mystics.[77] It is interesting to note that Sarrāj, contrary to his usual practice, here classifies Nūrī among the greatest Sufis. He explains that closeness equals establishing connection with God *(tawaṣṣul)*; however, while one is concerned with the problem of closeness or farness, he is evidently distanced from God. "Until the God-servant is in closeness [i.e., perceives closeness], there is no closeness [i.e., he does not attain to God], till he annihilates himself from closeness through closeness."[78] Sarrāj remarks that the meaning of Nūrī's message to Abū Ḥamza corresponds to the popular saying "the virtues of the pious *(abrār)* are the vices of those drawn near to God *(muqarrabūn)*" and "the sincerity of the seekers *(murīdūn)* is the hypocrisy of the knowers *(ʿārifūn)*,"[79] by which he means that speculation on mystical notions is adequate for the beginners, but must be superseded eventually.[80]

Several of the traditions attributed to Nūrī deal expressly with the problem of verbal expression and communication. These sometimes employ the paired concepts *lisān-bayān* (tongue and clarity), like the poem that has been discussed above:

> Let me weep with you over the tongue (*lisān*) of the Real, which
> vanished for long, and its remembrance faded from [our] imagination
> Let me weep with you over clarity (*bayān*) to which
> yield the ears of intelligent speakers whose speech is clear.[81]

Sarrāj dedicates a separate entry to these concepts in his glossary of Sufi terms. Each concept expresses a distinct aspect of the process of understanding and expressing a notion. *Bayān* signifies "being distinct and apparent," but also "making distinct and apparent," hence it refers to deep, clear understanding, and the intellectual action of clarification, clear exposition, and explanation. *Lisān* is the mode of expression by which the deeply understood concept (the *bayān)* is communicated. The distinction between the concepts of *bayān* and *lisān* is apparent in Ibn ʿArabī's words on letter-mysticism and the letters of the alphabet: "From the aspect of tongue, the letters give plain expression to the word [verbally]; from the aspect of clarity, they make it understood [semantically]."[82]

Sarrāj explains further the term *lisān* and quotes Shiblī's (d. 946) words on the concept: "Shiblī was asked: 'What is the difference between the tongue of learning *(lisān al-ʿilm)* and the tongue of reality *(lisān al-ḥaqīqa)*?' He said: 'The tongue of learning is that which reaches us through the intervention of a medium *(wāsiṭa),* and the tongue of reality is that which reaches us without the intervention of a medium.' He was asked further: 'And the tongue of the Real *(lisān al-ḥaqq),* what is it?' He said: 'That which is inaccessible for the creatures.' "[83] The threefold division represents the three stages of the Sufi path: *sharīʿa* (Muslim law), *ṭarīqa* (mystical path), and *ḥaqīqa* (true reality, the perfect realization and declaration of God's oneness).[84] The "tongue of learning" refers to religious sciences, law, and theology; the "tongue of reality" apparently comprises the beginning and advanced stages of the mystical path, while the "tongue of the Real" alludes to what is beyond human capacity, the incomprehensible and impenetrable hidden word of God.

Sarrāj mentions a letter written by Nūrī to Junayd praising him for his capacity of understanding and expressing his knowledge:

> Tongue (*lisān*) means the clarity (*bayān*) of what one has learnt about realities. Abū l-Ḥusayn al-Nūrī wrote a letter to Junayd, and he wrote in it: "Oh, Sir, you have tongue [with which to express] what can be learned about tribulation; you have blade [sharp wittedness with which to discern] what can be learned about the tribulation of tribulation." He meant by that the clarity of what he learnt.[85]

Sarrāj is likely referring to the same letter of Nūrī on tribulation *(balāʾ)* in the chapter treating the Sufi masters' correspondence, when he excuses himself for omitting it from his compilation due to its length: "their long letters, as for example the letter of Nūrī to Junayd concerning the issue of tribulation *(balā')* [. . .] and others could not have been quoted by us."[86] Nūrī's letter was not included in the Sufi works and collections by other authors either, and so it appeared to have been lost until recently. However, fortunately enough, the lost letter has been found in the Cairo Genizah, together with Junayd's answer to it. The letters include headings stating the names of the author and the addressee (Nūrī and Junayd), and their subject matter is *balā'*, or tribulation. Their text was preserved in fragmentary form, and the legible part does not contain verbatim the passage Sarrāj quoted on the "tongue [with which to express] what can be learned about tribulation," but it does comprise a longer section on the "tongue of tribulation" and praises Junayd for his mastery of the "tongues" (means of expression in general).[87]

The power of verbal expression is treated in the following verse attributed to Nūrī, as well:

> If a mother touched by the hunger of her child
> Feeds him with [saying] his name, forebears the child.[88]

The verse appears in Sarrāj's entry on the term "name" *(ism)*. According to his definition: "A name is composed of letters put together so that the person who utters the name could ask the confirmation of the thing named. If the letters are omitted, the meaning of the name does not become detached from the denominated thing."[89] Sarrāj includes the verse in a story on Shiblī, who used to say regarding God: "Creatures do not have anything of Him except His name." He also used to say: "Bring to me someone who is really worthy of uttering the name!" Sarrāj interjects a remark in the Shiblī narrative according to which Nūrī used to attest the meaning of the allusion concealed in Shiblī's words by the abovementioned verse. Shiblī continues explaining himself: "I mean someone who utters the name while realizing what he utters. Creation got lost respecting learning; learning got lost respecting the name; the name got lost respecting the essence."[90] Shiblī's words most likely serve as a reminder that the name of God is not identical with His essence; furthermore, even his name cannot be comprehended through learning since theological knowledge and religious sciences are in themselves misleading. No one is capable of uttering God's name with the full realization of the utterance save God himself.

Nūrī's verse may be interpreted in distinct ways. According to one possibility, the mother mentioned in the verse corresponds to God: only she is in the position of quieting her child merely by pronouncing his name (only she can utter the child's name with full realization of the utterance) since she has an incomparably unique status in their relationship, unattainable for anyone else. Following this line of thought, the conclusion drawn from Shiblī's and Nūrī's words might be that names are imperfect and do not have power in themselves. However, taking into consideration the context that treats uttering God's name especially, one might infer that the poem also refers to that; if the mother were truly capable of pronouncing the divine name, she could feed her child by merely uttering it. It should be observed here that in popular Sufism names have enormous importance and are attributed magical powers. Sufi masters are supposed to be familiar with mysterious and divine names by means of which they can accomplish supernatural objectives. This fact leaves the door open for an interpretation pointing toward the attribution of automatic power to names.[91]

The rest of Nūrī's sayings quoted in the *Book of Flashes* can be characterized with the same moderateness as the previous traditions. Sarrāj quotes Nūrī's saying on repentance, which Kalābādhī also cites (this is one of the two traditions that both compilators included in their collections).[92] Another saying treats friendship:

> A friend is not called to account for anything; and nothing is credited to an enemy's account.[93]

This proverb-like saying is quoted in the chapter in the Sufis' way of conduct with regard to affection and friendship. The sentential statements gathered in the chapter do not essentially differ from other wise aphorisms on the topic, like: "No way is too long if it leads to a friend, and no place is too tight if it is shared with an intimate"; "Avoiding the friend is preserving the friendship"; but also: "The affection, which is increased by the meetings is real affection."[94]

Finally, Nūrī's view on poverty should be discussed. Sarrāj quotes a saying similar in some ways to another tradition attributed to Nūrī and cited by Kalābādhī as well:

> Nūrī was asked about the sincere poor, and he said: "The sincere poor does not accuse God with regard to [the lack of] means (*asbāb*), and relies on Him under every circumstances."[95]

In both traditions poverty is connected with the idea of facing deprivation with calmness *(sukūn)*, relying on God *(yaskunu ilayhi)* calmly.[96] The term "means" *(asbāb,* plural of *sabab)* signifying "reasons, causes" primarily, refers in Sufi texts to all those things that appear to be causes of the existing phenomena and that may obscure the only true reason, or the first cause, which is God. Denying importance to the secondary, or worldly means is a fundamental Sufi doctrine, as it is illustrated by the following anecdotes, as well:

> The vizier of Muʿtaḍid gave some money to Abū l-Ḥusayn al-Nūrī in order to distribute it among the Sufis. He poured it into a room, then he gathered the Baghdadi Sufis, and said to them: "He who is in need for something from among you, shall enter the room and take what he needs!" So, some people took a hundred dirhams, some more and some less, and some of them did not take at all. When the dirhams disappeared and nothing there remained, he said to them: "The more dirhams you took, the farther you are from God; the more dirhams you left, the nearer you are to God."[97]

Religious and political leaders of the Muslim community were very much interested in the activity of the Baghdadi Sufis. Mystics were frequently detained and interrogated. One such case was the trial on charges of heresy brought against a group of Sufis including Nūrī by Ghulām al-Khalīl (d. 888/9), under the caliph Muʿtamid, which has been already discussed. At least one more incident Nūrī had with the caliph Muʿtaḍid is attested to: according to a story reported by Dhahabī, Nūrī broke the caliph's wine jugs and consequently was arrested. After an interrogation conducted by the caliph, Nūrī was set free unharmed.[98] The story in which Nūrī receives financial support from the vizier of the caliph Muʿtaḍid (892–902), the successor of Muʿtamid (870–892) may reflect Nūrī's actual position under the caliph's rule; or else, it may be a fictitious story destined to prove the caliph's support both to Nūrī and Baghdadi Sufis in general. The latter suggestion seems to be more plausible since the same story is reported on Shiblī.[99] A further anecdote reveals Nūrī's attitudes about property:

> A piece of land belonging to Nūrī was sold, and [its price], three hundred dinars were brought to him. He sat on the bridge on the Ṣarāt [canal in Baghdad] and threw the dinars one by one to the water, saying: "My Lord, do You want to deceive me from [dedicating myself to] You with these?"[100]

The story is preserved in a more complete version in the supplement to the *Book of Flashes* published by Arberry, and there it shows an interesting textual variant: Nūrī does not address God as "my Lord" there, but as "my Beloved" *(ḥabībī)*.[101] The transmitter of the story adds there that some of the people disapproved of Nūrī's act of throwing the money into the water, saying that it would have been better to spend it on a praiseworthy purpose. In the transmitter's view, if Nūrī knew that the wealth he received could divert him from God even for a second, it would have been proper to throw all the money in the river at once in order to get rid of the temptation. Supposing that the version published by Arberry is genuine, we might conclude that the text published in Nicholson's edition of the *Book of Flashes* deliberately opts for the neutral form of address and omits "Beloved," since it might appear controversial.

Conclusions

About a third of the traditions collected by Sarrāj are related to the ecstatic aspect of Nūrī's mysticism. The majority of the traditions, however, have no such bearing, and they do not differ in any sense from sayings or poems attributed to sober, moderate Sufis. Despite that, when Sarrāj expresses his view on Nūrī, he presents him as an ecstatic—as a mystic yet not fully accomplished—who died before reaching perfection in his spiritual quest. In his habitual scheme of classification by triads, Sarrāj usually places Nūrī's words and actions in the second, intermediate category, corresponding to the rank of advanced but not consummate Sufis. He does not criticize any of Nūrī's sayings or actions as inadequate but makes clear that his spiritual evolution did not reach the excellence of such mystics as Junayd. Sarrāj characterizes Nūrī as "one of the ecstatics,"[102] and indeed ecstatic behavior and enraptured sayings abound in the traditions related to him. He was a mystic who could not control his ecstasy or master the sensation of overwhelming love, which ultimately led to his death. He presents himself not merely as a lover *(muḥibb)* of God but as a person passionately in love with God *(ʿāshiq)*. Correspondingly, the central theme of the poems attributed to him is love; some of these are mystical poems in the guise of secular poetry following pre-Islamic models; some overflow with mystical terms while others completely lack these and are easily mistaken for profane love poetry. He evidently joined *samāʿ* sessions, and his poems were suitable for inducing ecstasy. The relation between Nūrī, and Junayd is not discussed in the *Book of Flashes*; the sole instance that bears witness to the tension between them is a sharp remark by Junayd blaming Nūrī for the liberties he took with God.

Nūrī's confrontation with the religious authorities is well described in the *Book of Flashes*. The accusations he had to face were due to his quasi-blasphemous utterances that were misunderstood by the people. He declared himself a lover of God, claimed an intimate relationship with God, and rejected established norms. Negative consequences of such conflicts are not mentioned; on the contrary, trials in the caliphal court followed identical schemes ending with the caliph bursting into tears and acknowledging Nūrī's supremacy in religious matters.

The duality of the traditions attributed to Nūrī (intoxicated and moderate) reflects the intrinsic nature of those mystical states that occur in pairs and that do not merely contradict but rather complement each other. The Sufi experiencing intoxicated ecstasy and uttering passionate or quasi-blasphemous words sobers down subsequently and expresses himself in a moderate way. However, a state may become dominant in the Sufi's personality and may become his characteristic disposition altered by other states only fugaciously.[103] The fact that Sarrāj distinguishes Nūrī as an intoxicated ecstatic is evidence of the permanent nature of these states in his personality. Notwithstanding that, he obviously expressed his mystical experiences in perfectly moderate ways as well, and such traditions cited in his name by Sarrāj even outnumber the ecstatic ones.

The *Book of Flashes* is contemporary with Kalābādhī's *Doctrine of the Sufis*, but despite that, the traditions concerning Nūrī preserved in them do not overlap, save in the case of two short sayings. The same holds true for the *Book of Flashes* and to the *Generations of the Sufis*, compiled some decades later by Sulamī. Kharkūshī's *Revision of the Secrets* contains a single tradition gathered in the *Book of Flashes* as well. Similarly, only one of the traditions quoted in the *Book of Flashes* was collected also in the *Ornament of God's Friends* compiled by Abū Nuʿaym. Parallels with Qushayrī's *Treatise* composed in 1045 are more significant (some eight sayings are quoted in it), although Qushayrī does not cite any of Nūrī's poems.

The principal themes of Nūrī's moderate sayings and poems are obtaining inspired knowledge by means of contemplation, unveiling the heart, and attaining to God's closeness. The traditions connected to his ecstatic inclination deal with love, recollection, and rapture. The recurring technical terms in the traditions are (in order of frequency): inspired knowledge *(maʿrifa)*, contemplation or witnessing *(mushāhada*, etc.), love *(maḥabba, muḥibb, ḥubb, ishq)*, intellect *(ʿaql)*, heart *(qalb)*, learning *(ʿilm)*, carnal soul *(nafs)*, inner heart or secret *(sirr)*, recollection *(dhikr)*, nearness *(qurb)*, farness *(buʿd)*, ecstasy *(wajd, tawājud)*, concealing (various forms deriving from the verbal root *STR)*, unveiling *(mukāshafa, kashf)*, certainty *(yaqīn)*, revelation *(tajallin)*, tongue *(lisān)*, allusion *(ishāra)*, audition *(samāʿ)*, means *(sabab)*.[104] The traditions employ some of the less frequent terms also *(shurūd, waṭan, lisān)*. It is interesting to note the quantity of the technical terms compared with the relatively reduced number of these in the traditions collected by the contemporary Kalābādhī.

CHAPTER 3

Sulamī

Generations of the Sufis *(Ṭabaqāt al-ṣūfiyya)*

Introduction

Abū ʿAbd al-Raḥmān al-Sulamī's (d. 1021) biographical work, entitled *Generations of the Sufis (Ṭabaqāt al-ṣūfiyya)*[1] is the first extant Sufi work that pertains to the genre of *ṭabaqāt*, that is, a collection of biographies arranged in chronological order.[2] In all probability, it was composed one or two decades later than Kalābādhī's *Doctrine of the Sufis* and Sarrāj's *Book of Flashes*, as Sulamī died some thirty years later than Kalābādhī and Sarrāj. Recently, Jean-Jacques Thibon has proposed that Sulamī completed his *Generations of the Sufis* (which is presumably the abbreviated version of his lost *Ta'rīkh al-ṣūfiyya)* after 997.[3] As opposed to the manuals written by Kalābādhī and Sarrāj, *Generations of the Sufis* is not a theoretical work systemizing the tenets of Sufism but a biographical lexicon containing the short biographies of 105 Sufis and presenting a selection of their sayings.

Sulamī was born in Nishapur in an Arab settler family, either in 937 or 942. He studied religious sciences with his grandfather, Abū ʿAmr Ismāʿīl b. Nujayd, a Shāfiʿī scholar, and was initiated in Sufism by Abū Sahl al-Ṣuʿlūkī, from whom he received licence to teach what he had learned from him *(ijāza)*. He was invested with the Sufi cloak (*khirqa*) by Abū l-Qāsim al-Naṣrābādhī, a disciple of Abū Bakr al-Shiblī from Baghdad. Sulamī traveled extensively in search of traditions and performed the pilgrimage to Mecca in the company of his master, Naṣrābādhī. Sulamī's grandfather bequeathed him a considerable sum of money, a library and house in Nishapur, which during Sulamī's activity became a small Sufi lodge. Sulamī compiled a great commentary of the Quran from earlier sources (which is studied in the next chapter), wrote Sufi biographies and many minor theoretical treatises on Sufism. Several of these works have been lost, but many of the minor works are published, and some are still in manuscript form.[4] He was interested in the teachings of the Malāmatiyya, with which he became familiar through his grandfather, Ibn Nujayd, who studied under Abū ʿUthmān al-Ḥīrī, the head of the Malāmatiyya in Nishapur. Upon his death, Sulamī was buried in the lodge he established.[5]

Although Sulamī's biographical work preserved important vestiges of the Iranian-style Sufism distinct from the prevalent Iraqi tradition since most of the Sufi masters included in the *Generations of the Sufis* are of Khorasanian origin, the work suggests a preference for the Sufis of Baghdad. As Mojaddedi pointed out, Baghdadi Sufis are assigned more authority as heads of most of the subsequent generations, and in general they are placed in positions of more hierarchical value.[6]

Sulamī introduced the sayings and stories he collected with proper chains of tradition, which, however, I do not reproduce in the English translation. Sulamī, as a biographer, did not comment upon the sayings; and their context does not offer clues to their interpretation. This is unlike the context of the traditions quoted in the theoretical works, where the sayings are normally integrated in a discursive setting expounding an idea. For that reason the interpretation of Nūrī's sayings is based here mostly on those relevant passages of Qushayrī's *Treatise* that discuss terms and concepts mentioned in the traditions Sulamī quoted.

Sulamī's entry on Nūrī begins, as usual in his lexicon, with biographical data. According to these, Nūrī was known as Abū l-Ḥusayn al-Nūrī, his name being either Aḥmad ibn Muḥammad, or (less probably) Muḥammad ibn Muḥammad. He was born and raised in Baghdad, but his family came from Khorasan, from the village Baghshūr, and therefore he was also called Ibn al-Baghawī. He was an eminent master and scholar of his time: "No one was better than him with regard to the [mystical] path *(ṭarīqa)*, and no one was more brilliant than him with regard to speech."[7] He studied under Sarī al-Saqaṭī, Muḥammad ibn ʿAlī al-Qaṣṣāb, and he had the opportunity "to see" the famous Syrian Sufi master, Aḥmad ibn Abī l-Ḥawārī.[8] He died in 295 AH (907/8 AD).[9] It has to be noted that the scandalous events of Nūrī's life are not mentioned in this brief résumé. The short biography is followed by a selection of traditions related to Nūrī. These do not have a central topic, and despite the genre of the collection, they are not related to the major events of Nūrī's biography. The reason might be that these events, especially the circumstances of his death or the trial he had to face for his blasphemous utterances, could easily be considered eccentric or suspicious incidents. Sulamī most probably deliberately omitted these from his biographical lexicon of authoritative personalities.

Despite that, the few reports on events of Nūrī's life include the description of an investigation in the ruler's presence:

> Nūrī was brought before the Sultan, who asked him: "Where do you eat from?" He said: "We do not have knowledge of the secondary means (*asbāb*) by which we gain our sustenance. We are a superintended group."[10]

Obviously, the question of the ruler concerns the community of the Sufis, although it is not clear whether he meant Sufis in general, or a more specific group. The story does not preserve any element of accusation or threat except for the setting of the inquiry that suggests a certain measure of coercion. It is interesting to note that in the *Ornament of God's Friends* complied by Abū Nuʿaym, Nūrī's words are connected to the Sufis' investigation before the Sultan that happened due to the instigation of Ghulām Khalīl, while in the rest of the sources the saying is presented as independent of that incident. The Sultan's question refers to the means by which the Sufis earn their living, and Nūrī's answer signifies that mystics are superintended by God alone, not by any worldly authority or even by themselves.[11]

Traditions Relevant to the Drunken Tendency

Another event related in the *Generations of the Sufis* may also be regarded as a biographical detail, at least with respect to Nūrī's relation to Junayd. The story narrates the opposing reactions of Nūrī and Junayd to illness, specified in the story as a state of ecstasy *(wajd)* afflicting both of them. Contrary to what might be expected considering the customary behavior of both mystics, in this case Nūrī conceals his ecstasy while Junayd gives free rein to his rapture.

> Both Abū l-Ḥusayn al-Nūrī and Junayd went through an illness. While Junayd expressed his ecstasy (*wajd*), Nūrī concealed it. So he was asked: "Why don't you express [your condition], like your friend?" He answered: "We are not apt to suffer from tribulations so it might appear as complaining." Then he recited:
>
> If sickness is my due
> Thanks are due to You
> Hurt me, for no heart remained
> To beg the sickness for delay
> When this was repeated to Junayd, he said: "We were not complaining, but wanted to
> reveal the Omnipotent (*ʿayn al-qudra*) in ourselves."
> Then he began to say:
> I exalt what appears from You
> Because it discloses something of You.
> For Yourself, my heart's intimate
> Are too sublime to be unveiled.
> You annihilated me from all my traits
> So how could I adhere to any place?[12]

According to the story, ecstasy *(wajd)* causes a state of illness, which is not unusual, since Sufis frequently compare ecstasy to disease, among them Nūrī himself: "Nūrī was asked about ecstasy and he said: By God, the tongue cannot describe its true reality, and the eloquence of the lettered is feeble to describe its essence, for it is the greatest matter, and there is no disease which heals better than the cure of ecstasy."[13] According to the Sufi conception, sickness is not a calamity but rather, much like other sufferings or trials affecting the body, a sign of God's care and concern. The appreciation of sickness is manifest in Abū Dharr's saying: "I prefer poverty to richness, and I prefer illness to health."[14] However, a mystic truly contended with God does not differentiate between favorable and disadvantageous situations but is confident in God's choice in either case.

Nevertheless, the social rules concerning the obligation of visiting the sick fall on the mystics, too. A story related in the *Tadhkirat al-awliyā* by Farīd al-Dīn al-ʿAṭṭār gives account of the difference between Nūrī's and Junayd's behavior on such occasions as well. When Nūrī fell ill, Junayd visited him and bought him a rose and a fruit as a present. Then Junayd fell ill, and Nūrī visited him with his companions. When they arrived, Nūrī ordered each of his companions to take a portion of Junayd's illness away in order to heal him. They did so, and Junayd recovered. Nūrī remarked: "If you come to visit me when I am sick, come, and do not bring rose and fruit!"[15] Both this story and the one related by Sulamī reflect an apparent tension between Nūrī and Junayd. In the *Tadhkirat al-awliyā* Nūrī criticizes Junayd, and the latter keeps silent, which means that Nūrī got the upper hand.

It is interesting to note that in Sulamī's story, the usual roles played by Junayd and Nūrī are inverted: Junayd is the one who expresses his ecstasy (although he is usually celebrated for hiding it under any conditions), while Nūrī, characterized by Sarrāj as an imperfect *mutawājid*, conceals his rapture. Such setting might have a polemical purpose: namely, to relativize or to challenge the conventional view on the spirituality of both. However, the disparity between Nūrī's and Junayd's behavior is seeming and superficial. They might react contradictorily to sickness, but the reason for their reaction is essentially the same: "No heart remained to beg" as Nūrī says, and "You annihilated me from all my traits" as Junayd maintains: both of their personalities had already been dissolved in God's will; neither of them has individual intents that diverg from God's purpose.

Nūrī's readiness to accept affliction is expressed in his following poem, as well:

> How many times I made my heart an endowment
> to suffocating, bitter pain because of Your trials (*balwā*)!
> What You inflicts and destroys me with, is due to me,
> whether I weep because of You or I am favoured with
> Your encounter.[16]

Although this poem is not cited in the rest of the collections studied here, the image of bitterness swallowed as water appears in another one of Nūrī's poems collected by Kalābādhī, which has been already discussed.[17] Here the image of suffocation (expressed with the Arabic verb *ghaṣṣa* meaning "to choke on food or drink") implies the act of swallowing in great quantities. In the poem quoted by Kalābādhī the cause of bitterness is not specified; here it is identified as trials and tribulations *(balwā,* plural of *balā')*: God is the cause of the mystic's suffering. It is a well-known *topos* of both secular love poetry and Sufi literature that the true lover takes pleasure in the afflictions caused by his beloved; he is content with whatever his lover does to him. Whatever comes from God should be accepted as a sign of His concern and care for His servant, and should be appreciated as a gift. Tribulations indicate God's closeness and suffering is dear to the mystic lover: "He is not sincere in his love who does not enjoy the stroke of the friend."[18]Apparently, *balā'* involves, first and foremost, corporeal sufferings like illness and physical pain, which test God's servant by means of the body *(imtiḥān al-ajsām)*. The mystic welcomes such trials, since according to Sufis his affliction is directly proportional to his nearness to God.[19]

Love is definitely a central element in Nūrī's mysticism. Despite that, Sulamī's portrayal of him does not abound in love-related traditions, except possibly for the previous poem, and certainly for the following saying:

> He who arrives at his Beloved (*man waṣala ilā' wuddihi*) finds intimacy in His closeness; and he who resorts to love (*tawassala bi-l-widād*) is chosen [by God] from among His servants.[20]

The beauty of the saying consists in an inner rhyme *(widād/ʿibād,* meaning "love/servants") on the one hand, and in a pun *(waṣala/tawassala)* on the other hand. Unfortunately, none of these can be reproduced in English. The pun is created by employing two verbs of very similar roots: WṢL and WSL. The former means "to arrive at," and it is the verbal root of the term *ittiṣāl* meaning "connection" (with God), which is the ultimate end of the Sufis' quest.

The other root, WSL, signifies "to make use of," and it is not a Sufi technical term. *Waṣl* ("arriving at") is self-annihilation in the attributes of God by means of replacing one's attributes with God's. Ultimate arrival *(waṣl al-waṣl)* is "returning to the station of reunion by following a way leading to God in God *(sulūk ilā Allāh fī Allāh)*, by connecting oneself to God through His attributes *(ittiṣāl bi-ṣifātihi)* and self-annihilation in God's substance, so that the real arrival could take place in eternity, in the same way as it existed in primordiality."[21]

Intimacy *(uns)* in Sufi terminology refers to the intimate, joyful aspect of man's relation with God. The spirit *(rūḥ)* takes pleasure in God's benevolence *(jamāl)*, the heart contemplates God's presence and the state of intimacy overpowers the Sufi. Intimacy is the opposite of fear *(hayba)* inspired by the majesty of God *(ʿaẓama)*.[22] Intimacy and fear form a pair of mystical states that mutually presuppose each other and that might be experienced at the same time, as Junayd said: "Intimacy means that modesty *(ḥishma)* passes away, although fear remains."[23] Kalābādhī commented upon Junayd's words saying that a person experiences intimacy with God when his hope *(rajā)* in God is greater than his awe *(khawf)* of Him.

Gaze (*naẓar*)

A further, peculiar episode of Nūrī's life is reported by Sulamī, which might reveal his intimate inclinations in the human sphere. The key term of the story is *naẓar* ("gaze"), which has a double meaning: looking at someone sensually or looking at something scrutinizingly. The story plays with the double meaning of the word, contrasting sensual and intellectual perception.

> I saw a beautiful young man (*ghulām*) in Baghdad, so I looked at him (*naẓartu*) and I wanted to look at him again. Therefore I told to him: You wear a creaking sandal and you are walking in the highway?! He said: You are right! [And you,] are you courting someone with [your] learning?![24] Then he recited:

Observe with the eye of the Real, if you look at (*kunta nāẓiran*)
An attribute (*ṣifa*), which manifests the originality of a creator.
Don't give your self (*nafs*) any share of it due to its quality
But look (*kun nāẓiran*) through Reality the potential of one [omni]potent.[25]

The story reflects the manners of the Abbasid society, which was relatively lenient toward sexual relations between males. Homosexual relations were tolerated during the Middle Ages and apparently were not unusual in religious brotherhoods and educational institutions. Male prostitution was common in the larger towns, homoerotic poetry had been in fashion ever since Abū Nuwās, and prose works on eroticism usually contained a chapter on techniques of seducing young men.[26]

Indulgence in such sensual pleasures was rejected by a fair number of mystics. The Egyptian Sufi master, Shaʿrānī (d. 1565), in his book concerning commendable behavior and character traits enumerates among the uncountable blessings with which God favored him that from his "childhood until the present moment" he has never committed any of the acts of Lot's people, and he describes vividly the divine punishment of such immoralities.[27] Suhrawardī (d. 1168) in his *Ādāb al-murīdīn (Rules for the Novice)* prohibits immodest glances at any person and rules that companionship with young people is reprehensible because it is harmful. He demands "those who are tried by the company of the youth"[28] to hold off their heart and body from them. He remarks that when young people seek the companionship of elders, it is a sign of their intelligence *(fiṭna)* and shows that God granted them prosperity *(tawfīq)*; but when elders seek the company of the youth, it is a sign of their stupidity and indicates that God failed to preserve them from committing evil actions. Consequently, Suhrawardī admits that companionship with youths is necessary and beneficial for the young but dangerous and troublesome for the elders. His demand of guarding not only the heart but also the body from young men indicates the delicate nature of the problems such companionship may entail.

Looking at another man lustfully, or even without any sensual desire, is deemed licentious. It is interesting to note that in his warnings against glances, Suhrawardī refers in the first place to gazing at another man, not at a woman: "The ethic of sight is lowering one's eyes before forbidden things. [. . .] As they say: 'He who yields to his eyes digs his own grave.' [. . .] It has been related that someone said: 'I looked at a person[29] *(shakhṣ)* with a sensuous glance, and I saw in my dream that someone said to me: <The world is My house, and the creatures in it are My servants and maids; whoever looks at one of them without having the right to do so, commits a perfidious act against Me.> When I woke up, I swore that I would not look at any person except in accordance with the religious obligation.' It has been related that Abū Yaʿqūb al-Nahrajūrī said: 'When I was circumambulating [the Kaʿba] I saw a one eyed man, who said: <I take refuge in You from You!> I asked him: <What is [the reason of] your supplication?> He answered: <Know, that I have been living in the vicinity [of the Kaʿba] for fifty years. One day I saw a person and I found pleasure in [looking at] him. But then, all of a sudden I was hit by a blow to my eye, and my eye flew out to my face! I screamed, and then I heard: One blow for one glance, and if you look again, you will be hit again.>' "[30]

Looking at handsome young men had also a spiritual connotation in some branches of Sufism. According to some masters, a beautiful young man is in fact the reflection of God's beauty, and therefore they regarded such a youngster as a *shāhid,* as evidence of the divine attributes. This issue is treated briefly in Qushayrī's *Treatise* at the end of the chapter entitled "Instructions for the Seekers" *(al-waṣāya lil-murīdīn),* in the subchapter "The Company of Youth" *(ṣuḥbat al-aḥdāth),* which is omitted in some editions of the text.[31] The practice of contemplating handsome youngsters as the reflections of divine beauty is criticized by Qushayrī and by other authors as well. The abovementioned Shaʿrānī dwelt on this issue in his summary of the rules of Sufism. According to him, one should not beguile oneself thinking that all beauty on Earth originates from divine beauty and therefore by contemplating a nice boy one contemplates God: "The One whose beauty you claim to contemplate prohibited to you such contemplation."[32] He also quotes ʿAlī al-Mawāzinī al-Shādhilī, who "was asked whether it was permitted for the wayfarer (*sālik*) to look at beautiful young boys *(amrad)*, and he said: 'As long as a man can differentiate between beautiful forms and not beautiful forms, he is [still engaged] in the obliteration of his nature and his carnal appetite, therefore it is not permitted for him to look at beautiful forms prohibited by law.' "[33]

Shaʿrānī adds that if a person attained such a degree of spiritual perfection that he could contemplate either a scarab or a frog as the supreme manifestation of human beauty then such contemplation was permitted: in that case his capacity to distinguish between the creatures was abolished, and he became absorbed in the Creator.

The "young man" *(ghulām)* whom Nūrī admires for his beauty is most probably a slave servant (*ghulām* means a youth, usually a slave, but also might refer to a young man in general, regardless of his social status). The youngster wears a special type of expensive sandal, which gets the attention of the passersby with its creaking;[34] furthermore, he walks on the highway, just as free men would do. Neither of these befits his status as a slave, and Nūrī makes an advance by means of lightly provoking him, to which the young man replies defiantly. His riposte (*"[And you,] are you courting someone with [your] learning?!"*) mocks Nūrī using the same argument with which Nūrī teased him: behaving in an inappropriate way, which does not befit his status. However, the youngster does not find fault with Nūrī's outer appearance and apparent behavior but reproaches him for his inner attitude. He criticizes theoretical knowledge acquired through learning *(ʿilm)* as an improper way to approach God. His remark means that God is not an object of cognition that can be grasped by intellectual faculties, but the Beloved, whose intimate nearness can be obtained through courting Him as lovers do.

The poem the youngster recites warns against falling victim to a deception: namely, instead of realizing the substance, letting oneself to be deluded by an accident. Interpreting the poem according to the context created by the story that introduces it, the misleading attribute *(ṣifa)* is probably beauty (embodied by the young man). The warning "don't give your self/carnal soul any share of it" advises against satisfying the carnal soul's appetite with regard to a desirable but nonessential attribute. Instead, one should "observe with the eye of the Real" the divine substance that manifests itself through the accidents. The expression "observe with the eye of the Real" *(ta'ammal bi-ʿayn al-ḥaqq)* has several senses. Since in Sufi phraseology *ʿayn* ("eye, source") in the genitive construction frequently refers to God, therefore the expression can be translated also as "observe the Real," that is, ultimate Reality (i.e., God). Furthermore, *ʿayn* may refer also to "substance" *(dhāt)*,[35] consequently the line can be interpreted as "observe the substance of the Real." Finally, if *ḥaqq* is not understood as denoting God but as a common noun meaning "reality," the translation is "observe with the eye of reality." Naturally, such double or triple meanings are completely intentional in Sufi texts.

Traditions Relevant to the Drunken Tendency

A theoretic saying of Nūrī elaborates further on the multiple meanings of the notion of *naẓar*.

> Those who are engaged in looking [at things carefully] (*ahl al-naẓar*) have various stances (*maqāmāt*) on looking. To some of them looking is distraction; to some looking is gaining benefit [through it]; to some looking is to see with the eyes of unveiling; to some looking is to compete in witnessing; to some looking is resemblance and similarity; to some looking is benevolence and observation; to some looking is supervision and overseeing. All of these are people who are engaged in looking.[36]

Besides the sensual aspect, *naẓar* denotes different mental processes as well. Its sense of "studying, considering" makes it synonymous with *fikr*, meaning ". . . the power of thought or cogitation, the ability of the soul to put together the data gathered by sense perception or acquired from imagination in order to reach rational conclusions."[37] The expression *ahl al-naẓar* originally denoted the Muʿtazila, and in several sources it is interchangeable with *ahl al-kalām* or *mutakallimūn* (scholastic theologians), but in a more general sense it refers to careful scholars who present well-founded opinion on any particular question.[38] Moreover, it is frequently used synonymously with "rational thinkers" (*ʿuqalā'*, plural of

ʿāqil) and thus does not refer to a specific, well-defined group of intellectuals, but to those who rely on their intellect in general, including all kind of thinkers or persons capable of deliberation.[39]

Since mystics deny the role of intellect in obtaining knowledge about God, they might be considered as the opposite pole of rational thinkers. Nūrī's saying, however, obviously includes mystics among the people engaged in *naẓar.* Those who look with "the eyes of unveiling" *(mukāshafa)* are evidently mystics. This inconsistency can be explained in two different ways. It might be suggested that some of the terms employed in the saying should not be understood according to their peculiar meaning as technical terms, but in a more commonsensical way. Accordingly, *ahl al-naẓar* might be used here in the vague, general sense of "people who study something carefully" instead of the technical meaning "rational thinkers." The same holds true to the term *maqām,* which is employed in the saying with its common meaning ("stance"), rather than as a Sufi technical term denoting spiritual station attained by the mystic wayfarer. The other possible interpretation supposes that the phraseology of the saying is exact and deliberate, not vague at all. In that case, it may be concluded that Nūrī intended to include mystics in the apparently exclusive class of careful scholars who might have impropriated that category to themselves, that is, to those who pursue study in a well-defined, peculiar scientific way. Supposing this, the saying can be interpreted as a sort of criticism directed at Muslim scholastic theologians in general or the Muʿtazila in particular, implying that these intellectual currents are by no means superior to mysticism.

In any case, the interpretation of a saying depends on its context. In Sulamī's collection, Nūrī's words are not connected to the previously discussed anecdote about the handsome youth. In the *Generations of the Sufis* the two texts are separated by three sayings and three poems, and they do not seem to be interrelated. However, the saying on *ahl al-naẓar* is also quoted in the *Black and White in the Words of Wisdom* complied by Sīrjānī, where it is included in the chapter on *naẓar* together with the anecdote about the young man in Baghdad, and another similar story about Nūrī falling in love with a youngster in Rayy, furthermore, a story about him giving advice not to look at young boys. In the context created by the chapter of Sīrjānī's *Black and White in the Words of Wisdom,* the meaning of looking acquires a more complex significance with special emphasis on the literal meaning of the verb as opposed to its figurative sense of "considering." The double meaning of the verb is clearly explained by a saying of Junayd, which in the *Black and White in the Words of Wisdom* precedes Nūrī's words. According to it, there are two kinds of looking: by way of ignorance *(jahl)* and by way of learning *(ʿilm).* The Quranic ordinance about averting the eyes *(ghaḍḍ al-naẓar,* cf. Quran 24:30) refers to the former. Fear should surround both kinds of looking; the former type because it is prohibited and the latter since it leads to the perception of God's unseen, hidden world *(al-ghayb).* "If the belief *(īmān)* of a person is correct, he is attached to the *ghayb,* and when he looks at the *ghayb,* he is taken from his looking by his looking, and he will look without returning to what is looked at."[40]

Several of the traditions Sulamī collected treat the limitations of cognition. Most of these traditions are intellectual and speculative, reflecting upon divergent aspects of the same phenomenon. Although the word "path" *(ṭarīqa)* does not occur in the following saying, the actions it mentions (stopping, making an advance, resting, losing the way) suggest that it describes phases of the path leading to God.

> Those who believe are stopped, those who witness that God is one are making an advance, those who are contended [with God] are resting, and those who detach themselves [from everything but God] are at a loss. Then he said: If the Real manifests Himself, everything He veiled and concealed disappears.[41]

It is interesting to note that the saying does not employ Sufi technical terms, and despite the metaphor of the wayfarers, which has a very strong Sufi mystical connotation, evidently not all of the different groups treading the path implied in the tradition are mystics. In early Sufism "path" referred to the special Sufi way of approaching God *(al-ṭarīqa al-ṣūfiyya),* not to particular Sufi orders or brotherhoods that emerged only in the thirteenth century. Treading the path is a metaphor much connected to Sufi mysticism but not exclusive to it. Nūrī's saying on the wayfarers differentiates between ordinarily religious people *(ahl al-diyāna),* true monotheists *(ahl al-tawḥīd),* "the people of contentment" *(ahl al-riḍā),* and "the people of detachment" *(ahl al-inqiṭāʿ).* Detachment from mundane affairs or "cutting the bonds" *(ḥadhf al-alā'iq)* is a prerequisite for entering the mystical way: the seeker is demanded to cut his attachment first to property, then to his social status or rank, and the appreciation of the people.[42] While the first group of the wayfarers has stopped and the second is moving forward, the third is taking a temporary rest before continuing on their way. Surprisingly enough, the last group, which seems to correspond to advanced Sufis who managed to liberate themselves from worldly concerns including bodily needs, social relations, psychological and emotional bonds, are nevertheless perplexed and lost *(yataḥayyarūn)* instead of advancing toward their goal. Their perplexity is probably because unlike those firmly rooted in the world and its conventions, mystics orientate themselves exclusively toward God and through Him. God, however, is veiled. The only consolation in this state is that which Nūrī offers: when God discloses Himself, every veil disappears.

The perplexity of the wayfarers is caused by some kind of cognitive dissonance: the perception of inconsistent ideas and actions. Although the Sufi reduces the role of the intellect and does not orientate according to it, uncontrolled thoughts may divert him from the path leading to God. Sulamī quotes a poem by Nūrī that distinguishes between disorientating ideas and thoughts inspired by God.

> How many times I desired that You benevolently
> avert a thing from me!
> May You never cease to grant my wishes mercifully
> and graciously!
> I decided not to perceive any sudden thought (*khāṭir*)
> coming to my heart (*qalb*),
> except when You are the one who originated it.
> [I decided that] You won't see me [abide] at any
> [sudden thought] alien to You,
> since You [alone] are exalted and glorified in my heart.[43]

Sudden thoughts *(khāṭir,* plural *khawāṭir)* are especially frequent during spiritual exercises and retreats, when the seeker suspends his ordinary activity in order to concentrate on spiritual and mystical realities. Uncontrolled thoughts may be correct and beneficial or quite the opposite: harmful and dangerous. The distinction between true and false impulses is not at all evident. Qushayrī's *Treatise* enumerates various types of thoughts and describes a possible way of distinguishing between them.[44] According to it, a thought is essentially a kind of speech that comes across the mind *(ḍamīr)* and originates either from an angel, a *shayṭān,* one's own self/carnal soul *(nafs),* or directly from God. When thoughts originate from an angel, they are inspiration *(ilhām)*; when they come from the self, they are concerns *(hawājis)*; when they come from a *shayṭān,* they are whispers and temptations *(waswās)*; when they proceed from God, they are real, genuine thoughts *(khāṭir ḥaqq).* The thought that originates from God always emerges in the heart *(qalb),* therefore one's heart never lies, while one's carnal soul never tells the truth; it is not reliable. A person may silence the self through spiritual struggle *(mujāhada),* and in that case their heart will be able to communicate by virtue of the person's endeavour; but a person can never force their spirit *(rūḥ)* to speak to them: "Even if you struggled with your outmost capacity to make your spirit talk to you, it would not ever talk to you."[45] As it has been already mentioned, Sufis contrast spirit *(rūḥ)* and soul *(nafs),* the first being the depository of praiseworthy qualities (similar to the heart), and the second that of blameworthy character traits. Angelic inspirations never contradict religious science *(ʿilm).* Satanic temptations, however, normally incite disobedience; whereas the concerns of the soul-self usually follow desires and passions and fill oneself with self-importance. According to Junayd,[46] the difference between Satanic temptations and the concerns of the self is that the latter are unchanging, like fixed obsessions, while the former are multifarious, always changing and renewing: if one succeeded in resisting a certain temptation, then that person will be exposed to another temptation immediately. The concerns of the self, however, never cease and can never be completely suppressed.

The idea that the Sufi's perception of the world, including intellectual cognition, may depend on God is expressed in Nūrī's following saying, as well:

> He who cognizes (*ʿaqala*) things through God, in every matter returns to God.[47]

Although cognition is an action performed by the intellect, according to the mystical approach the role of the intellectual faculty may be replaced by direct communication with God; this does not mean verbal communication but rather perceiving the world with the inner heart (intrinsically connected to God) instead of the mind. Denying the capacity of rational reasoning for perceiving God is also emphasized in Nūrī's definition of Sufism quoted by Sulamī:[48]

> Nūrī was asked about Sufism, and he said: "Sufism does not consist in formalities (*rusūm*) or learning (*ʿulūm*), but [spiritual] qualities (*akhlāq*)."[49]

Learning, or a theoretical approach, should be replaced by insight and inspiration; external manners should be replaced by spiritual qualities. Nūrī's saying is cited in the *Tadhkirat al-awliyā'* compiled by Farīd al-Dīn al-ʿAṭṭār (twelfth to thirteenth century) in a more extensive version that contains the explication of the utterance, too.[50] According to that saying, if Sufism consisted of formalities, it would be attainable through endeavor, and if it was a science, it could be learned. However, in fact, it resides essentially in one's morals, or more precisely, in replacing one's own qualities with those of God, in accordance with the *ḥadīth:* "Imitate the qualities of God *(takhallaqū bi-akhlāq Allāh)!*"[51] The *ḥadīth* is a reminder of the fundamental Sufi doctrine about "clothing oneself" with God's attributes *(ṣifāt)* after having eliminated one's own character traits.

Acquiring noble qualities supposes practice rather than mere theoretical knowledge. The dichotomy of theory and practice (*ʿilm* and *ʿamal)* is frequently treated in Sufi texts, giving preference invariably to the latter. Nūrī laments above those who do not convert their theoretical knowledge into deeds and criticizes those mystics who claim to possess inspired knowledge of God, but whose communication reveals that their claim is false:

> The greatest things in our days are two: a learned person (*ʿālim*) who practices what he has learnt, and a knower (*ʿārif*), who speaks about His true reality.[52]

To conclude, mention must be made of a tradition seemingly unrelated to the topic under discussion: Nūrī's saying on the eminence of Muḥammad.

> Nūrī was asked about al-Ḥabīb ["beloved," epithet of Muḥammad] and al-Khalīl ["bosom friend," epithet of Abraham] and he said: "He who was demanded to surrender [to God's command] (*taslīm*) is not like him who rushed to surrender."[53]

Muslims' general veneration of Muḥammad developed in later Sufism into an elaborate mystical theory of the primordial light *(al-nūr al-muḥammadiyya)* and the perfect man *(al-insān al-kāmil)*. For Sufis he is not only the ideal man, the model of perfect physical beauty and spiritual excellence, but also the archetype of the mystic. According to a *ḥadīth*[54] he announced that his *shayṭān* has become Muslim *(aslama shayṭānī). Shayṭān* is regarded as the representative of the lower self, the carnal soul. Muḥammad, thus, has reached the goal the mystics strive for: he succeeded in taming his *nafs* completely, to such an extent that even his base instincts obey God. Muḥammad's epithet "seal of all the Prophets" is evidence of his superiority, notwithstanding those traditions that prohibit the preference of one prophet over the other.[55] Muḥammad's unique position is even more emphasized in Sufi mysticism, maintaining that he literally precedes the prophets and all humankind in essence, since he is God's primal creation. According to this view (first expressed by Sahl al-Tustarī, d. 896), Muḥammad was created from the likeness of the divine light taking the shape of a luminous column genuflecting before the presence of God. God created man from the light of Muḥammad, and creation is nourished by his light.[56]

Looking for the underlying reason for the inclusion of the saying on Muḥammad in the selection of traditions attributed to Nūrī, we may conclude that the reason was its relevance to a major topic of the traditions: the preference of practice and experience over rationalization and theory. Seeking God's closeness through imitating the Prophet's example places acts and moral qualities above theological speculations. Moreover, the reference to the Prophet (especially by his epithet "the beloved") authenticates Sufi teachings in general, and Nūrī's spirituality in particular.[57]

Conclusions

The overall picture Sulamī presents of Nūrī is that of a sober mystic. Unlike Sarrāj, Sulamī does not include in his entry on Nūrī traditions anything that could be viewed as suspicious or provocative, except maybe the anecdote about Nūrī flirting with a handsome young man in Baghdad. The Ghulām Khalīl incident, however, is completely omitted from the biographical entry, notwithstanding that it was possibly the most remarkable episode of Nūrī's life.[58] Such an omission is telling in itself; it reveals Sulamī's intention of conforming Nūrī's figure to the accepted standards of Muslim religiosity. The sole incident that bears witness to the confrontation between Nūrī and the religious authorities is a question posed to him by the caliph. However, since the context of the question is omitted, the threatening nature of the event is hardly perceptible. Much like some of the material collected by Kalābādhī and Sarrāj, a certain contrast between Nūrī and Junayd is discernible in one of the traditions, but the apparent tension is dissolved by the poems justifying the behavior of both of them. In general, the subjects of the traditions collected in the entry are divergent, and no central topic can be indicated. General remarks can be made concerning their style and character only; most of the traditions are remarkably theoretical despite their recurring critique of the intellectual approach. Passionate love, overwhelming rapture, mystical concerts (*samāʿ* ceremonies) are not mentioned at all; ecstasy is referred to only once, and even then in the context of illness. What is more, Nūrī is presented as dominating and hiding his ecstasy, which is completely unusual.

It is interesting to note that the traditions collected by Sulamī employ on average more Sufi technical terms than those quoted by Kalābādhī and Sarrāj. The underlying reason may be that the traditions cited by Kalābādhī and Sarrāj are older and therefore possibly more authentic than those collected by Sulamī. The recurring Sufi terms are looking *(naẓar)*, which occurs twenty-one times; heart *(qalb)* four times; tribulation (*balāʾ* and verbal forms) four times; learning *(ʿilm)* four times; means *(asbāb)* twice; carnal soul *(nafs)* twice.[59] On the other hand, there are some words in the traditions that later became common Sufi terms, here however, most probably they are not used in a technical sense, like station *(maqām)* and state *(ḥāl)*. It should be noted also that the most frequently used word in the traditions is not a standard Sufi technical term. The word *naẓar* (gaze, looking, studying) appears twenty-one times, although only in two traditions, which might indicate that in Nūrī's usage it had special importance but did not develop into a full-fledged Sufi term (whereas it did become a technical term in the compound *ahl al-naẓar,* referring first and foremost to the *kalām* theologians).

CHAPTER 4

Sulamī

Realities of Interpretation *(Ḥaqā'iq al-tafsīr)*

Introduction

The *Realities of Interpretation (Ḥaqā'iq al-tafsīr,* henceforth: *Realities)*[1] is a commentary that addresses almost the complete text of the Quran in the order of the verses in a lemma plus comment format. Being a Quran commentary, its literary genre differs substantially from the sources previously discussed. While Sufi manuals and biographical lexicons frequently have apologetic purposes, such intention is not evident in the case of mystical commentaries of the Quran. The opposite opinion was held by Ignaz Goldziher, who argued that the primary aim of the mystical commentaries was to demonstrate that Sufi concepts were inherent in the Quran: a claim that in Goldziher's opinion was not true in reality. He maintained that Sufis read their own views into the Quran, even distorted the original meaning of the text, turning it into a showcase for their ideas.[2] A different approach was taken by Louis Massignon and Paul Nwyia, who concluded that Sufi terminology in fact depended on the Quran and originated from it.[3] The conclusions drawn by the latter scholars deny the covert apologetic purpose of the commentaries, and their opinion might be confirmed by Sulamī's introduction to his *Realities* (see below), for no apologetic aim whatsoever can be detected in it.

Sulamī wrote a short introduction to his commentary, in which he explained the work's purpose and method. He remarked that (1) although Sufi masters explained some of the hidden meanings of the Quran orally, they did not interpret the text in its entirety; (2) comments or commentaries on the Quran that were composed in writing usually treat its external, manifest aspects *(ẓāhir)*; (3) though two mystical commentaries had already been committed into writing, they, however, are fragmentary and do not extend to the whole text. Therefore, he decided to create a running commentary arranged according to the subsequent Quranic verses that interprets mystically the entire Quranic corpus.[4] The comments collected were not his own insights but the inspired revelations granted to his predecessors. As for the structure of the commentary, he wished to combine two genres: (1) *maqālāt,* that is, written sources that contain the interpretation *(fahm)* of sporadic Quranic verses *(āyāt mutafarriqa)* by Abū l-ʿAbbās b. ʿAṭāʾ (d. 309/921–2 or 311/923–4) and the interpretation of some verses by Jaʿfar b. Muḥammad al-Ṣādiq (d.148/765);[5] (2) *aqwāl,* that is, sayings of the Sufi masters.[6] It is important to note that although Sulamī's commentary became widely known under the title *Ḥaqāʾiq al-tafsīr,* it is not entirely clear whether he labeled his commentary as a *tafsīr,* which is the most general term for "commentary." His introduction to the compilation does not contain the title, and the earliest manuscripts date to the mid-twelfth century (more than a century later than Sulamī's death).[7] Medieval authors would usually include the titles of their works in the introduction; failing that, copyists may add slightly divergent titles according to their best knowledge. In any case, in the introduction Sulamī always uses the word *fahm* when referring to Sufi interpretations of the Quran, never the term *tafsīr*. The primary meaning of *fahm* is "understanding," and in the special context of Sufi texts it denotes mystical interpretation; Sarrāj, for example, uses consequently the term *fahm* in his long chapter on the Sufis' interpretation of the Quran.[8]

It should be noted here that there exists a unique manuscript entitled *Ziyādāt ḥaqāʾiq al-tafsīr (Appendix to the Realities of Interpretation)* attributed to Sulamī. It is preserved in the Gazi Husrev-Begova Biblioteka in Sarajevo (Bosnia), and it is undated. According to Böwering who published it, most probably it was copied in the Late Middle Ages. Its introduction explicitly identifies it as a supplement to the *Ḥaqāiq al-tafsīr ("sammaytuhu ziyādāt ḥaqā'iq al-tafsīr")*,[9] which might imply that Sulamī entitled his commentary as *tafsīr*. This conclusion, however, is uncertain, for the authenticity of the *Appendix* can be duly called into question for several reasons: (1) it is remarkable in itself that the Sarajevo manuscript is its single witness, while the *Realities* is preserved at least in about fifty manuscripts;[10] (2) apart from a single mention, no reference to it can be found either in the works of Islamic bibliography and biography, or in Sufi literature in general;[11] (3) although Böwering attaches great importance to the fact that Rūzbihān Baqlī's (d. 606/1209) *ʿArā'is al-bayān* has numerous parallels to the *Appendix*, this cannot prove the authenticity of the work, since Baqlī, as Böwering remarks "does not acknowledge his source but simply excerpts statements that fit his scheme of a Qur'anic commentary."[12] Therefore, it might be suggested that both works made use of a common source; or even that the anonymous author of the *Appendix* quoted Baqlī (without mentioning his source), and not vice versa.

The translation of the relevant passages of Sulamī's introduction goes as follows:

> Praise to God who selected the people of the realities *(ahl al-ḥaqā'iq)* in order to single them out as His select ones, and who made them the people interpreting mystically his discourse *(ahl fahm ḫiṭābihi)*, who know the subtleties of what He deposited in his revealed book 'to which falsehood does not approach either from before or from behind' [Q 41:42]. Accordingly, they gave a report of the hidden senses of His discourse *(maʿānī ḫiṭābihi)* according to the measure of God's inspiration to each them [reporting about] the subtleties of its secrets and hidden senses, and they talked about the mystical interpretation *(fahm)* of His book in accordance with what presented itself to them from its marvels. However, not one of them talked about the [true] reality of its realities [i.e., about its true reality in its entirety], but [everybody] reported according to the measure appropriate to his understanding *(fahm)*. [Their] understanding was short of grasping its realities and comprehending its utilities, except by way of revelations and inspirations. So, they were confused by the true

> allusions *(ishārāt ḥaqīqiyya)*, [incapable] of [understanding] some parts of it. Because these [allusions] are too delicate, except for their masters [i.e., the Messenger of God and the prophets]. Since it is a mighty book disclosed by a Mighty One to the mightiest of the creatures with regard to soul, and to the most noble of them with regard to graces, may God honor him and all of his prophets and messengers. When I saw that those engaged in external sciences *(ʿulūm al-ẓawāhir)* had composed works treating the different aspects of the Quran's excellences—like its forms of recitation *(qirā'āt)*, its commentaries *(tafāsīr)*, problems *(mushkilāt)*, regulations *(aḥkām)*, conjugation and declination *(ʿirāb)*, lexicography *(lugha)*, ambivalent and unequivocal verses *(mujmal wa-mufassar)*, abrogating and abrogated verses *(nāsikh wa-mansūkh)*—, but not one of them occupied himself with interpreting His whole discourse *(fahm ḫiṭābibi)* according to the tongue of reality, except for [the mystical interpretation *(faḥm)* of] some sporadic verses *(āyāt mutafarriqa)*, attributed to Abū l-Abbās b. ʿAṭā', and [except for the mystical interpretation of] some verses, transmitted in the name of Jaʿfar b. Muḥammad [al-Ṣādiq] unarranged; and when I have heard from them on this subject some words, I have found these appropriate, and I wished to add these to their writings *(maqālātihim)*, and to add the sayings of the Sufi masters *(aqwāl al-mashāyikh)* to this, and then to arrange it according to the Quranic verses, as my capacity and ability permit.[13]

As it can be seen from the last sentence, the arrangement of the sources had been a challenging task (cf. "as my capacity and ability permits"), which might indicate that part of the material was not linked clearly to specific verses, and their lemma should have been determined by the editor. Although the terms "sayings" and "writings" might suggest an oral/written dichotomy, this is not quite the case. Rather, the difference lays in the original formulation of the material: "sayings" *(aqwāl)* correspond to the oral teaching of the masters (that could have been recorded subsequently), while "writings" *(maqālāt)* were probably composed as such from the outset.

Some thirty comments attributed to Nūrī are preserved in the *Realities*, and most of them were not recorded in contemporary or even in later Sufi manuals or biographical lexicons (I could trace only six of the sayings in other compilations). That fact raises the question of how Nūrī's comments on the Quran relate to his other sayings, which were collected in the Sufi manuals. Böwering studied Sulamī's use of the sources, his priorities in attaching certain comments to certain verses. He concluded that many of the comments "may be taken up in total isolation from the actual context,"[14] consequently their inclusion was conditioned more by the term occurring in them than by the actual meaning of the Quranic verse in its original context. With regard to Nūrī, it can be asked whether his sayings included in the *Realities* were Quranic comments intended as such in the first place, or whether they were subsequently connected to lemmas by Sulamī, by virtue of specific terms occurring both in them and in the Quranic text. The following exposition aims to analyze the relation between the Quranic verses and the comments, and it intends to discuss the correlation between the comments and Nūrī's sayings also preserved in manuals. All translations of the Quran are mine, although the translations by Shakir, Yusuf Ali, and Pickthall were consulted. For the sake of legibility, in general I aimed at simplicity, with the exception of that part of the Quranic verse to which the comment refers in particular.

Q 2:29

"He is who created for you everything on earth, and then He turned to the sky and arranged it in seven heavens; for He knows everything."

> Abū l-Ḥasan al-Nūrī said: The highest station for the people of true realities is that they detach themselves from the creatures.[15]

Sulamī quotes several Sufi comments on the passage and enlists Nūrī's saying as the last of these. Compared with the preceding comments, Nūrī's saying does not seem to be directly related to the verse, but rather added here as a concluding remark due to its relevance to the subject (creation). This supposition is confirmed by the fact that the saying is cited also in the *Decoration of the Saints* composed by Abū Nuʿaym. There, however, it is not connected to the Quranic verse anyhow but forms part of a longer exposition by Nūrī, which describes divergent mystical ways leading toward one and the same goal: reaching the highest stage of spirituality.[16] Other comments on this verse gathered in the *Realities* were probably intended as interpretations of the words of the Quran, and they even include parts of the sentence they interpret: for example, "Ibn ʿAṭāʾ said: 'He is who created for you everything on earth'—so that everything would be yours entirely, and so that you would be God's entirely, turning away from occupation with yourself towards Him."[17]

Q 2:40

"OH, SONS OF ISRAEL! RECALL (*UDHKURŪ*, CF. *DHIKR*) THE BENEFACTION (*NIʿMA*) I GRANTED YOU, AND BE FAITHFUL (*AWFŪ*, CF. *WAFĀʾ*) TO MY COVENANT AND THEN I WILL BE FAITHFUL TO YOUR COVENANT; AND ME YOU SHOULD FEAR."

> Nūrī was asked how to understand this verse: "Be faithful to My covenant and then I will be faithful to your covenant." He said: Be faithful to my covenant in the realm of my trial[18] through my service by observing my sanctity, and then I will be faithful to your covenant in the realm of my benefaction through my nearness by the joy of my vision (*ru'ya*).[19]

The attribution of the saying to Nūrī is uncertain; on the basis of the manuscripts Nwyia consulted, he attributes it to Nūrī, but it is quoted in Thawrī's name (possibly Sufyān al-Thawrī, d. 778) in Sayyid ʿUmrān's edition of the *Realities*. In Arabic orthography, the difference between the two names is a single diacritical sign, which is not always indicated in manuscripts, resulting in a form (نورى) that can be read either way. Such confusion between the two names occurs also in Ṭabarī's *Comfort of the Mystics*.[20]

Sulamī arranged the comments he cited in two groups. The first expounds upon the dichotomy between Israel and the Muslims, emphasizing the purity of Islamic faith concerned solely with God, irrespective of His benefactions, while Israel recognizes God through divine guidance and benefits. The primacy of Muḥammad and the Muslim community is echoed also in a comment cited in the name of Sahl al-Tustarī (d. ca. 283/896), which, however, does not appear in Tustarī's own Quran commentary among his comments on this Quranic verse. According to the comment attributed to Tustarī, God singled out the Muslims over other nationalities or religions just as He singled out Muḥammad over other prophets, for God made Abraham see the realm of the Heavens and the Earth (cf. Q 2:75), while He "detached the inner heart *(sirr)* of Muḥammad and his vision *(ru'ya)* from anybody but Himself, for He said: 'Have you not seen your Lord, how He spread the shade?' [Q 25:45]"[21]

The remaining comments focus on the second half of the verse and ignore the reference to Israel. Instead, the Sufis understand it as conveying mystical messages addressed to their community and clarify this by paraphrasing the verse, intercalating words that specify the significance of the covenant with reference to both God and man. " 'Be faithful to my covenant'—to the primordial covenant made by uttering: 'Yes, You are [our Lord]' *(balā)* [Q 7:172], so do not return to seek anything but Me!"[22] Or: " 'Be faithful to my covenant'—preserve what I have entrusted to you, do not make it manifest *(ẓāhir)* to anyone except to whom it is destined; 'and then I will be faithful to my covenant'—I will give to you the keys of my treasuries and the keys of my nearness *(qurb),* and I will make you abide in the abodes of the pure."[23] Or, according to a saying attributed to an unnamed Iraqi master: " 'Be faithful to my covenant'—be for me creatures *(khalq)*; 'and then I will be faithful to my covenant'—I will be for you Real *(ḥaqq)*.[24] Nūrī's saying conforms to the style of these comments, although it is also linked to the first group of sayings as it echoes "vision" *(ru'ya)* of God.

Q 2:245

"Who could loan God a nice loan, so that He may return to him the double or more? For God constrains and extends, and you are returned to Him."

> Abū l-Ḥusayn al-Nūrī said concerning His saying: "For God constrains and extends"—God constrains you by Himself and extends you to Himself.[25]

The comments Sulamī quotes either elaborate on the meaning of the terms "constraint" and "extension," or operate with prepositions added to the verbs that modify and specify the meaning of the Quranic passage. "Ibn ʿAṭā said: 'He constrains you from yourself *(ʿanka)* and extends you by Himself *(bihi)* and to Himself *(lahu)*.' "[26] According to Wāsiṭī: "He constrains you from what you have and extends you in what He has."[27] Nūrī's saying is in line with these. It is important to note that this is Nūrī's only saying dealing with the concepts of expansion and constraint, and that it is attested to in Ṭabarī's collection, the *Comfort of the Mystics,* as well.[28] The wording of the saying is not exactly identical in both sources: the form of the prepositions varies, while their meaning remains essentially the same (Sulamī: *bi-iyyāhu* and *li-iyyāhu;* Ṭabarī: *bihi* and *lahu).*

Constraint *(qabḍ)* and expansion *(basṭ)* are complementary spiritual states generated by God: He constrains the human being as if holding him in the hollow of the hand, confining man's self and actions to the minimum and making him experience a state of anxious distress; or He lets him relax, enjoying serenity, or allowing him to be filled with enthusiasm.[29] Sulamī hints at the meaning of the terms with a saying attributed to an unnamed Baghdadi master, according to whom constraint inspires Sufis to turn away from the "vision of miracles/generous acts" *(ru'yat al-karāmāt),* and expansion allows them to "look at the Generous" *(naẓar ilā l-karīm)* instead.[30]

Q 2:273

"As for the poor who are in need on the path of God, who cannot make a journey in the land; the ignorant deem them rich because of their continence. You can recognize them by their mark: they do not beg from the people importunately. But if you spend any good thing, surely God knows it."

> Nūrī said: "You can recognize them by their mark"—by their rejoice in their poverty, and by their rightful states when tribulations descend upon them.[31]

The comments Sulamī cites relate to the false appearance of richness and poorness: the ignorant are deceived by apparent material richness and fail to recognize spiritual poverty, which consists in being in need of God while dispensing with everything else. Material poverty may be a means to reach the ultimate goal, spiritual poverty, but when the latter is attained, adhering to the former is unnecessary. Consequently, Sufis are not characterized by the outward display of asceticism or renunciation of material goods. Their distinguishing mark is their spiritual disposition, not their material circumstances. Nūrī's comment refers directly to the Quranic passage: it quotes a part of it and expounds on a word retaining the original structure of the sentence.

Q 3:35

"When the wife of ʿImrān said: My Lord, I have vowed to give you as a [person] consacrated [to Your service] what is in my womb. Accept it from me, for You hear and know everything!"

> Nūri said concerning His saying: "I have vowed to give You as a [person] consecrated [to Your service] what is in my womb"—as one freed from my occupation [with him] and from my forethought (*tadbīr*); he will be resigned (*muslam*) to Your forethought and to Your good choice for him.[32]

The passage of the Quran begins the story of Jesus, and the wife of ʿImrān mentioned in it is Mary's mother. Therefore, in the original context the phrase "I have vowed to give you as a [person] consecrated [to your service] what is in my womb" refers to Mary, although the pronouns are masculine since Mary's mother did not know in advance that she would deliver a female. The comments

Sulamī quotes interpret the word "consecrated" *(muḥarrar)*, focusing on the basic meaning of the word's verbal root ("to free, to liberate"). Most of the comments Sulamī cites seem to be directly linked to the passage. Jaʿfar al-Ṣādiq, for example, emphasizes the eminence of Mary quoting a dialogue between her and the prophet Zakariyyā (Q 3:37), and explains the meaning of consecration/liberation as "releasing from the slavery of the world and its people."[33] Sahl ibn ʿAbd Allāh comments on the idea in close connection to the Quranic expression *(nadhartu laka . . . muḥarraran)*, too: "He is released from the desires of his self *(nafs)* and from the dominion of his passion."[34] The use of masculine pronouns concords with the text of the Quran, and does not necessarily mean that the reference is to a male, and not to Mary. A comment by Muḥammad ibn al-Faḍl again elaborates on the term *muḥarrar:* "Freed from the occupation with earning."[35] Nūrī's comment corresponds to these: it completes the Quranic passage with a prepositional phrase that expounds the concept of consecration/liberation: delivering from human guidance to divine providence.

Nwyia's collection of Nūrī's comments in the *Realities* does not contain the tradition quoted above; it attributes another comment to Nūrī instead:

> "I have vowed to give You as a [person] consecrated [to Your service] what is in my womb"—Nūrī said: As a servant of Your choicest people (*ahl al-ṣafwa*).[36]

Again, the comment directly refers to the Quranic passage, although it does not complete or paraphrase it. Rather, it creates a pun by replacing the word *muḥarrar* (consecrated/liberated) with its opposite, *khādim* (servant), resulting in *"nadhartu laka . . . khādiman"* instead of *"nadhartu laka . . . muḥarraran,"* meaning "I vowed to give you as a servant" versus "I vowed to give you as a *libertus* (freedman). Freedom *(ḥūrriyya)* is one of the stations of the Sufi path. Qushayrī's *Treatise* explains the term much in the vein of Nūrī's saying, playing with the freedom-servanthood dichotomy. True servantship is the key to freedom, which is being in the service of God *(ʿubūdiyya)*, as Ḥusayn ibn Manṣūr al-Ḥallāj said: "He who wants freedom should arrive [in the spiritual path] to service [of God]" *(Man arāda l-ḥurriyya fa-l-yaṣil li-l-ʿubūdiyya.)*[37] The way toward the service of God (*ʿubūdiyya*) is taken up through the service (*khidma*) of God's intimate people, the Sufis: "The maximum of freedom is serving the poor (*khidmat al-fuqarāʾ*)."[38] Nūrī's comment corresponds to this conception: ultimate freedom means serving God's choicest people. Since one of the common etymologies of the word "Sufi" relates it to the verbal root ṢFW (basic meaning: "to be pure"; derived forms of the verb meaning "to select, chose"), the choicest people (*ṣafwa*) mentioned by Nūrī are evidently the Sufis themselves.[39] It is interesting to note that Nūrī's comment quoted in Nwyia's collection, unlike the comment attributed to him in Sayyid ʿUmrān's edition of the *Realities*, goes beyond the literal meaning of the Quranic text and extends it to the specific direction of Sufi mysticism.

Q 3:97

"There are clear signs in it, the station (*maqām*) of Abraham; whoever enters it is safe. He who can perform the pilgrimage to the House is obligated by God to do so; and whoever disbelieves: God is not in need of the world."

> Nūrī said: Whosever heart enters the rule of overseeing (*iṭṭilāʿ*) is safe from the concerns of his self and from the temptations of the Satan.[40]

The verse describes the Kaʿba, the House of God, and mentions legal prescriptions related to it, like the immunity of those who take refuge by it (cf. Q 2:125). The station of Abraham is a stone converted to a place of prayer in front of the Kaʿba's façade (where, according to Muslim tradition Abraham stood when building the Kaʿba, and where his footprints are preserved).

The comments Sulamī includes in his commentary elaborate on the meaning of "the station of Abraham" as a spiritual stage in which man renounces all of his belongings similar to Abraham. All the comments related to the phrase "whomever enters it is safe" dissociate it completely from the original Quranic context, albeit they paraphrase it and keep the structure of the sentence. Some comments add circumstantial modifiers to the verb "enters," defining the circumstances of the action; others specify its subject or direct object. While in the Quran the subject of the verb is an indefinite pronoun (whoever), and its direct object is the Kaʿba, the comments offer interpretations markedly distanced from the literal meaning. Some comments specify the subject as "faith" and the direct object as "heart" *(qalb),* resulting in sentences like: "Whosever heart faith enters, is safe from disbelief," or: "Whosever heart faith crosses, is safe from the levities of his self."[41] Nūrī's comment is one of these paraphrases, having as subject the term "overseeing" *(iṭṭilāʿ).* In Sufi texts, *iṭṭilāʿ* may be performed by God, and in that case denotes such ultimate control and knowledge that the human being is incapable of it, even regarding his own life. The term occurs five times in Qushayrī's *Treatise,* each time as an action definitely performed by God: "You can supervise *(ishrāf)* the inner heart, but the overseeing *(iṭṭilāʿ)* of the centre of the inner heart is exclusive to God."[42] However, it might be an action carried out by man, as well. Abū Ṭālib al-Makkī explains in his remarks regarding the term *muṭṭalaʿ* (place of overseeing) occurring in an enigmatic *ḥadīth:* "The Messenger of God said: 'The Quran was sent down according to seven letters. Each of these letters has an exterior *(ẓahr)* and an interior *(baṭn).* Each letter has a limit *(ḥadd),* and each limit has a place of overseeing *(muṭṭalaʿ).*' "[43] In his *Qūt al-qulūb,* Makkī asserts that "the place of overseeing is for the people of supervision *(ishrāf)*: they are the knowers *(ʿārifūn),* the lovers *(muḥibbūn),* the frightened; who oversaw *(iṭṭalaʿū)* the kindness of the Overseer *(muṭṭaliʿ),* after they were frightened by the horror of the place of overseeing *(muṭṭalaʿ)."*[44]

Q 3:128

"You have nothing to do with this, He may turn to them [mercifully] or may punish them, for they are wrongdoers."

> Nūrī said: "You have nothing to do with this"—for everything is [given] to you [by God].[45]

In the original context of the Quran, God addresses Muḥammad at the time of the battle of Uḥud, relieving him of the burden of punishing or forgiving unbelievers and sinners. Nūrī, however, detaches the first phrase of the passage and interprets it independently from the context: man has no control over anything, since God provides him everything. Alternatively, man should not be attached to anything, since his only true attachment is to God. The commentary quotes a parallel, more elaborate version of Nūrī's saying (apparently anonymous saying in Sayyid ʿUmrān's edition and attributed to Nūrī in Nwyia's publication), which adds: "It is above your capacity to perceive anything but the Real in what He begins or restores."[46] This sentence alludes to Q 85:13, praising God as He who "begins and restores" (creates and resurrects), and refers to the human being's ultimate goal in perceiving solely God in every action beginning with his creation until his return to God.

Q 3:152

"God fulfilled His promise when you slew them by His permission, until you failed and argued about the command, and you disobeyed after He had shown you what you had desired [that is, the booty]. Some of you seek the world, and some of you seek the world to come. Then He kept away you from them in order to test you, but He has already forgiven you, for God is generous towards the believers."

> Nūrī said: The common people wear the shirt of servanthood (*ʿubūdiyya*), and the elite wear the shirt of lordship (*rubūbiyya*) and they do not perceive servanthood, for the Real attracted the choicest people (*ahl al-ṣafwa*) and erased them from themselves.[47]

The original context of the verse is again a battle, but that is hardly touched upon by the comments. Since the verse contains the verbal root of the word *murīd* ("seeker," a term so central to Sufism), it is not surprising that most of the comments Sulamī quotes refer to this part of the sentence. Some of the comments, however, do not seem to be directly related to the passage at all, and that is the case with the comment cited in Nūrī's name. A slightly different version of the saying is also preserved in Sarrāj's *Book of Flashes*.[48] There common people and elite are both equalized as wearing the shirt of servanthood, that is, being servants of God. Here, however, the elite are distinguished as partaking in the divine act of *rubūbiyya* (lordship), usually exclusive to God. Compared with the version Sarrāj quotes, this saying expresses more boldly the concept of the elite's melting into God until they reach a spiritual state in which they cannot perceive their own personalities as distinct from the Creator. For another saying of Nūrī on the topic of servanthood and lordship, see his comment on Q 36:61 discussed below.

Q 4:128

"If a woman fears that her husband may treat her badly, or may avoid her, it won't do any harm if they make peace with each other, since peace is a good thing. Avarice was brought to the souls [of man], but if you act benevolently and fear God, He will surely know what you do."

> Nūrī said: Shades (*ashbāḥ*) are forced to oppose the Real under all circumstances,[49] and their avarice is that which compels them to covet the world.[50]

Nūrī's saying is the only comment Sulamī quotes with regard to the verse, and even this does not seem to be closely connected to it. Most probably, Sulamī chose to include the saying since the word "avarice" occurs in both of them. "Shade" (*shabaḥ*, plural: *ashbāḥ*) is a less common Sufi term. Material phenomena are perceived in mystical thought as shadows of spiritual realities, and the visible word is considered as a shade of the pure, perfect light.[51] The term emphasizes the apparent unreal character of worldly existence.

Q 6:9

"Had we sent an angel, we would have made him a man, and surely we would have confused them more regarding what they were already confused."

> Nūrī said: He would have shown mercy to them without their knowledge.[52]

Nūrī's sentence is deficient in itself and cannot be considered as a full utterance; therefore, it is reasonable to suppose that it was intended as a comment on this ambiguous Quranic phrase it complements. The verse explains that those failing to recognize God's message cannot be addressed in any way: were the message communicated in written form, they would regard it as an act of magic and demand oral communication by an angel. However, since an angel could be perceptible by the senses only if it is visible, they would get confused regarding its nature: whether it is transcendental or human and would not accept the message anyway. Consequently, they would not recognize God's mercy, as Nūrī explains.

Q 6:36

"ONLY THOSE WHO HEAR CAN ANSWER; GOD RESURRECTS THE DEAD AND THEY WILL BE RETURNED TO HIM."

> Nūrī said: Whoever opens his ear (*samʿ*) to hearing (*samāʿ*), makes flow his tongue with answers.[53]

Sulamī quotes only two sayings in respect of the verse, both of them praising the Sufi practice of audition ceremony (*samāʿ*, meaning literally "hearing"). Sulamī's position toward *samāʿ* is obviously positive, for the sayings he cites approve of the ceremony without reservation. According to Ibn ʿAṭā', God announced through this specific Quranic verse that "the people of hearing are the living, and they are the people of discourse and answer. He also announced that the others are the dead."[54] "Discourse" in this context denotes God's speech addressed to man, and by "answer" (*jawāb*) its acceptance is meant. Nūrī plays with the connotations of the words "hearing" and "answering," filling the trivial meaning of the sentence (i.e., only who hears the question is capable of answering) with the overtones of spirituality. The Sufi participating in the *samāʿ* session is overcome by a sensation of "flow," which urges his tongue to answer with incessant words of *dhikr*, recollection.

Q 6:83

"This is the argument we brought to Abraham against his people: We elevate the rank of those we wish; your Lord is wise and all-knowing."

> Nūrī said: "We elevate the rank of those we wish"—through being with God and receiving understanding from Him.[55]

The comments Sulamī quotes follow the same pattern: they complement the phrase "we elevate the rank of those we wish" with a clause expounding on the means by which the action is performed. These might be conventional, like "through obeying the Messenger and following his Sunna,"[56] or, like Nūrī's comment, may emphasize mystical concepts: being together with God and being illuminated by Him.

Q 7:2

"A book brought down to you so that you may warn [the people], and in order to be a reminder to the believers; so let there be no distress in your chest (*ṣadr*) because of it."

> Nūrī said: When the lights of realities descend upon the inner heart (*sirr*), it is unable to carry them; similarly to the sun: its rays prevent from perceiving their extremity (*nihāya*).[57]

Nūrī's saying does not directly relate to the verse, nor does it contain any word occurring in the passage of the Quran. The reason for its inclusion is thematic relevance on the one hand, and the semantic connection between the concepts of *ṣadr* (chest) and *sirr* (inner heart) on the other hand. In Sufi terminology, these are alternative denominations for the heart, emphasizing its different functions and aspects. Besides Nūrī's saying, Sulamī quotes Junayd with respect to the Quranic phrase "let there be no distress in your chest because of it." As opposed to Nūrī's saying, Junayd's words might well comment on the Quranic passage itself since they seem to paraphrase it: "Let not your heart *(qalb)* be too confined to bear its heaviness; for surely bearing the [divine] attributes *(ṣifāt)* is heavy, except for those who are aided by receiving contemplation *(mushāhada).*" The place of contemplation, witnessing God is normally the inner heart,[58] regarding which Nūrī formulates a paradox: when the inner heart receives the mystical realities *(ḥaqā'iq)* originating from the Real *(ḥaqq),* the very same realities obstruct the perception of God. The realities are similar to the rays of the Sun that enlighten the eyes, while blinding them from perceiving the Sun itself: the more directly one looks into the Sun, the less one can actually see it.

Q 7:29

"SAY: MY LORD HAS COMMANDED JUSTICE; SET UPRIGHT YOUR FACES AT EVERY PLACE OF PRAYER, AND CALL TO HIM WITH SINCERE RELIGIOSITY; YOU WILL REVERT TO [WHAT YOU WERE] WHEN HE CREATED YOU."

> Nūrī said: We will impose on you in infinity (*abad*) what we decreed on you in pre-eternity (*azal*).[59]

The saying is quoted in connection with the last part of the verse, although apparently it was not intended as a comment on it. The saying plays with the terms *azal* and *abad,* both meaning "eternity," but focusing on its opposing aspects: *azal* is "perpetuity of existence in the past," or preeternity, while *abad* is "perpetuity of existence in the future," infinity; and both are considered as attributes of God.[60] Nūrī's sentence is missing from Sayyid ʿUmrān's edition of the *Realities.* All of the comments Sulamī quotes with regard to the Quranic passage express the idea of predestination that apparent, transient acts do not alter.

Q 10:22

"HE ENABLES YOU TO TRAVEL BY LAND AND SEA; UNTIL [IT HAPPENS THAT] WHEN YOU ARE IN SHIPS SAILING WITH GOOD WIND, AND THEY REJOICE AT IT, [SUDDENLY] STORMY WIND COMES AROUND, AND WAVES FROM EVERY SIDE; THEY THINK THAT THEY ARE SURROUNDED, AND CALL TO GOD WITH SINCERE RELIGIOSITY: IF YOU SAVE US FROM THIS, WE WILL BE GRATEFUL."

> Nūrī said: Who calls [to God] in supplication sincerely does not associate anything to it from his self (*nafs*), except for his vision (*ru'ya*) of whom he calls to.[61]

Sulamī quotes a selection of short sayings related to sincerity (*ikhlāṣ*) that roughly corresponds to the beginning of the chapter on sincerity composed by Sarrāj in his *Book of Flashes*.[62] Evidently, these were not comments on the Quran originally; Sulamī chose to introduce them here due to their relevance to the Quranic phrase "call to God with sincere religiosity." Although Sarrāj's chapter contains a saying by Nūrī on sincerity, Sulamī does not include it here but quotes in his name another saying instead, which is more fitting to the Quranic verse since it does not treat sincerity in general but sincere supplication in particular. The word "vision" occurring in the sentence refers to the mental action of complete concentration, not to visual perception: "If you don't see the Real, you are not [seeing] by Him; and if you see other than Him, you do not see Him."[63] It is impossible to "see" God and anything other than God simultaneously.

Q 11:17

"VERILY, THOSE WHO FOLLOW THEIR LORD'S CLEAR SIGN (*BAYYINA*), RECITED BY HIS WITNESS, LIKE BEFOREHAND THE BOOK OF MOSES, AS A GUIDE AND MERCY—THOSE BELIEVE IN IT; BUT WHOEVER OF THE PARTIES DENIES IT, FIRE WILL BE HIS DESTINATION. DO NOT DOUBT IT; IT IS THE TRUTH FROM YOUR LORD, BUT MOST OF THE PEOPLE DO NOT BELIEVE."

> Nūrī said: Clear signs (*bayyināt*) are those which do not reveal mistakes and stumbling ultimately.[64]

Most of the comments explain the meaning of the word *bayyina,* which stands for "something that expresses something else clearly." In Junayd's words, "it is a reality confirmed by obvious knowledge *(ẓāhir al-ʿilm).*"[65] Nūrī's explication also emphasizes the concept of conclusiveness: *bayyina* is something that does not involve misconceptions and fallacies. In his commentary on the Quran, Sulamī rarely quotes pious stories about the Sufi masters. Here, however, he quite exceptionally interpolates such a story on Junayd's capacity of intuitive knowledge, which is usually called *firāsa* (intuition, insight) in Sufi texts: "A man came to Junayd, and said: 'I shall ask you about something in my heart *(ḍamīr).*' He said: 'Ask, then!' He said: 'I have already asked.' Junayd said: 'You have asked such-and-such, and the answer is such-and-such.' But the man said: 'No!' Junayd said: 'Yes, indeed! But you have changed the question to such-and-such, and the answer to that is such-and-such.'"[66] Both the story and most of the comments (including Nūrī's) seem to be unrelated to the original context of the Quran.

Q 14:10

"Their messengers said: Is there any doubt concerning God, the Creator *(fāṭir)* of the heavens and the earth? He calls you [to Himself] in order to forgive your sins and to delay the moment determined [for calling you to account]. They said: You are nothing but humans like us! You want to prevent us from [worshipping] what our fathers worshipped; bring to us an outright authority!"

> Nūrī said: God called the created beings to Himself by Himself, uttering the name Creator (*fāṭir*) from among His names, so that they may be free from attachment to any of the things that exist. Therefore He said: "the Creator of the heavens and the earth"—If you want what

> is in them, it is in My possession; if you want Me, do not turn towards them, but return from them to Me![67]

It is obvious that this short explanation was intended as a comment on the Quranic text from the outset. The point of the comment is the idea of cutting the attachments to everything except God.

Q 15:72

"By your life! They wandered about in their intoxication."

> Nūrī said concerning His saying "By your life"—by the life through which you are singled out from among the creatures, for they live by their spirits and you live by Me: your subsistence is connected (*muttaṣil*) to My subsistence, for you subsist in Me.[68]

The verse is from the story of Lot and the people of the cities of Sodom and Gomorrah, and the oath "By your life!" is uttered by God to Muhammad. Nūrī focuses on this detail, and his comment is unrelated to the broader context in other respects. As it has been already mentioned, spirit *(rūḥ)* is the counterpart of carnal soul *(nafs)*. The spirit is the life God breathed into man from His own spirit (cf. Q 15:29), it has a pronounced divine origin and character. The spirits were created before the bodies, and long to return to God. According to Nūrī's comment, the spiritual rank of Muhammad is above all humankind since while the latter live by the spirits God breathed into them, and are connected to God through the spirits, Muhammad subsists "in God," by God Himself, through his direct connection *(ittiṣāl)* to God.

Q 18:28

"Endure patiently with those who call to their Lord day and night, seeking His face, and let not your eyes bypass them, seeking the beauty of worldly life. Do not obey him whose heart We made neglect to recall Us, who follows his passion, and who carries matters to extremes."

> Nūrī said: Negligence is the reliance of the inner heart (*sirr*) on anything but the Real.[69]

Nūrī's sentence pertains to the genre of the Sufi masters' maxims, or short definitions of mystical concepts that were gathered in Sufi handbooks and biographical lexicons. Its inclusion here is due to its relevance to an expression occurring in the verse. The authors of the first Sufi handbooks usually did not dedicate a separate chapter to the term "negligence" *(ghafla)*, therefore the collection of sayings on the concept Sulamī includes in his commentary is highly interesting. For example: "Sahl said: Negligence is spending the [mystical] moment *(waqt)* in vain";[70] "Ibn al-Jalā' said: Negligence is what brings down to you indifference";[71] "Abū ʿUthmān was asked about negligence, and he said: Being careless about what you have been commanded and forgetting God's subsequent benefactions to you."[72] Sulamī quotes also anonymous sayings: "Negligence is following the appetite of the carnal soul *(nafs)*";[73] "Negligence is the punishment of the heart *(qalb)* consisting in veiling it from the Benefactor."[74]

Q 22:78

"Strive in [the way of] God as it befits Him. He has chosen you and has not imposed upon you any hardship in your religion, [it is] the faith of your forefather, Abraham. He named you Muslims [i.e., those who have surrendered to God] both previously and in this [Quranic passage], so that the Messenger may be witness against you, and you may be witnesses against the people. So perform the prayer and give the charity [prescribed], and hold fast to God; He is your Protector, how excellent a Protector and how excellent a Helper!"

> Nūrī said: Holding fast to God is for the [spiritual] elite, while holding fast the rope of God is for the common people. Holding fast the rope of God means to adhere to the commandments and to the Prophetic traditions, while holding fast to God means devoiding the heart (*qalb*) and the inner heart (*sirr*) of what distracts them from Him;

> and being occupied with [constantly] observing Him (*murāqaba*) and turning towards Him. God said: "hold fast to God, He is your Protector"—that is, He is who helps you if you engage in [the action of] holding fast.[75]

Nūrī interprets the expression "holding fast" *(iʿtiṣām)*[76] in the light of another verse of the Quran, which mentions "holding fast the rope of God," meaning that believers should preserve their unity and should beware of becoming divided into groups. The Quran expresses the idea with symbolic language, referring to a rope God stretched out to the people who may grab it without exception (cf. Q 3:103). It is a well-known hermeneutical device to interpret a verse by reference to another verse in which the same expression appears. Nūrī follows this hermeneutical principle when he distinguishes between the bearing of the term with regard to the common people and the elite. From the broader context of the verses it does not necessarily mean that they were addressed to two different groups; apparently both verses talk to the entire Muslim community. Nūrī, however, disregards this, and focuses on a semantical difference: holding fast the rope of God as opposed to holding fast to God Himself. The former requires some form of intermediation, while the latter implies direct connection. Nūrī's interpretation is obviously based on the text of the Quran, and it was not correlated with it by Sulamī subsequently. Nonetheless, it ignores the broader context of the Quran and concentrates instead on minimal units of discourse.

Q 24:63

"Do not make the Messenger's call to you like your call to each other. God knows those of you who steal away seeking refuge. So let him beware who diverges from his command, lest dissent *(fitna)* and painful chastisement may afflict them."

> Nūrī said: Dissent (*fitna*) is occupation with anything but the Real.[77]

The word *fitna* has double meaning: "dissent" (discord, even riot or civil strife), and "temptation." Here again, Sulamī includes a small collection of short sayings on a key term of the verse, unrelated to the original context. These perceive both aspects of the term but with slightly different emphasis. Junayd, for example, focuses more on the connotation of discord, disagreement with the accepted norms and God's commands: "*Fitna* is the inversion of the heart *(qalb)* until it does not recognize what is accepted and does not ignore what is unaccepted."[78] Other sayings contrast *fitna* with *balā'*, which is a Sufi technical term for trial and tribulation. "Ruwaym said: *Fitna* is for the common people, while *balā'* is for the [spiritual] elite." Or: "Abū Bakr b. al-Ṭāhir said: *Fitna* is taken on [by the people similarly to bad habits], while *balā'* is forgiven and rewarded." In light of these sayings, *fitna* consists in diverging from God's commands, adopting a behavior that contradicts divine will. Such behavior is initiated by the human being and causes a situation of trial, or test, in which man might deviate from the right way.[79] Obviously, this kind of dissent affects the common people. Conversely, *balā'* involves trials and tribulations originated by God that may be considered manifestations of divine communication with the chosen elite. Nūrī, however, broadens the meaning of the word *fitna* to include dissent, or deviation in the mystical sense of failing to concentrate on God exclusively.

Q 27:50

"So THEY PLOTTED A PLOT: AND WE PLOTTED A PLOT, WHILE THEY PERCEIVED NOT."[80]

> Nūrī said: If there were not for the plot, the life of God's friends would not be right.[81]

The attribution of the saying to Nūrī is highly uncertain; Nwyia reads Nūrī, while Sayyid ʿUmrān's edition ascribes the saying to Thawrī. Moreover, Sayyid ʿUmrān's edition includes here two sayings in the name of a certain Nawawī, one of which can be found in Sīrjānī's collection as attributed to Nūrī. The words Nūrī (النوري), Thawrī (الثوري) and Nawawī (النووي) are orthographically almost identical in Arabic, all the more so since manuscripts do not necessarily indicate the diacritical marks distinguishing between graphically similar letters. The saying Sīrjānī quotes ("Disobedience is not free from disappointment and obedience is not free from ruse"[82]) is not attested in the early collections among the sayings of Nūrī, and its occurrence in Sulamī's commentary with a different attribution might make its authenticity more uncertain.

According to Sufi mystics, divine ruse *(makr)* is aimed at testing the sincere devotion of man. In Muslim tradition God is frequently described as operating deceitfully—besides the present Quranic passage, see for example: "And they plotted and God plotted as well; and God is the best plotter" (Quran 3:54). The apparent success and material welfare of transgressors and oppressors is regarded as God's deception and artful plot; even spiritual states may be granted by God to undeserving persons who confront Him; miracles might be performed by unmeriting men who might enjoy God's apparent blessing temporarily. For that reason a Sufi should always fear a deceitful act from God; he may never feel secure in his spiritual attainment. He should ask himself whether his deeds are due to sheer hypocrisy, in which case God would evidently refuse them; and he should persist in the greatest wakefulness until his last day since God's judgment concerning his faith might change at any moment.[83]

The comment cited in Nūrī's name seems to be unrelated to the Quranic passage; most probably Sulamī opted for its inclusion since it elaborates on the term "plot" prominent in the verse.

Q 35:32

"Then we brought down the Book on those whom we have chosen from among our servants. Some of them do wrong to themselves, some adopt the middle course and some are foremost in good deeds by God's permission: that is the greatest grace."

> Nūrī was asked about God's saying: "Then we gave the Book as inheritance to those whom we have chosen from among our servants"—What does the word "then" refer to in God's saying? He said: It refers to the pre-eternal will and to the accomplished fact: Then we gave [it] as

> inheritance to those creatures whom we previously had chosen in pre-eternity.[84]

One of the hermeneutical premises of sacred texts is that they cannot contain any superfluous words. That explains the question regarding the meaning of the word "then," which Nūrī answers by paraphrasing the Quranic text. Evidently, this is an example of genuine exegetical activity on his part, not an originally unrelated saying connected to a Quranic lemma posteriorly.

Q 36:61

"And that you should serve Me? That is the right way."

> Nūrī said: Souls are of three types: souls in servanthood, souls in lordship and souls [existing] through the Lord.[85]

The sayings Sulamī connects to the Quranic verse refer to the verb "to serve" and to the noun "servant" derived from it. They seem to be equally unrelated to the Quranic passage as Nūrī's maxim. Another short saying by Nūrī on the topic of servanthood *(ʿubūdiyya)* and lordship *(rubūbiyya)* has been already discussed above (cf. his comment on Q 3:152). Contrary to that, this saying distinguishes three levels of connection with God: servanthood (the level of the common people), lordship (the level of the elite), and existence through the Lord (the level of the elite of the elite). On the other hand, it is similar to the formerly discussed comment with regard to the unusual connection between the elite and lordship: as it has been already noted, *rubūbiyya* (lordship) is exclusive normally to God, while here a select group of humans is distinguished by it.

Q 39:60

"The day of resurrection you will see those who lied about God, their faces will be blackened. Is there no place to settle for the haughty in the hell?"

> Nūrī said regarding this verse: Those who pretended to love God, but their love was not sincere.[86]

Sulamī quotes only two comments regarding the verse, both explaining the concept of lying about man's relation to God. Both comments paraphrase the concept with the word "pretension" *(iddiʿā')*. According to the other comment (by Yūsuf ibn al-Ḥusayn), pretension consists in simulating spiritual states, making undue claims of spiritual perfection. It would be probably supposed that the aim of such simulation is to beguile the people. However, considering the broader context of the Quran, another possibility emerges. In the Quran, the souls of the sinful plead diverse claims as excuses in order to avoid divine punishment on the Day of Judgment. In light of this, the act of pretension mentioned in both comments might be understood as an attempt to deceive God (and not the people) by false pretension of love.

Q 56:85

"And we are closer to you than you are, but you do not perceive."

> Abū l-Ḥusayn al-Nūrī said: The closest closeness in the sense to which we allude is the farthest farness.[87]

This saying is attributed to Nūrī also in Sarrāj's *Book of Flashes* and in Qushayrī's *Treatise*, where also the context of the saying is preserved in two slightly different versions.[88] Apparently, Sulamī detached the saying from the original story, which was a critique directed against a fellow mystic, Abū Ḥamza, and included in his commentary due to the relevance of the saying to the concept of closeness mentioned in the Quran.

Q 57:3

"He is the first and the last, the manifest and the hidden, and he knows everything."

> Abū l-Ḥusayn al-Nūrī said: Firstness is lastness, and lastness is firstness, and manifestness is hiddenness and hiddenness is manifestness, just like pre-eternity is infinity, and infinity is pre-eternity. There is no separation between them, but sometimes He makes you lose it and sometimes He makes you witness it, in order to renew pleasure and to show [your] servanthood to God.[89]

The tradition is included in Nwyia's collection of Nūrī's comments, but it is lacking from Sayyid ʿUmrān's edition of the *Realities*.[90] However, it can be found in Sarrāj's *Book of Flashes* in a fuller version.[91] Nūrī's words are evidently based on the Quran, but most probably were not intended as comment on it, rather—in accordance with Sarrāj's version—as an answer to a question posed to him about the incapacity of the intellect to apprehend God.

Q 72:3

"AND THAT HE—MAY OUR LORD'S MAJESTY *(JADD)* BE EXALTED—HAS TAKEN NEITHER CONSORT, NOR SON."

> Nūrī said: His mightiness (*ʿaẓama*) is more exalted than to be reached through any way, except through Him, or to be engendered by what He created. There is no indication (*dalīl*) of God, except [God] Himself, and nothing leaves a mark (*athar*) on Him, for He is who originated the marks.[92]

The text of the tradition is corrupt; there are minor differences between Nwyia's version (translated here) and the version in Sayyid ʿUmrān's edition. In any case, Nūrī's words do not seem to be in direct connection with the Quranic verse, and the link between the two are constructed by the expressions *taʿālā jadd rabbinā* ("may our Lord's majesty be exalted") and *taʿālat ʿaẓamatuhu* ("His mightiness is [more] exalted") that has identical syntactic structure in Arabic and that are also semantically related. The key term of Nūrī's saying is *dalīl*, "something that indicates something else," hence, "indication, sign," or "proof." Nūrī plays with synonyms of the word "sign" that express the opposite aspects of the same concept. *Dalīl* is a sign that points to something ("indication"), while *athar* is a sign produced as a trace, impression of something ("mark"). *Dalīl* is also a technical term of philosophy meaning "proof." In a tradition that has been already discussed, Nūrī is asked whether the intellect can guide to God *(dalīl ʿalā Allāh)*.[93] He replies that the intellect is incapable of that, and the only proof of God is God Himself. The saying Sulamī quotes formulates a similar idea: there is no way to approach God except for by His initiative and action.

Q 98:8

"Their reward at their Lord are gardens in Eden, beneath which rivers flow, living there immortals infinitely, God content with them and they content with Him: this is for him who fears his Lord."

> Nūrī said: Contentment means to accept [God]'s decrees happily.[94]

The saying is attributed to Nūrī in Sīrjānī's *Black and White in the Words of Wisdom*, too.[95] Most certainly it was unrelated to the Quranic verse originally; its inclusion in the commentary is due to the word "content," which triggers association with sayings on the Sufi technical term "contentment."

Conclusions

Although it is not always possible to determine the connection between the Quranic verse and Nūrī's words that Sulamī edited as comments, some conclusions might be drawn. Roughly half of the sayings seem to be completely unrelated to the Quran,[96] while half of them can be regarded as paraphrasing, complementing, and interpreting the text of the Quran from the outset.[97] The comments introduced by formulae such as "Nūrī was asked about God's saying," or "Nūrī said concerning His saying" are always directly related to the Quran, and most probably were uttered as comments on its text (see, for example, the comments on Q 2:40, 3:35, 15:72, 35:32). However, not all comments clearly related to the Quran are introduced by similar phrases; fragments of genuine Quranic exegesis may be introduced merely by the words "Nūrī said" (cf. the comments on Q 2:273, 3:128, 14:10). Six of Nūrī's sayings cited in the *Realities* are attributed to him also in the Sufi manuals studied here (in Sarrāj's *Book of Flashes,* Kharkūshī's *Revision of the Secrets,* Abū Nuʿaym's *Decoration of the Saints,* Qushayrī's *Treatise,* Sīrjānī's *Black and White in the Words of Wisdom).*[98] It is interesting to note that with the exception of a single comment (on Q 2:245), all of these are unrelated to the Quran and were certainly not intended as comments on its text. It might be of importance as well that Sulamī did not quote in the *Realities* any of Nūrī's sayings he included in the *Generations of the Sufis;* there is no overlap between his two compilations in this respect. The following conclusions might be drawn: although comments on the Quran by Nūrī (or by other masters) were not systematically collected in the Sufi manuals and biographical lexicons, not even in the *Generations of the Sufis* composed by Sulamī himself, obviously Nūrī (and his fellow Sufi masters) engaged in the interpretation of the Quran, and these comments were handed down similarly to their sayings. Apparently, the genre of the compositions defined their content substantially. Material pertaining to the genre of Quranic interpretation was normally not gathered in the manuals, although these compilations may include small selections of such comments occasionally. They certainly contain borrowings from the Quran *(iqtibās)* abundantly, not to mention the frequent references to the sacred text. On the other hand, while Sulamī's commentary aimed to edit as much mystical commentary on the Quran as possible, due to the scarcity of sources he also inserted a considerable amount of material that was probably unrelated but still relevant.

Sulamī's portrayal of Nūrī in the Quran commentary is consistent with the picture that emerges from his *Generations of the Sufis;* both compilations represent Nūrī primarily as a sober mystic, with minimal affinities toward the manifestations of ecstatic or unconventional behavior. In fact, such aspects are negligible in the material collected in the *Realities,* which transmits only one tradition of ecstatic nature: Nūrī's saying praising the otherwise controversial practice of audition ceremony, or mystical concert *(samāʿ).*

The survey of the technical terms occurring in the traditions cited by Sulamī in the *Realities* presents a different picture than the analysis of his *Generation of the Sufis*. The number and frequency of the Sufi technical terms are surprisingly low in comparison with both the *Generation of the Sufis* and the biographical lexicons and manuals composed by other authors. There are only four terms that recur in various traditions: carnal soul *(nafs)*, inner heart *(sirr)*, nearness *(qurb)*, and realities *(ḥaqā'iq)*.[99] This might suggest that Sufi terminology was still unestablished when the transmitted material was formulated, or else, this fact might follow from the genre, that is, comments on the Quran. In the latter case, the relative scarcity of the technical terms might allow us to draw the conclusion that Nūrī (at least) did not wish to "read into" the Quran Sufi ideas with the intention of legitimizing them, nor did he aim to transform the Quranic verses to proof-texts of central Sufi topics and concepts.

CHAPTER 5

Kharkūshī

Revision of the Secrets *(Tadhhīb al-asrār)*

Introduction

The *Revision of the Secrets (Tahdhīb al-asrār)* compiled by Kharkūshī (d. 1015/1016) is a lesser known Sufi manual that collects short sayings on principal Sufi concepts.[1] However, it also dedicates sections to subjects that are not treated in earlier or contemporary Sufi manuals, and most of these do not quote Sufi masters at all but reproduce mostly Prophetic *ḥadīth* (e.g., sections on awakening from sleep, use of the *siwāk,* nightly prayer, ritual ablution, etc.).[2] In Western scholarship Kharkūshī's manual is usually overlooked. The critical tone regarding this compilation was set by Arberry who introduced the manual in a short article in 1938, dismissing it as being too derivative of the *Book of Flashes*.[3] Arberry's critique was contested by Sara Sviri who argued that the *Revision of the Secrets* is essential for understanding the formative period of Islamic mysticism, as it contains much unknown material that cannot be found in other sources.[4] Her claim was partly confirmed but partly refused by Christopher Melchert, who despite acknowledging the significance of the *Revision of the Secrets,* ranked it among the less relevant sources.[5] Melchert repeated Arberry's critique of unoriginality and dependence on the *Book of Flashes* but held that precisely for that reason the *Revision of the Secrets* may make important contributions to scientific research by evidencing what was commonplace and what was extraordinary in the formative period of Sufism.

Although it is not among the objectives of the present study to take a stand on this issue, or even to formulate general statements on the *Revision of the Secrets,* the study of the material on Nūrī does not confirm Arberry's or Melchert's critiques placing it among irrelevant or less important sources. On the contrary, it proved to be the richest early source on Nūrī, containing a total of thirty-five traditions quoted in his name (more than twice as many as Sulamī's *Generations of the Sufis* and a third more than Kalābādhī's *Doctrine of the Sufis*). Moreover, its overlap with the early collections is insignificant: only three traditions overlap with Kalābādhī's *Doctrine of the Sufis,* a single one with Sarrāj's *Book of Flashes* (so much for Kharkūshī's dependence on it), again only one with Sulamī's *Generations of the Sufis* and another with his *Realities of Interpretation,* and four with the somewhat later *Ornament of God's Friends* by Abū Nuʿaym.[6]

The compilator, Abū Saʿd (or Saʿīd) ʿAbd al-Malik b. Muḥammad b. Ībrāhīm b. Yaʿqub al-Wāʿiẓ al-Kharkūshī was born about 951, lived in Nishapur, studied Shāfiʿī law, heard *ḥadīth* in Iraq after 980/1, made the pilgrimage to Mecca and spent three years there between ca. 1003–1005. He collected material for the *Revision of the Secrets* in Mecca, Fustat, Alexandria, Jerusalem, Sidon, and Nishapur.[7] Besides the *Revision of the Secrets,* he wrote a book on the interpretation of dreams and compiled a biography of the Prophet. Some other works attributed to him are lost, among them a work on asceticism *(K. al-Zuhd).*[8]

It is not entirely clear whether Kharkūshī should be considered a Sufi or not. Undoubtedly, the biographers praised him for his piety and *zuhd,*[9] but the pious and the ascetics are not necessarily Sufis too. Sviri holds that he belonged to "the same social and religious milieu" as Sulamī, and she points out that some of Kharkūshī's teachers (in *ḥadīth,* we may add, following Melchert's observation)[10] had an important role in Sulamī's life: Ibn Nujayd was Sulamī's grandfather, while Abū Sahl al-Ṣuʿlūkī initiated Sulamī to the mystical path. However, the biographers do not indicate who Kharkūshī's master was in Sufism, and there is no evidence that he had his own circle of Sufi disciples, directed a Sufi community, or at least been given a *khirqa* by any Sufi master. In this respect it might be interesting to raise the possibility that maybe Kharkūshī was connected more to the Malāmatiyya trend than to the Sufi tradition (his teacher, Ibn Nujayd, was a close disciple of the head of the Malāmatis in Nishapur, Abū ʿUthmān al-Ḥīrī), which might account for the obscurity that surrounds his spiritual affiliation. As Jacqueline Chabbi and Christopher Melchert have argued, there were two renunciant movements of local origin in Nishapur in the later ninth century, the Karrāmiyya and the Malāmatiyya, while Sufism (named as such expressly in the contemporary sources) spread from Iraq to Nishapur, where it absorbed the Malāmati trend in the eleventh century.[11] These movements did not develop in isolation but were in constant communication. The Malāmati trend (the so-called path of blame) was distinguished by the complete interiorization of religiosity, hiding piety entirely, which led the uninitiated "to blame" its followers for their supposed lack of piety. Now, Kharkūshi's chapter on the Malāmatiyya with which he introduces his manual seems to betray his sympathy toward the path of blame. Moreover, he declares categorically at the beginning of that chapter: "We explained what we could about the meaning of Sufism and the characteristics of the Sufis: and that is the path of the Iraqis. As for the Khorasanians, they tread the path of blame."[12] This might indicate that at the time Kharkūshi wrote his manual, Sufism was still regarded a distinctively Iraqi phenomenon; and since Kharkūshi himself was Nishapuri (i.e., Khorasanian), he most probably trod the path of blame himself, that is, he belonged to the Malāmatiyya.

Although Kharkūshī died a few years later than Sulamī, the *Revision of the Secrets* in its present form certainly postdates his death (for that reason Kharkūshī's work is discussed here after Sulamī). As Arberry has already discussed, the chains of tradition provided at the beginning of the book and elsewhere name two transmitters between Kharkūshī and the actual compilator—which is not strange at all in the case of Muslim authors and their compositions. The later transmitter, Abū ʿAbd Allāh al-Shīrāzī, died in 1047, and Arberry remarks that according to the information gathered on him by al-Khaṭīb al-Baghdādī (d. 1071) in his *Ta'rīkh Baghdād* "his reputation does not inspire confidence."[13] Allegedly, he made a show of his piety in order to deceive the masses but eventually became a sort of rich gang leader commanding a private army. According to al-Khaṭīb al-Baghdādī, he was considered a weak *(ḍāʿīf)* authority of *ḥadīth.*

The introduction of the *Revision of the Secrets* recounts (in first-person singular) that Kharkūshī composed it on the request of a (Sufi?) authority (*shaykh min arbāb hādhihi l-qiṣṣa)*[14] who asked him to describe the Sufis' customs, behavior, way of life, concepts and teachings, and also requested that he derive each Sufi practice and idea from a Quranic verse, the Sunna of the Prophet, or the tradition of the first pious generations *(salaf)*. Kharkūshī was unable to comply with the request of the sheik in the latter's lifetime, but after his death he kept this in mind until he finally decided to begin work. He related that after his decision the sheik appeared to one of Kharkūshī's companions *(aṣḥāb)* in his dream. The sheik looked wonderful, and he was preparing to pay a visit to Kharkūshī. This nightly vision reinforced Kharkūshī's determination, and he collected "part of what reached me from their traditions briefly and concisely, limiting this [work] to what can be easily understood and what is most close to the apprehension of the common people *(awām),* for the Prophet said: 'I was commanded to talk to the people according to the capacity of their apprehension.' [. . .] I left out their ecstatic utterances *(aqwālihim fī l-shaṭḥ)* and what is transmitted about them when being in the state of intoxication *(ḥāl al-sukr)*."[15] Of course, the request of the unnamed sheik might be regarded as a literary topos, but it might be given credit as well. The dream Kharkūshī mentioned must have had special importance for him, as he composed a work on the interpretation of dreams; and its impetus on Kharkūshī psychologically is perfectly reasonable. The book attests to the claim that it was composed for the common people, and that matters requiring more intellectual refinedness were omitted, especially those related to intoxication. It is important to note that Kharkūshī does not discriminate between sober and intoxicated mystics, wishing to include the former and to disregard the latter but also to represent Sufism, including intoxicated Sufis, in a selective manner. Consequently, controversial aspects of Sufism are hardly ever perceptible, and material that might be considered confusing or scandalous is excluded. On the other hand, the Sunna of the Prophet is systematically referred to not only as the source or forerunner of the fundamental Sufi ideas but as an exemplary form of behavior irrespective of any Sufi connotation (cf. the use of *siwāk* that has been already mentioned).

The *Revision of the Secrets* does not contain biographical entries but is arranged according to topics. Each chapter is introduced by quotations from the Prophet—that might be interpreted as projecting back Sufi ideas to the beginning of Islam (cf. Melchert's view[16]) but can also regarded as completely sincere efforts to find the antecedents of Sufi concepts in the Sunna of the Prophet. Kharkūshī seldom expounds upon the traditions he quotes or the notions he introduces, and the scarce explications are in fact frequently taken from the *Book of Flashes*. It is important to stress that the material Kharkūshī gathers in the *Revision of the Secrets* is not limited to Sufi wisdom and Prophetic traditions but is extracted also from *adab* literature. As Melchert has noted, the passages pertaining to the *adab* genre have more elegant style and are frequently even humorous. On the other hand, Sviri argued that the compilation incorporated Shiite material, and therefore it is relevant from the perspective of the Shiite impact on the evolution of Sufism (Melchert disagreed on this point).[17] The material Kharkūshī gathered is rarely introduced by chains of tradition (not even Prophetic *ḥadīth* is always provided with full chains of transmitters).

Evidently, the study of the traditions related to Nūrī in itself does not permit to draw general conclusions on the nature of the *Revision of the Secrets* or on Kharkūshī's intentions. However, it confirms Sviri's opinion on the importance of the compilation as an immensely rich source of information. As to be expected, Kharkūshī's portrayal of Nūrī is mostly unilateral since—in accordance with the preestablished methodology of his composition—he omitted Nūrī's ecstatic sayings and reports about eccentric or intoxicated behavior. Signs of these, however, still can be detected.

Sufism and Ecstasy

Although intoxication is suppressed in the collection, ecstatic behavior is not completely disregarded. Most of the traditions Kharkūshī quotes in Nūrī's name on the essence of Sufism present him as a sober mystic; but one saying betrays something of his intoxicated tendency. Kharkūshī cites five sayings of Nūrī on Sufism.[18] Some of these are also quoted in collections discussed before, like the tradition about confronting the carnal soul's desires (in two slightly divergent versions), or another about equanimity regarding material welfare.[19] A third saying emphasizes the importance of the concept of mystical moment: Sufism is seizing the moment.[20]

In fact, the saying is more expressive than the translation suggests: the original meaning of the verbal noun translated here as "seizing" is "springing, leaping, rushing upon" and hence: "attacking, laying violent hands upon someone, overpowering, subduing." According to a well-known saying, the Sufis are "the children of their [present] moment,"[21] that is, they are not concerned with the past and do not worry about the future; they are engaged solely in what their present state *(ḥāl)* requires. The present moment, its essential nature and requirements are chosen by God, not by the Sufi, and therefore "the moment is that which dominates man."[22] Nūrī turns the idea inside out: the moment dominates man, but man may dominate and seize his moment by living it wholeheartedly, experiencing it fully, but also by exercising self-control while experiencing a passing mystical moment, or state. Nūrī formulates this requirement in another saying as well:

> He who does not discipline himself (*yata'addab*) according to the moment (*waqt*), [makes] his moment loathsome.[23]

Each mystical moment or spiritual state has its own norms and requirements that the Sufi may observe. Since most of the states are opposing (or complementing) each other, the proper behavior *(adab)* related to a given state may contradict the conduct required by the other. However, since each state has its own *adab,* evidently the Sufi may comport himself as conforming to the standards of the specific state. For example, closeness to God entails forms of behavior that may be regarded inappropriate under other circumstances, as Junayd puts it: "If love is true, the rules of proper conduct are abolished."[24] The fact that Nūrī's saying praises composure and proper conduct whatever happens, even in the moments of mystical rapture, suggests a sober approach to overwhelming mystical experiences that may override established norms. Such attitude fairly contradicts uncontrolled, extreme forms of behavior generally associated with intoxicated, ecstatic mystics.

Despite that, one of Nūrī's definitions of Sufism singles out the display of ecstasy as a distinctive feature of Sufism:

> He who finds [God] (*wajada*) and displays ecstasy (*tawājada*), is a Sufi.[25]

The inherent beauty of the sentence—in the pun that exploits the multiple meanings of the verbal root WJD—cannot be translated into English. It creates semantic connection between "finding" *(wajada)* God, experiencing the sensation of ecstasy *(wajd)* and exhibiting ecstasy *(tawājada)* in public. Nūrī's sayings on proper behavior and those that equate Sufism with showing ecstasy are quoted in different chapters: the first is in the chapter on *adab,* which enumerates many traditions on norms of conduct both within the Sufi community and with God, and the second is in the chapter on "The Meaning of Sufism." Juxtaposing the sayings, we may conclude that Nūrī considers ecstasy as one of the distinctive peculiarities of Sufism but disapproves of improperly extreme ecstatic behavior. Ecstasy is a mystical state, or a moment that overpowers man and drives him to unconsciousness; however, a Sufi behaving properly may not act in an outrageous, uncontrolled manner incompatible with religious law even while passing the limits of consciousness.

> Nūrī was asked about ecstasy, and he said: By God, the tongue cannot describe its true reality, and the eloquence of the lettered is feeble to describe its essence, for it is the greatest matter, and there is no disease that heals better than the cure of ecstasy.[26]

Being an ecstatic mystic par excellence, it is only natural that Nūrī praises ecstasy as an indescribable experience. The association of illness and ecstasy has been already observed in a story narrated in Sulamī's *Generations of the Sufis*.[27]

Heart and Inner Heart

Among the traditions Kharkūshī cites in Nūrī's name, the texts related both to the outer heart *(qalb)* and to the inner heart *(sirr)* have special importance. The heart is the topic Nūrī most frequently addresses, and he singles it out as a decisive factor in his personal mysticism: he began to perceive intuitive, mystical knowledge once his heart and its inclinations became blocked:

> I was barred from my heart (*qalb*) for forty years; since I came to know God, I did not desire anything, I did not long for anything, and I was not fond of anything.[28]

"Knowing God" refers to intimate, inspired knowledge, or direct experience proper to the Sufis. The context of the saying discusses the reason why "knowers" do not commit sins: because they are feeling ashamed before God. Even if they were permitted to do as they wish, they would refrain from wrongdoing due to their sense of shame. Their hearts are veiled and their eyes are fixed on God. Nūrī apparently goes a step further: a mystic is not inclined toward sinful acts since he has no personal wishes at all. Nūrī does not praise ascetic equanimity in general; rather, he declares that knowledge of God entails blocking the heart's desires and impulses, abandoning personal preferences and choices to God. Consequently, the knower may even act as someone who desires or likes something, but the source of this desire is God, not his own personality. A desire diverting one from God may be hidden from consciousness, and therefore its abandonment may be even more challenging:

> Hidden desire (*shahwa khafiyya*) is when you desire something that God refuses, and you do not abandon it.[29]

Although the heart *(qalb)* in Sufi texts is usually conceived as a repository of praiseworthy character traits and of inspired knowledge—and an organ of cognition rather than the seat of desire and emotions[30]—in Nūrī's saying about the relation between blocking the heart and receiving mystical knowledge the heart is associated with passions and personal inclinations. A certain duality in the nature of the heart can be observed in Nūrī's following poem as well:

> The hearts are not in the position to love You
> (*tahwāka*)

Of course not, given that my eyes have no ability to
see You
My only wish is to be contended by You
Not by any of Your blessings
If we ransomed You by ourselves (*fadaynāka bi-l-nufūs*),
we wronged You
But You ransom a lover (*muḥibb*) who has ransomed
You
I do not cry because being blinded by desire
But fearing that I won't see You[31]

The poetic image of man ransoming God might be surprising, but according to Arab grammarians and lexicographers, this hyperbole is frequently used in rhetorical utterances or poems with the purpose of expressing glorification and exaltation.[32]

While in the previous traditions Nūrī perceives the heart as an imperfect organ incapable of loving God, and yielding to random inclinations, in the following poem he describes it corresponding to the usual conception of the heart attracted toward God, seeking the divine, capable of "seeing" the divine invisible for the eye:

My heart indicates towards You (*ashāra ilayka*)
In order to see what my eyes cannot see
Since You set in my innermost (*ḍamīr*)
The sweetness of beseeching and yearning
My heart wants me to follow my secret, inner will (*sirr*)
I had come to know what is wanted from me
Since I do not have destiny except You
Put me to test, no matter how[33]

The division of the heart into *qalb*, *ḍamīr*, and *sirr* can be observed in the poem. The outer heart *(qalb)* orientates toward God following a divine gift deposited in the inner heart *(ḍamīr, sirr)*, which is a secret *(sirr)* between man and God. The *qalb* "indicates" toward God by allusion *(ishāra)*. Allusion, or sign, is frequently contrasted with *ʿibāra* (utterance, expression). Mystical language prefers metaphoric and allusive ways of expression rather than exact definitions and precise expositions. Divine discourse itself has four registers determined by the communicative situation: "[Exact] expression

(ʿibāra) for the common people, allusion *(ishāra)* for the elite, subtleties *(laṭā'if)* for the friends of God, and realities *(ḥaqā'iq)* for the Prophets."[34] Kharkūshī quotes in Nūrī's name two traditions related to allusive language:

> Allusion (*ishāra*) is covert speech.[35]
>
> Abū l-Ḥusayn al-Nūrī was asked about allusion to the Real, and he said: Allusion makes [exact] expression (*ʿibāra*) superfluous; and the ecstasy (*wijdān*) of allusion to the Real is the absorption (*istighrāq*) of the inner hearts in trustworthiness (*ṣidq*).[36]

Trustworthiness—depending on the context—means the purity of intention, expression, behavior, and acts, free from any kind of falsity. Verbal communication is inherently imperfect, incapable of expressing the intended content or message: "If a trustful person wished to describe what was in his heart, his tongue would not utter it."[37] That is, his tongue would refuse to obey him, knowing that no utterance communicates exactly the intended meaning, and therefore speaking inevitably conveys certain falsities. According to Nūrī, allusive language is a superior form of communication that may provoke ecstasy when man's inner heart *(sirr)* becomes absorbed in the true experience of divine reality. Once the heart's *(qalb)* intentions are purified by being dedicated exclusively to God, the mystic may experience intimacy in his relation with the divine:

> Intimacy (*uns*) with God comes from the heart's purity towards God by being alone with Him (*tafarrud*).[38]

Abandoning all attachments to the world and directing the heart *(qalb)* exclusively toward God, engaging in intimate communication with Him, and recollecting Him constantly leads to certain knowledge, experience of God:

> Certainty of knowledge and trust (*al-yaqīn fī l-maʿrifa wa-l-tawakkul*) is attained solely by recollecting (*dhikr*) God constantly in the heart, and by engaging in inti-

> mate conversation (*munājāt*) with Him frequently, and by cutting (*qaṭ*ʿ) what detaches the heart from Him.[39]

Purification and training of the imperfect outer heart *(qalb)* is thus a prerequisite of spiritual advance. The inner heart *(sirr)*, however, is more intrinsically connected to God. While the outer heart is the organ of knowing God, the inner heart is the organ of contemplating God.[40] The double meaning of the word *sirr* (heart/secret) is perceived as an allusion to the partly divine nature of the inner heart, which is a shared sphere between the human being and God. As much as it is under God's control, it is a "secret" for man. The most secret part of the inner heart, the *sirr al-sirr*, is totally inaccessible to human consciousness and belongs to God exclusively. God's superintendence of the inner heart is treated in this Nūrī poem:

> The secrets of my inner heart were about to rejoice
> at a delight You brought upon me, which I won't
>   specify.
> But a secret of Yours, which guards my heart, cried at
>   my inner heart:
> How can you rejoice at a secret instead of Him, who
>   disclosed it?!
> And it continued to keep an eye on my inner heart
>   secretly in order to watch it
> And the Real watches me so that I might not look
>   after it
> So my inner heart began to annihilate (*yufnī*) my
>   attribute (*ṣifa*) from each and every thing
> and the Real began to annihilate me and to annihilate
>   it[41]

While contemplating God, the mystic should not let himself be beguiled by illusionary matters. Contemplation entails spiritual pleasure that might distract him from the very source of his delight. God, however, does not let him deviate from the path leading to real connection and discloses a secret *(sirr)* that warns him intimately of his delusion. The beauty of the poem lies in the pun employing words of distinct meanings that have identical consonantal stems (paronomasia). The words "inner heart," "secret" *(sirr, sarā'ir, asrār)*, and "rejoicing" *(surūr)*, are similar in sound, all of them deriving from the verbal root SRR, which creates the sensation of being interrelated semantically as well. Kharkūshī quotes another poem attributed to Nūrī that plays with the multiple meanings of the word *sirr*,[42] as well as a poetic (although not rhymed) description of the inner heart, which treats contemplation:

> When the fire of glorification mingles in the inner heart with the light of veneration (*hayba*), the breeze of love (*maḥabba*) from the realm of affection (*ʿaṭf*) stirs both fire and light; so that longing (*ishtiyāq*) arises from it and human condition fades; then contemplation takes place.[43]

Summing up the traditions discussed so far it is evident that the heart is a central topic in the traditions attributed to Nūrī that Kharkūshī chooses to cite. Although the outer heart is the organ of obtaining inspired knowledge of God, it may disorientate man. Consequently, it needs purification, that is, spiritual exercises like constant *dhikr*, in order to make it receptive of divine presence. When this is attained, man may experience God intimately in his heart. In the traditions attributed to Nūrī, the sensations of love, affection, longing, joy, delight, and ecstasy are connected to the inner heart; contemplation abolishes the limits of human condition; the inner heart becomes completely absorbed in the true reality of the divine; and it overflows with strong emotions.

Absence and Annihilation

Annihilation of the self *(fanā')* and absence both from the world and from the mystic's personality are among Nūrī's recurring themes in general, and Kharkūshī also includes a number of such traditions in his collection.

> Trust (*tawakkul*) is the annihilation (*fanā'*) of your disposal (*tadbīr*) in God's disposal and that you are content with divine agency and disposal.[44]

Trust in God *(tawakkul)* is one of the stations of the Sufi path, and the sayings that describe it usually operate with notions like being unperturbed by the circumstances, renouncing any preference, and investing God with full control over one's life. Some authors, including Kharkūshī, attach primordial importance to the concept, contrasting complete dependence on God with *kasb* "earning a living," and considering this distinction as a dividing line between Iraqi Sufism and the Khorasanian Malāmatiyya tendency.[45] In Nūrī's view trust is essentially annihilation of the self, that is, an inner spiritual disposition rather than an outer attitude toward worldly means.

> Nūrī was asked about annihilation (*fanā'*), and he said:
> I swear to Him who holds my soul in His hand, it is the first of the stations of Sufism.[46]

The peculiarity of the saying is that *fanā'* is not regarded as a station *(maqām)* normally, neither is it connected self-evidently to the ideas related to the most common initial stations, like repentance *(tawba)*, abstinence *(zuhd)*, struggle against the carnal soul *(mujāhada)*. Nūrī probably means that the stations most commonly regarded as the beginning of the path, do not necessarily suppose mystical connection to God, which, in fact begins with the self's annihilation in God, not with the subjugation of the body and its desires, neither with spiritual exercises that pertain to the sphere of mere ethics.

> If I knew the way to You, You would annihilate me (*afnaytanī*) from my entirety
> But now that I don't, I turn weeping to You[47]

Here again, annihilation is associated with the way *(tarīq)* leading to God. Had the mystic known the way, had he advanced on it properly, God would annihilate him: detaching him from everything, including his self-consciousness, so that he may not perceive himself, the world, or anything besides God. Once annihilation is complete, existence vanishes, and only God remains.

Some of Nūrī's poems treat the concept of absence. Absence *(ghayb* or *ghayba)* is a term that may refer either to man or God.

Usually, *ghayb* denotes God's hidden world and inner life, while *ghayba* means the mystic's withdrawal both from the external world and from his own inner world. Kharkūshī does not dedicate a separate chapter to the concept, nor does he explain it in his work. Therefore, Qushayrī's explication might be quoted here: "Absence *(ghayba)* is the absence of the heart from knowing what affects the circumstances of the creatures, since sensation is occupied with what descended upon it."[48] Absence is counterpoised by presence: "He is present before the Real, since when he becomes absent from the creatures, he enters into the presence of the Real, as if he were [in fact] present with Him. This happens because recollection takes full possession over his heart, and he is present in his heart before his Lord."[49] The process of such recollection is expressed in the following Nūrī poem:

> I recollected [God], but I did not recollect Him
> corresponding to the true reality of His recollection
> (*dhikr*)
> But the appearances (*bawādī*) of the Real made his
> reality apparent, so now I give utterance [to
> recollection correctly]
> Whenever a reminiscence (*dhikr*) of my recollection
> appears,
> He makes me absent (*yughībunī*) from the reminiscent
> of my recollection, and I submerge
> I submerge in the recollection I performed,
> forgetting the reminiscent of the former recollection[50]

Until the mystic is conscious of his recollection, his heart cannot be present with God. Proper recollection needs divine assistance: "appearances of the Real" direct the heart toward God. The term "appearance" *(al-bādī)* denotes the impression one's heart gains regarding a certain spiritual state. But "when the appearance of the Real appears, every appearance will perish, save the Real."[51]

Another poem grasps the concept of absence from the opposite perspective, complaining about suffering from God's absence from man:

> How sad it is that I call out for You indefatigably
> as if I was far away or as if You were absent (*ghā'ib*)

And I ask for Your grace reluctantly
for I've never seen craving for You like me any
abstinent (*zāhid*)[52]

The theme of the poem is a sense of melancholy and frustration. The mere fact that the mystic invokes God implies distance from God—an idea that the mystic rejects immediately, but voices his concern about "calling out for God" and "asking His grace." It is interesting to note that Nūrī pronounces his frustration with regard to prayer, that is, one of the religious obligations of Islam. The poem is also quoted in Abū Nuʿaym's *Ornament of God's Friends,* which locates the recital of the poem in Mecca, in front of the Kaʿba. This (possibly secondary) geographical setting might blunt the edge of the poem to a certain degree by demonstrating the orthodoxy of the concepts expressed: in the holiest site, where the presence of God can be felt, it is only natural that the believer would not find it necessary to "call out for" God. The poem itself, however, does not limit to the holy site the validity of the idea expressed but describes a general feeling of longing for God Himself instead of engaging in supplications or formal prayer.

Longing for the "country" of God, the invisible inner reality of God recurs in the following story:

> Abū l-Ḥusayn al-Nūrī said: I asked God to hide me in His country from His servants, and a voice called out: "Oh, Abū l-Ḥasan, nothing can veil God!"[53]

The tradition is included in the chapter on "heavenly voices" *(hawātif)* transmitting divine messages. A peculiarity of the chapter is that it also contains a story about Kharkūshī hearing such voices.[54] Nūrī's wish of being concealed from men in God's realm may be interpreted as a desire to disappear from the world and to partake in God's hidden life. The heavenly voice, however, warns him that Sufism is not a sort of escapism: nothing veils God, and the mystic attaining to God is not veiled from the people either. The story might be understood better in light of the Sufi concept of "return" *(rujūʿ).* The mystic, when reuniting God, vanishes from the world and even from his own self and will; when he regains consciousness of the creatures and of himself, he separates from God and subsists in the world. On a more advanced level, the mystic becomes capable of returning to the world without separating himself from God. He remains reunited with God, but he perceives the world and performs his duties connected with it. His perception of the creatures, including himself, is through God, whom he considers as the ultimate agent of every act. Kharkūshī quotes a further story about Nūrī being addressed by the heavenly voice:

> I asked God to make a state permanent for me, and a voice cried out to me: "Oh, Abū l-Ḥasan, no one endures what is permanent except for the Permanent!"[55]

Spiritual states are normally transitory, but a certain state may become characteristic of a specific Sufi, converting thus in his main disposition. Transient states may affect such person as passing "nightly visitors."[56] Most of the spiritual states occur in pairs that complement and mutually presuppose each other. Nūrī's request betrays a certain extremism: he prefers to stick to one of the extremities rather than seeking the equilibrium created by the alteration of the opposed and complementary states.

Spiritual Poverty and Contentment

Kharkūshī quotes several of Nūrī's sayings on poverty. The tradition of the poor being calm in the face of destitution, giving away property easily, and preferring others *(īthār)* when he has the possibility to do so has been already discussed.[57] Poverty in Sufi texts does not mean primarily lack of material means but "neediness with regard to God" *(iftqār ilā Allāh)*, being in need of God, orientating oneself toward Him exclusively. This concept of poverty permits puns that play on the double meaning of the word "needy." An example of that is Nūrī's comment on a saying of the Prophet Muḥammad:

> Nūrī was asked about the meaning of the Prophet's saying: "I had a look at the Paradise and I saw that most of its inhabitants were poor." He said: He who possesses Paradise in its entirety is poor, and he who is content with Paradise instead of God is poor.[58]

Those who "possess Paradise in its entirety" are those who have mastery over the means by which one can attain to Paradise. However, if they are content with Paradise itself, they substitute God with it, and they in fact remain in need of God. Thus, spiritual poverty entails contentment with God Himself instead of being content with His decree:

> Contentment (*riḍā*) is the lack of worry whatever decision is made.[59]

Comments on the Quran

A peculiarity of the *Revision of the Secrets* is that it collects many Sufi comments on the Quran, and these frequently constitute separate sections of the book. Kharkūshī also preserves a number of comments attributed to Nūrī. Some of these are also quoted in Sulamī's *Realities of Interpretation,* like Nūrī's comment on Q 39:60.[60] Another comment is attributed to Nūrī in Sulamī's *Realities,* but is quoted anonymously in the *Revision of the Secrets* (on Q 2:40).[61] A third comment is lacking from Sulamī's Quran commentary:

> Abū l-Ḥusayn al-Nūrī was asked about the meaning of the Quranic verse "prayer prohibits foul and reprehensible acts. [The continuation of the Quranic verse is: Recalling (*dhikr*) God is greater (Q 29:45)]." He said: It means that the reward for prayer may be accompanied by the punishment for fouls, but recalling God is greater than punishment for foul and reprehensible acts could subsist with whom who recalls God.[62]

The Quranic passage contains both the word prayer *(ṣalāt)* and recollection *(dhikr),* and it establishes the supremacy of *dhikr* over prayer. Nūrī's interpretation reads into the original context the special meaning of the Sufi *dhikr* to a certain extent: he differentiates between simple prayer, which remains in the sphere of reward and punishment, and the mystical sense of *dhikr,* which is not simply above that but also obliterates consciousness of sins and good deeds, reward and punishment. Evidently, it is a genuine comment and not a saying secondarily attached to the verse.

To conclude, a further commentlike saying may be mentioned, which is included in the chapter on "various wise sayings, admonitions and anecdotes."

> Abū l-Ḥusayn al-Nūrī said: When Joseph was sold, one of the company said: "Treat this stranger well!" Joseph replied: "If God is with you, you are not a stranger."[63]

This tradition is an addition to the Joseph story narrated in the Quran, according to which a passing caravan finds Joseph in the well, and they sell him to the Egyptians (Q 12:19–21). The dialogue itself is not recorded in the Quran but is included in the collection of traditions edited by Zamakhsharī (d. 1143), where it is not connected to Nūrī, and where the transmitter of the tradition is not mentioned.[64]

Biographical Details

Kharkūshī mentions three biographical details of Nūrī's life; an educating anecdote; an alternative version of his detention and intended execution; and an alternative version of his death. The anecdote presents Nūrī as a master capable of performing *karāmāt,* that is, miracles that make his special connection to God manifest.

> Nūrī entered a river, but a thief came and stole his clothes. So, he sat in the water, but before long the thief came back with the clothes, and put them in from of him. His right hand had become dry and lifeless. Nūrī said: "He gave back our clothes, so give back his hand!' "[65]

The story also manifests Nūrī's mercifulness: he does not insist on punishing the thief but asks God to heal him once he returned the stolen clothes (which in itself cannot be considered as proof of the thief's sincere repentance). Nūrī's humbleness making him prefer others to himself is also exposed in the story of his detention.

> A slanderer [in Qushayrī's Treatise: Ghulām al-Khalīl] slandered the Sufis to the caliph, saying: There is a group of heretics who reject the religious law (*sharīʿa*). Abū

l-Ḥusayn al-Nūrī, Abū Ḥamza and Raqqām [Qushayrī: Shaḥḥām, Raqqām, Nūrī and others] were arrested, while Junayd took cover in law [claiming that he was a jurist accepting religious law], since he talked according to the school of Abū Thawr. They were brought before the caliph, who gave the order to decapitate them. Then Nūrī stepped forward before the headsman in order to be beheaded first. The headsman said to him:

"You stepped forward from among your companions!"

Nūrī said:

"I prefer my companions to live even if only one moment."

The headsman and those present became perplexed. The caliph was informed about what happened, and he sent Nūrī back to the main judge in order to clarify his matter. Nūrī went to the judge, who asked him legal questions concerning ritual purity and prayer. After answering all of them, he said:

"Moreover, God has servants, who eat by God, dress by God, hear by God, go out by God, and go back by God."

When the judge heard what he said, he wept, and went to the caliph, saying:

"If these are heretics, then there is no monotheist (*muwaḥḥid*) [Qushayrī: Muslim] on the face of the earth."[66]

The story about Nūrī's detention and salvation is narrated first in the *Book of Flashes* by Sarrāj; however, that version differs considerably from this one.[67] Parallels of this version can be found in several early manuals, among them in Qushayrī's *Treatise*.[68] There the slanderer is identified with Ghulām Khalīl, as in Sarrāj's *Book of Flashes*. Unlike Sarrāj's text, the version cited by Kharkūshī, Qushayrī, etc. does not imply that the cause of the investigation was Nūrī's special way of articulating his connection to God, or the language related to love he occasionally used. Moreover, contrary to Sarrāj's version, here Nūrī was not accused alone, but with a whole group of Sufis including Junayd, the foremost representative of sober Sufism (although he managed to escape execution by posing himself as a jurist dealing with Islamic law). The inclusion of Junayd among the accused indicates that the charges did especially not concern the peculiar way of mysticism Nūrī followed, but Sufis, or the Sufis in Baghdad in general. The way of investigation and determining whether the Sufis were heretics or not was a kind of exam in Islamic law, meaning that the authorities wished to verify whether the Sufis conformed to the established and universally accepted legal schools, and apparently the investigation did not focus in particular on matters related to intoxicated Sufism.

Kharkūshī does not include in his collection the famous story of Nūrī's death caused by uncontrolled ecstasy that took hold of him when hearing a love poem.[69] Instead, he cites a tradition that hints at Nūrī's closeness to God.

> When Nūrī was dying, someone told him: "Say that there is no god save God!" He responded: "Am I not going to Him?"[70]

I prefer to interpret this story in light of a fifteenth-century Sufi commentary written by Zakariyyā al-Anṣārī to the corresponding locus of Qushayrī's *Treatise.* According to that, Nūrī's reaction to the demand requiring him to recite the formula of Muslim creed evidences the perfection of his spiritual state. In the narrations about the death of Sufi masters, such demands are made when those present at a person's agony suppose (erroneously) that physical pain diverted his attention from God, and therefore it was necessary to urge him to concentrate. Besides the fact that the person warning the master is mistaken, his interference might in fact distract the master from his communion with God. According to Anṣārī, that was the case with Shiblī and Yaḥyā al-Iṣṭakhrī, the former returning from "the preoccupation of the heart [being immersed in God's presence] to the occupation of the tongue [by reciting a verse as an answer]," while the latter was diverted from God by concerning himself with his disciples. Nūrī, however, did not depart from his perfect state while uttering his short and simple answer.[71]

Conclusions

Now that the expressed aim of the *Revision of the Secrets* is to offer an easily comprehensible compendium of Sufism for the common reader, leaving aside any aspects related to intoxication, ecstatic utterances, and potentially scandalizing manifestations, it is not surprising that Nūrī's portrayal is mostly unilateral, keeping silent about the intoxicated nature of his mysticism. Kharkūshī does not interpret any of the traditions he quotes in Nūrī's name, neither does he evaluate Nūrī in any (including indirect) way. The vast majority of the traditions Kharkūshī cites are perfectly "sober"—they do not even mention ideas or terms related to intoxicated mysticism. Two sayings on ecstasy may be regarded as exceptions: in the first place the definition of Sufism that expressly identifies it with the open and public display of ecstasy; and a saying that praises ecstasy as "the greatest matter." However, considering Nūrī's maxims on self-discipline while passing a mystical moment, and "seizing, dominating the moment," displaying ecstasy may not suppose uncontrolled rapture. It is also meaningful that Kharkūshī fails to mention Nūrī's death caused by such unrestrained ecstasy, and opts for including a markedly sober version of his death agony instead.

The most important topics of the traditions are the heart and the recollection of God. From a total of thirty-five traditions, five are related to the outer heart and five to the inner heart: the word *sirr* occurs twelve times, while the word *qalb* occurs six times; these are the most frequent terms in the traditions. Recollection *(dhikr)* is also repeatedly mentioned (fourteen times altogether), but most of these occur in one and the same poem. Allusion *(ishāra)* and the notion of preferring others *(īthār)* are also relatively overrepresented in the traditions (both occurring four times). Other recurring terms are: *riḍā* (4 times), *wajd* (3), *īthār* (3), *waqt* (3), *fanā'* (3), *maḥabba* (3), *faqīr* (3), *nafs* (2), *mushāhada* (2), *tawakkul* (2), *munājāt* (2), *ṣidq* (2), *ghayb* (2), *maʿrifa* (2). Terms occurring in only one tradition include *uns, tafarrud, hayba, yaqīn, ʿibāra, istighrāq, maqām, baʿīd, zāhid.* In general, the frequency of the technical terms is low: while in the Sufi manuals discussed previously the number of terms is greater than that of the traditions (meaning that on average each tradition employs at least one term), in Kharkūshī's collection the number of the traditions is greater than that of the terms occurring in them. The relatively reduced number of technical terms may suggest that Sufi terminology was still unestablished when these traditions were formulated; and it might point to the possibility that Kharkūshī's traditions are more authentic despite the fact that the compilations discussed previously predate his work.

CHAPTER 6

Abū Nuʿaym

Ornament of God's Friends (*Ḥilyat al-awliyāʾ*)

Introduction

The *Ornament of God's Friends (Ḥilyat al-awliyāʾ)*, a monumental biographical work composed by Abū Nuʿaym al-Iṣfahānī (d. 1038), is not limited to Sufi traditions but collects biographies and sayings of the pious in general, beginning with the four Rightly Guided caliphs, and including the Prophet's companions, the founders of the schools of law (with the exception of the founder of the Ḥanafī legal school, whose followers were opposed to the Shāfiʿī school to which Abū Nuʿaym pertained), and many Muslim scholars and ascetics.[1] These are also attributed some mystical utterances even if normally they are not remembered as transmitters of mystical knowledge.[2] The aim of the compilation seems to be apologetic since the inclusion of such forerunners legitimizes the Sufi doctrines and communities. Abū Nuʿaym had strong Sufi connections: he was the grandchild of Ibn al-Bannā (d. 899), one of the major Sufi masters of Iṣfahān. Abū Nuʿaym himself, however, was not a Sufi master but a *ḥadīth* scholar with dozens of students. His biographical work follows the norms of the science of the *ḥadīth* in that every tradition is introduced by detailed chains of tradition (which are omitted in my English translation).[3] Abū Nuʿaym studied under Sulamī in Nishapur, and the latter's influence is easily detectable in the *Ornament of God's Friends:* from the 103 biographies that can be found in Sulamī's *Generations of the Sufis,* 76 have a counterpart in the *Ornament of God's Friends,* and their material shows a great measure of overlap. To a certain extent, the same applies to Abū Nuʿaym's biographical entry on Nūrī, that includes seventeen traditions (sayings, stories and poems), four of which have already been discussed in the chapter on Sulamī's *Generations of the Sufis*[4] and four in Kharkūshī's *Revision of the Secrets.*[5] A further tradition has been treated in the chapter on the *Book of Flashes* by Sarrāj.[6] Four traditions are quoted in Qushayrī's *Treatise* that were composed shortly after Abū Nuʿaym's death.[7] In total, more than half of the traditions collected in the *Ornament of God's Friends* are quoted in other early sources as well.

Biographical Details

Abū Nuʿaym's entry on Nūrī begins with short biographical notes on Nūrī's life, containing his full name (Abū l-Ḥusayn Aḥmad b. Muḥammad, known as al-Nūrī and as Ibn al-Baghawī) and that of his teachers ("he met Aḥmad ibn Abī l-Ḥawārī and he accompanied Sarī al-Saqaṭī").[8] Abū Nuʿaym characterizes Nūrī as a person whose "healing tongue speaks with clarity about the inner hearts (secrets) of those who turn towards the Creator."[9] He relates several episodes of Nūrī's life (some of which have been already discussed): the thief stealing Nūrī's clothes,[10] Nūrī looking defiantly at a handsome youth in Baghdad,[11] and the following story on countering the carnal soul *(nafs).*

> I visited Nūrī one day and I saw that his feet were swollen. I asked him what happened, and he said: "My carnal soul demanded me to eat dates. At first I resisted, but my soul refused me. So I went out and bought some dates, and when I ate it, I told to my soul: 'Get up to pray!' But my soul refused. Therefore, I said: 'I owe to God [an oath as compensation]; I won't sit down for forty days!' And I did not sit down."[12]

The edifying anecdote presents Nūrī as engaging in severe ascetic practice in order to discipline his bodily wishes. Ascetic behavior is a well-known requirement of spiritual progress but does not constitute a Sufi distinguishing mark in itself: when the carnal soul is tamed, ascetic practices can be relinquished. Contrasting the story about the appetite for dates with the anecdote about Nūrī courting a young boy, the harsh reaction of Nūrī to the ephemeral wish of eating dates may be surprising, inconsistent with his levity in other matters related to carnal appetite. Evidently Abū Nuʿaym does not wish to depict Nūrī in a simplistic, one-sided way; he discloses inconsistencies of his personality deliberately.

The same applies to the incongruous relationship between Nūrī and Junayd: Abū Nuʿaym quotes the story about Nūrī's and Junayd's behavior during illness, when Junayd exhibits his suffering while Nūrī refuses to do so for fear it might seem like complaining about it.[13] Abū Nuʿaym also includes the story about Nūrī demanding God to perform a seemingly senseless miracle and Junayd's rebukes for Nūrī's caprices.[14] On the other hand, he cites from their exchange of letters evidencing Nūrī's reliance on Junayd in mystical matters (see below).

Furthermore, Abū Nuʿaym relates the Ghulām Khalīl incident in a version that corresponds roughly to the one related in Kharkūshī's *Revision of the Secrets* but differs substantially from the version quoted in the *Book of Flashes*.[15] Unlike the variant quoted in the *Revision of the Secrets*, the text in the *Ornament of God's Friends* mentions the name of the judge who investigated Nūrī's case (Ismāʿīl b. Isḥāq) but omits the names of the Sufis detained together with Nūrī (and does not mention Junayd's evasion of the investigation either). Finally, Abū Nuʿaym remarks that during the unstable years of persecution provoked by Ghulām Khalīl, Nūrī settled in Raqqa, withdrawing from the people. For the time he returned to Baghdad, he had already lost his followers *(unās)* and companions *(jullās)*. He refused to talk because his eyesight was weak, his body was exhausted, and his nourishment was restricted to the minimum.[16]

All these biographical details give the impression of a controversial, unstable personality whose weaknesses are not glossed over. However, neither his ecstatic utterances nor other peculiarities related to intoxicated mysticism are mentioned, and such omission is certainly deliberate.

Poems and Sayings

The central themes of the traditions cited in Nūrī's name in the *Ornament of God's Friends* are the inner heart, absence, and annihilation. His poems on the inner heart take full advantage of the double meaning of the term *sirr.* One of these has been already discussed in the previous chapter.[17] Another is a poetic question Nūrī addressed to Junayd:

> Nūrī wrote to Junayd asking him about the inner heart, describing it in his poem with three descriptions:
>
> About three things a heart (*sirr*) asks you confidently
> the secrets of which are concealed, and that are
> hidden, even if revealed.
> [First.] A man whose heart's concealment in his chest
> became lost for his awareness, until his heart disappeared.
> So he drew the veils of custody [over his speech]
> preventing
> any talk to give away the secret of his heart.
> For the concealment of a secret, if its concealment is
> conceivable,
> cannot be wholly achieved, [for] thinking of such
> secret entails its mentioning.
> So it was concealed by the hidden, and his chest
> concealed it from himself,
> for everything is reduced to naught, if so He wills.
> [Second.] A tenacious [man], [withholding] what he
> passionately desires. If something flashes up
> approximating it, speculation defends their[18]
> correctness.
> [Third.] A reticent [man], complying with hidden
> thoughts (*ḍamā'ir*), rides upon
> evasion for [a secret] imparted to him [avoids
> revealing your secret] and knows no betrayal.
> The crown of the Glorious blamed them, you mentioned[19]
> and from its drinking[20] in his state [originates an]
> overflowing source [of mystical states].
> Junayd said: "By God, I have never directed my inner
> heart to any of the two,[21] preferring one over the

> other, except when [God] attracted me towards it, and I postponed the decision concerning both [entrusting it] to God."[22]

The introductory remark helps the interpretation of the poem: it describes *sirr* (inner heart/secret) in three ways, apparently employing three metaphors: (1) a man concealing his *sirr* completely, limiting his communication in order not to disclose it—there is another poem by Nūrī that expresses the same idea and cited by both Sarrāj and Kharkūshī but not included by Abū Nuʿaym;[23] (2) a person withholding what he desires; (3) a reticent man, who guards the *sirr*. Evidently, the term *sirr* conveys both of its meanings at the same time, with major emphasis on one or the other significance in each line. (For that reason, the English translation is preferably now "heart," now "secret.") The three descriptions are obviously interrelated; they approach the same thing, although from different aspects (concealment, withholding, taciturnity). Junayd's answer does not contest the correctness of the descriptions, although he announces his perfect equanimity in the face of the different aspects, expressing his complete reliance on God. The correspondence between Nūrī and Junayd evidences their close relationship, and the fact that Nūrī turns with his question to Junayd suggests his dependence on him.

Some poems Abū Nuʿaym quotes are provided introductory remarks or even short stories that may serve as keys for their interpretation. The poems occur in other collections without such settings, which suggests that these narrative passages are secondary. The recital of a poem, which is also included in Kharkūshī's *Revision of the Secrets* (without geographical setting) is related to Mecca by Abū Nuʿaym, in front of the Kaʿba.[24] Similarly, another poem, which is included in the *Book of Flashes* in a shorter form and without any narrative introduction, is quoted in two slightly divergent versions by Abū Nuʿaym, both introduced by short narrations.

> Nūrī was a Sufi who talked[25] [to the people about God]. Once, when he came from Mecca, not in the season of pilgrimage, we went out and met him outside Baghdad. We saw that his face had changed, so we said to him: "Oh, Abū l-Ḥusayn, do the inner hearts (*asrār*) change

with the change of the skin [outer appearance]?"

He answered: "No! The Real took over Himself everything, and He took the burden off from the hearts of His friends." Then he recited:

"He drove me out of my abode
He treated me as you see
You see how He treated me
I live in forsaken ruins
When I absent myself (*ghibtu*), He appears (*badā*)
And if He appears, He makes me absent
I am in accord with Him, until every time
He is in accord with me, He differs from me
and says: You don't see what you see
Unless you see Me!"[26]

Here, Nūrī recites the poem when returning from Mecca, that is, after his encounter with God. In both variants, Nūrī's outer appearance is altered as a result of that: "his face has changed" in this version; in the parallel version even his physical existence is almost effaced: "Nūrī was seen when he returned from the Holy Place [al-Ḥaram, that is, Mecca], nothing remaining from him except his thought (*khāṭir*)"[27]—inspired by God at the holy place. The question addressed to him concerns the relation of the inner heart and outer appearance. The latter is expressed by the word "skin" in this version and "attribute" in the other: "Does what adhere to inner hearts (*asrār*), adhere to attributes (*ṣifāt*) as well?" In Nūrī's answer, the opposition of inner heart and skin/attribute is that of permanency versus temporariness. God overwhelms the heart and eliminates their burden (their distinct individuality). Nūrī's answer in the parallel version is more explicit: "No! [What adheres to inner hearts does not adhere to attributes.] The Real got engaged with inner hearts and carried them, but turned away from attributes and effaced them." The poem itself describes how the Sufi encounters God: his habits, character traits, own will and personality are eliminated: this is symbolized by his wandering in the desert. In the parallel version, the spiritual exile is expressed more passionately, using bitter terms: "Didn't He treat me like this?!

/ He stirred me up from my abode / He made me a stranger, chased me away." In such a vulnerable state, when man surrenders to God completely, giving up his personality, God appears: "When I absent myself, He appears / And if He appears, He makes me absent." However, once the mystic's personality manifests itself ("I am in accord with Him") God detaches Himself from man ("He differs from me," in the parallel version: "He separates from me") warning the wayfarer that everything apparently existent subsists only through God ("You don't see what you see / unless you see Me").

Absence and presence, annihilation and subsistence are only stations on the way leading to God, not permanent conditions:

> The highest station for the people of true realities (*ahl-ḥaqā'iq*) is that they detach themselves from the creatures (*khalā'iq*). The way of the lovers is taking delight in their Beloved. The way of the hopeful is to expect whom he expects. The way of those who seek annihilation [in God] (*fanā'*) is to annihilate themselves in their Beloved, whom they expect. The way of those who seek subsistence [with God] (*baqā'*) is to subsist through His subsistence. But for him who has left behind both annihilation and subsistence, there is neither annihilation nor subsistence. He said: The love for the Beloved intensifies due to the subtleties of the Beloved.[28]

The sayings might appear to be unrelated, but in fact they focus on one idea: the description of the ways through which mystics of different orientations can reach the highest station *(maqām)*. Those absorbed in true realities instead of apparent, transitory matters, achieve spiritual detachment *(inqiṭāʿ)* in various ways: taking delight in the Beloved, annihilating themselves in the Beloved, or subsisting through God. Eventually, however, the wayfarer should detach himself even from the notions of annihilation and subsistence. Those absorbed in true realities *(ḥaqā'iq)* are still treading the path, while he who detached himself completely from all notions and phenomena has attained to the Real *(al-ḥaqq)*.

The wayfarer's annihilation in God is imperfect while he is conscious of it and wants to communicate it:

> Abū l-Ḥasan al-Qannād said: "I wrote to Nūrī when I was young:
>
> When the totality of everything annihilates itself in the light
>
> Explain me, about which of the two existences (*wujūdayn*) shall I communicate?
>
> He answered me at once:
>
> When you annihilate yourself in what cannot be described
>
> the moment [you reserve] for description [shows your] confusion, I think."[29]

Sufis often exchanged letters on their mystical experience, describing it frequently in poetical form. Abū l-Ḥasan al-Qannād's poem plays on the meaning of the word *wujūd,* which expresses both the passive meaning "to be found" (to exist) and the active meaning "to find." In Sufi terminology it refers to encountering God, and it is closely related to the term *wajd* (ecstasy). The question of Abū l-Ḥasan al-Qannād thus signifies that when everything is annihilated in the encounter with God, about which aspect of *wujūd* should he communicate? Nūrī warns the young Abū l-Ḥasan al-Qannād that his question reveals the imperfection of his mystical quest, for communication necessarily detaches man from God.

The *Ornament of God's Friends* attributes to Nūrī a collection of spiritual advice that is not included in any of the early sources studied here, although the first counsel corresponds word for word with one of Nūrī's sayings quoted in Qushayrī's *Treatise.*[30] A section of such advice *(waṣāyā)* especially to disciples, that is, seekers *(murīdūn),* are frequently attached to Sufi manuals (see, for example, Qushayrī's *Treatise* and Sīrjānī's *Black and White in the Words of Wisdom).*[31]

> Abū Ḥusayn al-Nūrī said, advising some of his companions: There are ten things—and what ten things!—that you should beware of, and that you should do your utmost concerning them:
>
> First, if you see someone who claims that a state granted by God may make him violate religious law, keep away from him!

Second, if you see someone who relies upon people who are not of his kind, and mixes with them, keep away from him!

Third, if you see someone relying on leadership and on [men] praising him, keep away from him! Do not benefit from him even if he would benefit you, and don't wish him to succeed!

Fourth, the poor who returned to the world; keep away from him even if you were starving to death! Do not be friendly with him if he benefits you, for friendliness with him will harden your heart for forty mornings.

Fifth, if you see someone who is satisfied with his knowledge, do not feel safe from his ignorance!

Sixth, if you see someone who claims [to experience] a state, which is not proven by his inward [disposition] (*bāṭin*), and is not confirmed by the composure of his outward [behavior] (*ẓāhir*), doubt his religiosity!

Seventh, if you see someone who is pleased with his carnal soul, and is relying on his [mystical] moment (*waqṭ*), know that he is deceived, and be very cautious with him!

Eight, the seeker (*murīd*), who listens to [the recital of] poems and is inclined towards comfort[able life], do not expect any good from him!

Ninth, the poor whom you don't see to be present during audition (*samāʿ*), doubt in him, and know that he refuses its blissful effect, because his inner heart is confused and his concern (*hamm*) is scattered.

Tenth, if you see someone who is confident about his friends, brothers and companions, claiming the perfection of creatures on that basis, then you shall witness his feeble-mindedness and the weakness of his religion![32]

Nūrī's position toward *samāʿ* may be noted: he warns the seekers *(murīd)* against hearing the recital of poems, which evidently refers to audition sessions where love poetry was commonly recited. Such recitals may incite the carnal soul and confuse the unaccomplished. Advanced Sufis, (denoted *faqīr,* "poor" by Nūrī in this context), may attend audition ceremonies. What is more, in Nūrī's view the

Sufi who refuses to take part in the *samāʿ* is obviously imperfect, his inner heart is not purified, and he is not receptive to the divine inspiration transmitted by the *samāʿ*. Considering the controversy regarding *samāʿ*, this statement may be regarded as an early example of the apologetic position, since it considers audition an essential Sufi ceremony, not an optional practice.[33]

Finally, Abū Nuʿaym includes a saying that criticizes either contemporary Sufism in general, or the outward imitation of Sufi practices in particular.

> Tattered rugs were coverings for pearls; nowadays they have become dunghills upon corpses.[34]

Superficial, meaningless imitation of Sufi practices is a phenomenon that existed from the beginning of Sufi mysticism.[35] The position of the Sufi masters toward the imitators *(mutashabbihūn)* changed in the course of time. They most likely adopted a negative attitude in this respect in the formative period, as evidenced by Nūrī's saying—or that of his contemporary, Sahl al-Tustarī (d. 896)—quoted in the *Ādāb al-murīdīn (Rules for the Novice)* composed by Abū l-Najīb al-Suhrawardī (d. 1168): "The imitators called greediness 'enhancement', vices 'pure intention', abandoning correctness 'ecstatic utterances', taking pleasure in what is blameworthy 'goodness', following the passion 'trial', returning to the word 'arrival', bad morals 'arbitrariness', avarice 'renunciation', obscenity 'blame', although this is not the way the Sufis follow."[36] After the institutionalization of the mystical movement, however, the Sufi masters had no choice but to tolerate a certain measure of shallowness incidental to the generalization of Sufism. When Sufism became the dominant religious tendency, some of its outward marks lost their original functions and became false emblems of piety, like the golden beggar-bowls that the sultans possessed. The relative leniency with which the imitators were accepted is attested as early as in the twelfth century, as it is evidenced by the last chapter of the *Ādāb al-murīdīn*, which enumerates some forty dispensations *(rukhaṣ)*, that is, exemptions from the general code of behavior.[37] Suhrawardī closes the extensive list of dispensations with a statement of the Prophet, according to which "he who imitates [my] people is one of them."[38]

Conclusions

Abū Nuʿaym's *Ornament of God's Friends* is less genuine than the collections discussed before, its overlap with these is considerable. Despite that, one of Nūrī's central themes is absent entirely from Abū Nuʿaym's biographical lexicon: neither of the traditions treats *mushāhada*, "contemplation," which is the most frequent topic of Qushayrī's almost contemporary *Treatise*, and which is also exposed in the *Doctrine of the Sufis* and the *Book of Flashes*. The principal subject of the traditions collected by Abū Nuʿaym is the inner heart and God's secret deposited in it. The topic is treated mostly in poetical form, taking full advantage of paronomastic solutions offering themselves. Abū Nuʿaym put the focus on such traditions deliberately; his introductory remark in the entry on Nūrī, especially, characterizes him as a mystic describing the inner heart ingeniously. Corresponding to the genre of Abū Nuʿaym biographic lexicon, several details of Nūrī's life are included, although the most controversial aspects and incidents (such as ecstatic utterances) are omitted. Neither the circumstances of his extraordinary death are mentioned, despite the genre; biographies usually emphasize communication of such details, therefore their omission may be regarded as telling in itself. In general, ecstatic or drunken aspects of Nūrī's mysticism are not highlighted, though hints of these can be revealed, like his markedly supportive position toward audition ceremony. Love toward God is always expressed with moderate terms *(wadd, widād, maḥabba)*, and God is denoted "Beloved" *(muḥibb)*,[39] while the contentious term *ʿishq* is never used. Several traditions witness the strong relationship between Nūrī and Junayd, and the overall picture gives the impression of Nūrī being in a somehow subservient position to Junayd.

CHAPTER 7

Qushayrī

Treatise (*al-Risāla al-qushayriyya*)

Introduction

Abū l-Qāsim ʿAbd al-Karīm al-Qushayrī[1] (986–1072), a Sufi master and Sunni scholar, studied in Nishapur under the Sufi master Abū ʿAlī al-Ḥasan al-Daqqāq, who belonged to the Sufi tradition of Baghdad. Qushayrī became Daqqāq's foremost disciple, married his daughter, and later succeeded him as the head of his *madrasa.* After the death of Daqqāq in 1014 Qushayrī spent years under the guidance of Abū ʿAbd al-Raḥmān al-Sulamī (d. 1021) as his disciple. Apparently Qushayrī did not choose a new master after him but maintained himself a Sufi lodge in Nishapur and trained some disciples there, among them ʿAlī Faḍl b. Muḥammad al-Farmadhī, who later became the teacher of Abū Ḥāmid al-Ghazālī. In any case, the influence of Sulamī is clearly discernible in the biographical part of Qushayrī's *Treatise* modeled on the *Generations of the Sufis* written by Sulamī. Qushayrī was a Shafiʿī jurisprudent by profession, he was well versed in Ashʿarite theology and in the science of *ḥadīth.* In 1056 he held *ḥadīth* sessions at the caliph's palace in Baghdad by invitation of the caliph al-Qā'im. Because of the struggle between the Ḥanafī and the Shafiʿī schools, he could not return to Nishapur. He settled in Tus until the age of seventy-nine when he was finally able to return to Nishapur, where he spent the last decade of his life.

His main works include a Quran commentary *(Laṭā'if al-ishārāt)* compiled in 1019, and his famous *Treatise (al-Risāla al-qushayriyya)* written in 1045, both having evident apologetic aim, namely, to defend Sufism by demonstrating that it is compatible with Ashʿarite theology and to define it as a legitimate branch of Islamic science. The *Treatise* is justly held the most popular Sufi manual ever, which is still studied by Muslim mystics.[2] Besides summarizing the Sufis' tenets, discussing their customs and practices, and clarifying their terminology, it also contains eighty-three biographies of early masters arranged in chronological order. Qushayrī provided the material he collected with chains of traditions; these are omitted in the following discussion (similarly to several Muslim editions of the *Treatise*).

A number of commentaries were written on the *Treatise,* and two of them have been printed. *Aḥkām al-dalāla ʿalā taḥrīr al-risāla,* written in 1488 by Zakariyyā al-Anṣārī, was further extended by Muṣtafā Muḥammad al-ʿArūsī in his *Natā'ij al-afkār fī bayān maʿānī sharḥ al-Risāla al-qushayriyya* in 1854 (I consulted these, and their interpretation of Nūrī's texts will be reported when relevant).[3] Two commentaries are extant in manuscript form: *al-Dalāl ʿalā fawā'id al-Risāla* by Sadīd al-Dīn Abū Muḥammad al-Lakhmī (compiled in 1240), and another one by Mulla ʿAlī al-Qarī (d. 1605).[4]

Although Nūrī's short biography is included among those of the eighty-three Sufi masters, most of the material referring to him is scattered throughout the work according to the subject matters of the manual's chapters. The overlap of the traditions cited by Qushayrī with the collections discussed so far is considerable. It is not possible to give exact proportions since a tradition may be divided into separate units in one collection while originally independent passages may be combined into one text in another. Roughly two-thirds of the twenty-nine traditions collected by Qushayrī are cited in the earlier collections. The greatest overlap is with Kharkūshi's *Revision of the Secrets* and Sarrāj's *Book of Flashes* (eight and seven traditions respectively). The overlap with Abū Nuʿaym's *Ornament of God's Friends* and Kalābādhī's *Doctrine of the Sufis* is less significant (five and four traditions). Parallels with Sulamī are negligible: in his Quran commentary, Sulamī quotes a single sentence from a story that is preserved in a fuller version in Qushayrī's *Treatise* (the full version is also attested in Sarrāj's

Book of Flashes). Finally, Qushayrī cites two sayings preserved in Sulamī's *Generations of the Sufis.*

Nūrī's lack of poetic production is striking in Qushayrī's *Treatise,* even though it frequently includes poems by others. However, not even one of Nūrī's poems is quoted in the *Treatise.* Partly for that reason, one of Nūrī's central topics is absent entirely: Nūrī's poems (and sayings) on the inner heart cannot be found in the *Treatise.*

Biographical Details

The biographical data in Qushayrī's short entry dedicated to Nūrī is scarce; it is limited to the exact form of his name (Abū l-Ḥusayn Aḥmad ibn Muḥammad al-Nūrī), date of his death (295 AH/908 AD), place of birth and formation (Baghdad), place of origin (Baghwa), the name of his prominent teachers (Sarī al-Saqaṭī, Aḥmad ibn Abī l-Ḥawārī),[5] his most important colleague (Junayd), and a short remark on Nūrī's personality characterizing him as "of great importance" and describing him as a person of "gentle attitude and speech."[6] It might be mentioned here that the fifteenth-century commentator of Qushayrī, Zakariyyā al-Anṣārī, relates Nūrī's name to Nūr, which he identifies as a small village between Bukhārā and Samarqand. However, he offers a more spiritual explication, too, based on the meaning of the Arabic noun *nūr* ("light"), the adjective *nūrī* meaning "luminous, brilliant." He understands the name as a reference to Nūrī's "interior/hidden *(bāṭin)* and exterior/manifest *(ẓāhir)* light," or, offering a further explication, to the light that allegedly poured forth from his mouth illuminating the darkness whenever he spoke.[7] Qushayrī does not mention in the entry on Nūrī either the circumstances of his death or his arrest and trial for heresy; these details are scattered in other chapters. The only episode of Nūrī's life Qushayrī narrates there serves to illustrate how Nūrī wished to hide his piety. The story is not preserved in the earlier collections.

> It is related that he used to leave his house every day taking a loaf of bread with him, which he gave away as a charity on his way. Then he entered a mosque and

> prayed there until just before noon, when [after the midday prayer of the community] he left the mosque and opened his shop [in the market], where he kept fasting. Therefore, his family thought that he used to eat in the market, and the people of the market thought that he used to eat at home. He was following this practice for twenty years, at the beginning [of his mystical vocation].[8]

The entry also contains four short sayings: on equating Sufism with renouncing the realm of the carnal soul;[9] a critical remark on contemporary scholars and "knowers" (mystics);[10] another critical remark on contemporary Sufism;[11] and a warning against Sufis violating religious law.[12] Why does Qushayrī select especially these sayings in order to give a hint about Nūrī's personality? Are these sayings typical of Nūrī? Hardly so. It seems more likely that Qushayrī wishes to counterbalance other representations of Nūrī (like Sarrāj's entry), which depict him as controversial and something of a heretic. Besides Nūrī's sayings, Qushayrī also quotes two sayings on Nūrī by others.

> Junayd said: "Since Nūrī has died no one has given report about the true reality of trustworthiness (ṣidq)."[13]

Trustworthiness *(ṣidq)* is regarded as the basis and origin of sincerity *(ikhlāṣ)*, that is, pure intention directed toward God exclusively for God's sake, without any secondary thought or interest.[14] It does not entail rigidity or insistence on a certain attitude, on the contrary: it requires constant transformation and accommodation to the changing circumstances, to God's ever-renewing demands. As Junayd formulates: "A trustworthy man undergoes forty changes a day, while a hypocrite insists on the same single state during forty years."[15] The distinguishing mark of a trustworthy man according to Ḥārith al-Muḥāsibī is that he does not care in the least about the people's appreciation; he does not care whether or not the people have knowledge of his good deeds; and he is absolutely indifferent to their interest in his actions or their scrutinizing supervision of his acts. Trustworthiness may require the revelation of unpleasant facts and socially unacceptable behavior; at the highest level it involves ignoring both social norms and the laws of nature.[16]

Junayd's appreciative words to Nūrī, praising him especially for his trustworthiness, evidently legitimize extreme manifestations of his mystical behavior.

The other saying Qushayrī chooses to quote declares Nūrī's superiority to Junayd, or at least equality with him:

> Abū Aḥmad al-Maghāzilī said: "I have never seen a more perfect servant of God than Nūrī." He was asked: "Not even Junayd?" He replied: "Not even Junayd."[17]

Now that Junayd is the foremost authority of sober Sufism, and Nūrī is a representative of intoxicated Sufism, the saying may be interpreted as a stance taken regarding these tendencies. Intoxication *(sukr)* and sobriety *(ṣaḥw)* are essentially envisaged as two complementary phases that presuppose each other. The *Treatise* does not present any evidence of preferring either of the two states over the other. According to its definition, "Sobriety is returning to perception after absence *(ghayba),* and intoxication is absence caused by a strong oncoming impact *(wārid)* [originated by God]."[18] Thus, intoxication is associated with absence, that is, the mystics' spiritual withdrawal from the world while absenting himself in God's hidden, intimate, and unseen world, which is the aim of the mystical quest. Intoxication is not produced by one's own efforts but induced by an external agent, the *wārid* sent by God. Intoxication is tasted only by those who are used to experiencing ecstasy *(aṣḥāb al-mawājīd),* which indicates that unlike absence *(ghayba),* which is attainable for mystics in general, intoxication or drunkenness *(sukr)* is reserved for a class destined to experience it.[19] Furthermore, according to Harawī (d. 1088), *sukr* is intimately connected to love: "Intoxication [. . .] is a station reserved especially for the lovers *(min maqāmāt al-muḥibbīn khāṣṣatan).*"[20] The *Treatise* apparently equates the two states: "Know, that sobriety is commensurate with intoxication, and whose intoxication is true, his sobriety is also true. [. . .] Intoxication and sobriety point to [two] aspect[s] of separation [from God], but when there appears a sign from the might of reality, the attribute of the servant [of God] will be abolition and vanquishing. The following poem is recited in this sense: "If the light of dawn breaks on the stars of wine / drunken and sober will be equal in its light."[21]However, a tendency to hold sobriety in higher esteem than intoxication is also clearly discernible in other sources, like the *Kashf al-maḥjūb* by ʿAlī al-Hujwīrī (1072/77). Hujwīrī explains that the school of Junayd preferred sobriety to intoxication, which is the opinion that he himself accepted as well: "My Shaykh, who followed the doctrine of Junayd, used to say that intoxication is the playground of children, but sobriety is the death-field of men. I say, in agreement with my Shaykh, that the perfection of the state of the intoxicated man is sobriety"[22] (translation by Reynold A. Nicholson). The same idea is expressed by the abovementioned al-Harawī: "Sobriety is above intoxication [. . .] for intoxication is in the Real *(fī l-ḥaqq),* while sobriety is through the Real *(bi-l-ḥaqq).*"[23]

Although Qushayrī's entry on Nūrī evades controversial aspects of his mysticism, he did not completely purge his manual of such vestiges. Even though the portrayal of Nūrī in the entry dedicated to him may be simplistic, scandalous events of his life, even some of his ecstatic utterances, surface in other chapters of the *Treatise.* His quasi-blasphemous utterances concerning a muezzin and a dog, for example, are preserved apart from Sarrāj's *Book of Flashes* in Qushayrī's *Treatise.*[24] These utterances are included in the narration of Nūrī's trial instigated by Ghulām Khalīl in the *Book of Flashes,* while they are presented as unrelated in the *Treatise.* It is hard to tell whether Qushayrī chose to disintegrate the story narrated in the *Book of Flashes,* or whether Sarrāj combined independent fragments into one narrative.[25] However, the rest of Nūrī's scandalous utterances, or *shaṭaḥāt* quoted in the narration of the trial in the *Book of Flashes,* are missing from the *Treatise,* and Qushayrī's version of the Ghulām Khalīl incident and Nūrī's trial are identical to the variant narrated by Kharkūshī and Abū Nuʿaym.[26]

The story of Nūrī's death in Qushayrī's narration combines two elements (an intoxicated element and a sober element) that never occur together in the earlier collections.[27] Sarrāj relates that the cause of Nūrī's death was a love poem he heard, which triggered fatal ecstasy from which he never regained consciousness. On the other hand, Kharkūshī reports Nūrī's last words suggesting that his mind was clear and focused. Qushayrī is the first to bring the two events together, and the somewhat later Ṭabarī (d. ca. 1077), who relies on Qushayrī heavily, narrates Nūrī's death on the basis of Qushayrī's version, which combines the two traditions and thus creates a more balanced interpretative context.[28]

Stories revealing Nūrī's relation to miracles, or *karāmāt,* are also included in the *Treatise.* All of these are also known from the earlier collections: Nūrī bathing in the river while a thief steals his clothes;[29] Nūrī capriciously demanding God to perform a miracle for him and Junayd's rebukes;[30] and Nūrī humbly refusing to accept a miracle that was not requested.[31] These stories present Nūrī as a master capable of performing *karāmāt,* that is, miracles that make his special connection to God manifest. However, they are also evidence of his unstable personality. It is interesting to note that the setting of the three stories is identical: all of them occur either on the bank of a river or in the river itself. The second and the third are also connected syntactically: both employ the same characteristic oath formula: I swear "by Your might." The third story might even appear as a deliberate counterpointing of the second, aiming to modify Nūrī's image in a conformist way, disguising his true immoderate attitude. It is more plausible, however, that the inconsistency of the stories reflects the inconsistency in one's character in general, and the fact that all of them were included in the *Treatise* shows the general attitude of Muslim authors and compilers who may hand down contradictory traditions without wishing to unilaterally harmonize them.

Firāsa: Insight, Capacity of Reading Other People's Thoughts

The *Treatise* invests Nūrī with a capacity that is not mentioned in the earlier collections: the divine gift of *firāsa.* According to the *Treatise, firāsa* is a mental faculty that only a select few among the Sufis possess: those capable of seeing past, present, and future events and who can read the hidden thoughts of the people. The mystic endowed with the capacity of spiritual insight cannot freely choose when to utilize it since *firāsa* is a constant perception of concealed realities operating independently of one's will. Despite that, *firāsa* is listed among the spiritual stations (which are usually considered as *makāsib,* "acquisitions," degrees of spiritual perfection acquired by conscious effort): "Muḥammad al-Kattānī said: *Firāsa* is unveiling certainty, seeing the unseen world of God *(al-ghayb)*, and it is one of the stations of faith."[32]

> Someone asked Abū l-Ḥusayn al-Nūrī: "What is the origin of the insight (*firāsa*) of those who are able to read the thoughts of another person (*mutafarrisūn*)?" He said: "God's words: 'I breathed into him from My [own] spirit.' [Quran 15:29] He who receives a greater share from this light is more capable of contemplation, and his judgment by means of insight is more veracious. Don't you see how the fact that He breathed His spirit into man obliged [the angels] to bow down to him, as it is written: 'So, when I complete him and breath into Him from My [own] spirit, fall you down prostrating yourselves unto him!' [Quran 15:29]"[33]

Qushayrī explains that various Quranic precedents legitimize the concept of quasi-miraculous insight, and these passages are understood as referring to distinct classes of people capable of such perception.[34] For example, Abū Saʿīd al-Khazzāz interpreted the passage "those who inquire into things, *(yastanbiṭūn)* would have known it" (Quran 4:83) as referring to those who see the unseen world constantly and are always present in it.[35] Nothing is hidden for those who are known as *mustanbiṭūn,* that is, people who investigate the truth. A lower level of insight is that of the *mutawassimūn,* that is, those who discern signs and understand their significance. The origin of this word is the noun *wasm* meaning "brand, mark," indicating pertinence to someone or something. The *mutawassim* understands the marks and is guided by them; he reveals what is in the deepest folds of the heart by means of deduction, in accordance with the passage of the Quran: "Surely there are signs *(āyāt)* in this for those who understand the marks *(mutawassimūn)*" (Quran 15:75). The third category is *firāsa* proper: "He who is endowed with *firāsa* sees by divine light, that is, gleaming flashes shining in his heart that enable him to comprehend the meanings *(maʿānī).* It is one of the specialties *(khawwāṣ)* of faith, and those who are endowed with it in great measure are the godly ones *(rabbāniyyūn),* as God said: 'Be godly people!' [Quran 3:79]."[36] Although no Quranic passage mentions *firāsa* explicitly, the legitimacy of the concept is proven by Prophetic tradition: "Beware of the insight of the believer *(firāsat al-mu'min)*, for he sees by divine light!"[37] Qushayrī offers an etymological explication of the term, finding its derivation in the word *farīsa* signifying the prey of a wild animal. Accordingly, he concludes that *firāsa* is similar to a predatory force that descends upon the heart and seizes it completely, eliminating everything that opposes it. The *nafs* is incapable of countering it.[38] Possibly for that reason, *firāsa* is described by Abū Jafʿar al-Ḥaddād as a sudden thought *(khāṭir)* that has the immediate force of a conviction, without being countered by another thought. If it is followed by a second thought, then we know that the first one was not the product of insight but the often deceptive discourse of the carnal soul.[39] An anonymous saying on *firāsa* describes it with terms and ideas that recall magical concepts: "*Firāsa* means spirits *(arwāḥ)* that move about in the divine realm *(malakūt)* and oversee the meanings of the hidden world *(al-ghayb)*, therefore they can utter about the secrets/inner hearts of the creatures utterances [that are the result] of witnessing *(mushāhada)*."[40] The concept of spiritual beings, either angels or spirits—each of them in charge of special functions and capable of disclosing hidden events—is well known in Islamic magic.

The chapter on *firāsa* in the *Treatise* contains more stories that evidently surpass sayings both in number and in importance. The stories give account of the masters' potency of spiritual insight, both in trivial situations and in serious ones: the mystic senses the death of his fellow;[41] the master reads his disciple's thought concerning illicit connection with a woman;[42] he perceives wrong acts committed inadvertently by his disciples;[43] when the disciple thinks enviously about the cap *(qalansuwa)* of his teacher, wanting it for himself, the latter burns it so that he may not be tempted;[44] and so on. Qushayrī gives account of a direct, personal experience of *firāsa* connected to his own master, Abū ʿAlī al-Daqqāq: they were walking together to the master's class when it occurred to Qushayrī that Daqqāq could replace him and teach his courses for a while. At the same time, Daqqāq offered to replace him without being asked. Subsequently, when it crossed Qushayrī's mind that maybe substituting for Daqqāq twice a week would be too burdensome for his master given his state of health, the latter added that if he was unable to substitute for him twice a week, he would do it once a week instead.[45]

Although Qushayrī, like medieval Muslim compilers in general, may sometimes interpret the sayings and stories he gathered, he refrains from criticizing these save for exceptional cases. Nūrī's words on *firāsa* is one of these extraordinary occurrences, for Qushayrī remarks that Nūrī's explication of the Quranic passage is "somehow obscure,"[46] for it might give the impression that according to Nūrī spirits are preexistents. Anṣārī's commentary expounds on Qushayrī's observation: Nūrī apparently regarded God's act of breathing His spirit into man as a prerequisite for the angels' prostration, while the reason for their prostration before man was solely God's order, as evidenced by the Quranic verse: "So, when I complete him and breath into Him from My [own] spirit, fall you down prostrating yourselves unto him!" (Quran 15:29). Moreover, Nūrī's saying might mislead the simple minded, causing them to believe that spirits are not created, while something that can be detached from, attached to, or breathed into is evidently subject to change and therefore created.[47] ʿArūsī adds that the preeternity of the spirits was one of the tenets of the Muʿtazila,[48] which is quite surprising, since the Muʿtazila never held that the spirits were preeternal; moreover, they strictly refuted the possibility of multiple preeternals, and it is for this well-known reason that they denied the concept of the uncreated Quran and the existence of attributes distinct from the divine substance. Nūrī's capacity for *firāsa* is evidenced by the following story:

> It was related by Zaytūna, the maidservant of Abū l-Ḥusayn al-Nūrī, who served him, and had served also Abū Ḥamza and Junayd: "It was a cold day. I told Nūrī:
>
> 'I bring you something [to eat].'
>
> 'Fine.'
>
> 'What do you want?'
>
> 'Some bread and milk.'
>
> So I brought it to him. He had some charcoal in front of him, which he stirred with his hand. He started to eat the bread having just reached into the charcoal with his hand, and the milk was running down on his hand black with soot. I thought:

'My God, how dirty are Your friends! There is not a single one among them who is clean.'

Then I left him and went out, but a woman took hold on me saying:

'She has stolen a bundle of cloths!'

So I was taken to the police officer. Nūrī was informed about what happened, so he came and said to the police:

'Don't detain her, for she is one of God's friends!'

The police officer replied:

'So what shall I do? That woman accuses her!'

But then a maidservant came, bringing with her the bundle of clothes which the woman sought for. Nūrī brought me back [to home], and said:

'After all that, do you still say: How dirty are Your friends?'

I said:

'I have repented and returned to God Most High.' "[49]

Sayings Relevant to the Drunken Tendency

These traditions comprise the sayings on ecstasy, love, and *samā*ʿ. Sayings on these subjects are scarce in the *Treatise*. Nūrī is not reported to have attended *samā*ʿ sessions, although his definition of Sufism singling out audition as a distinctive feature is quoted: when asked who is a Sufi, he answers:

> He who listens to audition, but prefers [its underlying] reasons.[50]

The restriction in the second half of the sentence indicates a certain reservation, however, or at least suggests that some people attended the *samā*ʿ ceremony with unjustified motives (like mere amusement, for example). Nūrī's fifteenth-century commentator, Anṣārī, expounds upon the legitimate reasons for attending the mystical audition,[51] while the later commentator, ʿArūsī, remarks that Nūrī might have meant the beginning of the mystical quest: for someone advanced on the path *samā*ʿ loses importance since one should hear with his heart and not with his ears.[52] ʿArūsī illustrates this with the well-known poetic metaphor of the caravan leader, or camel driver, who urges the camels forward by singing. He who is at the beginning of the path, implores the "camel-driver," that is, God, to sing for him in order to peace his longing and desire; while he who is at the end of his path does not request from the camel driver anything else than his mere presence. A somewhat similar idea is expressed in an anonymous poem ʿArūsī cites: "I never ceased to hear [the song of] your camel-driver filling us with longing / Until we met [finally] and there was no camel-driver nor longing"[53]

Nūrī's death caused by the ecstasy due to a love poem he heard is obviously connected to the idea of *samāʿ*, although it did not necessarily take place at an audition session. Nūrī describes himself as constantly oscillating between ecstasy and self-consciousness:

> I have been for twenty years between finding (*wajd*) and losing (*faqd*). If I find my Lord, I lose my heart; and if I find my heart, I lose my Lord.[54]

Unfortunately, the English translation of the saying cannot reflect its inherent beauty due to the double meaning of the verbal root WJD ("to find; to experience strong emotional excitement"). The verbal noun *wajd* denotes ecstasy, while the idea of finding and encountering God is usually expressed with the verbal noun *wujūd*. The distinction is explained in the *Treatise* as well, superimposing *wujūd* to *wajd*.[55] According to Qushayrī, ecstasy overcomes one's heart unexpectedly, without any inducement or effort, but "finding, encountering" *(wujūd)* takes place only after having risen above the state of ecstasy *(wajd)*. Finding God presupposes losing every trace of human nature since this is incompatible with the presence of God. Qushayrī illustrates his explication with Nūrī's saying about finding God while losing the heart and losing the heart while finding God. But since Nūrī employs the term *wajd*, and not *wujūd*, the phraseology of his saying is unique, a single word conveying both meanings through association. It implies that Nūrī finds God in the state of ecstasy; finding and ecstasy take place simultaneously. As an ecstatic mystic, Nūrī does not aim to hide his ecstasy, as it is evidenced by the story of his death, which tells us that when hearing the love poem, he "showed his ecstasy" *(tawājada).*[56] According to Qushayrī, *wajd* (experiencing ecstasy) is more perfect than *tawājud* (showing, displaying ecstasy) since the latter means to summon up ecstasy by one's own choice, while real ecstasy comes upon the heart unexpectedly. On the other hand, *tawājud* means also to exhibit the real ecstasy as opposed to concealing it, a meaning that Qushayrī exemplifies with the following story: "Abū Muḥammad al-Jurayrī (d. 924) said: 'I was at Junayd's place, and Ibn Masrūq was also there. Ibn Masrūq and others stood up, and Junayd kept silent. I asked him: Master, don't you have anything to say concerning audition *(samāʿ)?* Junayd said: You see the mountains and you suppose that they are firm, but they are moving like passing clouds. [Quran 27:90] Then he said: And you, Abū Muḥammad, don't you have anything to say concerning audition? I said: Master, if I attend a place where an audition is celebrated, and there is someone of high esteem present, I keep my ecstasy in myself, and when I remain alone, I let my ecstasy free and I show my ecstasy *(tawājadtu).*' [Qushayrī remarks:] He approved of showing ecstasy according to this story, and Junayd did not disapprove that."[57]

Finally, it might be important to mention Nūrī's passionate saying on love evoking the bridegroom's act of uncovering the bride on the wedding night:

> Love (*maḥabba*) means to tear the veils and to uncover the secrets."[58]

Qushayrī's interpretation of the saying differs from that of Sarrāj, who quoted it in the *Book of Flashes* as an example of the righteous *(ṣādiq)* and accomplished mystic *(muḥaqqaq)* love for God. Qushayrī, however, explains the difference between human love and divine love, establishing that the love of God for man manifests itself in divine mercy *(raḥma)* and grace *(niʿma),* and it shows itself in the special state to which God elevates man. Actions that characterize human love, like predilection *(mayl)* and seeking intimacy with the beloved *(ist'inās),* however, cannot be attributed to God.[59] If Nūrī's saying is interpreted as conforming to Qushayrī's explication, then it might not be understood as referring to man's love of God, but vice versa. That supposition is all the more plausible since the agent of unveiling *(mukāshafa)* is normally God, not man. Consequently, the saying might describe symbolically God's action of revealing and exposing Himself to man as an expression of His love.

Anṣārī, however, explains the saying differently. In his view, "Whose love is perfect, seeks impatiently [the companionship] of his beloved, and his love becomes manifest in his speech and in his body. He becomes overwhelmed [by love] and his secret *(sirr)* is disclosed to the creatures, and what was covered before them becomes exposed."[60] ʿArūsī adds to Anṣārī's comment that man might reach such a point unintentionally if he is carried away by his love and is incapable of bearing the burning heat of its fire.[61]

Sayings Related to the Sober Tendency

As already noted, Nūrī's central topic in the earlier collections, the inner heart, is not mentioned in the traditions Qushayrī gathered. Even the traditions on contemplation, another of Nūrī's favorite subjects, are underrepresented. Qushayrī quotes only two sayings related to the concept; a saying equating contemplation with certainty[62] and another that seemingly states that man cannot witness God in this life:

> The servant of God cannot truly witness God until he has a single vein functioning. He [also] said: There is no need of lightener (*miṣbāḥ*) at morning light (*ṣabāḥ*).[63]

This tradition attributed to Nūrī appears only in Qushayrī's *Treatise*: the rest of the sources studied here do not include it. The first saying has a similar version in some editions of the *Treatise*, which reads as follows:

> Nūrī said: The servant of God cannot truly witness God until he is alive.[64]

ʿAnṣārī explains that one's heart must be completely absorbed in the contemplation of God's essence and attributes in order to witness God. When such a state is attained, and man contemplates divine light, secondary means *(asbāb)*—exemplified in the saying by a device providing light—become superfluous.[65] According to

ʿArūsī, the image of the functioning vein stands for "firm knowledge of anything else than the Real."[66] Both explications exclude the possibility of interpreting the expression "until he has a single vein functioning" as meaning "until he is alive." According to both commentators, witnessing God is possible for the mystic in this world and does not presuppose his death and transition to the world to come.

Nūrī's relation to secondary means, or worldly matters, is exemplified by the following story:

> Nūrī was starving in the desert when he heard a voice: "What do you prefer, a means (*sabab*) or sufficiency (*kifāya*)?" He said: "Sufficiency—nothing is above that." And he remained seventeen days more without having eaten anything.[67]

Sabab literally means "reason," but in Sufi texts it might refer to false reasons that camouflage the real actor, God. In that sense, *sabab* corresponds to a means by which something is attained, especially some transitory material resource or fallacious mundane idea: "The word *sabab* means a medium *(wāsiṭa):* the *asbāb* and the mediums are those which are between the creatures and God."[68] In the context of the story, *sabab* refers to the means by which one may obtain sustenance, while sufficiency alludes to what is necessary in order to endure starvation or any other deprivation, like patience, endurance, and so on. The significance of the question is whether the mystic prefers a means of obtaining food or will look to God for the necessary virtues to endure hunger. The story is included in the chapter on *tawakkul* (trust in God) among several similar accounts about starving and depending on God exclusively for one's basic needs. A parallel version of the same story is narrated in the chapter on miracles about Abū Saʿīd al-Kharrāz, with the difference being that the dichotomy is related to means or strength *(sabab aw quwwa)*: "I went out on one of my journeys, and every third day there appeared something to me to eat and to manage with. Then three days' time passed, and nothing there appeared, so I grew weak. I sat down, and heard a voice: 'What do you prefer, a means or strength?' I said: 'Strength!' I got up at once, and kept walking for ten days without tasting anything, and without growing weak."[69]

Anṣārī most probably had this version in mind when commenting on the story about Nūrī, since he explained the question about means or sufficiency as follows: "Sufficiency—and strength through God['s action of] going behind what is ordinary for your sake in that He makes you more independent of eating and drinking than what He has already made you and has already strengthened you."[70]

According to Nūrī, the person who truly relies on God, who is fully content with divine providence, is not merely indifferent in the face of adversity but even rejoices over hardships since these help him to detach himself mentally from the apparently existent secondary means.

> Contentment (*riḍā*) is the heart's rejoicing at the bitterness of fate (*qaḍā*).[71]

Although in this form the saying is unique to the *Treatise*, contentment and bitterness are interconnected in other traditions attributed to Nūrī as well, most obviously manifested in his poem quoted by Kalābādhī: "Contentment is bitterness swallowed regardless of satisfaction / Every time that turbid [water] is found sweet."[72] Another poem collected by Sulamī operates via the very same image of the suffocating bitterness that the mystic chokes on: "How many times I made my heart an endowment / to suffocating, bitter pain because of Your trials!"[73] The commentators explain that the carnal soul desires sweetness: therefore, the seeker must prefer hardships over well-being. But the advanced Sufi who has succeeded in taming his soul does not differentiate between sweetness and bitterness at all. He tends to be wary of sweetness since he recognizes the dangerous temptation it involves.[74] The God-fearing person turns to God trustingly even when he realizes the tremendous power of the divine:

> He who fears [God] flees from his Lord to his Lord.[75]

Nūrī's saying on fear *(khawf)* is outwardly paradoxical, since one normally would not ask for the protection of someone or something he is afraid of. But God is exceptional in this sense, as noted by Abū l-Qāsim al-Ḥakīm: "He who fears something, flees from it; he who fears God, flees to Him."[76] ʿArūsī explains the plain meaning of Nūrī's words, saying that since no real actor save God exists, he who fears him necessary flees to Him, for nothing really exists except Him.[77] ʿAnṣārī, however, completes the saying and interprets it as referring to obeying and disobeying God: he who fears God, flees from the disobedience of his Lord to the obedience of his Lord.[78] In Sufi mysticism, fear is usually regarded as a station of the path. It is counterbalanced by hope: "Fear and hope are two reins that hold back the *nafs* so that it won't rush carelessly. When the Real manifests Himself to the inner hearts, nothing remains there for fear or hope."[79] Qushayrī explains that "when the signs of the Real seize the inner hearts, He conquers them [entirely], and no possibility remains for them to remember anything created. Fear and hope are, however, traces [indicating] that the sensation of human rules still persists."[80] In other words, fear and hope are related to the human condition, but when divine presence seizes and appropriates the inner heart, it becomes void of such temporary concerns. The implication here is that although fear and hope are necessary for advancing on the mystical path—hence they are included among the stations by Qushayrī as well—ultimately, they must be superseded. Nūrī's saying on fear alludes to perception going beyond sensations and focusing on the ultimate existent, that is, realizing true *tawḥīd*.

> Bearing witness of God's oneness (*tawḥīd*) means that every uncontrolled thought (*khāṭir*) points toward God without being countered by thoughts of making Him similar (*tashbīh*) [to anything].[81]

Nūrī's saying on monotheism expresses the Sufi conception of *tawḥīd, w*hich besides recognizing, acknowledging, and affirming that God is one, requires that one attribute everything to Him: to see one's actions, both manifest and hidden acts and experiences, as happening through God and originating from God. Such a person considers his own acts annihilated in God's acts, contemplates God in the creatures, and does not perceive the existing beings or even his own self due to his complete annihilation in God.[82]

Finally, Nūrī's saying on Muḥammad should be mentioned. In later Sufism Muḥammad became considered the archetype of the mystic, and the beginnings of this tendency can already be observed in the formative period.

> The Real beheld the hearts and He did not see a heart longing for Him more than the heart of Muḥammad. Therefore, God honored him with the ascension to heaven (*miʿrāj*) granting him in advance the vision [of God during his life in this world, not in the hereafter] and the conversation [of God with him].[83]

The saying does not employ distinctly Sufi terms (except for *shawq* "longing"). "Conversation," for example, is expressed by the word *mukāmala* and not with the terms *najwā* or *munāja,* which would have more explicit Sufi connotations. The nineteenth-century commentator ʿArūsī, however, interprets the saying against the background of a fully developed mystical tradition formulated by Jīlānī (eleventh century) concerning the primordial covenant between God and all humanity, which is referred to in Quran 7:172. God called forth the future descendants of Adam, the whole of humanity, and addressed them, asking: "Am I not your Lord (*a-lastu bi-rabbikum*)?" To which they answered and testified, unanimously acknowledging His lordship. According to ʿArūsī's explication, God's act of beholding the hearts and singling out the heart of Muḥammad was one of the divine manifestations similar to the primordial covenant. He describes that in poetical terms employing a metaphor of birds escaping from their cages that symbolizes the spirits leaving behind the yet unformed, unborn body and the heart. A messenger addressed the spirits hidden in the "moulds" (*qawālib;* note the pun on *qalb,* meaning "heart") of the yet-unborn humans, stirring up their passion from its placidity and passivity. The spirits took wings like birds and flew up to the atmosphere of love *(maḥabba)* and alighted on the twigs of mad love *(hayamān)* listening to the song of the nightingales filled with yearning and nostalgia for the sacred bounty of God. They became agitated from the rising breeze and the breath of passion, willing to repeat once again the event of the primordial covenant itself, when God asked humanity: "Am I not your Lord?" Some of them left the cage of the chest and beheld the place from where they took wing in preeternity, that is, their original position in the closeness of God. They inhaled the breath rising from the place where speech became articulated and heard the man of "the substance of existence" (*ʿayn al-wujūd*), the man of God, Muḥammad, invoking God in human language. His invocation remained engraved on the spirits, shook the trees' branches, agitated the hearts' anxieties, and the minds' comprehension of the primary forms became confused. And because of that, the spirits' longing for God became a secret (*sirr*) from among the secrets of preeternity, and their madly passionate love for God became a subtlety (*laṭīfa*) from among the subtleties of divine predestination.[84]

Conclusions

The most striking peculiarity of the material Qushayrī collected on Nūrī is that there are no poems written by him, although poetry as such is not absent from the *Treatise* in general: Qushayrī frequently cites poems in explaining the subject matter of a certain chapter. As for Nūrī, who is otherwise celebrated for his mystical poems, the situation is different: not one of his poems is quoted, not even in the biographical section dedicated to him and not to a specific Sufi concept or tenet. On the other hand, a new genre is getting more attention in the *Treatise* than in the former compilations: that of short anecdotes and instructive stories. Some eight of such narrations were collected by Qushayrī. While the sayings are sometimes obscure, paradoxical, and difficult to decipher, the anecdotes have a very clear message.[85]

The image of Nūrī that takes shape on the basis of the sayings and stories is not entirely consistent: on the one hand he seems to strictly adhere to the orthodox Muslim tenets, whose teachings are in line with moderate, sober judiciousness. On the evidence of some stories and passionate sayings, however, he appears to be an enraptured mystic, a lover who occasionally even tries to manipulate God by emotional blackmail. His paradoxical or scandalous acts and utterances are countered by others that may override these, like the two stories on his attitude concerning *karāmāt* that are juxtaposed by the compiler without any explication (although they have completely contradictory bearings). In the same vein, Qushayrī counterbalances Junayd's harsh rebuke of Nūrī's behavior by also citing Junayd's opinion that reveals a full appreciation for him and by including a tradition that equates both of them as perfect servants of God. Other outrageous utterances are readily explained as completely justified: for example his quasi-blasphemous reaction to the muezzin's call to prayer and the dog's barking. His well-known saying on love, "tearing the veils and uncovering the secrets," however, remains unraveled, and only Qushayrī's immediate interpretation of love might blunt its edge in case the reader decides to interrelate them. It has to be noted also that while in the *Book of Flashes* the accusations of Ghulām Khalīl are related to Nūrī's unconventional way of speaking about God using the language of passionate love, Qushayrī's narrative is void of any such vestiges, and the investigation conducted against him seems to be unrelated to the ecstatic form of mysticism. It is telling in itself that the entry Qushayrī dedicated to Nūrī in the biographical section of the *Treatise* ignores the contentious aspects of his mysticism and portrays him as a perfectly sober Sufi. In fact, his most important life events and his most characteristic sayings are scattered in the theoretical part of the manual.

The number of recurring Sufi technical terms in the traditions related to Nūrī are relatively scarce, despite the many sayings and narratives Qushayrī collected. Terms that recur in various traditions include heart *(qalb),* occurring six times; ecstasy/finding (*wajd, wajada, tawāgada)* (five times); nearness (*qurb,* including a verbal form) (four times); giving preference (*īthār,* including verbal forms) (three times); insight *(firāsa, mutafarrisūn)* (three times); contemplation (*mushāhada)* (two times); secondary means *(asbāb)* (two times); mystical moment *(waqṭ)* (two times); farness *(buʿd)* (two times); sudden thought *(khāṭir)* (two times); repentance *(tawba)* (two times); learning *(ʿilm)* (two times). Terms that occur only once are more numerous, which is attributable to the wide spectrum of themes the material connected to Nūrī covers.[86]

CHAPTER 8

Sīrjānī

Black and White in the Words of Wisdom
(Kitāb al-bayāḍ wa-l-sawād)

Introduction

The *Kitāb al-bayāḍ wa-l-sawād min khaṣā'iṣ ḥikam al-ʿibād fī naʿt al-murīd wa-l-murād* (translated by its editors as *Black and White in the Words of Wisdom by Bondsmen Describing the Seeker and the Mystic Quest*)[1] is a handbook that explains basic Sufi concepts and describes the Sufis' habits, behaviors, and spiritual practices. According to the book's introduction, its intended audience is mainly those disciples, or seekers *(murīd)* capable of understanding mystical traditions and who strive for advancement on the Sufi path. From the point of view of genre, this book is similar to Sarrāj's *Book of Flashes* (although it does not contain anything similar to commentaries on the Sufis' quasi-blasphemous utterances, discussions about heretical doctrines, and the enumeration of mystics attracted to these), to Kalābādhī's *Doctrine of the Sufis* (although it is not as elaborate as Kalābādhī's manual), and to Kharkūshī's *Revision of the Secrets*. It shares certain similarities with the theoretical part of Qushayrī's *Treatise*, but it does not contain long biographical sections dedicated to individual Sufis, with the exception of seven prominent personalities (Abū Turāb al-Nakhshabī, Abū Yazīd al-Bisṭāmī, Shāh ibn Shujāʿ al-Kirmānī, ʿAlī ibn Sahl al-Iṣfahānī, Sahl al-Tustarī, Ibrāhīm al-Khawwāṣ and Abū ʿAbd Allāh al-Maghribī). Some seventy more Sufis are listed according to the geographical region they were active in, but there are only two or three sentences about each. Chains of traditions are completely suppressed throughout the book, and the chapters are patterned on a uniform structure, each one beginning with the relevant Quranic passages accompanied by short comments; then a selection of Prophetic traditions follows, authenticating the Sufi concepts by indicating that they are rooted in orthodox religion. Most preferably those Quranic passages and Prophetic traditions are quoted that contain the exact Sufi term that is being treated in the chapter (even if it has a different meaning to a certain extent in its original context), but also synonyms or parallel concepts and utterances are cited. In each chapter, such quotations introduce the collection of Sufi sayings, many of which have short and even rhyming dicta. Sīrjānī usually refrains from commenting upon the sayings; he creates, however, an interpretative context that helps to understand even obscure utterances or cryptic poems. The didactic purpose of the book is discernible in its structure and style.

Not much is known about Sīrjānī's life and works. He was a disciple of Abū Ismāʿīl Aḥmad al-Ṣūfī, called also Sheikh ʿAmmū (d. 1049). After the death of his master, Sīrjānī undertook the guidance of his own disciples in a *ribāṭ* (Sufi lodge) in Sīrjān.[2]

The *Black and White in the Words of Wisdom* mentions Nūrī more than forty times, but most of the traditions attributed to him are also collected in other early sources that have been already treated in the previous chapters of this study. Therefore, the discussion will be restricted to those traditions that do not appear in any of the earlier compilations. As previously noted, Sīrjānī's book does not include detailed biographical sections, and his remarks concerning Nūrī are limited to two sentences. He mentions him among the sheiks of Iraq with the epitheton ornans "support of the hearts and sword of his people" *(sanad al-qulūb wa-sayf ahlihi)*, adding: "He was one of the sincere ones in his time, and one of those who speak about the Real in each of the diverse ways."[3] Sīrjānī also comments upon the name of Nūrī: "He used to devote himself to the service of God in a hermitage in the desert, and the people got up to look at him at night, and behold, light *(nūr)* was radiating from his hermitage, and he was called Nūrī ("luminous") because of that."[4]

Mystical Knowledge and Theoretical Learning

Early Sufi works generally begin by demonstrating that Sufism is a branch of science and by no means inferior to Islamic law, the science of the *ḥadīth*, or theology. The legitimacy and also the superiority of Sufism are usually justified by passages from the Quran and the Prophetic tradition. Sīrjānī dedicates a separate chapter to this topic, entitled "The Similarity Between the Two Types of Learning and the Difference Between Them." He quotes a Quranic passage that establishes the preeminence of those capable of understanding the hidden meanings of the Quran by the method of *istinbāṭ*,[5] that is, mystical interpretation: "If they had referred it to the Messenger and to those who are in charge among them, those of them who derive its hidden sense *(yastanbiṭūnahu)* would have learned about it" (Quran 4:83). Sīrjānī explains that "those who are in charge" are "the people of learning" *(ahl al-ʿilm)*, of which "the people of mystical interpretation" *(ahl al-istinbāṭ)* is a subcategory. He refers also to the words of the Prophet: "Learning is of two kinds: there is a learning which is established in the heart *(thābit fī l-qalb)* and there is a learning which flows on the tongue."[6] Sīrjānī cites several sayings that express the distinct peculiarities of mystical doctrine as opposed to the science of Islamic religious law *(sharīʿa)*: the former is hidden *(bāṭin)*, derived *(yustanbaṭ)* from what is manifest *(ẓāhir)*; consequently it cannot contradict the latter, since "a hidden [sense] which is not supported by a manifest [meaning of the Quran] is false."[7] Furthermore, "The science of the tongue is the science of argumentation *(ʿilm al-ḥujja)*, while the science of the heart is the science of the destination *(ʿilm al-maḥajja.)*."[8] The word "destination" *(maḥajja)* means, more concretely, the place to where the pilgrimage's route leads and therefore alludes to the spiritual path the seekers follow, as opposed to the method of rational reasoning characteristic of nonmystical doctrines. Sufism is distinguished by its peculiar way of expression that uses allusions rather than plain statements. Hidden meanings cannot be communicated by unambiguous, clear-cut declarations, as Abū ʿAlī al-Rūdhbārī put it: "We have learnt it by way of allusions, and had it been expressed [explicitly], it would have disappeared."[9] Mystical expressions have universal and perpetual validity and do not share the transient nature of worldly phenomena: "Knowers possess treasures, which they formulated as extraordinary branches of learning and marvellous tidings, and they speak about it in the language of eternity and they communicate about it by expressing endlessness."[10] Learning (even mystical learning) may lead man astray, and ignorance is preferable than relying on what one has already learned: "The ignorant is in the darkness of their ignorance, how else it could be, since even the learned is in the darkness of their ignorance, and the darkness of learning is heavier?"[11] In the chapter on theoretical learning and mystical knowledge, Sīrjānī quotes a poem attributed to Nūrī, which describes the conscious effort of the Sufis to free themselves from the rigid formulations of theoretical sciences.

> We erased [what we learned], and you recorded [it] in
> a draft, then in a fair copy
> arranging words on brand-new sheets
> You veiled yourself with them from understanding
> how to draw out a [hidden] sense
> about the ultimate ends in endless eternity
> From absence (*ghayba*) there appeared ways of
> understanding to their hearts
> like heavy rains the downpour of which is help.[12]

People of religious learning may strive for recording, establishing, and perpetuating their learning, which ultimately blocks the way of true understanding. Sufis, however, seek to obliterate what they have learned, similar to the act of erasing writing from a sheet to make it capable of receiving anything. The hearts of the mystics receive understanding as a divine gift originating from God's hidden world. The communication of inspired knowledge requires the use of symbolic language:

> In Egypt, Nūrī was asked about Sufism, and he said: Subtlety of allusion (ishāra) and excellence of expression (*ʿibāra*).[13]

Although the saying is not attested in the earlier compilations, and Nūrī is not likely to have visited Egypt (such journey is not mentioned in the sources treating his biography), the tradition befits both Nūrī's general attitude and the authors' appreciation of his refined ways of expression (cf. the remarks by Abū Nuʿaym, Qushayrī, and Sīrjānī). Allusion (*ʿishāra*) and clear expression (*ʿibāra*) are juxtaposed in one of Nūrī's sayings that was collected by Kharkūshī, and allusive communication is established as superior.[14] Nūrī does not merely praise the Sufi way of communication but also delivers a harsh criticism of religious scholars, which betrays the danger involved in the Sufis' divergence from the established religious norms:

> I do not fear for my blood [that it might be shed], except for the Quran reciters and the learned people (*ʿulamāʾ*).[15]

Sīrjānī cites Nūrī's remark in a subchapter on Quran reciters (*qurrāʾ*). In fact, the attribution of the saying to Nūrī is not entirely certain, for in one of the manuscripts it is attributed to Thawrī,[16] and it cannot be found among Nūrī's sayings in the earlier compilations. The Sufis' critique of theoretical learning is well known; however, their aversion to Quran reciters is less manifest. The sayings Sīrjānī collected about this subject do not elaborate on the reasons for such hatred; most of them merely advise against the companion of Quran reciters or describe the otherworldly punishment they will inevitably suffer. The few sayings that inform about their deeds and character traits affirm that Quran reciters are conceited, presumptuous, and envious. It might be suggested that accusations that led to official investigations against the Sufis (cf. "I do not fear for my blood") were made both by religious scholars and by Quran reciters, which may account for the Sufis' suspicion.

Murīd and *Murād*

The disciple of the Sufi sheik is called *murīd* ("seeker"), or in literal translation: "he who wants," that is, to get to the closeness of God. Being a *murīd* is the beginning of the Sufi path. Since Sīrjānī's manual is dedicated primarily to the seekers, it is not surprising that it contains a chapter about traditions related to the seeker's condition, among them, sayings attributed to Nūrī, as well.

> Nūrī was asked about being a *murīd*, and he said: "[It means] to desist from what is habitual."[17]

The saying is cited in the broader context of the *murīd*'s relation to the master. The preeminent importance of the master in Sufi tradition is well known: "Even if a person had been supreme to such an extent that he had been inspired [by God directly], had he not followed a teacher, nothing would result from him."[18] Sīrjānī quotes several sayings related to the verbal root of the term *murīd* (the root means "to want"), for example: "The *murīd* is him who wants what God wants to him, and accompanies [takes as a teacher] him who wants what he wants."[19] He also collects sayings on the condition of being a *murīd*, that is, *irāda:* "The distinguishing mark of being a *murīd* is following and obeying one's instructor";[20] "Being a *murīd* means to master the determination of baring *(tajrīd)* [everything] to the secrets *(asrār)*, and to be keen on the remembrance of God."[21] The first sentences refer to the cooperation of the *murīd* and his sheik: the disciple relinquishes the dominion over his personality and actions to his master, who guides and instructs him until the disciple becomes capable of ruling himself on his own. The last definition establishes that the beginning of the mystical path involves the resolution to attain God, which requires one to discard everything except God and to concentrate on Him exclusively. That is what is meant by "baring [everything] to the secrets *(asrār)*" of God, and these secrets are deposited in the inner hearts *(sarā'ir)*: the expression evokes the image of a man divesting himself of everything except his inner heart.[22] The process of discarding mundane attachments must be controlled by the master, so that the disciple does not go astray. The sayings Sīrjānī collects enumerate several requirements a *murīd* has to meet: serving his master and his companions; avoiding comfort; engaging in constant toil and exertion; unconditioned obedience to the master; self-denial, etc. These prerequisites are evidently alien to the normal course of life, and that is precisely the aspect that Nūrī formulates: being a *murīd* means to break away from what is habitual in ordinary life. The same idea is expressed in a more elaborate way in the following anonymous saying: "Being a *murīd* means to extinguish the fires of what concerns [man by his] nature and habit."[23] Another saying attributed to Nūrī differentiates between the *murīd* ("he who wants") and the *murād* ("him who is wanted"):

> He who wants is thirsty, and him who is wanted is drunken.[24]

Besides those who want to get close to God *(murīd)*, there are those who are drawn close to God by God Himself. They are wanted by God *(murād)*, or, as it is more frequently said, attracted *(majdhūb)*. In the chapter Sīrjānī dedicates to the topic, he derives the concept from the Quran: "God choses to Himself whomever He wishes, and leads to Himself him who turns to Him" (Quran 42:13). Abū Saʿīd al-Qurashī interpreted the passage and added that God wants the *murād* unconditionally, without demanding any action on the *murād*'s part, while He requires active initiative from the *murīd*. The *murīd* is led by his master and strives to arrive to God's closeness, while the *murād's* arrival *(wuṣūl)* precedes his striving to arrive.[25] However, once the *murād* is attracted to God, his passivity should end, according to the view of al-Ḥusayn ibn Manṣūr al-Ḥallāj: "The *murīd* is him whose efforts precede his unveilings, while the *murād* is him whose unveilings precede his efforts."[26] The expression "his unveilings" *(kushūfuhu)* refers to God's act of unveiling Himself to man. Although most sayings emphasize the dichotomy of activity and passivity (for example, "The *murīd* attracts his Lord's mercy upon himself, while the *murād* is attracted by the lights of His sanctity"),[27] some do refer to the action of God in the case of the *murīd* as well: "The *murīd* is the seeker *(ṭālib)*, and the *murād* is the one sought for *(maṭlūb)*; him who is sought for is accepted *(maqbūl)*, and the seeker is desired *(marghūb)*."[28]

Nūrī's words describe the difference between the *murīḍ* and the *murād* in a figurative way. The *murīd*'s state is characterized by imperfection: he is thirsty, longs for God's closeness, and strives to get there. The *murād*, in turn, has already reached what his counterpart desires and does not even know how he got there: being drunken with the love of God, he became unconscious of his actions.

Tripartite Division of the Heart

> The chest (*ṣadr*) is the mine of surrender [to God], the heart (*qalb*) is the mine of certainty, and the innermost (*ḍamīr*) is the mine of the secret.[29]

It has been already discussed that in the mystical tradition the heart is conceptualized as composed of parts with special functions. Qushayrī's *Treatise,* for example, differentiates between the outer heart *(qalb),* the inner heart *(sirr),* and the center of the inner heart *(sirr al-sirr).*[30]

One of the most elaborate early descriptions of the heart is that of Tirmīdhī (d. ca. 932), who distinguished between the *ṣadr,* the *qalb,* the *fu'ād,* and the *lubb.*[31] With the exception of the first word, which usually refers to the chest, the meaning of all these is "heart" in English, although with different connotations. *Qalb* is the most common word in Arabic for "heart"; according to some Arabic lexicographers, *fu'ād* refers to the pericardium, the membrane enclosing the heart; but others say that it is precisely the middle, or interior of the *qalb.*[32] *Lubb* means the kernel, the pith, or the middle of a nut, a date, or the like; figuratively it refers to the purest part of anything (or to its substance). In Tirmīdhī's description these constitute concentric spheres with special functions. The chest is the repository of learning necessary to cope with the requirements of Islam *(ʿilm al-sharīʿa);* the outer heart is the seat of mystical learning *(ʿilm al-bāṭin)* leading to faith *(īmān);* the inner heart is the abode of spiritual perception, vision *(ru'ya)* conveying inspired knowledge *(maʿrifa);* and finally, the center of the heart reflects the light of real monotheism *(nūr al-tawḥīd)* granted by divine grace. Tirmīdhī called the different parts of the heart subsequent "stations" *(maqāmāt)* that depend on one another. He who reaches the subsequent stations is regarded as *Muslim,* then *mu'min* (believer), after that *ʿārif* (possessor of inspired knowledge, mystic), and finally *muwaḥḥid* (real monotheist).[33]

A treatise attributed to Nūrī, the *Stations of the Hearts (Maqāmāt al-qulūb)*[34] operates with the same notions and structure that Tirmīdhī uses: it distinguishes between the same four parts of the heart *(ṣadr, qalb, fu'ād,* and *lubb),* and each part is regarded as the mine *(miʿdan)* of the concepts *islām, īmān, maʿrifa,* and *tawḥīd* respectively.

However, the saying Sīrjānī quotes in Nūrī's name employs a tripartite division, which does not conform to the structure described in the *Stations of the Heart*, although the first layer of the heart shows a marked similarity. The outer part of the heart, indicated with the word "chest" *(ṣadr)* both in the saying and in the treatise attributed to Nūrī, corresponds in the saying to *taslīm*, "to surrender to God," and in the treatise to *islām* "to resign oneself to the will of God." The second part of the heart is called *qalb* in the saying, just like in the *Stations of the Hearts*, but its function is different: it is the source of certainty *(yaqīn)*, a term that has peculiar meaning in Sufi terminology, as opposed to the more common concept of belief *(īmān)* mentioned in the *Stations of the Hearts*. The third section is called, as in Nūrī's saying, *ḍamīr*, meaning "something hidden" (heart, mine, innermost), which conceals the secret *(sirr)* that God deposited in man's innermost heart. This does not correspond to the third section of the *Stations of the Hearts'* division. The fourth section mentioned in the *Stations of the Heart* does not appear in Nūrī's saying at all. On the other hand, the structure described in the *Stations of the Hearts* corresponds to Tirmīdhī's description (both the names of the parts and their functions).

However, Nūrī's division of the heart is in line with a description attributed to Jaʿfar al-Ṣādiq (eighth century), according to which the *ṣadr* (chest) is the place of *taslīm* (surrender to God), the *qalb* (heart) is the place of *yaqīn* (certainty), the *fu'ād* (interior of the heart) is the place of *naẓar* (looking, considering), and the *ḍamīr* (innermost) is the place of *sirr* (secret).[35] As it can be seen, Nūrī's saying is identical to Jaʿfar al-Ṣādiq's description except for the third part of the heart *(fu'ād)*, which is missing from Nūrī's version.

Gaze *(naẓar)*

The significance of looking has been already discussed in connection with an anecdote quoted by Sulamī, according to which Nūrī looked at a young man lustfully and defiantly, trying to court him. "Looking" covers a wide range of concepts: it may refer to looking at another person or at his belongings, which is prohibited. But it may stand for various ways of "considering, studying" mystical or other branches of knowledge that may lead ultimately to God and to the vision of his hidden world.[36] Sīrjānī's *Black and White in the Words of Wisdom* includes a chapter on *naẓar* that covers both basic meanings of the term, although the overwhelming majority of the traditions cited there treat the issue of looking at handsome young men, which is, according to several sayings, the major vice of Sufism. Nūrī is mentioned surprisingly frequently in the chapter: Sīrjānī quotes the anecdote about Nūrī and the young man in Baghdad[37] and also his saying about "those engaged in looking" whether by way of distraction or with the aim of understanding rationally or intuitively.[38] These two traditions are collected by Sulamī as well.[39] In addition, Sīrjānī relates the following stories:

> Jaʿfar al-Khuldī said: "We were in the Shūnīziyya mosque, me, Junayd and some of our companions. Someone came to us and said: 'Oh, Abū l-Qāsim [al-Junayd], I have tried hard everything that can be tried, but my [mystical] moment did not become pure.' He said: 'Go to Abū l-Ḥusayn al-Nūrī, and ask him!' Abū l-Ḥusayn told him: 'It seems to me that you have asked from Junayd such-and-such a thing, and he sent you to me!' The man said: 'Yes.' He said to him: 'Tell me, aren't you inclined to look at youngsters?' He said: 'Yes.' [Nūrī] said: 'That is your veil, and that is the most powerful veil. Stop doing that, so that your moment may become pure and your heart may become empty [of mundane attachments].' "[40]

> Jaʿfar al-Khuldī said: "I have heard that Nūrī said: 'Once I entered the city of Rayy and I saw a young man sitting on a bench. I knew that God had [put] a secret in him, and my attention was focused on him. I entered the mosque, and behold, the young man has stopped at my side. He sat down and it did not seem proper to him to initiate a conversation with me, except by way of the Quran. So he told me: 'Oh, sheikh, do you know the Quran by heart?' I said: 'Yes.' He said: 'What do you demand from me?' I said: 'In the name of God . . .' So he begun to recite, but I told him: 'Make it short, for I want to go!' He said: 'From where [are you coming] and to where

> [are you going]?' I said: '[I come] from Baghdad, and I want to return [there]!' He said: 'I go with you!' I said: 'Are your parents alive?' He said: 'Yes.' I said: 'Then go and ask their permission!' So he asked their permission, and they allowed him to go. They bid him farewell and they handed him over to me. When we entered Baghdad I greeted Abū l-Qāsim Junayd, and he said: 'Oh, Abū l-Ḥusayn! God has made your reward great in this young man until three days!' And after three days, the young man died. Junayd was asked: 'How did you know that this would happen?' He said: 'I saw that he conquered the heart of Abū l-Ḥusayn, and I know that the Real is jealous if his friend's hearts incline towards other than Himself.' "[41]

Considering the traditions Sīrjānī quotes regarding Nūrī, the picture that emerges is complex: he appears much exposed to the temptations of young men, which he might not be able to resist. On the other hand, or maybe precisely because of his inclination toward them, he is well aware both of the intricate nature of *naẓar* and the dangers it involves. It must be noted that dedicating a separate chapter to *naẓar,* and to assemble dozens of delicate stories about the Sufi masters' predilection toward boys in the *Black and White in the Words of Wisdom,* is quite unique since early Sufi manuals usually do not treat the subject so exhaustively.

Abstinence and Contentment

Sīrjānī quotes some of Nūrī's sayings on the Sufis' relation to worldly matters that are not cited in the earlier collections. One of these treats the Sufis' relation to food and eating:

> We were sitting around Ibrāhīm al-Khawwāṣ one day, and Nūrī was sitting on his side. One of those present turned to Nūrī and asked: "How do this people take their food?" Nūrī said: "Like the pious in the house of eternity." Then he turned to Ibrāhīm al-Khawwāṣ and asked him about this, and he said: "Like the sick takes

> the medicine he expects to cure him." We got up and went to Abū l-Qāsim al-Junayd, and we repeated him both answers [asking which one was correct]. He said: "Certainly, [both answers are correct], for Abū l-Ḥusayn talked about contemplation of a true reality, and Abū l-Isḥāq talked about the state of striving (mujāhada)."[42]

The story appears in the chapter on food and the Sufi customs related to it. Most of the sayings collected in the chapter discuss practical aspects of eating, like insisting on only consuming food permitted by religious law, moderateness, sharing one's food with others, accepting invitations to join others for a meal, suppressing one's appetite and desire for specific foods, accepting with equanimity whatever is offered—even if nothing is offered at all. The sayings of Nūrī and Ibrāhīm al-Khawwāṣ, however, approach the issue from different perspectives. They describe how the mystic's relation with God is reflected in his manner of eating. According to their different spiritual states, their actions may be static (corresponding to "contemplation" meant by Nūrī) or dynamic (corresponding to "striving" meant by Ibrāhīm al-Khawwāṣ). Nūrī's saying about the pious in "the house of eternity" *(dār al-qarār)* does not refer to the hereafter but to their presence with God even in this world. Presence entails contemplation, although in this case in a limited, imperfect sense: according to Junayd's explication, they do not contemplate the Real God *(ḥaqq)* but only a true reality *(ḥaqīqa).* The parable of Ibrāhīm al-Khawwāṣ on taking medicine describes a more dynamic state characterized by struggle. Both answers, therefore, express distinct facets of the mystical experience, and neither of them is more authentic or authoritative than the other.

Another tradition attributed to Nūrī mentions eating in the context of abstinence *(zuhd)*, again focusing on its purpose as opposed to its outward aspects.

> Abstaining (*zuhd*) from the world means to give up expectations, not to eat tough food or to wear coarse garments.[43]

Spiritual independence from the world is attained by physical practices that aim to break one's dependence on material and sensual pleasures. Such self-discipline, however, constitutes only the first steps on the way to spiritual perfection, as Abū Saʿīd al-Kharrāz affirms: "The beginning of abstinence is making the resolution to confront the carnal soul regarding all its wishes, and to prevent it from [enjoying] comfort and [satisfying its] passions, like excesses in eating, drinking, clothing, dwelling, sleeping, speaking, looking and hearing."[44] Naturally, Nūrī does not deny the necessity of these external aspects of renunciation, but he warns not to mistake outward practices for the ultimate end, which is to refrain from entertaining hopes related to this world. On the other hand, Nūrī affirms the importance of tribulations *(balā')* for attaining mystical perfection:

> The servant will not find the sweetness of faith until tribulation comes over him from every place.[45]

This tradition is in line with a previously discussed Nūrī saying that establishes a connection between "rejoicing at the bitterness of fate" and contentment.[46] Sīrjānī collects many sayings that praise tribulation, like that of Sahl ibn ʿAbd Allāh: "Had it not been for the tribulation originating from God, the servant would have had no path to God."[47] According to Abū Saʿīd al-Kharrāz, trials and tribulations urge the mystic to seek connection with God: "The trial with which God visits His lovers is a gift and a present that stimulates their connection [to God] *(muwāṣala)* in their heart *(ḍamīr)*.[48] Tribulation is sometimes associated with bitterness, which must be tasted in order to perceive sweetness, in accordance with Dhū l-Nūn's saying: "Tribulation is the salt of the believer, and if the believer lacks tribulations, he does not find sweetness in his state."[49] Accepting tribulations gratefully brings about contentment:

> Contentment means to accept [God's] decrees happily.[50]

Ecstasy and Recollection

Several of Nūrī's poems and sayings that have been discussed before exploit the inherent opportunities in the multiple meanings of the word "ecstasy," implying both "finding, encountering" but also "loving passionately, experiencing great agitation" (and also pain). Sīrjānī quotes one more similar poem from Nūrī:

> Ecstasy enraptures him whose relaxation is in ecstasy
> But ecstasy is lost in the presence (ḥuḍūr) of the Real
> My ecstasy used to enrapture me, but Him who is
> found (mawjūd) in ecstasy
> Distracted me from perceiving the ecstasy (wajd).[51]

Here again, *wajd* evokes multiple connotations: "ecstasy is lost" means also "finding is lost," which conveys a double meaning: the ecstatic agitation in which the mystic encounters God passes away when the encounter takes place, since (ecstatic) emotions related to the encounter distract man from God. On the other hand, even the consciousness of the "encounter is lost": when God enraptures man, neither ecstasy nor consciousness of the encounter persists. Nūrī expresses a similar idea regarding recollection in his following saying:

> Everything has a punishment, and the punishment of the knower is the disruption of recollection.[52]

The purpose of the Sufi is constant recollection of God: "Recollection is leaving the field of negligence for the space of contemplation despite the supremacy of fear and the intensity of love."[53] Through recollection, the mystic overcomes his state of negligence caused by the sensation of fear or love that may overwhelm him and thus may divert him from God. However, even recollection might be a form of negligence since the act of remembering God and repeating His attributes or names in a contemplative way may equally appropriate man's consciousness and distract him from the ultimate goal: "The true reality (i.e., the full realization) of recollection is forgetting about recollection through perceiving Him who is recollected."[54] Sīrjānī mentions the cessation of recollection in two cases; when it occurs as a kind of punishment (as in Nūrī's saying); and its opposite, when it is connected to a paradisiac state (and therefore to the concept of reward): "Is there recollection in Paradise? He said: Recollection is dispelling negligence, but when negligence is abolished, recollection has no sense."[55] Naturally, the effacement of *dhikr* is basically a concomitant of ethereal perfection and not a kind of divine reward.

Both ecstasy and recollection may be forms of deception that divert man from God. Seeking to comply with God's orders, mere obedience may constitute a trial, a ruse distracting man from the ultimate goal, as Nūrī says:

> Disobedience is not free from disappointment and obedience is not free from ruse (*makr*).[56]

Sīrjānī dedicates a separate chapter to the concept of *makr* ("ruse, deception"). The immediate context of Nūrī's saying stresses that Sufism particularly incurs the risk of deception, for example, according to Shiblī's words: "We have chosen the path of Sufism in order to be safe from deception, and behold, all of it is deception!"[57] In the Sufi context, deception is attributed first and foremost to God: He is the one who leads man astray by artful ruses, and the ethical problem involved in this idea is quite evident: "Sumnūn was asked about God's saying [Quran 27:50]: 'So they plotted a plot: and We plotted a plot *(wa-makarū makran wa-makarnā makran),* [while they perceived not.]'[58] Is it permitted to ascribe ruse[ful acts] to God? So he recited: "A thing, done by other than You, I hold mean / But done by You, I do esteem."[59] God's ruse means essentially that the apparent state of affairs masks their true nature: "God concealed things in things, He concealed His ruse in His patience; He concealed His treachery in His kindness *(luṭf);* He concealed His punishments in His miracles *(karāmāt).*"[60] Everything perceptible may be an illusion; even the process of spiritual progress, in the way it is interpreted by Sufism, might be an illusion since the wayfarer might attach more importance to the stations of the path than to its goal: "All the stations are veils or deceptions; deceptions for those who are close, and veils for those who are far."[61] The stations are necessarily veils since they are between God and man, and until one strives for progress from one stage to the other, he is evidently distant from God. The accomplished mystic, who traversed the stations of the path and attained closeness to God, might be beguiled by his progress, cherishing an illusion of God instead of God Himself. Nūrī's saying articulates a similar idea: acts of obedience and piety entail deception, while sinful acts of disobedience inevitably result in disillusion.

Acts of obedience, worship, and service to God (*ʿibāda)* for Sufis obviously exceed common religious service. A saying by Abū l-ʿAbbās ibn ʿAṭā' grasps the essence of servanthood: "The true reality of the servant is not to possess anything."[62] This entails that the servant must divest himself of his own personality, as Abū Muḥammad al-Jurayrī says: "The true reality of the servant is to be patterned on the model of his Lord."[63] "True reality" *(ḥaqīqa)* is a noun derived from the verb *ḥaqqaqa* meaning "to fully realize something." Jurayrī states, thus, that man realizes his full potency when he assumes the qualities *(akhlāq)* of God. Consequently, God's real servant focuses exclusively on his Master and liberates himself from every worldly or even spiritual attachment: "Junayd was asked: 'When can a servant know [for sure] that he is a servant [in fact]?' He said: 'When he is free from everything except God, then he is [indeed] a servant."[64] Servanthood is perceived as man's relation to God and regarded as the full realization of human potential and condition. True servanthood, or a perfect relation with God, does not consist of performing acts (like the ceremony of recollection), or in experiencing mystical states (like ecstasy) but in contemplating divine sovereignty and what follows from that with regard to the human condition:

> Abū l-Ḥusayn al-Nūrī was asked about servanthood (*ʿubūdiyya*), and he said: It means to contemplate lordship (*rubūbiyya*).[65]

Conclusions

Besides the traditions discussed above, Sīrjānī collected in the *Black and White in the Words of Wisdom* twenty-six more traditions attributed to Nūrī; these, however, occur in earlier collections as well, and most of them are cited in at least two separate compilations.[66] Twelve traditions are quoted in the *Book of Flashes* by Sarrāj, nine in the *Doctrine of the Sufis* by Kalābādhī, nine in the *Ṭabaqāt al-ṣūfiyya* by Sulamī, eight in Qushayrī's *Treatise*, five in the *Ornament of God's Friends* by Abū Nuʿaym, and three in Kharkūshī's *Revision of the Secrets*. Those traditions that are peculiar to the *Black and White in the Words of Wisdom* are mostly in line with the material quoted in the earlier collections, and some of them seem to be parallels or alternative formulations of previously expressed ideas.

The peculiarity of Sīrjānī's collection is that the problem of gaze or looking *(naẓar)* and Nūrī's involvement in related issues is quite marked. A stylistic observation can be made regarding Nūrī's short sayings that were not collected in the rest of the compilations studied: namely, that most of them are decidedly short and concise (the average length of the sayings is six words), and almost half of them rhyme. Such a pronounced prevalence of this stylistic feature cannot be detected in the sayings attributed to Nūrī in the earlier compilations.

CHAPTER 9

Correspondence between Nūrī and Junayd Preserved in the Cairo Genizah

Description of the Manuscript

A manuscript originating from the Cairo Genizah contains a fragmentary correspondence between Nūrī and Junayd on the subject of tribulation *(balā')*, which is one of the recurring themes of Nūrī's sayings. Reference to an exchange of letters on that subject is made by Sarrāj in the *Book of Flashes,* a fact that might be considered an argument in favor of the text's authenticity.[1]

The manuscript contains twenty pages written in the Arabic language and in Arabic script, possibly between the eleventh to thirteenth centuries.[2] The pages contain between twenty-two and twenty-six lines, but some words and lines are barely legible. The beginning and the end of the text is missing, and its remaining parts do not belong to just one literary genre. The first unit contains *shaṭaḥāt,* ecstatic utterances by Abū Yazīd al-Bisṭāmī, commented upon by a certain ʿAbd al-Raḥmān b. Muḥammad. The second unit begins with the sayings of the same ʿAbd al-Raḥmān b. Muḥammad, but much of the chapter consists of long stories about Sufi masters. The third part contains the correspondence between Nūrī and Junayd. In all probability, the owner of the manuscript selected these texts from different sources and copied them into one collection that served his own needs and interests, and apparently the copy was intended for his personal use. It does not seem plausible that it would be a continuous text copied from one compilation.

Unfortunately, I could not identify specific signs pointing either toward the identity of the copyist or the owners. Since the manuscript was found in the Cairo Genizah, in the storeroom of the Ibn Ezra synagogue in Fustat that had preserved several hundred thousand medieval manuscripts, it was evidently owned by Jews at a certain point, but it is not clear whether it was originally copied by a Jew or not. The text does not contain any words in Hebrew or in Judaeo-Arabic, but it presents grammatical features corresponding to Middle Arabic: for example, imperfect indicative P/3 m. ending *ū* instead of *ūna* (*wa-yakūnū* instead of *wa-yakūnūna*); the use of plural suffix *-īna* instead of *-ūna* in nominative; disappearance of *tanwīn -an (kāna ḥaddād, kuntu ḥaddād)*; words terminating in *ḥamza* are usually written with *-yā*; inconsistencies in verbal agreement: verb conjugated in the plural before a plural subject *(wa-yakūnū hā'ulā'i al-thalātha)*; erroneous form of the imperative: *qūm* instead of *qum*; use of dialectal forms (*esh anta* and *fa-esh taʿmal*). It has to be noted that these deviations from classical Arabic occur exclusively in the chapters comprising the sayings of Bisṭāmī and the stories about Sufi masters, but they are completely absent from the correspondence of Nūrī and Junayd, which might be considered again as a feature supporting the authenticity of the letters.

The first part of the manuscript (fols. 1a–3b) contains *shaṭaḥāt* of Abū Yazīd al-Bisṭāmī. The *shaṭaḥāt* are ecstatic sayings that mystics utter when they are absorbed in the divine to such a degree that they lose consciousness of their own selves.[3] In the state of ecstasy they announce their direct experience of God in the form of unconscious utterances that border on blasphemy if they are taken out of their specific context: that is, the state of intoxicated ecstasy. Mystics themselves regard these sayings as if they were uttered by God directly through the tongue of the mystic who passes away from his self while subsisting with God. Some of the *shaṭaḥāt* of Abū Yazīd al-Bisṭāmī preserved in this Genizah fragment have parallels in the manuscripts published by Badawī[4] and Qāsim Muḥammad ʿAbbās.[5] A few of them can also be found in widely known Sufi manuals, like the *Ornament of God's Friends*. Parts of the sayings, however, apparently were not left to us in other sources. Furthermore, the *shaṭaḥāt* preserved in the manuscript were commented on and interpreted almost one by one by ʿAbd al-Raḥmān b. Muḥammad. His commentary could serve as an interesting complement to the commentaries in the *Book of Flashes*, which contains two commentaries on Bisṭāmī, one attributed to Junayd, and another written by Sarrāj. The interpretation of ʿAbd al-Raḥmān is characterized by justifying Bisṭāmī's sayings with the concept of *fanā'* and *ghayba*, stating that the mystic in the state of annihilation is detached from his self and transmits mystical experiences originating exclusively from God.

Moving on to the second part of the manuscript (fols. 3b–7b) the genre of the text changes.[6] The main theme of this part *(tawakkul,* "trust in God") is indicated by the chapter heading. This section includes sayings of ʿAbd al-Raḥmān, short sayings of various sheikhs and also longer stories. These address the theme of traveling, wandering while dealing with hunger, thirst, and heat—and relying completely on God. The element of miracle is present in most narratives, but some describe everyday situations. The point of the stories is that the attitude of the mystic toward God is not affected in the slightest by the circumstances. The narrations promote the ideal of equanimity, self-possession, composure, and steadiness, in line with the central Sufi concept of *ṣabr* ("patience, forbearance").

Correspondence between Nūrī and Junayd Mentioned in the Previous Sources

The last part of the fragment (fols. 7b–10b), which contains the correspondence of Nūrī and Junayd, is completely different from the foregoing chapters in its literary genre, linguistic features, and style. Several of the letters written by or addressed to Junayd have been included in the *Book of Flashes*, in the *Ornament of God's Friends*, while others were published by Abdel-Kader,[7] Jamāl Rajab Saydabī,[8] and Suʿād al-Ḥakīm.[9] The *Book of Flashes* dedicates two chapters to the correspondence of Sufi masters, in which Sarrāj quotes various short letters. However, he deliberately omits letters he considered too long to include in his manual: "As for their correspondence and exchange of letters, it is impossible to quote all of them with their numerous parts, therefore we cited only some of them, as time permitted us, since their long letters, as for example the letter of Nūrī to Junayd about *balā'* [. . .] and others could not have been quoted by us."[10] Sarrāj enumerates several other letters he omitted; most of these have been lost forever since then. Apparently the same applied to the correspondence between Nūrī and Junayd concerning tribulation, which cannot be found in the early sources and is not included among the letters published by modern scholars either. Sarrāj refers to this letter in another chapter as well: "Abū l-Ḥusayn al-Nūrī wrote a letter to Junayd, and he wrote in it: 'Oh, Sir, you have a tongue [with which you can express] what can be learned about tribulation; you have a blade [sharp wittedness with which you can discern] what can be learned about the tribulation of tribulation."[11]

Fortunately, the Genizah fragment published here seems to have preserved the letter mentioned by Sarrāj. It contains both Nūrī's letter to Junayd on *balā'* and also a long fragment from Junayd's answer to it.

Style and Topic of the Letters: Tribulations *(balā')*, Limits of Verbal Expression

Nūrī's letter is characterized by a passionate style, colorful symbolism, and powerful expression of imagery. He uses the allegory of the storming sea to describe the overwhelming sovereignty of God and the absolute feebleness of man who drifts with the vehement currents of the endless sea, under constant trials and tribulations. An interesting peculiarity of Nūrī's letter is that it employs an expression almost exclusively connected to Niffarī (d. 965). The expression *awqafanī* "He made me stand" introduces each one of Niffarī's visionary "standings" *(mawāqif)* that he describes in his *Kitāb al-mawāqif* (which was composed apparently by his son, for Niffarī himself never composed any book; rather, he drafted his revelations on scraps of paper).[12] In Nūrī's letter, the expression is not as emphatic as in Niffarī's texts; it is used only once, and not even as an introductory formula. Further difference is that while the verb consequently takes the preposition *fī* in Niffarī's texts, in Nūrī's letter it stands with *ʿalā*. Despite that, it must be noted that one of Niffarī's *mawāqif*, "the standing of the sea" *(mawqif al-baḥr)* shows a certain similarity to Nūrī's letter in its imagery and symbols, including the stormy sea, rising and falling waves, ships, and drowning. The sea itself is a means by which God puts the mystic to the test; whether he drowns in it or makes it disappear and annihilates himself in God.[13]

The central theme of Nūrī's and Junayd's exchange of letters is *balā'*, that is, tribulation that God inflicts on the mystic. Although the topic of *balā'* is not central in Nūrī's sayings and poems quoted in the early Sufi manuals, it is certainly one of his recurring themes. Traditions concerning *balā'* attributed to Nūrī were included in the manuals of Sarrāj, Sulamī, Abū Nuʿaym, and Sīrjānī.[14] The letter Nūrī wrote to Junayd abounds in expressive poetical images, as well as passionate and exaggerated expressions, while, as expected, the tone of Junayd's response is moderate, rational, and interpretative. Nūrī praises Junayd for his ability to understand the different "languages" of the existent phenomena and to speak in all the "tongues" of human actions. Speaking and understanding means in this context the capacity for discerning the hidden mystical implications, aims, and causes of both worldly and spiritual matters. It may be noted that the nature of mystical communication, the limits of verbal expression, "tongue," "allusion," "clarity," and "expression" are also frequently treated in Nūrī's sayings and poems collected in the early manuals.[15] Although the compilators of these usually regard Nūrī as a master of expression and interpretation,[16] in his letter to Junayd he admits deficiencies in this respect and turns humbly to Junayd for interpretation of the unbearable state he experiences. He praises Junayd for being familiar with each and every "tongue," mystical experience and the way it can be communicated: "Oh you, to whom all tongues are gathered, every tongue speaking according to the variation of their meanings!"[17] The term "tongue" *(lisān)* alludes both to understanding and expressing the sense of hidden meanings. Nūrī mentions, for example, the tongues of trials, tribulations, benefactions, inspired knowledge, and practice. He continues stating that from all of these, only one language—that of tribulation—was disclosed to him therefore his only tool of communication and mode of cognition is the language of tribulation. Tribulation is also his "way of practice" *(ʿamal)*, which is a reference to the duality of *ʿilm* and *ʿamal*, knowledge and practice, mutually presupposing each other in Sufi thought. He complains about the mystical state of tribulation he faces with hyperbole describing how insufferable his pain and despair are and how confused and disoriented he is. He perceives both his inner, mental and psychological state and the outer world, the company of men and communication with them, as highly trying and demanding. Even contacting Junayd to ask for his help in interpreting his condition is exhausting. He compares his state to a stormy sea that washes over him and sweeps him away with its rising and falling waves. He realizes that he has to cross the turbulent water, so that it may become annihilated from his consciousness *(fanā')*, but when he believes to have reached his aim, an even bigger sea appears in front of him. Finally, God carries him through the stormy seas of tribulation amid frights, afflictions, and despair—saving him but also delivering him to suffering again. He feels completely defenseless, destroyed, and confused. He addresses Junayd with exaggerated terms of admiration and asks him to interpret his situation.

Junayd explains that Nūrī's state is not unique and that its cause is God's ardent love toward the mystic. God's jealousy results in demanding the mystic exclusively to Himself and in isolating the beloved from everything other than Himself. Suffering is like a veil with which God separates man both from the world and from his own self, setting apart the mystic to Himself alone. By means of tribulations, God imparts confusing and disorienting thoughts to the mystic in order to bewilder him completely. Junayd interprets the metaphor of the wildly rolling sea as the manifestation of transcendental inspiration: ". . . this is similar to a stormy sea, which devastates with its vehemently returning heavy waves. He realizes in every falling wave *(mawja wārida)* something mighty, something new, and something disquieting."[18] The adjective *wārida,* "falling, descending" alludes to the Sufi term *wārid* meaning oncoming thought, stimulus sent by God, and inspiration descending upon the mystic. Junayd plays with the words deriving from the verbal root "to descend" (WRD) creating ingenious puns. According to his words, this procedure "falls outside the habitual decrees," and man cannot comprehend it since it "is in contradiction with his existing ways of understanding."[19] God takes away from man everything he firmly holds, removes everything he knows, and destroys everything he possesses. He turns matters upside down, reverses logic, and eliminates rationality. In his ultimate confusion, the mystic experiences the closeness of death, but he fails to perceive that his mystical experience is in fact subsistence with God *(baqā')*, that is, the aim of the mystic quest. In Junayd's view, this state is experienced by those whom God attracts and demands for Himself; not by those who seek God's closeness by their own initiative. Junayd admits modestly that he would be unable to endure such a mystical state, and he closes his answer with references to their earlier correspondence on mystical matters as evidence that he habitually interpreted Nūrī's mystical experiences and kept answering his questions.

Authenticity of the Letters

Naturally, the authenticity of the letters cannot be established with certainty. In any case, the setting, theme, and terminology of the letters correspond to the extant material related to Nūrī and Junayd, and the same holds true when it comes to the style of Junayd's letter. The correspondence witnesses the close relationship between Nūrī and Junayd but also reveals a certain tension (cf. Nūrī's words complaining about how Junayd has admonished him; fol. 8a, line 9). The theme of the correspondence (i.e., *balā'*) recurs in Nūrī's sayings and poems collected in the early sources. The most important technical terms of Nūrī's letter *(balā', shuhūd, lisān, fanā', wujūd, sirr, wiṣāl, kashf, ghayb)* are found frequently in the sayings and poems attributed to him. Unfortunately, since this is the only epistle attributed to Nūrī, its literary style cannot be compared to other such texts authored by him but only to his short sayings and poems preserved in the early sources. The style of these is not uniform; on the contrary, it ranges from an analytical, theoretical tone to passionately scandalous modes of expression. His epistle evidently squares with the latter style. Notwithstanding all these facts, and the reference in Sarrāj's *Book of Flashes* to the correspondence of Nūrī and Junayd on *balā'*, obviously the authorship of the text cannot be established beyond all doubt—but the same applies also to the traditions attributed to Nūrī in the early sources. Be it as it may, the Genizah fragment is the longest continuous text attributed to Nūrī that survived in a medieval manuscript, and for that reason it obviously deserves the reader's attention.

Translation of the Correspondence between Nūrī and Junayd on Tribulation *(Balā')*

CAMBRIDGE UNIVERSITY LIBRARY, TAYLOR-SCHECHTER ARABIC 41.1

Fol. 7b

[17] In the name of God, the Compassionate, the Merciful. Letter of Abū l-Ḥusayn al-Nūrī to Abū l-Qāsim [18] al-Junayd (may God have mercy on both of them)

[19] May God sanctify you with the purities of glory in the highest degree! May He make your turning toward Him [20] the closest closeness, the most perfect unveiling (*kashf*), and the most delightful reunion (*wiṣāl*)! May He enable you [21] to witness (*shuhūd*) His lights through the love of His encounter (*bi-waddi wujūdihi*)! May He single you out for His unveilings (*kushūf*)! [22] May He remove from you proudness[20] through his bounties when you witness (*shuhūd*) Him! May He [enable you] to adorn yourself [23] with His attributes (*ṣifāt*)! [May He enable you] to receive by way of inspiration (*istīrād*)[21] what [permits] you to arrive (*wāṣil*) at Him, by affirming His oneness, [24] and [what permits you] to descend (*wārid*) from Him to Him! Nay, may He unveil for you the companion of His proof (*rafīq hujjatihi*)[22]! May He make you witness [25] the chosen one of His love! May He attract you to Himself from the nearness of His nearness! May He single you out for Himself [26] from those who worship Him! May He make you meet Him through His grace, so that you could dispense by His means[23]

Fol. 8a

[1] with every [hidden] sense (*ma'nā*), but Him! You will be then concealed in the concealments [2] of His unseen world (*ghayb*), hidden in the foldings of [His] inner heart. You will be then preserved in pure [3] knowledge of [His] oneness; you will be

sheltered and preserved eternally [there]. Oh you, to whom all tongues are gathered, [4] every tongue speaking according to the variation of their meanings! So one of the tongues became to him [5] the tongue of tribulation, another tongue the tongue of benefactions, another tongue [became] the tongue of trials, [6] another tongue [became] the tongue of practice (*ʿamal*), another tongue [became] the tongue of the knower (*ʿārif*). [. . .] [7] And a tongue from among these has appeared to me. And I speak in this tongue about what I have learned (*ʿilm*) concerning all [8] the tongues, each and every one of them, since the tongue of tribulation is the tongue of my way of practice (*ʿamal*). [9] Abū l-Qāsim has admonished me with regard to every [hidden] idea, although I witnessed only what He wanted me [to witness].[24] [10] Tribulation became primal and ultimate for me; but I endured until He poured upon me trials [11] and tribulations infinitely, and He squeezed me, and He afflicted me even more [12] with tribulations. He revealed to me from this tribulation a source [pouring out] tribulation, or even more, [13] which cannot be endured. And I remained in tribulation. He afflicted me with more tribulation. Then, above all this, [14] He poured upon me the tribulation of all the creatures, and there was no repose for me among the creatures [15] and no relief among them. If I incline toward them, my inclination afflicts me; [16] but if I avoid them, my avoidance becomes tribulation for me. And in some moments it occurs to me [17] to complain or to implore for relief, and I beg but [. . .]. [18] I was afflicted more with tribulation, and if I complain, it becomes tribulation for me. Know, [19] oh Abū l-Qāsim, that if I write to you, it becomes a tribulation for me; but if I did not write to you, [that also] would be [20] tribulation for me. I realized this, and I made my choice. I wrote to you since I am equally [21] afflicted [whether I write or not]. But my choice became tribulation for me. Then, above all this, there appeared a sea of tribulation [22] and a sea in which there were boats of tribulation, so that I may cross the sea. When I thought that it became annihilated *(faniya)*, [23] and that salvation was getting closer, a greater sea appeared before me, flowing with its tribulations and its frights. [24] Then He carried me across it as He wanted and the way He wanted. I saw His will [25] concerning me, and it afflicted me. Oh, Abū l-Qāsim, how could one be saved

Fol. 8b

[1] from what there is no salvation; or how could one seek escape for whom seeking escape [2] is tribulation; or how could one annihilate himself [in God] for whom annihilation (*fanā'*) is tribulation? For I am immersed in tribulation; [3] I am burning in the fire of tribulation; I am thrown into the fright of tribulation; [4] I am lost in the darkness of tribulation! My origin is from tribulation, and my termination is in tribulation. [5] Tribulation is my potation; and in tribulation is my dwelling. When tribulation drowns me, [6] to tribulation He thrusts me. When He saves me from tribulation, to the sea of its frights He brings me. [7] When He stations me (*awqafanī ʿalā*) over tribulation, He increases it on me. What could the state (*ḥāl*) of someone be like, [8] whose state is like this? Or what could the state of someone be like, whose state is tribulation for him? And for whom it is a tribulation to remember his state? [9] Oh, you, who achieved this station! [God] alone has set up meaning to everything! I have offered you [10] my beginning and my end! Talk to me like a despotic tyrant, like a king [11] who rules over the people of his kingdom imperiously, and don't soften your words so you make [12] that a tribulation for me! For what is the totality of tribulation? All tribulations with every tribulation I have described. [13] Thereafter trials were multiplied upon me until they reached a hundred times more than what was [14] due to me. My speech is tribulation upon me, so do not force me to speak! Tell me, if there is refuge for someone whose [15] state is like this, or if there is no refuge for him! Whether from the attributes of the Real (*al-ḥaqq*), [16] or from the attributes of Glory (*al-majd*) appeared to me [a state] like this, and others? Do I have a [17] share with you? Have you opened a door for me, or have you closed it?[25] Is there [18] any hope that the closed door will be opened? Oh, Abū l-Qāsim, you are the [only] one who [. . .][26] [19] all of them from you, and you are the only one who can lead [anyone] toward yourself.[27] Reveal[28] to me a word concerning [my state] [20] that includes [that is, answers] everything I have asked. I do not want you to ease my situation, but to increase tribulation upon me by reading it [that is, your answer]. [21] Since what I have fulfilled from my state was only a bit.[29] [. . .]

[22] Answer of [23] Abū l-Qāsim al-Junayd, may have God mercy upon him

[24] [. . .] in his place and in his abodes (*awṭān*), unique in his generation [25] [. . .] among his friends, associates and companions.

Fol. 9a

[1] [. . .] who is hidden both from those who associate with him and those who are foreign to him; [2] whose [hidden] essence (*maʿnā*) cannot be grasped either by his friends or his contemporaries. What is more wonderful is [3] that he is unaware of his self in himself and does not discern any [hidden] sense (*maʿnā*) that could save him from his tribulations.[4] May he be brought to perfection by Him, Who had prolonged his life, Who had thickened the layers covering him, [5] plastering them together. Earth and heavens became heaped one above the other, and he became confined in the narrowest [6] spot of moist earth [. . .] in the most horrible isolation of tribulations. He became distressed because of his anxiety, [7] and [God's] sentence was pronounced upon him, and his complaining prevented him from finding relief. [8] But he endures the horrible and extreme tribulations that affect him. His voice is not heard, [9] his supplication is not answered, his tears are not pitied, his weeping does not help him, [10] and his misery is infinite. So he expects the end; he is anxious [11] and pained because of the despair that perplexes him and conceals him in what he knows not. [12] Peace be with you! I praise to you God, who alone is praised [even] for the worst of afflictions, [13] who created all things by His will, arranged them by His knowledge, ordained and decreed upon them [14] what He wished to ordain and to decree. Therefore, they are bound by His supremacy and subjected to His authority [15] according to the degrees (*marātib*) of His creation and the performance of His will. Those who know Him best are those who [16] fear Him most, who most submissively and humbly humiliate themselves before His might, [17] who apply themselves to inquire about what He appropriated to Himself exclusively. [18] Therefore, if those who know Him (*ahl al-ʿilm bihi*) are like that, what do you think about those who are

far away from that? [19] Your letter has reached me, and I have understood what you exposed in it concerning your conditions. [20] I answer to the expressions of what has descended upon you as inspiration (*īrād*). I have understood that you think that you alone are in this state of yours [21] [. . .] Know, (may God have mercy upon you), [22] that others have experienced it before you. [. . .]

Fol. 9b

[1] They drunk from the finest [. . .] the taste of death unmixed, and they became completely unable to perceive [2] what happened to them because of a thick, impenetrable [3] dense covering, so they remained like this. There is no putting to death in this [state] nor bringing to life. [4] In my opinion, it means that He wants them to Himself, so He, Whose command is mighty, has selected them through His purest [5] quality. He protected them against themselves, and veiled them from themselves in every way [6] and in every sense, inspiring in them (*yūriduhum*) thoughts about how He demands them [to Himself]. [7] But then the springs (*mawārid*) of [God's] decisions diverged, and [God's] decrees assumed most extreme tribulations. [8] By means of their divergence they constantly brought about things that cannot be put in writing, so that [9] he who is demanded [by God] (*maṭlūb*) should not rely, through the tribulations [he suffers], on something he adheres to, and so that he should not seek refuge in a saying he understands. [10] When that happens, [God's] decree concerning him falls outside the habitual decrees, and his understanding [11] contradicts his existing ways of understanding since he refuses some of what he ignores [12] and knows some of what he refuses. Then he reverses turning over [13] and the [constant] changing of all this becomes manifest. Then he becomes confounded because [14] he is utterly incapable of comprehending this. So he stays in this situation [15] and in this condition, his matters turning upside down, confused and unsettled, [16] tasting the reality of death, his evanescent complexion, and the closeness of moist earth [that is, death]. [17] He is retained in this [state] during the period of subsistence (*baqā'*) [in or with God] but he does not despair, since there is [18] relief for him in his despair. But he does not perceive it[30] [that he is with God] because he yearns to leave behind tribulations [19] that have

already filled their[31] flesh, bones, skin, hair, and nerves with [20] abhorrence. When [tribulation] overcomes, it is too excessive to let him settle himself anyhow [21] because of its [extreme] measure, since further inspirations (*wārid*) constantly descend upon him in every [mystical] moment (*waqt*) [22] to the extent that it seems to him that because of their excessiveness he is returned

Fol. 10a

[1] to himself [that is, he is refused by God]. He who can be described like this is similar to a stormy sea, which devastates [2] with its vehemently returning heavy waves. He [3] realizes in every falling wave (*mawja wārida*) something mighty, something new, and something disquieting. And he [4] remains under these conditions until he is commanded otherwise. But [5] it would take too long to describe in this letter the characteristics [of this state], [6] and these are only hints of what could be set forth. Know, my brother, that this [7] does not result from the demands of the one demanded [by God to Himself] (*maṭlūb*), but only because of the ardent love of the Beloved (*maḥbūb*), [8] and because of His jealousy that isolates him from everything other than Himself, and because of His envy that keeps him away from anything but Himself. Since He preferred [9] him over anybody else, He subdued him due to his high [spiritual] position and because of the mightiness of what he does with him. [10] Furthermore, this is a way for one drawn close [to God], a pure [state of] astonishing absence (*mujarrad ghayba ʿajība*). [11] Part of this way belongs to the most wonderful wonders. It is such a way that all other paths[32] are destroyed, [12] and the traces of signs leading to it and the waymarks indicating its whereabouts are erased, [13] and even unique persons scarcely ever seek it. [14] Verily, how far is his state (*ḥāl*), and how incapable I would be of enduring [15] this state! His state [. . .] and if [. . .] [16] [. . .] his arrogance would triumph [. . .] and prevail. [17] He rose against his contemporaries boasting of his state, [. . .] talking and acting [18] to an extent that cannot be resisted. Moreover, I hope that [19] your deliverance is close and that you will obtain what a sincere, obedient, chosen [20] lover and beloved obtains. You have mentioned in your letter that in [the letter] you received, I answered you [21] concerning the characteristic (*rasm*)

of the name (*ism*), but your experience (*wujūd*) was other than what I have described. [22] That is because the answer should be like that; the answer should be only according to what the [23] letter contains. You have mentioned in your letter changes [alternating states] that affect you [24] and things you receive from me differently [that is, I explain your states in a different way]. I have understood what you described concerning these.

Fol. 10b

[1] You have mentioned [. . .] [2] [. . .] He who is demanded [by God] (*al-maṭlūb*) is drawn out from all of his states, [3] so that he does not have anything to rely on and cannot cleave to knowledge (*maʿrifa*) about a state in which he would take shelter. [4] Or he experiences diverse [divine] decrees, and then he experiences His intimacy (*ta'āluf*), which cannot be put into writing. [5] But he moves from one decree[33] to the other, so that he who is demanded [by God] should not cleave either to [6] anything he knows, or to what he considers established. Therefore, he finds that opposites are wrestling in himself. [7] Then [the situation] changes, and he finds himself in the opposite [extreme] at once, and [8] even certainty comes hastily concerning it. All this concerns what I have [already] described to you. You have mentioned that you suffer more and more excessive tribulations [9]. This is inevitable and unavoidable:[10] but when a similar thing happens, although it is hard and excessive, its reward can be expected. Even if you ignore it [. . .] [11] but I do not ignore it. The decrees of God must be carried out completely. Tribulations last until the time of [12] [. . .] the termination. You have mentioned that you speculate, but you cannot acquire knowledge because of the changes [13] that affect you in your connection (*ittiṣāl*) [to God], and that you can't find the reason for the changes, and that you are not satisfied with the knowledge (*maʿrifa*) of [14] [. . .] concerning your state. It is as you have described and related. For how [15] could you be satisfied[34] with learning (*ʿilm*) about a state, which does not remain with you, which is not lasting for you, and nothing [16] [. . .] from it corresponds to the [hidden] sense (*maʿnā*) that you hold to be right, or to what you regard as truth? All this [17] afflicts you because of those things through which you are demanded [by

God to Himself]. Since He who demands you (*ṭālib*) afflicts you, [18] taking from you everything He founds; removing everything you know; eliminating everything you [19] firmly hold; turning every state upside down and in such a way that the reason [for what happens] could not be understood.[20] For this exists through your separation from Him and through your absence (*ghayb*) [21] from Him. But if the [significance] of your state becomes manifest to you,[35] [the end of] this will be close, and the termination of all this will come in no time. [22] You have mentioned that some of my words resemble [23] what is in your soul. These are incentives I release [encouragements to what I hold good] and impediments [24] I confine [dissuasions from what I deem wrong]. Verily, you have understood that well! The [hidden] meaning of this is that he who is demanded [25] by this state is found by his comrades seeking him, until [. . .].

CHAPTER 10

Stations of the Hearts
(Maqāmāt al-qulūb)

Nwyia's Arguments in Favor of the Authenticity of the Tractate

The *Stations of the Hearts* is a short tractate attributed to Nūrī that was reconstructed and published by Paul Nwyia in 1968 on the basis of four manuscripts preserved in Istanbul, two of them dated (1218 AH / 1803–4 AD and 1294 AH / 1877 AD) and two undated.[1] None of the manuscripts contains the whole text. Nwyia did not comment upon the approximate age of the undated manuscripts; most likely they are not early copies. The first mention of the treatise can be found in the bibliographic encyclopedia composed by Kātib Çelebi (Ḥajjī Khalīfa) in the seventeenth century, which gives its title and indicates Nūrī as its author.[2]

Nwyia stressed the fact that Nūrī was a poet and therefore described spiritual experience through images and symbols instead of abstract language, employing the method of allusion *(ishāra)* rather than discursive arguments. Nwyia compared the structure of the tractate to that of a prose poem, which does not follow a logical scheme but develops through images that evoke others either by way of similarity or dissimilarity. In Nwyia's view, considering that Nūrī was a poet and used allusive methods of expression, the authenticity of the treatise is certain. In fact, Kalābādhī mentioned Nūrī among those Sufi authors who wrote about mysticism employing allusion ("promulgated the science of allusion *(ʿulūm al-ishāra)* in books and letters").[3] Nwyia even refused some of the possible counterarguments that may challenge Nūrī's authorship. He admitted that the sole clue as to the attribution of the treatise to Nurī is the incipit of the text, which in three of the four manuscripts mentions Abū l-Ḥasan al-Nūrī, while the fourth one attributes the text to a certain Abū l-Ḥasan al-Nawawī. As Nwyia rightly observed, that must be an orthographical mistake due to the easily confoundable letters "w" and "r" resulting in نووي instead of نوري. He remarked also that chapter 6 of the tractate might raise further questions regarding Nūrī's authorship since it contains an anonymous saying introduced by the formula "he said," which Sulamī attributes to Abū ʿUthmān al-Ḥīrī (d. 910), a disciple of Shāh Kirmānī. Furthermore, the same chapter cites a saying in the name of Shāh Kirmānī (d. before AH 300/AD 912/913), which is also ascribed to him by Sulamī.[4] Nwyia explained that the authorship of short, detached mystical dictions was frequently uncertain, and the same saying was often quoted in the name of various personalities. He added that Sufi masters often cited the sayings of their contemporaries, therefore the inclusion of the passages related to Abū ʿUthmān and Shāh Kirmānī does not call into question the authenticity of the treatise.[5] Nwyia concluded that the tractate was indeed authored by Nūrī and that it was not an apocryphal work that was written after his death.

Counterarguments Questioning Nūrī's Authorship

As already noted in the introduction, Nwyia's arguments are not completely convincing, and the attribution of the treatise to Nurī seems dubious for several reasons: (1) The manuscripts of the text are relatively recent (those that have colophons are dated to the nineteenth century). (2) No part of the text is quoted in any of the early works collecting Nūrī's sayings, although the treatise is composed of rather brief chapters that may stand alone, regardless of their ample context. Some of the chapters consist of not much more than one or two sentences, which are mostly formulated as maxims or aphorisms. The literary genre of these short passages is similar to that of Nūrī's sayings quoted in the various Sufi collections; therefore it seems strange that none of these passages is cited by the medieval compilators. (3) Nūrī's one and only saying that describes the structure of the heart is quoted in Sīrjānī's *Black and White in the Words of Wisdom.*[6] In that saying, the heart has a tripartite division of *ṣadr, qalb,* and *ḍamīr* ("chest," "heart," and "innermost"), which is inconsistent with the structure of the heart sketched in the *Stations of the Hearts,* according to which the parts of the heart are *ṣadr, qalb, fu'ād,* and *lubb* ("chest," "heart," "core of the heart" and "sense"). (4) The functions of the parts in Nūrī's saying also do not correspond to the *Stations of the Heart.* In the saying, the functions of the part are *taslīm, yaqīn,* and *sirr* ("surrender to God," "certainty," and "secret"), while in the *Stations of the Hearts* these are *islām, īmān, maʿrifa,* and *tawḥīd* ("resigning oneself to the will of God," "faith," "inspired knowledge," and "assertion of God's unity"). Obviously only the first division of the heart *(ṣadr)* and its function *(taslīm/islām)* are more or less identical in the saying and in the treatise. (5) The treatise employs imagery that does not recur in Nūrī's sayings, and some of its concepts seem to contradict Nūrī's ideas expressed in several of his sayings collected by the medieval authors. For example, learning *(ʿilm),* learned people or scholars *(ʿulamā')* and intelligence *(ʿaql)* are considered meritorious in the treatise, while they are vehemently criticized in Nūrī's sayings preserved in the early compilations.[7] (6) Some passages and basic concepts of the treatise are markedly similar to Tirmīdhī's *Bayān al-farq bayna l-ṣadr wa-l-qalb wa-l-fu'ād wa-l-lubb,* including the number, the names, and the functions of the parts of the heart.[8] Both Tirmīdhī and the *Stations of the Hearts* enumerate four parts of the heart, having the names *ṣadr, qalb, fu'ād,* and *lubb* ("chest," "heart," "core of the heart" and "sense"), and regard these parts as the mine *(miʿdan)* of *islām, īmān, maʿrifa* and *tawḥīd* (Islam, faith, inspired knowledge and assertion of God's unity). Furthermore, some of the symbols and mental images Tirmīdhī employs are similar to those of the *Stations of the Hearts* ("house," "treasury," "king," "fire," "light," "sea," "garden," "tree," "fruit," "wall," etc.). Although Tirmīdhī is more or less contemporary with Nūrī (he died around AH 300), his works attained wide popularity only in the thirteenth century;[9] therefore, it cannot be automatically supposed that Nūrī was familiar with Tirmīdhī's concept, while such familiarity might be assumed with regard to a thirteenth-century author. (7) The introductory part of the *Stations of the Hearts* also shows certain similarity to a thirteenth-century mystical-magical description of the heart by Būnī in his very popular *Shams al-maʿārif*,[10] according to which the heart has three cavities *(tajwīf):* the outer one is the *qalb* ("heart"), the middle cavity is the *shaghaf* ("pericardium"), and the inner one is the *fu'ād* ("center of the heart"). These contain three types of love: *wudd, ʿishq,* and *ḥubb,* respectively. Furthermore, each cavity has special functions, and again, the outer one (which is the *qalb* in the *Shams al-maʿārif*) is the place of Islam *(maḥall al-islām).* The concept of *īmān* is associated with the inner cavity, the *fu'ād.* The structure depicted in the *Shams al-maʿārif* is not as precise and carefully elaborated as the system of al-Ḥakīm al-Tirmīdhī or the one detailed in the *Stations of the Hearts* attributed to Nūrī, and it does not correspond entirely to that of the *Stations of the Hearts* or to Tirmīdhī's ideas. However, it evidences that in the thirteenth century, mystical-magical speculations about the structure of the heart had certain currency. (8) Both the phraseology (including imagery and vocabulary of Sufi technical terms) and the theoretical background of the *Stations of the Hearts* seem to be fully established and elaborate to such an extent that we might question its dating to the formative period of Sufism.

My conclusion is that the treatise originated in a much later period, at the earliest in the thirteenth century, when similar speculations about the mystical structure of the heart began to have wide circulation. The attribution of the treatise to Nūrī might be due to the symbol of light *(nūr)* that recurs in the treatise (the word "light" occurs twenty-seven times in the text).

The Symbolism of the Heart

The symbolism of the heart in early Sufi tradition was studied by Yazaki in relation to Makkī's *Qūt al-qulūb* (*The Nourishment of the Hearts*).[11] Yazaki proves that in the formative period of Sufism the heart was already considered the organ of spiritual knowledge. According to the earliest mystics, the heart reflects the light of certainty emanating from God, by which the human being may "see" God. The heart must be polished as a mirror, so that its perception does not fade away. The hidden is seen by the heart, not by the eye; the heart is directed toward God and orientates man toward the divine; when spiritual perfection is realized, all members of the body may become "hearts." Yazaki enumerates al-Ḥasan al-Baṣrī (d. 728), Rābiʿa al-ʿAdawiyya (d. 801), al-Ḥārith al-Muḥāsibī (d. 857), Nūrī, Sahl al-Tustarī (d. 896), al-Ḥākim al-Tirmīdhī (d. ca. 912) and Ḥallāj (d. 922) as the forerunners of Makkī, remarking that some of them influenced Makkī more than others. She also mentions that Makkī referred to Nūrī only twice in the *Qūt al-qulūb*, clearly placing Nūrī among the Sufis who had less influence on Makkī. However, in connection with Nūrī, Yazaki mentions the *Stations of the Hearts* exclusively (unquestioningly accepting Nūrī's authorship), which might create in the reader the false impression that Makkī indeed quoted the *Stations of the Hearts* in his *Qūt al-qulūb*, which is not the case. Although Makkī's work contain a chapter that details the mystical conception of the heart, and it includes some metaphorical images as well (like the image of the heart as a lamp or as a treasury), neither this section nor the *Qūt al-qulūb* in general shows similarity to the *Stations of the Hearts* attributed to Nūrī.

Tirmīdhī's *Bayān al-farq bayna l-ṣadr wa-l-qalb wa-l-fu'ād wa-l-lubb* explains that the word "heart" *(qalb)* is a general name that designates both the heart in its entirety and its parts that have special functions. These parts are regarded as "stations" *(maqāmāt)* of the heart. The metaphorical image of the heart is compared to the eye, the house, the Holy place (Mecca), the lamp, and the almond: all of them envisaged as concentric spheres. Tirmīdhī designates the parts of the heart as *ṣadr,* the *qalb,* the *fu'ād,* and the *lubb.* Except for the first word, which means "chest," all of these terms are synonymous, with special semantic bearings on which Arabic lexicographers do not agree completely. For example, according to some, *fu'ād* denotes the pericardium, while according to others it designates the very center of the heart. In Tirmīdhī's symbolism, the outermost sphere of the heart, its first station is the chest, which corresponds to the courtyard of a house, where strangers, dangerous and impure things can enter. Similarly, selfish appetites, desires, harmful thoughts, and temptations may easily enter the outermost sphere of the heart. It is also compared to the white of the eye, the territory that surrounds Mecca, the water that the lamp contains, and the gray-green outer hull of the almond. The carnal soul that incites to evil *(al-nafs al-ammāra bi-l-sū')* can enter the chest and therefore control it. It is also the place of *islām* and theoretical learning including law, *ḥadīth,* and religious sciences. The second station, the heart proper *(qalb),* is inside the chest. It is like the house, the black of the eye, Mecca, the part of the lamp that holds the wick, and the almond in its hard shell. It is the mine of the light of faith *(īmān),* humility, piety, love, contentment, certainty, fear, hope, and patience. It is the place of the principles of learning, or theoretical science *(uṣūl al-ʿilm),* for it is like the spring of the water that fills the pool of the chest. The heart pours forth certainty, learning *(ʿilm),* and intention to the chest since the heart is the "root" *(aṣl),* the principal source, while the chest is "branch" *(farʿ),* that is, secondary. The soundness of the bodily members depends on the heart, just as the quality of the lamp depends on the light of the burning wick. The third station is the core of the heart *(fu'ād).*[12] It is like the pupil of the eye, the mosque in Mecca, the inner chamber in the house, the wick of the lamp, and the seed of the almond. The core of the heart is the place of inspired knowledge *(maʿrifa),* of inspired thoughts *(khawāṭir),* and vision *(ru'ya).* The fourth station is *lubb,* which means "kernel, pith, choice part, heart, mind, sense, intelligence." Tirmīdhī compares it to the light of the eye or of the lamp, the oil in the seed of the almond. It is the place of the light of *tawḥīd* and the assertion of God's unity. Tirmīdhī affirms that beyond these four stations there are other subtle stations, all of which originate in *tawḥīd.* But he does not dwell on these. The short tractate dedicates a separate chapter to each one of these parts detailing their special functions and introducing new symbols besides those mentioned above. It must be noted that Tirmīdhī does not include *sirr* (inner heart), or *sirr al-sirr* (center of the inner heart) in this structure, although these concepts have primordial importance for other Sufi authors and thinkers, like Qushayrī for example. Although Qushayrī's *Treatise* does not elaborate on the structure of the heart, it does dedicate a subchapter to the inner heart, and his conception of the heart can be reconstructed to some extent from his scattered remarks and the traditions he quotes.[13] Apparently Qushayrī operates with a tripartite division of the heart: (1) the outer heart *(qalb)* is the seat of praiseworthy character traits and of inspired knowledge *(maʿrifa)*;

(2) the inner heart *(sirr)* is a more subtle part of the heart—the seat of witnessing God. Both the outer and the inner heart are accessible to man; (3) the center of the inner heart is a "secret" for man because he has no access to it. It is divine in nature, and so human acts cannot corrupt it. In any case, the early Sufi manuals constantly use both the term *sirr* and *sirr al-sirr,* therefore the absence of these terms from Tirmīdhī's essay is striking.

Style and Content of the Tractate

The *Stations of the Hearts,* attributed to Nūrī, shows marked similarity to Tirmīdhī's concept of the heart. The tractate may be divided in two main parts according to genre: a mostly theoretic introduction, and subsequent chapters that are mainly symbolic and rife with poetic and metaphoric images. The first part does not employ poetic images at all. It serves as a kind of introduction expounding upon the four names of the heart that correspond to the four parts, or receptacles, within the heart proper. Each receptacle represents an increasingly elevated spiritual station to which the heart rises; therefore on the one hand these parts can be conceptualized as stations on the mystical path the heart traverses and, on the other hand, as concentric circles containing and presupposing each other. The four names of the heart are taken from the Quran. The tractate cites Quranic passages in order to justify the mystical function attributed to each station of the heart, preferably passages in which the name of the station and the function attributed to it occur together (chest: *islām;* heart: faith), or other passages in which instead of the specific function, a quality related to it is mentioned (core of the heart: does not lie; sense: understands the signs). The enumeration of the parts proceeds from the outermost part *(ṣadr,* meaning "chest") to the innermost *(lubb,* that is, "kernel, sense"). Each part is the mine *(miʿdan),* or receptacle *(wiʿāʾ)* of a spiritual quality, some of which are usually regarded as stations in Sufi literature *(tawḥīd, maʿrifa),* and some of which are not normally enlisted among the mystical stations *(islām, īmān).* However, the author also explains that the outer qualities presuppose the inner ones; consequently, the existence of the outermost and most manifest quality depends on the existence of the innermost and most hidden quality. Considering this, it appears that the subsequent stations of the heart do not only develop from the outer toward the inner but vice versa as well, which teaches us that these spiritual qualities are completely interdependent. The author briefly explains the practical aspects of each quality: its actual meaning, the kind of spiritual practices it requires, the way it can be achieved. In the course of this exposition, besides the four terms denoting the stations or parts of the heart, the author uses also the terms *sirr* (inner heart) and *ḍamīr* (heart, innermost self) repeatedly, but he does not combine all of these terms into one coherent structure. Apparently he does not aim at constructing a new, all-comprehensive structure but merely to offer a different approach to the conception of the heart, which is not meant to invalidate or override other approaches.

The introduction of the treatise is followed by twenty short chapters. Some of these chapters contain poetical images that depict intellectual concepts symbolically elaborating on relatively simple mental pictures (the house, the garden, the fortress, the meadow, the sea, the tree), which, however, usually cannot be visualized as actual, realistic images. What I mean by this is that the images combine real (material) and abstract elements. Abstractions act like physical beings: for example, the heart grazes (as a sheep) in different kinds of meadows, etc. This and similar figures of speech are characteristic of the Arab poetical language. Some of the images recur and are further elaborated on (the house, the tree, the garden), but again, the images are not wholly consistent; for example, the two parables describing the believer's heart as a house (chapters I and XVI) seem to be parallel rather than complementary to each other, although the latter interpretation is also feasible. Note that some of the images relate to the heart of the "believer," while others relate to that of the "knower," which might justify the duplication of certain images: for example, the tree of knowledge in the heart of the believer (chapter XVII) and the same in the heart of the knower (chapter XIV). However, even this distinction is inconsistent. The chapter heading may refer to the "believer," while the text may relate to the "knower" (see, for example, chapter IX); or the object of the description may be the "believing knower," conflating the two categories (see, for example, chapters X and XV).

On the other hand, the literal style of the treatise is consistent: almost all of the chapters are constructed as enumerations, based mostly on the numbers seven and three (seven fortresses, seven branches of the tree of knowledge, seven acts of God toward the heart, seven futile passions; three meadows, three lights, three signs of the heart, etc.). The usual pattern of a chapter starts with a statement including a number: "there are three lights"; "there are four fires"; "there are ten gardens"; "it is like a tree that has seven branches"; "the knower must traverse three seas"; "the knower's heart grazes three meadows"; "God made seven fortresses"; "it involves seven things." That is followed by the specification of the general notion or idea mentioned, always in the form of enumeration ("the first kind is"; "the second kind is," etc.) After that, the author returns to the first item and expounds upon it, then continues with the second item and details it, and so on. The tractate does not have a formal conclusion; it simply ends with a poetic image about the two kinds of rain affecting the hearts of God's friends and enemies.

Chapter VIII of the treatise deserves special attention, for it has been suggested that it was a source of inspiration for Saint Teresa de Ávila's Interior Castle, which is probably the most famous symbol of Spanish medieval mysticism. As is well known, Saint Teresa in her *Moradas del castillo interior* (written in 1577) envisaged the soul as a castle composed of seven concentric dwellings *(moradas)*, which are themselves also castles. The walls of the seven concentric castles are made of crystal, and they serve as protection from the devil, who tries to penetrate these walls. The castles or dwellings symbolize stages of the mystical quest, until the soul reaches the innermost castle where it joins God and dwells together with Him. According to the proposition of Lúce López-Baralt (which has been accepted as convincing, for example, by Annemarie Schimmel as well),[14] Nūrī's allegorical interpretation of the heart inspired Saint Teresa's famous symbol, although somewhat indirectly.[15] As López-Baralt explains, already Miguel Asín Palacios had detected a Sufi mystical precedent in Saint Teresa's concept, which he found in the *Nawādir* attributed to Aḥmad al-Qalyūbī (d. 1659), which was actually redacted toward the end of the sixteenth century.[16] That source is, consequently, most probably later than Saint Teresa's vision. However, López-Baralt calls attention to the fact that this passage of the *Nawādir* has a parallel in the *Stations of the Hearts,* which undoubtedly predates Saint Teresa. In fact, the two passages resemble each other, but they are far from identical. Both short passages describe the soul as composed of seven concentric fortresses (or castles, in Asín Palacios's translation). The Satan is hanging around the outermost wall of the fortresses as a dog seeking to slip inside. If the believer neglects the walls, the Satan enters. In both traditions the seven walls are made of seven different materials. In the *Nawādir,* which enumerates the walls from outside to inside, these are pearl, emerald, porcelain, rock, iron, silver, and gold—the sequence of the materials does not seem to reflect a logical arrangement based on their value or other quality. Conversely, in the *Stations of the Hearts* the description of the walls proceeds from the innermost fortress, which is made of the most valuable material, toward the outermost and less valuable wall (the sequence is sapphire, gold, silver, iron, copper, brass, and mud). The spiritual qualities the materials represent are similar (but not identical) in both passages. On the basis of this textual evidence, López-Baralt concludes that the image is probably a "metaphoric motif recurrent in Islamic thought and writing" having "a long literary tradition" and "replaying itself across the centuries."[17] Accordingly, she does not argue that Nūrī's treatise would have been the immediate source of Saint Teresa's complex system of the seven castles or dwellings, but that the symbol of the seven concentric castles as representing the soul was taken from Muslim tradition, which indeed might be reasonable to suppose.

Stations of the Hearts

In the name of the merciful and the compassionate God!

May God be praised, the Master of the universe, and may His peace be with His chosen servants!

May He bless our lord, Muḥammad, his family and companions, all of them!

The sheik Abū l-Ḥasan al-Nūrī said:

The stations of the hearts are four, since God gave the heart four names: He denominated it as chest (*ṣadr*), heart (*qalb*), core of the heart (*fu'ād*) and sense (*lubb*). The chest is the mine of surrender [to God] (*islām*), as God said: "Whose chest God opened for surrender [to Him]" [Quran 39:22]. The heart is the mine of faith (*īmān*), as God said: "But God endeared to you faith, and He made it desired in your heart" [Quran 49:7]. The core of the heart is the mine of inspired knowledge (*maʿrifa*), as God said: "The core of his heart did not lie about what he saw" [Quran 53:11]. Sense is the mine of asserting God's unity (*tawḥīd*), as God said: "They are indeed signs for those who have sense." [Quran 3:190]

Therefore, the sense is the receptacle of God's unity, the core of the heart is the receptacle of inspired knowledge, the heart is the receptacle of faith, and the chest is the receptacle of surrender [to God]. For asserting God's unity means to deem the Real ungraspable; inspired knowledge means to acknowledge the Real with regard to His sublime attributes and most beautiful names; faith means to fasten the heart through rejecting everything that frenzies the hearts, either harmful or useful, except God; and surrender to God means to commit everything to God both in a hidden and in an overt way. These lights are present in the inner hearts (*asrār*) of the those who assert the unity of God (*muwaḥḥidūn*).

Inspired knowledge is not correct without asserting God's unity, faith is not correct without inspired knowledge, and surrender to God is not correct without faith. Therefore, those who do not acknowledge the unity of God do not have inspired knowledge at all. He who has no inspired knowledge has no faith at all. And he who has no faith does not surrender to God at all. Acts, practices, and morals are of no use to those who do not surrender to God. The light of surrender to God is through remembering the consequences (*ʿawāqib*), and the light of faith is through attentiveness to the calamities. The light of inspired knowledge is through remembering the antecedents (*sawābiq*), and the light of acknowledging God's unity is through unveiling (*kashf*) the true realities. Remembering the consequences necessitates dominating the soul (*siyāsat al-nafs*), while attentiveness to the calamities necessitates training the soul (*riyāḍat al-nafs*). Remembering the antecedents necessitates safeguarding the heart (*ḥirāsat al-qalb*). Witnessing the true realities necessitates respecting [divine] rights and [human] duties (*riʿāyat al-ḥuqūq*).[18] The servant of God attains to the confirmation of his belief (*taṣdīq*) through dominating [the soul]; [he attains to] realization (*taḥqīq*) through safeguarding [the heart]; to divine assistance (*tawfīq*) through training [the soul], and to the Real [God] through respecting [divine] rights and [human] duties. Domination means to preserve the soul and its inspired knowledge; training means to discipline and to control the soul; safeguarding means to reflect upon the benevolence of God in the innermost self (*ḍamīr*); and respecting rights and obligations means to comply with the laws of the Lord in the inner heart (*sirr*). For observance necessitates fulfilling the obligations; safeguarding necessitates keeping the law; training necessitates contentment with what is available (*riḍā bi-l-mawjūd*); domination necessitates renouncing what is lacking (*ṣabr ʿan al-mafqūd*).

These qualities are those that God entrusted to his servants regarding servanthood secretly and expressly, in both a hidden and in an overt way.

I. Description of the Believer's Heart as a House

Know that God created a house inside the believer, which is called "heart" (*qalb*). Then He sent a breeze from His generosity (*karam*) that purified this house from polytheism (*shirk*), doubt, hypocrisy, and discord. Then He dispatched clouds from his gracefulness and showered this house with rain, causing all kinds of plants to sprout around it, like certainty, trust, sincerity, fear, hope, and love. Then He placed in the foremost part of this house a couch (*sarīr*) made of God's unity, and He spread (*basaṭa*) on the couch a sheet (*bisāṭ*) made of contentment. Then

He planted the tree of inspired knowledge in front of the house. Its roots are in the heart of the believer, and its branches are in the heaven,[19] under the Throne. On the left and on the right of the couch He made a resting place from His laws, and He opened a door leading from it to the garden of His mercy. And he planted in it, as aromatic plants, glorification, praise, exaltation, and recollection. Then He poured water from the sea of guidance to the river of grace (*faḍl*) so that it may irrigate this garden. Then He hung a lamp from the lamps of his grace, from the door of the most Elevated, and He lit it with the oil of purity, and its light shined with the radiance of piety. Then He locked the door of the house in order to hold back the evil. Then He [himself] took the key of the house, and He did not entrust it to any of his creatures, neither to Gabriel, nor to Mikael, nor to Israfel. Then the Lord said: That is my safe place upon my earth; this is the mine of my perception (*naẓar*) and the dwelling place of my unity (*tawḥīd*)! I [myself] dwell in this shelter! What a perfect dweller and what a perfect dwelling place!

II. God's Gentleness toward the Heart of the Believer until It Got to Know Him

Know that besides the heart of the believer, God created seven [other] things, until the heart got to know Him (*ʿarafahu*).[20] First, its tenderness (*līn*) so that it may be led, as He said: "Their skins and their hearts become tender to God's recollection" (Quran 39:23). Then, after tenderness, broadening (*tawassuʿ*), as He said: "Whose chest God opened for surrender [to Him] is enlightened" (Quran 39:22). That is, whose chest God broadened until it could accommodate the knowledge (*maʿrifa*), which heaven, the earth, and the mountains were unable to bear.[21] Then, after these, healing from illness (*shifāʾ min al-maraḍ*), as He said: "[God] will heal the chests of those who believe" (Quran 9:14). Then, guidance (*hidāya*), as He said: "But God endeared to you faith, and He made it desired in your heart" (Quran 49:7). Then, calmness (*sakīna*) and reassurance (*ṭuma'nīna*), so that it may be reassured with Him and may not rely on (*yaskun ilā*) other than Him, as He said: "It is he who sent down calmness (*sakīna*) to the hearts of the believers" (Quran 48:4). Finally, enlightening (*tanwīr*), as He said: "God guides to his light whom he wants" (Quran 24:35).

III. God's Dealing with the Hearts of His Enemies Until They Ignored Him

It involves seven things. First, constraint, so that their hearts cannot accommodate knowledge and cannot assert the unity of God, as He said: "He constrains and tightens the chests of those whom He wants to lead astray" (Quran 6:125). Then He hardened them so that they may not yield tenderly to the words of the prophets, God's friends (*awliyā'*) and the learned ones (*ʿulamā'*), as He said: "After that, your hearts rigidified" (Quran 2:74). Then He blackened them, as He said: "Nay! But their hearts were stained by what they earned" (Quran 83:14). Then He put darkness in their hearts, as He said: "They said: Our hearts are covered" (Quran 2:88). Then He sealed them, so that it may not be opened, as He said: "God sealed their hearts" (Quran 2:7). Then He locked them, as He said: "There are locks on the hearts" (Quran 47:24). Then, after all these, He denied them His inspired knowledge (maʿrifa), as He said: "Those who do not believe in the hereafter, their hearts refuse to know" (Quran 16:22). For this reason they refuse to acknowledge His unity, His lordship, and to remember His messengers, His promise, and His threats.

IV. The Three Kinds of Heart

The first kind is the heart of the disobedient, which is destruction and the realm of the Satans, in which there is uncleanliness and defilement. The second kind is the heart of the obedient, which is the home of the people of sincere learning and practice (*al-ʿālimīn ʿwa-l-āmilīn al-mukhliṣīn*), in which He gathered things and set custodians over them in order to guard them. The third is the heart of the knower, which is like the treasury of the kings in which there are jewels, pearls, and sapphires, and the king [himself] guards, protects, and watches over it, and He is the only king that looks at it.

V. Description of the Knowers' Hearts

Verily, God has gardens on the face of the earth. He who smelled their fragrance is not longing after the Paradise—these are the hearts of the knowers.

VI. Description of the Sound Heart

He indicates with his heart from its lower part to faithfulness (*wafā'*), from its upper part to contentment (*riḍā'*), from its right to donations (*ʿaṭā'*), from its left to destiny (*manan*), from its frontal part to encounter (*liqā'*), and from its rear part to subsistence (*baqā'*).[22]

He said,[23] it has four stations (*manzila*): first, the safeness of the heat from doubt (*shakk*); second, the safeness of the heart from deceptive passion (*al-hawā l-muḍill*); third, the safeness of the heart from hypocrisy (*riyā'*) and conceit (*ʿujb*); and fourth, the safeness of the heart from recollecting (*dhikr*) anything except God.

The most accomplished Sufi, Shāh Shujāʿ al-Dīn al-Kirmānī, said: "Three signs of the safeness of the heart are putting trust in everyone, seeing people's goodness, and founding excuses to everybody."

VII. Description of the Beloved Ones' Hearts[24]

God said to Moses: bare your heart to my love (*ḥubb*), for I made your heart the domain of my love. I spread out in your heart a land of knowing Me (*maʿrifa*); I built in your heart a house of faith in Me (*īmān*); I set in your heart a sun of longing after Me (*shawq*); I raised in your heart a moon of My love (*maḥabba*); I made come up in your heart stars of my inspirations (*mawārid*); I made in your heart clouds of reflection on Me (*tafakkur*); I made a breeze of My assistance blow in your heart (*tawfīq*); I showered in your heart a rain of my preference [for you] (*tafḍīl*); I planted in your heart a plantation of my trustworthiness (*ṣidq*); I grew in your heart a tree of obedience to Me, and I made sprout it leaves of My faithfulness (*wafā'*); I made it bear fruits of wisdom from intimate conversation with Me (*munājāt*); I made rivers in your heart flow—rivers of the subtleties of the knowledge (*ʿulūm*) of My eternity; and I placed in your heart love originating from My certainty.

VIII. The Fortresses of the Believer's Heart

Know that God made in the believers' heart seven fortresses (*ḥuṣūn*), each one having seven walls surrounding them. He ordered the believers to enter these fortresses, and He shut out the Satan from all of the fortresses. Therefore, the Satan yells and howls at them like a dog beyond [the walls of] the fortresses.

The walls of the first fortress are made of sapphire, which is the inspired knowledge of God (*maʿrifat Allāh*). It is surrounded by a fortress made of gold, which is trust in God (*īmān*). It is surrounded by a fortress made of silver, which is sincerity (*ikhlāṣ*) in speech and acts. It is surrounded by a fortress made of iron, which is contentment (*riḍā'*) with God's decree. It is surrounded by a fortress made of copper, which is performing the religious duties imposed by God (*al-qiyām bi-farā'iḍ Allāh*). It is surrounded by a fortress made of brass, which is complying with God's commands and prohibitions (*al-qiyām bi-amr Allāh wa-nahyihi*). It is surrounded by a fortress made of mud, which is disciplining the carnal soul (*al-qiyām bi-adab al-nafs*) regarding all its acts, in accordance with God's saying: "Over my servants you do not have authority" (Quran 15:42). For the believer is inside these fortresses, in the fortress of sapphire.

The Satan cannot penetrate the fortresses as long as the servant disciplines his carnal soul. But when he belittles the fortresses and says, "They are not necessary," the Satan seizes from him the fortress made of mud and covets another. And when he fails to comply with any of God's commands and prohibitions, the Satan seizes from him the fortress made of brass and covets the third one. When he falls short of contentment with God's decree, the Satan seizes the fortress made of copper and covets the fourth one, and so on.

IX. The Fires in the Heart of the Believer

There are four fires in the heart of the knower: the fire of fear (*khawf*), the fire of love (*maḥabba*), the fire of knowledge (*maʿrifa*), and the fire of longing (*shawq*). The fire of fear consumes the sweetness of disobedience, the fire of love consumes the sweetness of obedience,[25] the fire of knowledge consumes the sweetness of attachments (*ʿalāʾiq*), and the fire of longing consumes the sweetness of happiness (*rawḥ*) so that it arrives [at God] through the contentment of the Beloved.

X. The Meadows of the Believing Knower's Heart

The knower's heart grazes three meadows: the meadow (*rawḍa*) of harshness, the meadow of favors, and the meadow of graces. When it grazes the meadow of harshness, timidity overcomes it; when it grazes the meadow of benefits, hope (*rajāʾ*) fills it; when it grazes the meadow of graces, it acts with faithfulness (*wafāʾ*).

XI. The Lights of the Knower's Heart

There are three lights in his heart: the light of knowledge (*maʿrifa*), the light of intelligence (*ʿaql*), and the light of learning (*ʿilm*). Knowledge is like the sun, intelligence is like the moon, and learning is like the stars. The light of knowledge veils passion (*hawā*); the light of intelligence veils sensual desires (*shahwa*); and the light of learning veils ignorance (*jahl*). By the light of knowledge he sees the Lord. By the light of intelligence he accepts the Real. And by the light of learning he acts according to the Real (*bi-l-ḥaqq*).

XII. The First Thing That Appears in the Heart of the Knower

A light is the first thing that appears in the heart of a person whose felicity God wants. Then this light becomes a flash and then a ray—then a moon and a sun. When the light manifests itself in the heart, the world and everything it contains grows cold in his heart. And when it becomes a moon, he abstains from (*zahada fī*) the world to come and from everything it contains. And when it becomes a sun, he does not see either this world or the other, and he does not recognize anything except his Lord. For his body is [from] light, his heart is [from] light, and his speech is [from] light, "light upon light, God guides to his light whom he wants" (Quran 24:35).

XIII. The Seas of the Knower's Heart

The knower must traverse three seas in order to arrive at the majesty of his Lord: the sea of lordship (*rubūbiyya*), the sea of divine hegemony (*muhaymaniyya*), and the sea of godship (*lāhūtiyya*). When he plunges into the sea of lordship he shall recognize that God is the Lord, and that man is dominated. So his heart shall plunge in the sea of meditation (*fikr*), his tongue in recollection (*dhikr*) of His favors, his eye in beholding His graces, his soul in service [of God] (*khidma*), and in striving for the contentment [of God]. He must make obedience a sea, and service [of God] a boat, and meditation on the graces its sails, and recollection of the favors the wind with which it sails, and beholding the graces the boat's pilot who steers it. The wind of benevolence directs the boat, and it sails until the knower reaches the sea of supremacy. But there will be no boat there. So he must make a bridge from longing (*shawq*), love, and repentance (*ināba*), and he shall traverse it in order to reach the sea of godship. And when he reaches that sea, there will be no boat, nor bridge. He must resign himself [to the will of God] and throw himself into the sea so that the wind of affection and the waves of generosity shall cast him upon the shore. There he will get to know (*yaʿrif*)[26] the majesty of the Lord. Then, when he gets to know His majesty and splendour, his heart will be adorned with four things: the lamp of knowledge in its center; [self] revelation (*tajallin*) of majesty on the right, splendor in front, and might behind. So, when the servant looks by the light of knowledge, by the way of meditation, he is shown awe and fright through [God's] knowledge; and when he looks forward, he is shown dread and dismay through [God's] splendor; and when he looks behind, he is shown humility and humbleness through [God's] might.[27] He will know his heart through the graces of God, and he will impose fear as a nature on his tongue so that it shall not speak except about Him; and he will impose awe on his eyes so that they shall not look except at Him; and he will impose fright as shackles on his hands so that they shall not take except from Him; and he will impose dread as fetter on his legs so that they shall not walk except to Him. Then the veils of the heavens will be lifted, and the angles will take him.

XIV. The Tree of Knowledge in the Heart of the Knower

At first, the rain of generosity showers on his heart, and then the tree of knowledge grows in his heart. The tree shoots forth five branches: the first reaches to the Throne, the second to the East, the third to the West, the fourth to the right horizon, the fifth to the left horizon. The branch that reaches to the Throne is watered by felicity, and its fruit is intimate conversation [with God] (*munājāt*). That which reaches to the East is watered by generosity, and its fruit is the fruit of service [of God]. That which reaches to the West is watered by mercy, and its fruit is the fruit of learning and admonition (*ʿibra*); and under admonition, meditation and obedience is to be found.[28] That which reaches to the right horizon is watered by love, and its fruit is the fruit of recollection. That which reaches to the left horizon is watered by repentance (*ināba*), and its fruit is the fruit of vision originating from Him.

XV. The Tongue of the Knower's Heart, Its Sayings, Signs and [the Believer] Listening [to It]

There are three signs of the believing knower's heart: it veils acts of disobedience with the veil of repentance; it veils good deeds with the veil of recollection; and it veils all things with the veil of loving God, until no existing phenomenon remains in his heart except love for his Lord. Its sayings concern guarding the carnal soul and recollecting God's favors and graces. It speaks with inspired knowledge by means of four things: the tongue of praise, the tongue of gratefulness, the tongue of complaint, and the tongue of [asking for] forgiveness (*maʿdhira*). The tongue of praise is between him and God's graces. The tongue of gratefulness is between him and God's creatures, by which he expresses his gratitude to God before His creatures. With the tongue of complaint he complains of his self (*nafs*) to his Lord. With the tongue of asking forgiveness he asks his Lord to forgive his sins. The knower listens to three things: to revelation (*tanzīl*), to exegesis (*tafsīr*), and to [mystical] interpretation (*ta'wīl*).[29] When he hears the revelation, he believes in it; when he hears the exegesis, he acts according to it; when he hears the [mystical] interpretation, he turns to the learned ones [concerning] its learning.[30]

XVI. Parable of the Believer's Heart and Its Dweller

It is similar to a house that has two doors: a door that leads to this world, and a door that leads to the word to come. The door of this world is admonition (*ʿibra*), and the door of the world to come is meditation (*fikra*). There is a throne (*sarīr*) in this house that has four legs:[31] the majesty of reverence,[32] the humility of obedience,[33] forsaking disobedience, and fearing from the end. There is a king on the throne, who has two viziers. The king is certainty, the vizier on his right is fear, and the vizier on his left is hope. Twelve chiefs are standing before the throne, on the right side: first, attesting [the Islamic creed] (*shahāda*), which is the adornment of Islam; second, prayer, which is the pillar of Islam; third, almsgiving, which is the purity of Islam; fourth, fasting, which is the perfection of Islam; fifth, pilgrimage, which is the cornerstone of Islam; sixth, custom (*ʿurf*), which is the force of Islam; seventh, commanding what is proper (*amr bi-l-maʿarūf*), which is the protection of Islam; eighth, forbidding what is improper (*nahy ʿan il-munkar*), which is the proof of Islam; ninth, the Muslim community (*jamāʿa*), which is the ornament of Islam; tenth, charity (*ṣadaqa*), which is the essence of Islam; eleventh, maintaining family ties (*ṣilat al-raḥim*), which is the compassion of Islam; twelfth, the goodness of the end (*ḥusn al-khātima*),[34] which is the preservation of Islam.

XVII. Parable of the Tree of Knowledge in the Heart of the Believer

[Inspired] knowledge in the heart of the believer is like a tree that has seven branches: the first branch is toward the eyes of the believer; the second is toward his tongue; the third is toward his heart; the fourth is toward his carnal soul; the fifth is toward the creatures of his Lord; the sixth is toward the world to come; the seventh is toward his Lord. Each branch bears two fruits: the fruits of the branch toward the eyes are weeping and tears; the fruits of the branch toward the tongue are learning (*ʿilm*) and wisdom; the fruits of the branch toward the heart are longing (*shawq*) and repentance (*ināba*); the fruits of the branch toward the carnal soul are abstention (*zuhd*) and worship (*ʿibāda*); the fruits of the branch towards the creatures are faithfulness (*wafā'*) and reliability (*amāna*); the fruits of the branch toward the world to come are God's grace and Paradise; the fruits of the branch toward the Lord are vision [of God] (*ru'ya*) and closeness [to God].

XVIII. Parable of the Tree of Futile Passion

Passion (*hawā*) in the heart of man is like a tree that has seven branches: the first is toward his eyes; the second is toward his tongue; the third is toward his heart; the fourth is toward his carnal soul; the fifth is toward the creatures; the sixth is toward the world; the seventh is toward the world to come. The fruits of the branch toward the eyes are greed and sensual desire; the [fruits] of [the branch] toward the tongue are prying and slandering; the [fruits] of [the branch] toward the heart are hatred and animosity; the [fruits] of [the branch] toward the carnal soul are the legally prohibited and suspicious things; the [fruits] of [the branch] toward the creatures are ruse and deceit; the [fruits] of [the branch] toward the world are embellishment[35] and simulation; the [fruits] of [the branch] toward the world to come are grief and regret.

XIX. Description of the Gardens of the Knower's Heart

There are ten gardens in the heart of the knower: the first is the garden of affirming God's unity; the second is the garden of the path (*sabīl*)[36]; the third is the garden of certainty; the fourth is the garden of humility; the fifth is the garden of lawfulness; the sixth is the garden of forbearance; the seventh is the garden of open-handedness; the eight is the garden of contentment; the ninth is the garden of sincerity; and the tenth is the garden of learning (*ʿilm*). The believer roams about in the gardens and takes care of them. If he finds the thorn of polytheism and hypocrisy (*nifāq*) in the garden of God's unity he tears it out and throws it away. If he finds futile passion (*hawā*) and heretical innovation (*bidaʿ*) in the garden of the path, he uproots it. If he finds doubt (*shakk*) and hesitation (*ẓann*) in the garden of certainty he uproots it. If he finds conceit and haughtiness in the garden of humility he uproots it. If he finds something legally prohibited and suspicious in the garden of lawfulness he uproots it. If he finds hatred and coercion in the garden of forbearance he uproots it. If he finds avarice and niggardliness in the garden of open-handedness he uproots it. If he finds simulation (*riyā'*) and pretence (*samʿa*) in the garden of sincerity he uproots it. If he finds anxiety and complaint in the garden of contentment he uproots it. And if he finds ignorance and negligence in the garden of learning he uproots it.

XX. The Rains of the Hearts of God's Friends and Enemies

Rain is of two kinds: the rain of mercy and the rain of vengeance. The rain of mercy is a sign of felicity, and the rain of vengeance is a sign of misery. Shortage of rain of mercy may be due to three things: first, the heart's mingling with simulation (*riyā'*); second, the intelligence's mingling with pretentiousness (*daʿwā*); third, the innermost self's (*ḍamīr*) mingling with hypocrisy (*nifāq*). The rain of vengeance may shower on the heart due to three things: first, eating what is prohibited; second, forsaking what is permitted; third, evil inclinations.

The rain of mercy consists of four things: the thunder of awe, the lightning of longing, the showers of generosity, and the breeze of happiness (*rīḥ al-rawḥ*). The thunder of awe crashes in the heart of the repentant (*tā'ib*); the lightning of longing flashes in the heart of the abstinent (*zāhid*); the showers of generosity are pouring in the heart of the beloved (*muḥibb*); and the breeze of happiness blows in the heart of the knower (ʿārif).

The rain of vengeance consists of four things: the thunder of separation; the lightning of hatred, the rainfall of animosity, and the wind of veiling. The thunder of separation is in the heart of the infidel (*kāfir*); the lightning of hatred is in the heart of the hypocrite (*munāfiq*); the rainfall of animosity is in the heart of the unjust (*ẓālim*); and the wind of veiling is in the heart of the disobedient (*ʿāṣin*).

CHAPTER 11

Conclusions

How Ecstatic Is an Ecstatic Mystic in Fact?

To what extent has our picture of Nūrī—and in general, our understanding of ecstatic mysticism—been modified in the light of the texts studied? Does the usual conception of an ecstatic mystic as an eccentric—or even lunatic—figure hold true with regard to Nūrī?

Without indulging in statistics and overestimating their value by supposing that quantity has more to say about a phenomenon than its quality, a survey of the proportion of moderate versus ecstatic traditions related to Nūrī may be instructive. Although no clear line of distinction can always be traced between sober and drunken manifestations of spirituality, the predominant nature of a certain expression or act may be perceived, however. Considering the five earliest collections that this study has analyzed in great detail, the overall proportion of traditions of mainly moderate nature in contrast with those of mostly ecstatic character is three to one. The greatest proportion of traditions connected to the drunken aspect of Nūrī's character is recorded in the *Ornament of God's Friends* (about 40 percent) and in the *Book of Flashes* (almost 30 percent), while lesser proportions can be found in Sulamī's *Generations of the Sufis* (about 10 percent), his *Realities of Interpretation* (3 percent), and Kharkūshī's *Revision of the Secrets* (about 5 percent).[1] These include his *shaṭaḥāt* (ecstatic utterances), passionate love poems, highly uncommon forms of behavior, references to ecstasy *(wajd),* and mystical concerts or recitals *(samāʿ)* inducing ecstasy. It is interesting to note that even the same event may be narrated as connected to ecstatic behavior by one author while positioned as perfectly moderate by another. The Ghulām Khalīl episode has no scandalous, ecstatic bearing whatsoever in the narration of Kharkūshī or Qushayrī, while it is formulated as an apologia of drunken mysticism in Sarrāj's narrative. Such inconsistencies can be explained by the general aim each author sought to achieve with his respective compilation.

Evidently, ecstatic behavior constituted only one aspect of the complex spirituality of those mystics who, much like Nūrī, were regarded as "ecstatics" (*arbāb al-mawājīd,* to use Junayd's expression)[2] even by their contemporaries. Considering the sources, however, the question arises whether in fact unconscious rapture was the paramount facet of their mystical devotion. Clearly it was a distinctive feature, but as has been shown in the case of Nūrī, it was complemented, probably even overridden, by serene and self-possessed forms of attitude: finding expression both in theoretical and practical terms. Most of the traditions related to Nūrī do not differ in any way from statements made by sober mystics. This observation holds true especially with regard to his short sayings akin to definitions, determining the meaning of mystical terms in a concise way. The majority of his utterances are perfectly moderate, and only a limited number of his sayings seem to express raw ecstatic experience, articulating mostly sensations of rapture and love. Such unconscious encounters and extreme manifestations of passionate love are verbalized primarily in his poems, which does not mean, however, that the majority of his poems would be of an ecstatic nature. The most obvious ecstatic manifestations of Nūrī's spirituality are those that were regarded as such by his contemporaries as well, like his state of constant rapture in the mosque while repeating the name of God for days without eating, drinking, or sleeping; or his unconscious straying in the field of reeds until being mortally wounded. These instances are not as prominently represented in the traditions related to Nūrī, which is telling in itself, even if we suppose that most authors deliberately omitted controversial traditions from their compilations.

Narrative Structures

Nūrī's literary legacy is variegated from a formal point of view, as well: several major types of traditions may be distinguished. Lines of division may be traced between texts of oral and written communication; poetry and prose; Nūrī's words *versus* anecdotes or dictions regarding him. The proportion of the diverse genres differs from source to source (see below). Naturally, a certain tradition may pertain to more than one category with different aspects in view. The basic types of traditions are the following:

1. Spontaneous answers to actual questions. Although a considerable portion of the sayings pertains to this category formally, the spontaneity of some sayings is questionable, especially in cases when they employ word plays or other literary devices that presuppose careful meditation on the saying's formulation. An example might be Nūrī's relatively long discourse on the limitations of intellect, which is characterized by high rhetorical quality and innovative phrasing, including the creation of new words.[3] Unless we suppose that both the question and the answer originated in written form (which would not be unusual), it is plausible to suppose that the spontaneity of Nūrī's discourse is a literary convention rather than a fact. Almost half of the traditions introduced by the formula "Nūrī was asked about . . . and he said" are divergent definitions of Sufism. A saying recorded in one source as an answer to an actual question may appear as an independent diction in another.[4] Despite these observations, the genuineness of the question-answer structure as a method of transmitting mystical teaching is beyond question; the introductory formula is a reminiscence of the master-disciple relationship finding expression in dialogues in which the roles of transmitter and receiver never change.

2. Verbal reactions to specific events. This type may be exemplified by Nūrī's meeting with a disciple of a fellow Sufi, Abū l-Ḥamza,[5] or Nūrī's reaction to Junayd's request of talking to him and his disciples.[6] Again, the context of the sayings may be fictional, and the same saying may appear embedded into slightly different narratives or without the narrative context at all.[7] Sometimes the reaction takes poetic form; for example, when returning

from Mecca, Nūrī met a group of Sufis who inquired about his state.[8] Once more, the poem may be quoted in another source without the narrative context.[9]

3. Short sentential sayings recorded without any context. The majority of the traditions pertain to this category. The sayings frequently employ literary devices like *jinās* (repetition of similar sequences of sounds) or inner rhymes, and in general, they are very compact (the shortest saying consists of merely two words).[10]

4. Longer discourses recorded without any context or with a minimal introduction, like Nūrī's advice *(waṣāyā)* to his companions.[11]

5. Poems recorded without any context.

6. Anecdotes about Nūrī's behavior, customs, or actions. The anecdotes may cite Nūrī's words, but in these cases, they are not intended to convey mystical knowledge. Examples may be Nūrī's long dialogue with his maidservant, or his oaths either when requesting God to perform an idle miracle, or when refusing to avail himself of another.

7. Ecstatic utterances, or *shaṭaḥāt,* regarded as blasphemous by the uninitiated. These utterances are usually embedded in a narrative context that asserts explicitly their controversial nature. When called to account, Nūrī explains the hidden meaning of his words.

8. Comments on the Quran and the Prophet's sayings.

9. Letters. Besides both the poetic and the prosaic letters mentioned in the early Sufi manuals (exchange of letters with Abū l-Ḥasan al-Qannād and especially with Junayd),[12] the letter of Nūrī and Junayd's answer preserved in the Cairo Genizah pertain to this category.

10. Finally, the only long discursive text attributed to Nūrī may be mentioned, the *Stations of the Hearts,* the authorship of which is highly questionable.

Nūrī's Portrayal in the Different Sources: Themes, Genres, and Purposes

This study surveyed the mystical legacy of Nūrī and examined the spirituality attributed to him by different Sufi authors. It seems to be appropriate to recapitulate briefly his portrayal in the various compilations, conditioned to a large extent by the main purpose of each source. Both the main themes of the traditions and their literary genre show considerable variation from source to source.

Kalābādhī gives an account of the ecstatic and intoxicated tendencies of Nūrī's mysticism but stresses that such behavior does not lead him to antinomian acts. While most of the traditions Kalābādhī quotes are "sober," he also depicts Nūrī as an enraptured lover of God refusing and condemning rational discourse with the people about God. According to Nūrī, man's intellectual faculty is incapable of encompassing the divine, and certainty about God can be obtained only by means of contemplation. Contemplation is not an intellectual process but rather witnessing God through being present with Him. God's presence can be witnessed by drawing close to Him, which entails the annihilation of the mystic's self. The mystic's presence with God is commensurate with his absence both from the world and from himself. Presence, contemplation, annihilation, and absence are key terms that recur in Nūrī's thoughts, primarily in his poems. The mystic's endeavor of getting into God's closeness may mislead him; his efforts may in fact confirm his self instead of obliterating it. The disillusionment the mystic suffers in such cases is devastating, and the distance separating him from God may appear unsurmountable. Separation from God, however, is followed by reunion with Him; the mystic in the course of his spiritual quest experiences states of intoxicated ecstasy induced by immoderate love, and when both his strain and his ecstasy disappears, he finally encounters God. The poetical vein of Nūrī appears to be especially rich in Kalābādhī's portrayal: ten out of the twenty-one traditions attributed to him are poems, most of them addressing God directly in an intimately passionate tone.

Sarrāj represents Nūrī as an imperfect mystic unable to control his ecstasy, uttering apparently blasphemous sayings that scandalize the believers. His love of God induces a clear feeling of intimacy that he does not hide from the people: he speaks overtly about his passionate love for God and also about God's passionate love for him; he discloses their intimate relation saying that he was "at home with God"; and he describes love as "tearing the veils and uncovering the secrets." He curses the muezzin calling to prayer but answers with an expression of utmost humility to a dog's barking. His personality has certain defects: he blackmails God and demands Him to perform an otherwise senseless miracle, with the sole purpose of demonstrating God's favorable disposition toward him. Could this be considered as a hysterical manifestation of love? The harsh reaction of the religious authorities was to be expected: Nūrī is detained, and an investigation is conducted against him. Finally, he is exempted and the true nature of his acts and utterances is revealed. His death is caused by uncontrolled ecstasy provoked by a love poem, and thus he ends up as a martyr of love. Again, the lyrical facet of Nūrī's personality is marked; the traditions associated with him include seven poems (taking into account the poem that caused the uncontrollable ecstasy leading to his death, although that poem was not composed by him). Nūrī's frenetic behavior and impassioned sayings are counterbalanced by traditions that give expression to a less emotional aspect of his personality. His lengthy exposure on the role of the intellect manifests Nūrī's rhetorical talent and originality with respect to the language: he even creates words spontaneously. Some of his sayings are in fact short, straightforward definitions and answers that lack the deliberate ambiguity characteristic of mystical communication. The most frequent subjects of Nūrī's sayings and poems in Sarrāj's collection are, again, contemplation and love.

Sulamī's portrayal of Nūrī tends to eliminate all traces of nonconformity and irregularity from Nūrī's image. The biographical entry Sulamī composed presents Nūrī almost as a theoretical thinker engaged primarily in formulating definitions and establishing abstract categories. The most frequently occurring terms in the traditions quoted in his name are "looking carefully, studying" and "learning," besides others like "tribulations" and "heart." Subjects like ecstasy, intoxication, self-annihilation, absence, and witnessing are barely treated in the traditions cited. Although Sulamī is a biographer, he omits Nūrī's detention and investigation by the religious authorities; likewise, he passes over Nūrī's extravagant death and does not mention any of his scandalous deeds or utterances. The one and only unconventional incident Sulamī reports is the anecdote about Nūrī "looking" (and making a pass) at a young man, but the inclusion of that episode might be conditioned by the term "looking carefully" that recurs in it, and to its message that criticizes "learning" as opposed to the mystical way of obtaining direct knowledge of God. Almost one third of the traditions related to Nūrī include poems (four out of fifteen), taking into consideration the poem that the abovementioned youngster recited in response to Nūrī's flirting. Two of the poems treat the theme of affliction and pain, while the other two are more abstract and theoretical, dealing with the nature of cognition.

Sulamī's Quran commentary presents a picture of Nūrī very much similar to that of the biographical lexicon. Although there is no overlap whatsoever between the two sources—none of the traditions attributed to Nūrī appears in both—his portrayal in the sources is entirely consistent. In Sulamī's Quran commentary, Nūrī's one and only saying that reveals an ecstatic aspect of his personality are his words praising *samāʿ* (audition ceremony). No poem is transmitted in his name in the commentary, a fact that can be easily explained by the genre of the compilation.

Since the expressed purpose of Kharkūshī's *Revision of the Secrets* is to summarize basic tenets of Sufism excluding controversial aspects, ecstatic utterances, and intoxicated behavior, it is not surprising that his composition offers a unilateral portrayal of Nūrī. The ecstatic facet of his mysticism can be traced only sporadically, in some sayings praising ecstasy and even considering it as the essential feature of Sufism. Most traditions handed down in Nūrī's name, however, deal with theoretical problems like the role of the heart and the inner heart, recollection, absence, and annihilation. His poetic production is well represented by the selection of poems Kharkūshī quotes, most of them addressing God or describing mystical experiences in an intimate tone. The scant biographical details Kharkūshī mentions do not reveal anything of Nūrī's eccentric, enraptured actions or character traits; they are perfectly compatible with orthodox religiosity.

Abū Nuʿaym does not evade unconventional or even eccentric aspects of Nūrī's character and life; he reports the anecdotes about Nūrī blackmailing God, flirting with the young man, and also a less scandalous version of the Ghulām Khalīl incident. These, together with the passionate love poems and sayings about love emphasize the nonconforming aspect of Nūrī's personage. The number of poems among the traditions Abū Nuʿaym collected is quite significant; he quotes eight poems (besides nine traditions of other genres, including both sayings and anecdotes). Some of the poems are markedly emotional, while others are conceptual and intellectual. The latter display great linguistic originality exploiting double meanings, playing on the ambiguity of words, producing puns—especially homographic and homophonic paronomasia. A central topic of the poems is the inner heart and God's secret deposited in it.

The most striking peculiarity of Qushayrī's *Treatise* is that none of Nūrī's poems is quoted in it (even though the compilation contains many poems composed by others). Regarding Nūrī's poems in the other sources, it must be noted that their attribution to Nūrī, in most cases, seems to be uncertain. Some thirty poems are quoted in the sources in Nūrī's name (some are attested to in slightly different versions as well), and two more are associated with him, although they are not attributed to him: the poem, which the young man recited to Nūrī, and the poem that Nūrī kept repeating during his ecstasy (and that finally led to his death). The majority of the poems ascribed to Nūrī, that is, twenty-four out of the thirty are quoted in one of the sources only. Five poems are cited in two different sources and only three in three different compilations. Besides that, two poems (not attributed to Nūrī)[13] that are quoted in anecdotes related to Nūrī are quoted in three different sources. None of the poems associated with Nūrī is quoted in more than three different sources. It can be observed that those poems that have a narrative frame relating them to Nūrī are more likely to appear in various compilations. Supposing that the authorship of Nūrī's poems is more dubious than the authenticity of the sayings, the reason for their omission from the *Treatise* might be Qushayrī's uncertainty about their genuineness. On the other hand, Qushayrī narrates a fair number of stories and anecdotes related to Nūrī, and the common characteristic of these is that unlike his poems and short sayings, they lack ambiguity and can be easily understood even by those not familiar with Sufi notions. Despite that, Qushayrī's portrayal of Nūrī is not simplistic; he does not expose a certain character trait while hiding or denying another. On the contrary, he presents both the moderate and the deviant aspects of Nūrī's life and personality and hands down both conventional and scandalous utterances.

Sīrjānī's compilation is less original than the previous ones; it relies mostly on the material quoted in the former sources. The number of new traditions it quotes is quite limited. It is interesting to note the relatively large number of "frivolous" traditions collected by Sīrjānī in connection with the concept of "looking," which, in Nūrī's case frequently must be understood in its literal (and disapproved) sense.

The Genizah fragment containing the correspondence of Junayd and Nūrī has special importance for two reasons. First of all, it is the longest continuous text attributed to Nūrī preserved in a medieval manuscript, and it is the only extant letter written in prose that is ascribed to him. Moreover, it sheds light on the relationship between Junayd and Nūrī, revealing the confidential nature of their relation. It certainly exposes the inner dynamics of the sober and intoxicated tendencies of Sufism, showing how the representatives of these engaged in communication with each other without questioning the authenticity and the validity of the "opposite" mystical attitude. Even if we do not accept the letters as authentic, they are still informative regarding the period in which the manuscript was copied (according to its paleographic features, sometimes between the eleventh and the thirteenth centuries), and they are relevant to the sober-drunken dichotomy. A mystic considered as ecstatic—in a letter clearly pertaining to the extreme, intoxicated genre—seeks the advice of a moderate companion, who in turn interprets the mystical state of the former without any sign of disapproval or reservation. Whether it is conjecture or fact, in any case it proves that sober and intoxicated forms of mysticism were not rival or incompatible trends.

The attribution of the *Stations of the Hearts* to Nūrī seems dubious, and several factors suggest that it was composed at a later period, probably around the thirteenth century. The manuscripts of the treatise are relatively recent. Despite its literary style, which is similar to Nūrī's sayings collected by the early compilers, no part of the treatise is quoted in any of these compilations; it has, however, parallels in other works that were composed or aspired to popularity in the thirteenth century. The terminology of the treatise is not consistent with that of the other texts attributed to Nūrī, and some of its concepts plainly contradict Nūrī's views exposed in the early collections.

All in all, Nūrī's personality, his teachings, and his literary production show a marked complexity, which might be explained by the disparity of sources and the compilers' varying intentions;

but this complexity may also reflect the inconsistencies and the intricateness of his character. Nūrī's impassioned poems and sayings on the one hand, his observations of theoretical nature on the other—and above all, his strong attachment to Junayd, unaffected by the occasional divergence of their views and behavior: all these evidence that sobriety and intoxication, moderateness, and ecstatic (or otherwise exalted actions) were not mutually exclusive or irreconcilable trends in early Sufism. Moderate acts and utterances might have been equally characteristic of the so-called ecstatic mystics as unconscious or extreme behavior; drunkenness and sobriety were not regarded as permanent conditions but complementary and equally legitimate states of mind. Despite that, the scandalous nature of intoxicated actions was a challenge that Sufism had to face and a problem it had to handle. The compilers of the first Sufi manuals evidently made great efforts to fit such extravagances into the framework of standard religiosity, either explaining and justifying the manifestations of ecstatic disposition or by divesting them of their most controversial peculiarities. A close study of Nūrī's legacy contributes to the better understanding of the early period of Sufism by observing the complexity of the sober-intoxicated polarity, the dynamics of the relationship between Junayd and Nūrī, and its relevance to the nature of the so-called Baghdadi school of mysticism.

APPENDIX A

Arabic Texts

Ch. 1. Kalābādhī's *Doctrine of the Sufis*

(*Kitāb al-taʿarruf li-madhhab ahl al-taṣawwuf*. Ed. Arberry. Cairo: al-Khānajī, 1994)

On Sufism *(nafs*, carnal soul)

ص 9) وسئل أبو الحسن النوري ما التصوف فقال ترك كل حظ للنفس.

On the guide to God *(ʿaql*, intellect)

ص 37) وقال رجل للنوري ما الدليل على الله قال الله قال فما العقل قال العقل عاجز والعاجز لا يدل الا على عاجز مثله.

On Sufism *(maqām*, promulgating a station)

ص 63) سئل النوري عن التصوف فقال نشر مقام واتصال بقوام. قيل له فما أخلاقهم قال ادخال السرور على غيرهم والأعراض عن أذاهم.

Poem on the impossibility of describing mystical states *(ḥāl)* "You discouraged me . . ."

ص 63) أزعجتني عن نعوت الحال بالحال / وكيف ينعت من [ما] لا قال بالقال
ما كل من يدعى حالا تصدقه / حتى يترجم عنه صاحب الحال

On repentance *(tawba)*

ص 64) وقال النوري التوبة أن تتوب من ذكر كل شيء سوى الله جل وعز.

On the poor/Sufi (preferring others, *īthār)*

ص 67) قال النوري نعت الفقير السكون عند العدم والبذل والايثار عند الوجود.

Poem on fearing God *(taqwā)* "I fear You without being afraid . . ."

ص 70) اني أتقيتك لا مهابة من محاذرة المصير
أني وكيف وأنت لي الف يفوق مدى السمير
توفي السرائر سرها وتحوط مكنون الضمير
لكن أجلك أن أجل سواك للخطر الحقير

Poem on gratitude *(shukr)* "I express my gratitude"

ص 71) سأشكر لا أني أجازيك منعما / بشكري ولكن كي يقال له الشكر
وأذكر أيامي لديك وحسنها / وآخر ما يبقى على الشاكر الذكر

Poem on contentment *(riḍā)* "Contentment is bitterness . . ."

ص 73) ان الرضا لمرارات تجرعها / عن القنوع اذا ما ستعذب الكدر
عواقب أشهدت بعض الحضور فما / يرعى التكثر الا ناقة نزر

On certainty and witnessing *(yaqīn, mushāhada)*

ص 73) قال النوري اليقين هو المشاهدة.

Poem on ecstasy and recollection *(wajd, dhikr, farṭ al-ḥubb)* "My love is so immoderate . . ."

ص 75) أريد دوام الذكر من فرط حبه / فيا عجبا من غيبة الذكر في الوجد
وأعجب منه غيبة الوجد تارة / وغيبة عين الذكر في القرب والبعد

Poem on reunion *(jamʿ, fanā', taqarrub)* "My reunion [. . .] showed me . . ."

ص 78) أراني جمعي في فنائي تقربا / وهيهات الا منك عنك التقرب
فما عنك لي صبر ولا فيك حيلة / ولا منك لي بد ولا عنك مهرب
تقرب قوم بالرجا فوصلتهم / فما لي بعيدا منك والكل يعطب

Poem on nearness and witnessing *(qurb, mushāhada, shuhūd)* "Oh You, whom I witness . . ."

ص 78) يا من اشاهده [عندي] (عني) فأحسبه / مني قريبا وقد عزت مطالبه
اذا سمت نفسي سلوة عنه ردني / اليه شهود ليس تفنى عجائبه

On connection and unveiling *(ittiṣāl, mukāshafa, qalb, mushāhada, sirr)*

ص 78) الاتصال مكاشفات القلوب ومشاهدات الاسرار.

On ecstasy compared to a flame *(wajd, sirr)*

ص 82) وقال النوري الوجد لهيب ينشأ في الأسرار ويسنح عن الشوق فتضطرب الجوارح طربا أو حزنا عند ذلك الوارد.

Poem on absence and witnessing *(ghayb, shuhūd)* "I witnessed [Him] perceiving . . ."

ص 87) شهدت ولم أشهد لحاظا لحظته / وحسب لحاظ شاهد غير مشهد
وغبت مغيبا غاب للغيب غيبه / فلاح ظهور غيبه غير مفقد

Poem on absence and veiling oneself *(ghayb, satr)* "I veiled myself from the world"

ص 88) تسترت عن دهري بستر همومه / محيرة في قدر من جل عن قدري
فلا الدهر يدري أنني عنه غائب / ولا أنا أدري بالخطوب اذا تجري

Story on Junayd's view on Nūrī's intoxicated ecstasy in the mosque

ص 99) قال الجنيد وقيل له ان أبا الحسين النوري قائم في مسجد الشونيزي منذ أيام لا يأكل ولا يشرب ولا ينام وهو يقول الله الله ويصلي الصلوات لأوقاتها فقال بعض من حضره انه صاح فقال الجنيد لا ولكن أرباب المواجيد محفوظون بين يدي الله في مواجيدهم.

Poem on spiritual struggle *(jihād)* "I say: I have almost reached the limit . . ."

ص 110) أقول أكاد اليوم أن أبلغ المدى / فيبعد عني ما أقول أكاد
فما لي جهاد غير أني مقصر/ وعجزي عن طول الجهاد جهاد
وان رجائي عودة منك بالرضا / والا فحظي في المعاد بعاد

On public discourse *(kalām)*

ص 111) قيل للنوري متى يستحق الانسان الكلام على الناس قال اذا فهم عن الله جل جلاله صلح أن يفهم عباد الله واذا لم يفهم عن الله كان بلاؤه عاما في بلاده وعلى عباده.

Story on Nūrī's and Junayd's attitude towards public discourse *(kalām)*

ص 112) سمعت فارسا يقول سمعت أبا عمرو الانماطي يقول كنا عند الجنيد اذ مر به النوري فسلم فقال له الجنيد وعليك السلام يا أمير القلوب تكلم فقال النوري يا أبا القاسم غششتهم فأجلسوك على المنابر ونصحتهم فرموني في المزابل. فقال الجنيد ما رأيت قلبي أحزن منه في ذلك الوقت. ثم خرج علينا في الجمعة الأخرى فقال اذا رأيتم الصوفي يتكلم على الناس فاعلموا أنه فارغ.

Ch. 2. Sarrāj's *Book of Flashes*

(*Kitāb al-luma*ʿ *fī l-taṣawwuf*. Ed. Nicholson. Leiden and London: Brill and Luzac, 1914)

On the Sufi *(samāʿ)*

ص 26) وقيل لأبي الحسين أحمد بن محمد النوري رحمه الله من الصوفي فقال من سمع السماع وآثر بالأسباب.

On the intellect *(ʿaql)*

ص 37–38) وقيل لابي الحسين النوري رحمه الله كيف لا تدركه العقول ولا يعرف الا بالعقول فقال كيف يدرك ذو أمد من لا أمد له أم كيف يدرك ذو عاهة من لا عاهة له ولا آفة أم كيف يكون مكيفا من كيف الكيف أم كيف يكون محيثا من حيث الحيث فسماه حيثا وكذلك أول الأول وأخر الآخر فسماه أولا وآخرا فلولا أنه أول الأول وأخر الآخر ما عرف ما الأولية وما الآخرية ثم قال وما الأزلية في الحقيقة الا الأبدية ليس بينهما حاجز كما ان الأولية هي الآخرية والآخرية هي الأولية وكذلك الظاهرية والباطنية الا أنه يفقدك وقتا ويشهدك وقتا لتجديد اللذة ورؤية العبودية لأن من عرفه بالخلقة لم يعرفه بالمباشرة لأن الخلقة على معنى قوله كن والمباشرة اظهار حرمة لا استهانة فيه.

On the guide to God (intellect, *ʿaql)*

ص 40) قيل لأبي الحسين النوري رحمه الله بما عرفت الله تعالى فقال بالله قيل فما بال العقل قال العقل عاجز لا يدل الا على عاجز مثله لما خلق الله العقل قال له من أنا فسكت فكحله بنور الوحدانية فقال أنت الله فلم يكن للعقل أن يعرف الله الا بالله وسئل عن أول فرض افترض الله تعالى على عباده ما هو فقال المعرفة لقوله تعالى وما خلقت الجن والانس الا ليعبدون وقال ابن عباس رضي الله عنه ليعرفون.

On repentance *(tawba)*

ص 44) التوبة أن تتوب من كل شيء سوى الله تعالى.

To Abū Ḥamza's disciple on nearness *(qurb, buʿd)*

ص 57) فاما حال الكبراء واهل النهايات فهو على ما قال أبو الحسين النوري رحمه الله لرجل دخل عليه فقال من أين أنت قال من بغداد قال من صحبت بها قال أبا حمزة قال اذا رجعت الى بغداد فقل لأبي حمزة قرب القرب في معنى ما نحن نشير اليه بعد البعد.

On love and tearing the veils *(maḥabba, sitr, kashf, sirr)*

ص 59) حكي عن أبي الحسين النوري رحمه الله أنه سئل عن المحبة فقال هتك الأستار وكشف الأسرار.

On certainty *(yaqīn)*

ص 81) اليقين المشاهدة.

On the sincere poor *(faqīr ṣādiq, sabab)*

ص 108) وسئل النوري رحمه الله عن الفقير الصادق فقال الفقير الصادق الذي لا يتهم الله تعالى في الاسباب ويسكن اليه في كل حال.

Story on Nūrī throwing money to the canal

ص 193–194) حمل الى أبي الحسين النوري رحمه الله ثلثمائة دينار قد باعوا عقارا له فجلس على قنطرة الصراة وهو يحذف بواحد واحد منها الى الماء ويقول سيدي تريد أن تخدعني عنك بهذا.

Story on Nūrī offering money to the Sufis *(qurb, buʿd)*

ص 195) ودفع وزير المعتضد مالا الى ابي الحسين النوري رحمه الله تعالى حتى يفرقه على المتصوفة فصبه في بيت وجمع صوفية بغداد فقال لهم كل من يحتاج منكم الى شيء فليدخل البيت وليأخذ حاجته منه فكان يأخذ الرجل مائة درهم والآخر أكثر والآخر أقل ومنهم من لا يأخذ شيئا فلما فنيت الدراهم ولم يبق شيء قال لهم بعدكم من الله تعالى على مقدار أخذكم من الدراهم وقربكم من الله تعالى على مقدار ترككم لها.

On the friend and the enemy

ص 209) الصديق لا يحاسب بشيء والعدو لا يحسب له شيء.

On reunion and separation *(jamʿ, tafriqa)*

ص 212) وقال أظنه النوري الجمع بالحق تفرقة عن غيره والتفرقة عن غيره جمع به.

On sincerity *(ikhlāṣ)*

ص 218–219) وسئل أظنه أبا الحسين النوري رحمه الله تعالى عن الإخلاص فقال ترك الموافقة للخلق.

On the Sufis' denomination *(wājid, inqiṭāʿ)*

ص 225) مسئلة لم سميت هذه الطائفة بهذا الاسم [. . .] وقال النوري رحمه الله تعالى سميت بهذا الاسم لاشتمالها عن الخلق بظاهر العابدين وانقطاعها الى الحق بمراتب الواجدين.

Poem on *sirr*

ص 232, 248) لعمري ما استودعت سري وسرها / سوانا حذارا أن تشيع السرائر
ولا لاحظته مقلتاي بلحظة / فتشهد نجوانا العيون النواظر
ولكن جعلت الوهم بيني وبينه / رسولا فأدى ما تكن الضمائر

Poem on nostalgia for a mystical state

ص 248) أنعى اليك إشارات القلوب معا / لم يبق منهن الا دارس العلم
أنعى اليك قلوبا طال ما هطلت / سحائب الجود منها أبحر الحكم
أنعى اليك نفوسا طاح شاهدها / فيما وراء الحيث بل في شاهد القدم

أنعى اليك لسان الحق مذ زمن / أودى وأذكاره في الوهم كالعدم
أنعى اليك بيانا تستكين له / أسماع كل فصيح مقول فهم
أنعى وحقك أخلاقا لطائفة / كانت مطاياهم في مكمن الكظم

Story on Nūrī's death

ص 290) وعن أبي الحسين النوري رحمه الله أنه حضر مجلسا فيه سماع فسمع هذا البيت
ما زلت أنزل من ودادك منزلا / تتحير الالباب عند نزوله
قال فقام وتواجد وهام على وجهه فوقع في أجمة قصب قد كسحت وبقي أصولها مثل السيوف فأقبل يمشي عليها ويعيد البيت الى الغداة والدم يخرج من رجليه ثم ورمت قدماه وساقاه وعاش بعد ذلك أياما قلائل ومات.

Poem inducing ecstasy *(tawājud)* "How many times a wailing dove . . ."

ص 304–305) وذكر عن أبي الحسين النوري رحمه الله أنه اجتمع مع جماعة من المشايخ في دعوة فجرى بينهم مسئلة في العلم وأبو الحسين النوري رحمه الله ساكت قال ثم رفع رأسه فأنشدهم هذه الأبيات
رب ورقاء هتوف في الضحى / ذات شجو صدحت في فنن
فبكائي ربما أرقها / وبكاءها ربما أرقني
هي ان تشكو فلا أفهمها / واذا أشكو فلا تفهمني
غير أني بالجوى أعرفها / وهي أيضا بالجوى تعرفني
قال فما بقي في القوم أحد الا قام وتواجد لما أنشد النوري هذه الابيات.

Story on Nūrī refusing to avail himself of a miracle

ص 325) وذكر عن النوري رحمه الله أنه وافى ليلة الى الدجلة قال فوجدتها وقد التزق الشط بالشط قال فقلت وعزتك لا عبرتها الا في زروق.

Story on Nūrī demanding a miracle

ص 327) قال ابن عطاء سمعت أبا الحسين النوري يقول كان في نفسي من هذه الكرامات شيء فأخذت قصبة من الصبيان وقمت بين زروقين ثم قلت وعزتك لئن لم تخرج لي سمكة فيها ثلاثة أرطال فلأغرقن نفسي قال فخرج لي سمكة فيها ثلاثة أرطال قال بلغ ذلك الجنيد رحمه الله فقال كان حكمه أن يخرج له أفعى تلدغه.

Saying on unveiling and connection *(mukāshafa, qalb, ittisāl)*

ص 346) مكاشفات العيون بالأبصار ومكاشفات القلوب بالاتصال.

Verse on the power of names

ص 350) اذا أم طفل مسها جوع طفلها / غذته باسم الطفل فاستعصم الطفل.

Fragment of Nūrī's letter to Junayd on expressing tribulation *(lisān, balā', bayān)*

ص 353) واللسان معناه البيان عن علم الحقائق كتب أبو الحسين النوري رحمه الله الى الجنيد كتابا فقال فيه يا سيدي لك في علم البلاء لسان وفي علم بلاء البلاء سنان يعني بيان عن علمه.

On erasure, common people and the elite *(maḥw)*

ص 355) الخاص والعام في قميص العبودية الا أن من يكون منهم أرفع جذبهم الحق ومحاهم عن نفوسهم في حركاتهم وأثبتهم عند نفسه.

On learning and certainty *(ʿilm, yaqīn)*

ص 359) كلما رأته العيون نسب الى العلم وكلما علمته القلوب نسب الى اليقين.

On theophany and creation *(tajallin, khalq)*

ص 363) تجلى لخلقه بخلقه واستتر عن خلقه بخلقه.

On theophany and good deeds *(tajallin, maḥāsin)*

ص 363) بتجليه حسنت المحاسن وجملت وباستتاره قبحت وسمجت.

Poem on absence *(ghayb)* "Don't you see that He captivated me?"

ص 369) أما ترى هيمني / شردني عن وطني
اذا تغيبت بدا / وان بدا غيبني
يقول لا تشهد ما / تشهد أو تشهدني

Line from the poem (on p. 248) on nostalgia for a mystical state

ص 382) مضى الجميع فلا عين ولا أثر / مضي عاد وفقدان الالى [الاولى] ارم

ARTHUR JOHN ARBERRY, PAGES FROM THE *KITĀB AL-LUMAʿ* OF *ABŪ NAṢR AL-SARRĀJ* BEING THE LACUNA IN THE EDITION OF R. A. NICHOLSON (LONDON: LUZAC, 1947)

Ghulām Khalīl incident and blasphemous sayings

ص 5) قال أبو نصر وفيما بلغني أن أبا الحسين أحمد بن محمد النوري رحمه الله كان في أيام الموفق وكان ينكر عليه غلام الخليل فرفع الى الموفق وهو يومئذ أمير المؤمنين أن ببغداد رجلا من الزنادقة دمه حلال فان قتله أمير المؤمنين فدمه في عنقي قال فبعث الخليفة في طلبه فحمل اليه فشهد عليه غلام الخليل أنا سمعته يقول أنا أعشق الله وهو يعشقني فقال النوري رحمه الله سمعت الله تعالى ذكره يقول يحبهم ويحبونه وليس العشق بأكثر من المحبة غير أن العاشق ممنوع والمحب يتمتع بحبه قال فبكى الموفق من رقة

كلامه وشهدوا عليه أيضا أنه سمع أذان المؤذن فقال طعنة وسم الموت وسمع نباح الكلاب فقال لبيك وسعديك فقيل له في ذلك فقال أما المؤذن فأنا أغار عليه أن يذكر الله وهو غافل وبأخذ عليه الأجرة ولولا الأجرة القليل من حطام الدنيا التي يأخذها لما ذكر الله فلذلك قلت له طعنة وسم الموت وقد قال الله جل ذكره وان من شيء الا يسبح بحمده ولكن لا تفقهون تسبيحهم فالكلب وكل شيء يذكرون الله بلا رياء ولا سمعة ولا طلبا للعوض فلذلك قلت ما قلت قال وحمل النوري مرة أخرى الى الخليفة وشهدوا عليه بأنه قال كنت البارحة في بيتي مع الله فسئل عن ذلك فقال صدق وأنا أيضا الساعة مع الله واذا كنت في البيت فأنا مع الله واذا كنت في البرية فأنا مع الله ومن كان في الدنيا مع الله فهو في الآخرة مع الله أليس يقول الله جل ذكره ولقد خلقنا الانسان ونعلم ما توسوس به نفسه ونحن أقرب اليه من حبل الوريد قال فغلفه الخليفة بيده وقال تكلم بما شئت فتكلم النوري بكلام لم يسمعوا مثله قط فبكى الخليفة وبكوا جميعا وقالوا هؤلاء أعرف بالله من غيرهم.

Ch. 3. Sulamī's *Generations of the Sufis*

(*Ṭabaqāt al-ṣūfiyya*. Ed. Nūr al-Dīn Shurayba. Cairo: al-Khānjī, 1997)

On reunion and separation *(jamʿ, tafriqa)*

ص 166) الجمع بالحق تفرقة عن غيره والتفرقة عن غيره جمع به.

On Sufism *(nafs, carnal soul)*

ص 166) التصوف ترك كل حظ للنفس.

On intimacy and love *(uns, wudd, qurb)*

ص 166) من وصل الى وده أنس بقربه ومن توسل بالوداد فقد اصطفاه من بين العباد.

Poem on tribulations *(balā')* "How many times I made my heart . . ."

ص 166) كم حسرة لي قد غصت مرارتها / جعلت قلبي لها وقفا لبلواكا
وحق ما منك يبليني ويتلفني / لأبكينك أو أحظى بلقياكا

On the Ḥabīb and the Khalīl

ص 166) وسئل النوري عن الحبيب وعن الخليل فقال ليس من طولب بالتسليم كمن بادر بالتسليم.

Nūrī and the handsome young man *(naẓar)*

ص 166–167) رأيت غلاما جميلا ببغداد فنظرت اليه ثم أردت أن أردد النظر فقلت له تلبسون النعال الصرارة وتمشون في الطرقات قال أحسنت أتجمش بالعلم ثم أنشأ يقول
تأمل بعين الحق ان كنت ناظرا / الى صفة فيها بدائع فاطر
ولا تعط حظ النفس منها لما بها / وكن ناظرا بالحق قدرة قادر

On Sufism as developing spiritual qualities *(akhlāq)*

ص 167) وسئل النوري عن التصوف فقال ليس التصوف رسوما ولا علوما ولكنها أخلاق.

On phases of the mystical path and the different groups of wayfarers

ص 167) أهل الديانة موقوفون وأهل التوحيد يسيرون وأهل الرضا يستروحون وأهل الانقطاع يتحيرون ثم قال ان الحق اذا ظهر تلاشى كل ما حجب وستر.

Nūrī's and Junayd's behaviour during illness *(wajd, fanā')*

ص 167–168) لحق ابا الحسين النوري علة والجنيد علة فالجنيد أخبر عن وجده والنوري كتم فقيل له لم لم تخبر كما أخبر صاحبك فقال ما كنا لنبتلى ببلوى فتوقع عليها اسم الشكوى ثم أنِشأ يقول

ان كنت للسقم أهلا / فأنت للشكر اهلا
عذب فلم يبق قلب / يقول للسقم مهلا
فأعيد ذلك على الجنيد فقال ما كنا شاكين ولكن أردنا أن نكشف عن عين القدرة فينا ثم بدأ يقول
أجل ما منك يبدو / لأنه عنك جلا
وأنت يا أنس قلبي / أجل من أن تجلا
أفنيتني عن جميعي / فكيف أرعى المحلا

On looking at things *(naẓar)*

ص 169) مقامات أهل النظر في النظر شتى فمنهم من كان نظره نظر التسلي ومنهم من كان نظره نظر استفادة ومنهم من كان نظره نظر عيان المكاشفة ومنهم من كان نظره نظر المنافسة في المشاهدة ومنهم من كان نظره نظر المشاكلة والمماثلة ومنهم من كان نظره نظر طيبة وملاحظة ومنهم من كان نظره نظر اشراف ومطالعة وكل واحد منهم أهل النظر.

On learning and mystical knowledge *(ʿilm, maʿrifa)*

ص 169) أعز الاشياء في زماننا شيئان عالم يعمل بعلمه وعارف ينطق عن حقيقته.

On cognition *(ʿaql, rujūʿ)*

ص 169) من عقل الاشياء بالله فرجوعه في كل شيء الى الله.

On the sincere poor *(faqīr ṣādiq, asbāb)*

ص 169) وسئل النوري عن الفقير الصادق فقال الذي لا يتهم الله تعالى في الاسباب ويسكن اليه في كل حال.

Poem on uncontrolled thoughts (khawāṭir) "How many times I desired . . ."

ص 169) وكم رمت أمرا خرت لي في انصرافه / فلا زلت بي مني أبر وأرحما
عزمت على ألا أحس بخاطر / على القلب الا كنت أنت المقدما
والا تراني عند ما قد كرهته / لأنك في قلبي كبيرا معظما

On secondary means *(asbāb)*

ص 169) وأخضر النوري مجلسا للسلطان فقال له من أين تأكلون فقال لسنا نعرف الاسباب التي تستجلب بها الارزاق نحن قوم مدبرون.

Ch. 4. Sulamī's *Realities of Interpretation*

For the Arabic text of Nūrī's comments in the *Ḥaqā'iq al-tafsīr*, see: Paul Nwyia, "Textes mystiques inédits d'Abū-l-Ḥasan al-Nūrī." *Mélanges de l'Université Saint-Joseph* 46 (1968): 144–47

Ch. 5. Kharkūshī's *Revision of the Secrets*

(*Tahdhīb al-asrār*. Ed. Bassām M. Bārūd. Abu Dhabi: al-Majmaʿ al-Thaʿqāfī, 1999)

On Sufism *(nafs)*

ص 28) وعن أبي الحسين النوري قال التصوف هو ترك كل حظ النفس وقال أيضا نعت الصوفي السكون عند العدم والايثار عند الوجدود وقال مرة أخرى الصوفي هو التارك لحظوظ نفسه لحظ الحق فيه وقال أيضا التصوف الصولة على الوقت وقال أيضا من وجد وتواجد فهو صوفي.

On the heart *(qalb)*

ص 54) وعن ابي الحسين النوري أنه قال قد حيل بيني وبين قلبي مذ أربعين سنة وما اشتهيت شيئا ولا تمنيت شيئا ولا استحسنت شيئا منذ عرفت ربي عز وجل.

On intimacy with God *(uns, qalb, tafarrud)*

ص 82) وقال النوري الأنس بالله تعالى من صفاء القلب مع الله عز وجل بالتفرد به.

On contemplation *(mushāhada, sirr, hayba, ishtiyāq)*

ص 85) وقال النوري اذا امتزجت نار التعظيم مع نور الهيبة في السر هاجت ريح المحبة من حجر العطف على النار والنور فظهر منه الاشتياق وتلاشت البشرية فصارت المشاهدة.

On certainty and recollection *(yaqīn, maʿrifa, tawakkul, munājāt, dhikr)*

ص 92) وقال النوري لن ينال أحد اليقين في المعرفة والتوكل الا بدوام ذكر الله تعالى بالقلب وكثرة مناجاته وقطع ما يشغل القلب عنه.

On contentment (riḍā)

ص 130) وقال النوري الرضا ارتفاع الجزع في أي حكم كان.

On trust in God and annihilation *(tawakkul, fanā')*

ص 135) وقال النوري التوكل أن يفنى تدبيرك في تدبيره وترضى بالله عز وجل وكيلا ومدبرا.

On a saying of the Prophet on poverty

ص 154) وسئل النوري عن معنى قول النبي صلى الله عليه وسلم اطلعت في الجنة فرأيت أكثر أهلها الفقراء فقال من ملك الجنة. بأسرها فهو فقير ان من رضي بالجنة عوضا من الله عز وجل فهو فقير

On the poor/Sufi *(preferring others, īthār)*

ص 157) وعن ابي الحسين النوري نعت الفقير السكون عند العدم والبذل والايثار عند الوجود.

On hidden desire *(shahwa khafiyya)*

ص 177) وروي عن النوري أنه قال الشهوة الخفية أن يكون الرجل يشتهي الشيء مما يكره الله تعالى فلا يتركه.

Comment on Q 39:60

ص 186) وقال النوري في قول الله عز وجل ويوم القيمة ترى الذين كذبوا على الله وجوههم مسودة قال هم الذين ادعوا محبة الله تعالى ولم يكونوا فيها صادقين.

Comment on Q 29:45

ص 203) وسئل أبو الحسين النوري عن معنى قوله عز وجل ان الصلوة تنهى عن الفحشاء والمنكر قال معناه ثواب الصلاة يذهب بها عقاب الفحشاء ولذكر الله أكبر من أن يبقى على صاحبه عقاب الفحشاء والمنكر.

Saying on the mystical moment and proper behavior *(waqt, adab)*

ص 216) وقال النوري من لم يتأدب للوقت فوقته مقت.

Ghulām Khalīl incident

ص 286) وقال ابن عطاء سعى ساع بالصوفية الى الخليفة فقال ان هاهنا قوما من الزنادقة يرفضون الشريعة فأخذ أبو الحسين النوري وأبو حمزة والرقام وتستر الجنيد بالفقه وكان يتكلم على مذهب أبي ثور فأدخلوا على الخليفة فأمر بضرب أعناقهم فبدر أبو الحسين الى السياف ليضرب عنقه فقال له السياف بدرت من بين اصحابك قال أحببت أن أوثر أصحابي بحياة هذه اللحظة فتعجب السياف وجميع من حضر من ذلك وكتب الى الخليفة فرد امرهم الى قاضي القضاة فقام اليه النوري فسأله عم أصول الفرائض في الطهارة والصلاة فأجابه

ثم قال وبعد هذا فان لله عبادا يأكلون بالله ويلبسون بالله ويسمعون بالله ويصدرون بالله ويوردون بالله فلما سمع القاضي كلامه بكى بكاء شديدا ثم دخل على الخليفة فقال ان كان هؤلاء القوم زنادقة فما على وجه الارض موحد.

On allusion to the Real *(ishāra ilā l-ḥaqq, ʿibāra, istighrāq, sirr, ṣidq)*
ص 322) وسئل أبو الحسين النوري عن الإشارة الى الحق فقال تعبر [تغني] الإشارة عن العبارة ووجل [ووجدان] الإشارة الى الحق استغراق السرائر بالصدق.

On allusion *(ishāra)*
ص 322) وقال النوري الإشارة الكلام الخفي.

On ecstasy *(wajd)*
ص 345) وسئل أبو الحسين النوري عن الوجد فقال يمتنع والله اللسان عن نعت حقيقته وتكل بلاغة الأديب عن وصف جوهره فان خطبه من أعظم الخطوب ولا داع أعيا معالجة من الوجد.

On veiling *(satr)*
ص 352) وعن أبي الحسين النوري قال سألت الله عز وجل أن يخفيني في بلاده عن عباده فنوديت يا أبا الحسن ان الحق لا يستره شيء.

On making a spiritual state permanent
ص 356) وقال أبو الحسن النوري سألت الله تعالى أن يديم لي حالة فهتف بي هاتف يا أبا الحسن لا يصبر على الدائم الا الدائم.

On annihilation and the stations of Sufism *(fanā', maqām)*
ص 385) وسئل أبو الحسين النوري عن الفناء فقال والذي نفسي بيده انه أول مقام من مقام التصوف.

Story on Nūrī and the thief
ص 412) وعن جعفر الدبيلي قال دخل أبو الحسين النوري الماء فجاء لص فسرق ثيابه فجلس وسط الماء فلم يكن الا قليلا حتى أقبل اللص مع ثيابه فوضعها بين يديه وقد جفت يده اليمنى فقال النوري قد رد على ثيابي فرد الله يده عليه.

Poem on recollection and absence *(dhikr, ghayb)* "I recollected . . ."
ص 499) ذكرت ولم أذكر حقيقة ذكره / ولكن بوادي الحق تبدي فأنطق
اذا ما بدا ذكر لذكر ذكرته / يغيبني عن ذكر ذكري فأغرق
وأغرق بالذكر الذي قد ذكرته / عن الذكر بالذكر الذي هو أسبق

Poem on the heart *(qalb)* "My heart indicates towards You . . ."

ص 500) أشار قلبي اليك كيما / يرى الذي لا تراه عيني
وأنت تلقي على ضميري/ حلاوة السؤل والتمني
يريد مني اختيار سري / وقد علمت المراد مني
فليس لي سواك حظ / فكيف ما شئت فاختبرني

Poem on the heart *(qalb)* "The hearts are not in the position to love You . . ."

ص 501) ما محل القلوب أن تهواكا / لا ولا قدر ناظري أن يراكا
رغبتي في رضاك لا في نعيم / أي عيش يطيب لي مع سواكا
ان فديناك بالنفوس ظلمناك / ولكن تفدي محبا فداكا
ما بكائي ذهاب عيني لغيني / بل بكائي مخافة الا أراكا

Poem on annihilation *(fanā')* "If I knew the way to You . . ."

ص 506) لا كنت ان كنت أدري كيف الطريق اليكا / أفنيتني عن جميعي فصرت أبكي عليكا

Poem on the inner heart *(sirr)* "The secrets of my inner heart."

ص 506) سرائر سري أن تسر بما / أوليتني من سرور أسميه
فصاح بالسر سر منك يرقبه / كيف السرور بسر دون مبديه
فظل يلحظني حظي لألحظه / والحق يلحظني أن لا أراعيه
فأقبل السر يفني الكل عن صفتي / وأقبل الحق يفنيني وأفنيه

Poem on absence *(ghayb)* "How said it is . . ."

ص 510) كفى حزنا أني أناديك دائبا / كأني بعيد أو كأنك غائب
وأسأل منك الفضل من غير رغبة / ولم أر مثلي زاهد فيك راغب

A tradition on Joseph

ص 523) لما بيع يوسف عليه السلام قال انسان من أهل الرفقة استوصوا بهذا الغريب خيرا فقال يوسف من كان الله تعالى معه فليس بغريب.

Poem on *sirr* ("By my life! I have never entrusted my secret . . .")

ص 539) لعمري ما استودعت سري وسره / سوانا حذارا أن تشيع السرائر
ولا لاحظته مقلتاي بنظرة / فتشهد نجوانا العيون النواظر
ولكن جعلت الوهم بيني وبينه / رسولا فأدى ما تكن الضمائر

Nūrī's last words

ص 549) ولما حضر النوري الوفاة قيل له قل لا اله الا الله فقال أليس الي ثم أمر

Ch. 6. Abū Nuʿaym's *Ornament of God's Friends*

(*Ḥilyat al-awliyāʾ wa-ṭabaqāt al-aṣfiyāʾ*. Beirut: Dār al-Kutub al-ʿIlmiyya, 1988)

Report on Nūrī's circumstances during the persecutions provoked by Ghulām Khalīl

ص 249) سمعت عبد المنعم بن حيان يحكي عن أبي سعيد الأعرابي محنته وغيبته عن اخوانه في أيام محنة غلام الخليل وأنه أقام بالرقة سنين متخليا عن الايناس ثم عاد بعد المدة المديدة الى بغداد وفقد أناسه وجلاسه وأشكاله وانقبض عن الكلام لضعف في بصره وانحلال في جسمه وقوته

Longer version of the poem on absence (short version quoted by Sarrāj)

ص 250) قدم أبو الحسين النوري وكان صوفيا متكلما في بعض قدماته من مكة في غير أوان الحج فخرجنا فاستقبلناه فوق بغداد فرأينا في وجهه تغيرا فقلنا يا أبا الحسين تغير الاسرار من تغير الأبشار فقال لا ان الحق تحمل كل وثقل عن قلوب أوليائه ثم أنشدنا

أخرجني من وطني / كما ترى صيرني
صيرني كما ترى / أسكن قفر الدمن
اذا تغيبت بدا / وان بدا غيبني
وافقته حتى اذا / وافقني خالفني
وقال لا تشهد ما / تشهد أو تشهدني

Another longer version of the poem on absence (short version quoted by Sarrāj)

ص 250) رئي النوري في رجوعه من الحرم ولم يبق منه الا خاطره فقال له رجل هل يلحق الاسرار ما يلحق الصفات فقال لا ان الحق أقبل على الاسرار فحملها وأعرض عن الصفات فمحقها ثم أنشأ يقول

أهكذا صيرني / أزعجني من وطني
غربني شردني / شردني غربني
حتى اذا غبت بدا / وان بدا غيبني
واصلني حتى اذا / واصلته فاصلني
يقول لا تشهد ما / تشهد أو تشهدني

Ghulām Khalīl inicident

ص 250) لما كانت محنة غلام الخليل ونسب الصوفية الا الزندقة أمر الخليفة بالقبض عليهم فأخذ في الجملة من أخذ النوري في الجماعة فادخلوا على الخليفة فأمر بضرب أعناقهم فتقدم النوري مبتدرا الى السياف ليضرب عنقه فقال له السياف ما دعاك الى الابتدار الى القتل من بين أصحابك فقال آثرت حياتهم على حياتي هذه اللحظة فتوقف

السياف والحاضرون عن قتله ورفع أمره الى الخليفة فرد أمرهم الى قاض القضاء وكان يلي القضاء يومئذ إسماعيل بن اسحاق فقدم اليه النوري فساله عن مسائل في العبادات والطهارات والصلاة فأجابه ثم قال له وبعد هذا لله عباد يسمعون بالله وينظرون بالله ويصدرون بالله ويردون بالله ويأكلون بالله ويلبسون بالله فلما سمع إسماعيل كلامه بكى بكاء طويلا ثم دخل على الخليفة وقال ان كان هؤلاء القوم زنادقة فليس في الارض موحد فامر بتخليتهم. وسأله السلطان يومئذ من اين يأكلون فقال لسنا نعرف الاسباب التي يستجلب بها الارزاق نحن قوم مدبرون.

On intimacy and love *(uns, wudd)*

ص 250) من وصل الى وده أنس بقربه ومن توصل بالوداد فقد اصطفاه من بين العباد

Story on Nūrī and the thief

ص 251) حدثنا [. . .] أن أبا الحسين النوري دخل يوما الماء فجاء لص فأخذ ثيابه فبقي في وسط الماء فلم يلبث الا قليلا حتى رجع اليه اللص معه ثيابه فوضعه بين يديه وقد جفت يمينه فقال النوري رب قد رد على ثيابي فرد عليه يمينه فرد الله عليه يده ومضى.

Story on Nūrī's countering the carnal soul *(nafs)*

ص 251) دخلت على النوري ذات يوم فرأيت رجليه منتفختين فسألته عن أمره فقال طالبتني نفسي بأكل التمر فجعلت أدافعها فتأبى علي فخرجت فاشتريت فلما أن أكلت قلت لها قومي حتى تصلي فأبت فقلت لله علي وعلى ان قعدت على الأرض أربعين يوما فما قعدت.

Story on Nūrī demanding a miracle

ص 251) سمعت أبا الحسين النوري يقول كان في نفسي من هذه الآيات شيء فأخذت من الصبيان قصبة وقمت بين زورقين وقلت وعزتك لان لم تخرج لي سمكة فيها ثلاثة أرطال لأغرقن نفسي قال فخرجت لي سمكة فيها ثلاثة أرطال قال فبلغ ذلك الجنيد فقال كان حكمه أن يخرج له أفعى فتلدغه.

On outward imitation of Sufism

ص 251) كانت المراقع غطاء على الدر فصارت مزابل على جيف.

Nūrī's and Junayd's behavior during illness *(wajd, fanā')*

ص 252) لحق ابا الحسين النوري علة والجنيد علة فالجنيد أخبر عن وجده والنوري كتم فقيل للبوري لم تخبر كما أخبر صاحبك فقال ما كنا لنبتلى ببلوى فتوقع عليه الشكوى ثم أنشأ يقول

ان كنت للسقم أهلا / فأنت للشكر اهلا
عذب فلم يبق قلبا / يقول للسقم مهلا

فأعيد على الجنيد ذلك فقال الجنيد ما كنا شاكين ولكن أردنا أن نكشف عن عين القدرة فينا ثم بدأ يقول

أجل ما منك يبدو / لأنه عنك جلا

وأنت يا أنس قلبي / أجل من أن تجلا
أفنيتني عن جميعي / فكيف أرعني المحلا

Spiritual advices *(waṣāyā)*

ص 252) سمعت أبا الحسين النوري يقول ويوصي بعض أصحابه عشرة وأي عشرة احتفظ بهن واعمل عليهن جهدك فأولى ذلك من رأيته يدعي مع الله عز وجل حالة تخرجه عن حد علم الشرع فلا تقربن منه والثانية من رأيته يركن الى غير أبناء جنسه ويخالطهم فلا تقربن منه والثالثة من رأيته يسكن الى الرئاسة والتعظيم له فلا تقربن منه ولا ترتفق به وان أرفقك ولا ترج له فلاحا والرابعة فقير رجع الى الدنيا ان مت جوعا فلا تقربن منه ولا ترفق به ان أرفقك فان رفقه يقسي قلبك أربعين صباحا والخامسة من رأيته مستغنيا بعلمه فلا تأمن جهله والسادسة من رأيته مدعيا حالة باطنه لا يدل عليها ولا يشهد عليها حفظ ظاهره فاتهمه على دينه والسابعة من رأيته يرضى عن نفسه ويسكن الى وقته فاعلم أنه مخدوع فاحذره أشد الحذر والثامنة مريد يسمع القصائد ويميل الى الرفاهة لا ترجون خيره والتاسعة فقير لا تراه عند السماع حاضرا فاتهمه واعلم أنه منع بركة ذلك لتشويش سره وتبديد همه والعاشرة من رأيته مطمئنا الى أصدقائه واخوانه وأصحابه مدعيا لكمال الخلق بذلك فاشهد بسخافة عقله ووهن ديانته.

Poem on absence *(ghayb)* "How said it is . . ."

ص 253) رأيت أبا الحسن النوري قائما حيال الكعبة يحرك شفتيه كأنه يسأل شيئا ثم أنشأ يقول
كفى حزنا أني أناديك دائبا / كأني بعيد أو كأنك غائب
وأسأل منك الفضل من غير رغبة / ولم أر مثلي زاهدا فيك راغب

On the ways to God (fuller version of Comment on Q 2:29 quoted by Sulamī)

ص 253) أعلى مقامات أهل الحقائق انقطاعهم عن الخلائق وسبيل المحبين التلذذ بمحبوبهم وسبيل الراجين التأميل لمأمولهم وسبيل الفانين الفناء في محبوبهم ومأمولهم وسبيل الباقين البقاء ببقائه ومن ارتفع عن الفناء والبقاء فحينئذ لا فناء ولا بقاء وقال ان المحبة للمحبوب تتزايد من لطائف المحبوب.

Poem on the inner heart *(sirr)* "The secrets of my inner heart."

ص 253) كادت سرائر سري أن تسر بما / أوليتني من سرور لا أسميه
فصاح للسر سر منك يرقبه / كيف السرور بسر دون مبديه
فظل يلحظه سرا ليلحظه / والحق يلحظني ألا أراعيه
وأقبل السر يغني الكل عن صفتي / وأقبل الحق يغنيني ويغنيه

Poetic correspondence on annihilation *(fanā')*

ص 253) سمعت أبا الحسن القناد يقول كتبت الي النوري وأنا حديث
اذا كان كل الكل في النور فانيا / أبن لي عن أي الوجودين أخبر
فأجابني في الحال
اذا كنت فيما ليس بالوصف فانيا / فوقتك في الاوصاف عندي تحير

Poem on the inner heart *(sirr)* and Junayd's answer

ص 254) كتب النوري الي الجنيد يسأله عن السر ووصفه في شعره ثلاثة أوصاف
يناجيك سر سائل عن ثلاثة / سرائرهم كتم واعلانهم ستر
فتى ضاع كتم السر بين ضلوعه / عن ادراكه حتى كان لم يكن سر
فأسبل أستار التخفر صائنا / لكل حديث ان يكون هو السر
فكتام سر مدرك الكتم لم ينل/ سوى حد كتم السر من ظنه ذكر
فكاتمه المكنون ثم تكاتمت / جوانحه فالكل من بته صفر
ضنين بما يهواه ما لاح لائح / يقاربه الا احتمى صوابها الفكر
ومكتتم وافقى الضمائر وامتطى/ لمودعه جحدا وليس به غدر
لامهم تاج الفخار ذكرته / ومن شربه في حاله المنهل الغمر
فقال الجنيد والله ما رميت بسري الى أحدهما لأفضله على الآخر الا جذبني اليه
وقد أرجأت أمرهما الى الله.

Nūrī and the handsome young man *(naẓar)*

ص 254) رأيت غلاما جميلا ببغداد فنظرت اليه ثم أردت أن أردد النظر فقلت له لم تلبسون النعال الصرارة وتمشون في الطرقات قال أحسنت أتحسن العلم ثم أنشأ يقول
تأمل بعين الحق ان كنت ناظرا / الى صفة فيها بدائع فاطر
ولا تعط حظ النفس منها لما بها / وكن ناظرا بالحق قدرة قادر

Ch. 7. Qushayrī's *Treatise*

(*al-Risāla al-qushayriyya*, ed. M. Zurayq and A. Balṭajī. Beirut: Dār al-Jīl, n.d.)

Saying on Muḥammad *(qalb, miʿrāj, ru'ya)*

ص 43) شاهد الحق القلوب فلم ير قلبا أشوق اليه من قلب محمد صلى الله اليه وسلم فأكرمه بالمعراج تعجيلا للرؤية ومكاملة.

On tawḥīd *(khāṭir)*

ص 45) التوحيد كل خاطر يشير الى الله تعالى بعد أن لا تزاحمه خواطر التشبيه.

On ecstasy, finding and loosing *(wajd, faqd)*

ص 62) أنا منذ عشرين سنة بين الوجد والفقد أي اذا وجدت ربي فقدت قلبي واذا وجدت قلبي فقدت ربي.

To Abū Ḥamza's disciple on nearness *(qurb)*

ص 82) ورأى أبو الحسين النوري بعض أصحاب أبي حمزة فقال أنت من أصحاب أبي حمزة الذي يشير الى القرب اذا لقيته فقل له ان أبا الحسين النوري يقرئك السلام ويقول لك قرب القرب فيما نحن فيه بعد البعد.

On repentance *(tawba)*

ص 95) التوبة أن تتوب من كل شيء سوى الله عز وجل.

On fearing God *(khawf)*

ص 127) الخائف يهرب من ربه الى ربه.

Story on Nūrī starving in the desert *(sabab)*

ص 169) وقيل جاع النوري في البادية فهتف به هاتف ايما أحب اليك سبب أو كفاية فقال الكفاية ليس فوقها نهاية فبقي سبعة عشر يوما لم يأكل.

On certainty and witnessing *(yaqīn, mushāhada)*

ص 181) اليقين المشاهدة.

On contentment *(riḍā, qalb, qaḍā')*

ص 196) الرضا سرور القلب بمر القضاء.

On insight *(firāsa)*

ص 234) وسئل أبو الحسن النوري من أين تولدت فراسة المتفرسين فقال من قوله تعالى ونفخت فيه من روحي فمن كان حظه من ذلك النور أتم كانت مشاهدته أحكم وحكمه بالفراسة أصدق ألا ترى كيف أوجب نفخ الروح فيه السجود له بقوله تعالى فاذا سويته ونفخت فيه من روحي فقعوا له ساجدين.

Ghulām Khalīl incident

ص 248–249) لما سعى غلام الخليل بالصوفية الى الخليفة أمر بضرب أعناقهم فأما الجنيد فانه تستر بالفقه وكان يفتى على مذهب أبي ثور وأما الشحام والرقام والنوري وجماعة فقبض عليهم فبسط النطع لضرب أعناكهم فتقدم النوري فقال له السياف تدري الى ماذا تبادر فقال نعم فقال وما يعجلك فقال أوثر علي أصحابي بحياة ساعة فتحير السياف وأنهى الخبر الى الخليفة فردهم الى القاضي ليتعرف حالهم فألقى القاضي على أبي الحسين النوري مسائل فقهية فأجابه الكل ثم أخذ يقول وبعد فانه لله عبادا قاموا بالله واذا نطقوا نطقوا بالله وسرد ألفاظا أبكى بها القاضي فأرسل القاضي الى الخليفة وقال ان كان هؤلاء زنادقة فما على وجه الارض مسلم.

Blasphemous saying on the muezzin and the dog

ص 258–259) وسمع النوري رجلا يؤذن فقال طعنة وسم الموت وسمع كلبا ينبح فقال لبيك وسعديك فقيل له ان هذا ترك للدين فانه يقول للمؤذن في تشهده طعنة وسم الموت ويلبي عند نباح الكلاب فسئل عن ذلك فقال أما ذلك فكان ذكره لله على رأس الغفلة وأما الكلب فقال تعالى وان من شيء الا يسبح بحمده.

On the poor/Sufi (preferring others, *īthār*)

ص 278, 281) نعت الفقير / الصوفي السكون عند العدم والايثار عند الوجود.

On the Sufi *(samāʿ)*
ص 282, 341)وسئل أحمد النوري عن الصوفي فقال هو الذي سمع السماع وآثر الأسباب.

Saying on the mystical moment and proper behavior *(waqt, adab)*
ص 287) من لم يتأدب للوقت فوقته مقت.

Story on Nūrī's death
ص 306–307) كان سبب وفاة أبي الحسين النوري أنه سمع هذا البيت
لا زلت أنزل في ودادك منزلا / تتحير الالباب عند نزوله
فتواجد النوري وهام في الصحراء فوقع في أجمة قصب قد قطعت وبقي
أصولها مثل السيوف فكان يمشي عليها ويعيد البيت الى الغداة والدم يسيل
من رجليه ثم وقع مثل السكران فتورمت قدماه ومات وروي أنه قيل له
عند النزع قل لا اله الا الله فقال أليس اليه أعود.

On love and tearing the veils *(maḥabba, sitr, kashf, sirr)*
ص 324) المحبة هتك الاستار وكشف الاسرار.

On Sufism *(nafs)*
ص 439) التصوف ترك كل حظ للنفس.

On learning and mystical knowledge *(ʿilm, maʿrifa)*
ص 439) أعز الاشياء في زماننا شيئان عالم يعمل بعلمه وعارف بالله ينطق عن حقيقة.

On violating the religious law (=one of Nūrī's spiritual advices *(waṣāyā)* quoted by Abū Nuʿaym)
ص 439) من رأيته يدعي مع الله تعالى حالة تخرجه عن حد العلم الشرعي فلا تقربن منه.

Junayd's estimation of Nūrī *(ṣidq)*
ص 439) وقال الجنيد منذ مات النوري لم يخبر عن حقيقة الصدق أحد.

Nūrī's equality with Junayd
ص 439) قال أبو أحمد المغازلي ما رأيت أعبد من النوري قيل ولا الجنيد قال ولا الجنيد.

On outward imitation of Sufism
ص 439) كانت المراقع غطاء على الدر فصارت اليوم مزابل على جيف.

Story on Nūrī hiding his piety
ص 439) وقيل كان يخرج كل يوم من داره ويحمل الخبز معه ثم يتصدق به في الطريق ويدخل مسجدا يصلي فيه الى قريب الظهر ثم يخرج ويفتح باب حانوته ويصوم فكان أهله يتوهمون أنه يأكل في السوق وأهل السوق يتوهمون أنه يأكل في البيت بقي على هذا في ابتدائه عشرين سنة.

(*AL-RISĀLA AL-QUSHAYRIYYA*, ED. A. MAḤMŪD AND M. IBN AL-SHARĪF. CAIRO: DĀR AL-SHAʿB, 1989)

On the possibility of witnessing God *(mushāhada)*

ص 160) لا يصح للعبد المشاهدة وقد بقي له عرق قائم وقال اذا طلع الصباح استغني عن المصباح.

Story on Nūrī demanding a miracle

ص 575) وذكر عن ابن عطاء أنه قال سمعت أبا الحسين النوري يقول كان في نفسي شيء من هذه الكرامات فأخذت قصبة من الصبيان وقمت بين زورقين ثم قلت وعزتك ان لم تخرج لي سمكة فيها ثلاثة أرطال لأغرقن نفسي قال فخرج لي سمكة فيها ثلاثة أرطال فبلغ ذلك الجنيد فقال كان حكمه أن تخرج له أفعى تلدغه.

Story on Nūrī refusing to avail himself of a miracle

ص 575) وحكي عن النوري أنه خرج ليلة الى شط دجلة فوجدها وقد التزق الشطان فانصرف وقال وعزتك لا أجوزها الا في زروق.

Story on Nūrī's capacity of insight *(firāsa)*

ص 594) سمعت زيتونة خادمة أبي الحسين النوري وكانت تخدمه وخدمت أبا حمزة والجنيد فقالت كان يوم بارد فقلت للنوري أحمل اليك شيئا فقال نعم فقلت ماذا تريد قال خبز ولبن فحملت وكان بين يديه فحم وكان يقلبها بيده وقد اشتغلت يده فأخذ يأكل الخبز واللبن يسيل على يده وعليها سواد الفحم فقلت في نفسي ما أقذر أولياءك يا رب ما فيهم احد نظيف قالت فخرجت من عنده فتعلقت بي امرأة وقالت سرقت لي رزمة ثياب وجروني الى الشرطي فأخبر النوري بذلك فخرج وقال للشرطي لا تتعرضوا لها فانها ولية من أولياء الله تعالى فقال الشرطي كيف أصنع والمرأة تدعي قال فجاءت جارية ومعها الرزمة المطلوبة فاسترد النوري المرأة وقال لها تقولين بعد هذا ما أقذر أولياءك قالت فقلت قد تبت الى الله تعالى.

ص 599) دخل النوري الماء فجاء لص فأخذ ث يابه ثم انه جاء ومعه الثياب وقد جفت يده فقال النوري قد رد علينا الثياب فرد عليه يده فعوفي.

Ch. 8. Sīrjānī's *Black and White in the Words of Wisdom*

(*KITĀB AL-BAYĀḌ WA-L-SAWĀD*, ED. B. ORFALI AND N. SAAB. LEIDEN AND BOSTON: BRILL, 2012) THE LIST CONTAINS ONLY THOSE TRADITIONS THAT ARE NOT QUOTED IN THE EARLIER COLLECTIONS

Poem on theoretical learning and mystical knowledge "We ereased . . ."

ص 33) محونا وأثبتم سوادا ومعجما / بتقويم ألفاظ على ورق جدد
حجبتم بها عن فهم مستنبط النهى / الى منتهى الغايات في سرمد الأبد
فهوم بدت من غيبة لقلوبهم / تكاثف أمطار هواطلها مدد

On Sufism *(ishāra, ʿibāra)*

ص 44) وسئل النوري بمصر عن التصوف فقال لطف إشارة وحسن عبارة.

On abstinence *(zuhd)*

ص 97) الزهد في الدنيا قصر الامل ليس بأكل الغليظ ولا بلبس الخشن.

On the *murīd*

ص 104) سئل النوري عن الإرادة فقال ترك ما عليه العادة.

On tribulation *(balā', īmān)*

ص 116) لا يجد العبد حلاوة الايمان حتى يأتيه البلاء من كل مكان.

On eating; Gunayd's interpretation of Nūrī's words

ص 156) كنا يوما حوالى إبراهيم الخواص والنوري جالس الى جنبه فأقبل بعض القوم وسأل النوري كيف يتناول هؤلاء القوم الطعام قال النوري تناول الابرار في دار القرار ثم أقبل على إبراهيم الخواص وسأله في ذلك فقال تناول العليل الدواء يرتجى به الشفاء قال فقمنا ودخلنا على ابي القاسم الجنيد فأعدنا عليه العبارتين قال بلى أما أبو الحسين فأخبر عن مشاهدة حقيقة واما أبو إسحاق فأخبر عن حال مجاهدة.

On servanthood (ʿubūdiyya)

ص 161) وسئل أبو الحسين النوري عن العبودية فقال مشاهدة الربوبية.

Story on inclination to look at youngsters (*naẓar,* Junayd sending the inquirer to Nūrī)

ص 237) وقال جعفر الخلدي كنا بمسجد الشونيزية أنا وجنيد وجماعة من أصحابنا فدخل علينا رجل فقال يا أبا القاسم قد عالجت بكل ما يعالج فلم يصف وقتي فقال اذهب الى أبي الحسين النوري فسله قال فذهب الى أبي الحسين فقال له أبو الحسين كأني بك وقد سألت جنيدا كذا وكذا فأرسلك الي فقال الرجل نعم فقال له أخبرني هل تميل النظر الى الاحداث قال نعم قال هذا حجابك وهو أعز الحجاب اترك هذا حتى يصفو لك الوقت ويخلو لك القلب.

Story on Nūrī losing his heart to a young man (Junayd interpreting what happened)

ص 239) وقال جعفر الخلدي سمعت النوري يقول دخلت الري مرة ورأيت شابا جالسا على دكان فعلمت أن لله تعالى فيه سرا فجمعت همي له ودخلت المسجد فاذا أنا بشاب قد وقف على رأسي قال فجلس فلم يحسن أن يداخلني الا من طريق القرآن فقال يا شيخ تحفظ

القرآن قلت نعم قال ما تأخذ علي قلت بسم الله قال فابتدأ يقرأ فقلت خفف فاني أريد أن أخرج فقال من أين والى أين فقلت من بغداد وأنا اريد أن أرجع فقال وأنا معك فقلت ألك الوالدان فقال نعم فقلت فاستأذنهما فاستأذنهما فأذنا له فشيعاه وسلماه الي فلما دخلنا بغداد سلمت على أبي القاسم جنيد فقال يا أبا الحسين عظم الله أجرك في هذا الشاب الى ثلاثة أيام فمات الشاب بعد ثلاثة أيام قال وقيل للجنيد من أين حكمت على الشاب فقال رأيته أخذ قلب أبي الحسين فعلمت أن الحق يغار على قلوب أوليائه أن يسكنوا الى سواه.

On the tripartite division of the heart

ص 287) وقال أبو الحسين النوري الصدر معدن التسليم والقلب معدن اليقين والضمير معدن السر.

On the punishment of the knower *(dhikr)*

ص 307) وقال النوري لكل شيء عقوبة وعقوبة العارف انقطاعه عن الذكر.

On the *murīd* and the *murād*

ص 308) وقال أبو الحسين النوري المريد عطشان والمراد سكران.

On contentment

ص 313) وقال النوري الرضا استقبال الأحكام بالفرح.

On disobedience, obedience, and ruse *(makr)*

ص 337) وقال النوري المعصية لا تخلو من الخذلان والطاعة لا تخلو من المكر.

Poem on ecstasy *(wajd)* "Ecstasy enraptures . . ."

ص 368) الوجد يطرب من في الوجد راحته / والوجد عند حضور الحق مفقود
قد كان يطربني وجدي فأذهلني / عن رؤية الوجد من في الوجد موجود

On Quran reciters and learned people

ص 402) وقال النوري ما أخاف على دمي الا القراء والعلماء.

Ch. 9. Correspondence between Nūrī and Junayd

Cambridge University Library, Taylor-Schechter Arabic 41.1, fols. 7b–10b

Fol. 7b

17 بسم الله الرحمن الرحيم رسالة ابي الحسين النوري الى ابي القسم
18 الجنيد رحمهما الله

19 قدسك الله بطهارات المجد في اعلا الدرجات وجعل منقلبك اليه
20 من اقرب القرب واتم الكشف واهنا الوصالات وامكنك
21 من انوار شهوده وبود وجوده والبسك تفريد كشوفه
22 واذهب عنك في شهوده الانتصاب بجوايده والتحلى
23 بصفاته والاستيراد[1] بتوحيده ما تكون به اليه واصلا
24 ومنه عليه واردا بل كشف لك رفيق حجته واشهدك
25 صفى حبه واجذبك اليه من قرب قربه وانتخبك لنفسه
26 من اهل عبادته و[القا بك؟] بنعمته لنفسه تستغني[2]

Fol. 8a

1 به عن كل معنى سواه فانت عند ذلك مخفى في مخفيات
2 غيبه مكنون في طوايات سر المكاتمات محروز في خا
3 لص علم التوحيد مخلد مصون يا من جمعت له الالسن
4 كلها ينطق كل لسان بتلوين معانيها فصار له لسان
5 البلا لسان ولسان النعما لسان ولسان المحن لسان ولسان
6 العمل لسان ولسان العارف لسان كلها داخلة في ال[. . .]
7 وقد بدا لي منها لسان وانا اتكلم فيها على علمي بجميع
8 الالسنة كلها وذلك ان لسان البلا لسان عملي[3] وقد اخذ
9 على ابو القسم في كل معنى فلم اشهد شيا الا [ا]رادني[4] له صار
10 البلا لي اولا واخرا ثم لم ازل مع ذلك حتى صب على من البلا
11 بلا ومن البلا بلا الى ما لا نهاية له فضمني وهو يزيد على من
12 البلا بلا وكشف لي من ذلك البلا عيبا من البلا او فوق ذلك
13 لما لا يطاق حمله فبقيت في بلاى زاد لي بلا ثم مع ذلك كله
14 صب على بلا الخليقة كلها فلم تكن لي في الخلق راحة
15 ولا معهم فرج فان سكنت اليهم بسكوني بلا على وان
16 هربت منهم صار هربي بلا على فيقع لي في الاوقات ان
17 اشكو او اسل الفرج فاتضرع فيفقد ان طير ان ذلك
18 على قلبي زيد لي من البلا فان شكوت كان بلا على ○ واعلم
19 يا با القسم ان كتابي اليك صار بلا على ولو لم اكتب كان
20 بلا على فميزت ذلك فاخترت فكاتبتك اذ استويت في
21 البلا فصار اختياري بلا على ثم مع ذلك ابتدا بحر البلا
22 وبحر فيه سفن البلا حتى اسير فلما ظننت انه قد فنى
23 وقرب الخلاص بدا لى بحر اعظم منه فجرى ببلايه واهو
24 اله ثم حملني فيه كما شا كيف شا واشاهد مشيته
25 في فصار بلا على ○ يا با القسم كيف السبيل الى الخلاص

Fol. 8b

1 مما لا خلاص منه ام كيف يطلب النجاة من طلب النجاة
2 بلا عليه ام كيف يفنى عنه من فناوه بلا عليه فانا في البلا

3 مغموس وبنار البلا محروق والى هول البلا مدفوع وفي
4 ظلمة البلا تايه فمن البلا مصدري وعلى البلا موردي
5 ومن البلا مشربي وفي البلا مسكني فان غرقني البلا فالي
6 البلا يدفعني وان نجاني البلا فالى بحر اهواله منه يوردني فان
7 اوقفني عليه فمن نفس البلا يزيد لي فكيف حال من هذه
8 حاله ام كيف يكون حال من حاله بلا عليه وذكره لحاله بلا
9 عليه فيا من اقيم اقام لكل شي معنى وحده قد اهديت اليك
10 ابتدايي ومنتهايي خاطبني مخاطبة جبار عنيد وملك قد
11 ملك على اهل مملكته بالسطوة ولا تلين لي في القول فتجعل
12 ذلك بلا على فاي جمع البلا كل البلا مع كل بلوى وصفته
13 ثم زيد على اضعاف ذلك ما بلغ عشر عشير ما انا به
14 متحقق وكلامي بلا على فلا تلجني ان اتكلم اخبرني بمن هذه
15 حالته اله ماوى ام لا ماوى له وهل من صفات الحق ابدا مثل
16 هذا ام من صفات المجد وغير ما انا به وهل لي في مكانك
17 نصيب ام هل فتحت لي بابا اليك او جعلت فتحها غلقا ام لهذا
18 المغلق ما يرجا فتحه ○ ابا القسم انت الواحد الذي [. . .]
19 كلهم عنك وبقيت وحدك معك اليك ابدى الى منها كلمة
20 تجمع لي فيها كلما سالت ولا باسطني فتزيدني بقراته
21 بلا اذ كان كلما[؟] اديت منها ذرة [. . .] ابديه
22 [. . .] جواب
23 [. . .] ابي القسم جنيد رحمه الله
24 [. . .] في محله واوطانه المنفرد من اهل دهره
25 [. . .] من اخلايه واقاربه واخدانه

Fol. 9a

1[. . .] المنطوى من ساير طرايه واقرانه المجهول
2 معناه عند معارفه واسنانه واعجب من ذلك انه لا
3 يقف في نفسه على نفسه ولا يميز معنى ينجوا[5] به من بلواه
4 وحققه الذي قد عمره وتكاثف عليه مطابق الغطا
5 وتلاصق عليه فتراكب الارض والسما وحبس في اضيق
6 امكنة الثرى [. . .] بافظع معزل البلا وشقى من كربه
7 فاجرى به ا[. . .]ر والقضا ومنع من ذلك التروح بالشكوى
8 فهو عظيم على فظيع فرط بلايه لا يسمع منه صوته ولا
9 يجاب عند ندايه لا ترحم عبرته ولا ينفعه بكاوه ولا
10 لمكروهه غاية فيومل انقضايه فهو لذلك قلق
11 موجع من ياس متوه مغيب به فيما لا يعرف ○
12 سلام عليك فاني احمد اليك الله الذي لا يحمد على عظيم المكاره
13غيره الذي خلق الخلق بمشيته ودبرهم بعلمه واجرى عليهم

ما اراد من قضايه وحكمه فهم في اسر قوته وقهر سلطانه
على مراتب تكوينه ونفاذ مشيته فاعلمهم به اشدهم
خشية له واخضعهم في ذلة التواضع لعظمته وابعد
هم تعرضا لمطالبة الاطلاع على شي مما استااثر[6] به
فاذا كان اهل العلم به كذلك فما ظنك بمن بعد عن ذلك ○
وصل الى كتابك وفهمت ما ضمنته من اخبارك مجيبك
عن تعابر[7] ايرادك[8] ورايت انك تظن انك قد انفردت بحالك
[. . .] باحد قبلك ○ واعلم رحمك الله
[. . .] قد سبق اليها قبلك [. . .]

Fol. 9b

وجرعوا من الذ عا[. . .] مذاق الموت[9] صرفا وقطعوا عن الا
طلاع على شي مما وقع بهم قطعا من مترادف متكاثف
متوالى الغطا فهم كذلك بذلك لا اماتة فيها ولا احياء وما
ذاك عندي الا انه ارادهم لنفسه واستخلصهم من خالص خا
لصته الجليل امره فحماهم منهم وسترهم عنهم بكل وجه
وبكل معنى يوردهم على فهم شي مما به طلبهم فاختلف
عند ذلك موارد القضايا والبست الاحكام بأفظع البلايا
وتوالت باختلافها بامور خرجت عن حد التاليف ليلا
يسكن المطلوب بها الى شيء تعلقه ولا ياوى الى قول يفهمه
فحكمه اذ كان كذلك خارج من معروف الاحكام وفهمه
منعكس عن حاضر الافهام فهو يجد فيما لا يعرفه
ما ينكره ويجد فيما ينكره ما يعرفه ثم ينقلب متكفيا
فيصير مشهورا تغير[؟] ذلك كله ثم يلتبس بقصور
ما لا يوقف عليه ولا يستدرك شي منه فهو على هذا النعت
وهذه الصفة تنقلب عليه اموره متكفية متكدرة
مذاق حقيقة الموت ومزاجه التلف ومحاضرة الثرى
وهو محتبس في ذلك مدة البقاء فلا هو مويس فيكون له
في الاياس فرجا ولا يلاحظه طمعا بارتحاله[10] من البلا قد
ملى منهم اللحم والعظم والبشر والشعر والعصب
مكر[و]ها افرط عند وقوعه من ان يوقفه على شي
من حده وهو على توالى الاوقات في مزيد وارد بحد
ما هذا منه يورا[11] لما وقع من فرطه انه مردود

Fol. 10a

الى عنده وانما مثل من هذه وصفته مثل البحر المثير المتلف
بامواجه المتكاثف المرتجع بشدة ارتجاعه فهو

3 في كل موجة واردة يظهر على عظيم بديع هايع وهو
4 لا يزال كذلك ما كان ماموراً بذلك وبعد فان ذكر
5 ما هذا نعته يكثر وصفه ويطول نعته به الكتاب
6 وهذه اطراف مما حضر من ذكره ○ واعلم ياخي ان ذلك
7 ليس من المطالب للمطلوب الا لعظيم شدة المحبة للمحبوب
8 وغيره عليه من غيره وضنه به عن من سواه واستيثارا
9 به عن من دونه غلبه عليه لعلو مكانه ولعظيم ما يزيده
10 وبعد فان هذا طريق متقرب مجرد غيبه عجيبه يوجد
11 بعضه في اعجب العجب وهو طريق عورت المسلك دونه
12 وقطع اثار الدلايل عليه ومحيت معالم الاشارة الدالة
13 على شي منه وليس يطلب به الا الفرد من الرجال في الازمنة
14 البعيدة هيهات وهيهات ما ابعد [حا]له واعجز كوني من
15 هذه الحال حاله [. . .] فلو[. . .]لك صاح وبدا على
16 الحقيقة هنالك [. . .] لغلبت [. . .] وقهرت سطوته
17 وثار افتخارا بها على اهل زمانه [. . .]بسط من القول والفعل
18 الى ما لا يمكن احد مقاومته وبعد فاني اومل لك ان يكون
19 خروجك قريب وان تنال ما ناله [ا]لمخلص المطيع المنتجب
20 الحبيب المحبوب ○ وذكرت في كتابك اني اجبتك في الواصل
21 اليك على رسم الاسم وكان وجودك على غير ما رسمت
22 فكذي يكون الجواب انما يكون الجواب على حسب ما تضمنه
23 الكتاب ○ وذكرت في كتابك ما يقع لك من اختلاف
24 واشيا تقع لك مني مختلفة ○ وفهمت وصفك لها

Fol. 10b

1 وقد ذكرت[. . .]
2 منها وال[. . .] فيها ان المطلوب يوخذ من كل احواله
3 ليلا يكون له شي يسكن اليه ولا يقر على معرفة حال ياوي اليها
4 او تقع احكامه مختلفة ثم يقع من تالفه ما ليس من جنس
5 التاليف ولكن ينتقل في احكامه وليلا يقر المطلوب اما على
6 شي يعرفه او يقر عنده فهو يجد الاضداد متقاومة عنده
7 ثم يختلف ذلك فيقع بالضد من ساعته كذلك بل يسرع
8 اليقين فيه وذلك كله لما وصفت لك ○ وذكرت تزايد البلا
9 عليك وفرطه وهذا ما لا بد منه ولا محيص عنه وبوقوع مثل
10 ذلك على شدته وفرطه يومل اجره وانت ان انكرت ذلك
11 [. . .] ك فاني لا انكره ولا بد من تمام احكام الله البلا الى مدة
12 [. . .] الانقضا ○ وذكرت انك تنظر فلا تعرف لاختلاف
13 ما يقع بك اتصلا [اتصالا] ولا تجد له سببا وانك لا تستغنى بمعرفة
14 [. . .] عن حالك والامر كما وصفته واخبرت به وكيف

قد تستغني [؟] بعلم حال لا يقف معك ولا يدوم ولا شا
[. . .] منها على معنى تصح ولا الذي تعتد بحق وكل
ذلك جاز عليك لما انت به مطلوب والطالب واقع عليك
باخذ كلما يجده وبذهاب كلما يعرفه [تعرفه][12] وبزوال كلما
تعقده وبانقلاب الاحوال كلها ليس من حيث يستدرك
علة ذلك فيها لان ذلك كاين بذهابك عنه ويغيبك [وبغيبك؟][13]
منه فان بدا لك منه بادى حال ذلك عن قريب وزوال ذلك كله[14]
في وقت يسير وذكرت شيا وجدته من كلامي يشبه
بعض ما هو في نفسك وهو بواعث ارسلتها وموانع
حبستها نعم هو شي فهمته ومعنى ذلك ان المطلوب
بهذه الحال تجده الاسنة تطلبه من ورايه حتى

Ch. 10. *Stations of the Hearts*

For the Arabic text of this treatise, see: Paul Nwyia, "Textes mystiques inédits d'Abū-l-Ḥasan al-Nūrī." *Mélanges de l'Université Saint-Joseph* 46 (1968): 130–43.

Appendix B

Comparative Table of the Material Related to Nūrī

The following table lists Nūrī's short sayings, poems, and the stories related to him that are collected in the early sources. A certain tradition associated with Nūrī in one source may be anonymous, or it may be attributed to another person in another source. The order of the traditions listed in the table is identical with that of the Arabic texts included in the Appendix. The short titles of the traditions also correspond to those of the Arabic texts in the Appendix; remarks and technical terms in parentheses help to distinguish between traditions on the same subject. The texts of the traditions may display considerable textual variations in the different sources; this is not indicated in the table. Traditions repeated in the sources are listed only once, with the exception of Nūrī's comments on the Quran collected by Sulamī, each of which is enlisted in separate line. If a comment is identical with a saying quoted also in any of the sources, the corresponding saying is indicated.

	Kalābādhī	Sarrāj	Sulamī: Generations	Sulamī: Realities	Kharkūshī	Abū Nuʿaym	Qushayrī	Sirjānī
On Sufism (*nafs*)	+	–	+	–	–	–	+	–
On the guide to God (intellect, *ʿaql*)	+	+	–	–	–	–	–	+
On Sufism (promulgating a station)	+	–	–	–	–	–	–	+
Poem on the impossibility of describing mystical states	+	–	–	–	–	–	–	–
On repentance	+	+	–	–	–	–	+	+
On the poor/Sufi (preferring others, *īthār*)	+	–	–	–	+	–	+	+
Poem on fearing God ("I fear You without being afraid . . .")	+	–	–	–	–	–	–	–
Poem on gratitude ("I express my gratitude . . .")	+	–	–	–	–	–	–	–
Poem on contentment ("Contentment is bitterness . . .")	+	–	–	–	–	–	–	+
On certainty and witnessing	+	+	–	–	–	–	+	+
Poem on ecstasy and recollection ("My love is so immoderate . . .")	+	–	–	–	–	–	–	–
Poem on reunion ("My reunion [. . .] showed me . . .")	+	–	–	–	–	–	–	–
Poem on nearness and witnessing ("Oh You, whom I witness . . .")	+	–	–	–	–	–	–	+
On connection and unveiling	+	+	–	–	–	–	–	–
On ecstasy compared to a flame	+	–	–	–	–	–	–	–

	Kalābādhī	Sarrāj	Sulamī: Generations	Sulamī: Realities	Kharkūshī	Abū Nuʿaym	Qushayrī	Sirjānī
Poem on absence and witnessing ("I witnessed [Him] perceiving . . .")	+	–	–	–	–	–	–	–
Poem on absence and veiling oneself ("I veiled myself from the world")	+	–	–	–	–	–	–	–
Story on Junayd's view on Nūrī's intoxicated ecstasy in the mosque	+	–	–	–	–	–	–	+
Poem on spiritual struggle ("I say: I have almost reached the limit . . .")	+	–	–	–	–	–	–	–
On public discourse (*kalām*)	+	–	–	–	–	–	–	–
Story on Nūrī's and Junayd's attitude towards public discourse	+	–	–	–	–	–	–	–
On the Sufi (*samāʿ*)	–	+	–	–	–	–	+	+
On the intellect (*ʿaql*)	–	+	–	–	–	–	–	+
To Abū Ḥamza's disciple on nearness	–	+	–	–	–	–	+	–
On love and tearing the veils	–	+	–	–	–	–	+	–
On the sincere poor (*faqīr ṣādiq, asbāb*)	–	+	+	–	–	–	–	+
Story on Nūrī throwing money to the canal	–	+	–	–	–	–	–	+
Story on Nūrī offering money to the Sufis	–	+	–	–	–	–	–	–
On the friend and the enemy	–	+	–	–	–	–	–	–
On reunion and separation	–	+	+	–	–	–	–	+
On sincerity	–	+	–	–	–	–	–	–

	Kalābādhī	Sarrāj	Sulamī: Generations	Sulamī: Realities	Kharkūshī	Abū Nuʿaym	Qushayrī	Sirjānī
On the Sufis' denomination (*wājid*)	–	+	–	–	–	–	–	–
Poem on *sirr* ("By my life! I have never entrusted my secret . . .")	–	+	–	–	+	–	–	+
Poem on nostalgia for a mystical state ("Let me weep . . .")	–	+	–	–	–	–	–	–
Story on Nūrī's death	–	+	–	–	–	–	+	+
Poem inducing ecstasy ("How many times a wailing dove . . .")	–	+	–	–	–	–	–	–
Story on Nūrī refusing to avail himself of a miracle	–	+	–	–	–	–	+	+
Story on Nūrī demanding a miracle	–	+	–	–	–	+	+	+
Verse on the power of names	–	+	–	–	–	–	–	–
Fragment of Nūrī's letter to Junayd on expressing tribulation	–	+	–	–	–	–	–	–
On erasure (*maḥw*), common people and the elite = Comment on Q 3:152	–	+	–	+	–	–	–	–
On learning and certainty	–	+	–	–	–	–	–	–
On theophany and creation	–	+	+	–	–	–	–	+
On theophany and good deeds	–	+	–	–	–	–	–	–
Poem on absence ("Don't you see that He captivated me?")	–	+	–	–	–	+	–	+
Ghulām Khalīl incident (different versions)	–	+	–	–	–	+	+	+

	Kalābādhī	Sarrāj	Sulamī: Generations	Sulamī: Realities	Kharkūshī	Abū Nuʿaym	Qushayrī	Sirjānī
Blasphemous saying on the muezzin and the dog	–	+	–	–	–	–	+	–
On intimacy and love	–	–	+	–	–	+	–	–
Poem on tribulations ("How many times I made my heart . . .")	–	–	+	–	–	–	–	–
On the Ḥabīb and the Khalīl	–	–	+	–	–	–	–	+
Nūrī and the handsome young man (*naẓar*)	–	–	+	–	–	+	–	+
On Sufism as developing spiritual qualities (*akhlāq*)	–	–	+	–	–	–	–	+
On phases of the mystical path and the different groups of wayfarers	–	–	+	–	–	–	–	–
Nūrī's and Junayd's behaviour during illness	–	–	+	–	–	+	–	+
On looking at things (*naẓar*)	–	–	+	–	–	–	–	+
On learning and mystical knowledge	–	–	+	–	–	–	+	–
On cognition (*ʿaql, rujūʿ*)	–	–	+	–	–	–	–	–
Poem on uncontrolled thoughts ("How many times I desired . . .")	–	–	+	–	–	–	–	+
On secondary means (*asbāb*)	–	–	+	–	–	+	–	+
Comment on Q 2:29 = First sentence of Nūrī's saying on the ways to God quoted by Abū Nuʿaym	–	–	–	+	–	+	–	–
Comment on Q 2:40	–	–	–	+	–	–	–	–
Comment on Q 2:245	–	–	–	+	–	–	–	–

	Kalābādhī	Sarrāj	Sulamī: Generations	Sulamī: Realities	Kharkūshī	Abū Nuʿaym	Qushayrī	Sirjānī
Comment on Q 2:273	–	–	–	+	–	–	–	–
Comment on Q 3:35	–	–	–	+	–	–	–	–
Comment on Q 3:97	–	–	–	+	–	–	–	–
Comment on Q 3:128	–	–	–	+	–	–	–	–
Comment on Q 3:152 = On erasure, common people and the elite (*maḥw*)	–	+	–	+	–	–	–	–
Comment on Q 4:128	–	–	–	+	–	–	–	–
Comment on Q 6:9	–	–	–	+	–	–	–	–
Comment on Q 6:36	–	–	–	+	–	–	–	–
Comment on Q 6:83	–	–	–	+	–	–	–	–
Comment on Q 7:2	–	–	–	+	–	–	–	–
Comment on Q 7:29	–	–	–	+	–	–	–	–
Comment on Q 10:22	–	–	–	+	–	–	–	–
Comment on Q 11:17	–	–	–	+	–	–	–	–
Comment on Q 14:10	–	–	–	+	–	–	–	–
Comment on Q 15:72	–	–	–	+	–	–	–	–
Comment on Q 18:28	–	–	–	+	–	–	–	–
Comment on Q 22:78	–	–	–	+	–	–	–	–
Comment on Q 24:63	–	–	–	+	–	–	–	–
Comment on Q 27:50	–	–	–	+	–	–	–	–
Comment on Q 35:32	–	–	–	+	–	–	–	–
Comment on Q 36:61	–	–	–	+	–	–	–	–
Comment on Q 39:60	–	–	–	+	+	–	–	–
Comment on Q 56:85 = [To Abū Ḥamza's disciple] on nearness	–	+	–	+	–	–	+	–

	Kalābādhī	Sarrāj	Sulamī: Generations	Sulamī: Realities	Kharkūshī	Abū Nuʿaym	Qushayrī	Sirjānī
Comment on Q 57:3 = On the intellect (*ʿaql*)	–	+	–	+	–	–	–	–
Comment on Q 72:3	–	–	–	+	–	–	–	–
Comment on Q 98:8 = On contentment (*riḍā*)	–	–	–	+	+	–	+	+
On the heart (*qalb*)	–	–	–	–	+	–	–	–
On intimacy with God (*uns*)	–	–	–	–	+	–	–	–
On contemplation (*mushāhada, sirr, hayba, ishtiyāq*)	–	–	–	–	+	–	–	–
On certainty and recollection (*yaqīn, maʿrifa, tawakkul, munājāt, dhikr*)	–	–	–	–	+	–	–	–
On contentment (*riḍā*)	–	–	–	+	+	–	+	+
On trust in God and annihilation	–	–	–	–	+	–	–	–
On a saying of the Prophet on poverty	–	–	–	–	+	–	–	–
On hidden desire	–	–	–	–	+	–	–	–
Comment on Q 29:45	–	–	–	–	+	–	–	–
Saying on the mystical moment and proper behavior	–	–	–	–	+	–	+	–
On allusion to the Real (*ishāra, ʿibāra, sirr*)	–	–	–	–	+	–	–	–
On allusion (*ishāra*)	–	–	–	–	+	–	–	–
On ecstasy	–	–	–	–	+	–	–	–
On veiling (*satr*)	–	–	–	–	+	–	–	–
On making a spiritual state permanent	–	–	–	–	+	–	–	–

	Kalābādhī	Sarrāj	Sulamī: Generations	Sulamī: Realities	Kharkūshī	Abū Nuʿaym	Qushayrī	Sirjānī
On annihilation and the stations of Sufism	–	–	–	–	+	–	–	–
Story on Nūrī and the thief	–	–	–	–	+	+	+	–
Poem on recollection and absence	–	–	–	–	+	–	–	–
Poem on the heart ("My heart indicates towards You . . .")	–	–	–	–	+	–	–	–
Poem on the heart ("The hearts are not in the position to love You")	–	–	–	–	+	–	–	–
Poem on annihilation ("If I knew the way to You")								
Poem on the inner heart ("The secrets of my inner heart . . .")	–	–	–	–	+	+	–	–
Poem on absence ("How said it is . . .")	–	–	–	–	+	+	–	–
A tradition on Joseph	–	–	–	–	+	–	–	–
Nūrī's last words	–	–	–	–	+	–	+	–
Report on Nūrī's circumstances during the persecutions provoked by Ghulām Khalīl	–	–	–	–	–	+	–	–
Story on Nūrī's countering the carnal soul (*nafs*)	–	–	–	–	–	+	–	–
On outward imitation of Sufism	–	–	–	–	–	+	+	+
Spiritual advices (*waṣāyā*)	–	–	–	–	–	+	–	–
Poetic correspondence on annihilation (*fanā'*)	–	–	–	–	–	+	–	–

	Kalābādhī	Sarrāj	Sulamī: Generations	Sulamī: Realities	Kharkūshī	Abū Nuʿaym	Qushayrī	Sirjānī
Poem on the inner heart (*sirr*) and Junayd's answer	–	–	–	–	–	+	–	–
On Muḥammad	–	–	–	–	–	–	+	–
On *tawḥīd*	–	–	–	–	–	–	+	–
On ecstasy, finding and loosing (*wajd, faqd*)	–	–	–	–	–	–	+	–
On fearing God	–	–	–	–	–	–	+	–
Story on Nūrī starving in the desert	–	–	–	–	–	–	+	–
On insight (*firāsa*)	–	–	–	–	–	–	+	–
On violating the religious law (=one of Nūrī's spiritual advices (*waṣāyā*) quoted by Abū Nuʿaym)	–	–	–	–	–	+	+	–
Junayd's estimation of Nūrī (*ṣidq*)	–	–	–	–	–	–	+	–
Nūrī's equality with Junayd	–	–	–	–	–	–	+	–
Story on Nūrī hiding his piety	–	–	–	–	–	–	+	–
On the possibility of witnessing God	–	–	–	–	–	–	+	–
Story on Nūrī's capacity of insight (*firāsa*)	–	–	–	–	–	–	+	–
Poem on theoretical learning and mystical knowledge	–	–	–	–	–	–	–	+
On Sufism (*ishāra, ʿibāra*)	–	–	–	–	–	–	–	+
On abstinence (*zuhd*)	–	–	–	–	–	–	–	+
On the *murīd*	–	–	–	–	–	–	–	+
On tribulation (*balā', īmān*)	–	–	–	–	–	–	–	+

	Kalābādhī	Sarrāj	Sulamī: Generations	Sulamī: Realities	Kharkūshī	Abū Nuʿaym	Qushayrī	Sirjānī
On eating; Gunayd's interpretation of Nūrī's words	–	–	–	–	–	–	–	+
On servanthood (*ʿubūdiyya*)	–	–	–	–	–	–	–	+
Story on inclination to look at youngsters (*naẓar*, with Junayd sending the inquirer to Nūrī)	–	–	–	–	–	–	–	+
Story on Nūrī losing his heart to a young man (Junayd interpreting what happened)	–	–	–	–	–	–	–	+
On the tripartite division of the heart	–	–	–	–	–	–	–	+
On the punishment of the knower (*dhikr*)	–	–	–	–	–	–	–	+
On the *murīd* and the *murād*	–	–	–	–	–	–	–	+
On disobedience and ruse (*makr*)	–	–	–	–	–	–	–	+
Poem on ecstasy ("Ecstasy enraptures . . .")	–	–	–	–	–	–	–	+
On Quran reciters and learned people	–	–	–	–	–	–	–	+

Appendix C

Technical Terms

ʿamal: practice
ʿaql: intellect
ʿārif: possessor of inspired knowledge
balāʾ: tribulation, trial, affliction
baqāʾ: subsistence, permanence
bāṭin: internal, hidden
bayān: clarity
buʿd: farness
ḍamīr: mind, heart, innermost
dhāt: substance
dhawq: tasting, experiencing directly
dhikr: recollection, recalling, remembering, and enunciating
fanāʾ: annihilation of the self, passing away
faqīr: poor, person depending on God, Sufi
ghayb, ghayba: absence (of the mystic from this world), withdrawal, inner and unseen world of God
ḥāl: mystical state
ḥaqīqa: true reality
al-ḥaqq: the Real (one of God's names)
hayba: fear
ikhlāṣ: sincerity
ʿilm: learning, science
ishāra: allusion
istighrāq: absorption
ittiṣāl: connection

jadhb: attraction
jamʿ: reunion, togetherness
jalāl: splendor, majesty
jamāl: benevolence
jihād: spiritual struggle
khāṭir, (pl: *khawāṭir):* sudden, uncontrolled thought
lisān: tongue, language
maḥabba: love
maḥw: erasure
maqām: station of the mystical path leading to God
maʿrifa: inspired knowledge
mujāhada: spiritual struggle
mukāshafa: unveiling
murīd: disciple, seeker
mushāhada: witnessing, contemplation
nafs: carnal soul, self
najwā: intimate conversation
naẓar: gaze, looking, considering, studying
qalb: (outer) heart
qurb: closeness
riḍā: contentment
rūḥ: spirit
rujūʿ: returning from God to the world
sabab: (plural: *asbāb)*reason, means
ṣahw: sobriety
samāʿ: hearing, audition, ceremony consisting in recitation of poems accompanied by music
ṣidq: trustworthiness
ṣifa: attribute
shuhūd: seeing, witnessing
shukr: gratitude
shurūd: running away, roaming, straying
sirr: inner heart, secret
sukr: intoxication
sukūn: calmness
sukūn ilā: reliance on
tafriqa: separation
tajallin: revelation, theophany
tawājud: exhibiting ecstasy

tawakkul: trust in God
tawba: repentance
tazkiyat al-nafs: purification of the self
uns: intimacy
wajd: ecstasy, encounter
wārid: oncoming event, thought, inspiration
waṣl: arriving at, connection with
waṭan: abode
wiṣāl: being together, reunion
wujūd: finding, being found, existence
wuṣūl: arrival (at God)
yaqīn: certainty
ẓāhir: external, manifest
zuhd: abstinence

Notes

Introduction

1. Qushayrī, *Risāla.* (Henceforth: *Treatise.),* ed. Zurayq (Beirut: Dār al-Ǧīl, n.d.), 71.

2. For a detailed study of the problem, see Jawid A. Mojaddedi, "Getting Drunk with Abū Yazīd or Staying Sober with Junayd: The Creation of a Popular Typology of Sufism." *Bulletin of the School of Oriental and African Studies* 66, no. 1 (2003): 1–13.

3. On the formation of these schools and especially on the school of Nishapur see Sara Sviri: "Hakim Tirmidhi and the Malamati movement in Early Sufism" in *The Heritage of Sufism,* ed. Leonard Lewisohn (Oxford: Oneworld, 1999), 1:583–613; Sara Sviri: "The Early Mystical Schools of Baghdad and Nīshāpūr or: In Search of Ibn Munāzil," *Jerusalem Studies in Arabic and Islam* 30 (2005): 450–82. On the Sufis of Baghdad see for example Ahmet T. Karamustafa, *Sufism. The Formative Period* (Edinburgh: Edinburgh University Press, 2007), 1–37.

4. Cf. for example the Baghdadi Sufis enumerated by Sīrjānī in Bilal Orfali and Nada Saav, eds., *Sufism, Black and White. A Critical Edition of Kitāb al-Bayāḍ wa-l-Sawād by Abū l-Ḥasan al-Sīrjānī* (Henceforth: Sīrjānī, *Black and White in the Words of Wisdom.)* (Leiden and Boston: Brill, 2012), 251. But see also Kharkūshī, *Tahdhīb al-asrār* (Henceforth: *Revision of the Secrets),* (Abu Dhabi: al-Majmaʿ al-Thaqāfī, 1999), 39, who differentiates between two branches of mysticism: Sufism, "which is the path *(ṭarīqa)* of Iraq," and Malāmatiyya, which is "the path of Khorasan."

5. Abdel Kader and Ali Hassan, *The Life, Personality and Writings of al-Junayd,* (London: Luzac, 1976), IX.

6. Cf. Abū Nuʿaym, *Ḥilyat al-awliyā'.* (Henceforth: Abū Nuʿaym, *Ornament of God's Friends.*) (Beirut: Dār al-Kutub al-ʿIlmiyya, 1988), 10:249–50; and Hujwírí, *The Kashf al-Maḥjúb.* The Oldest Persian Treatise

on Sufism. Translated by Reynold A. Nicholson (Leyden: Brill; London: Luzac and co., 1911), 130, 176, 189–90.

7. See for example Alexander Knysh, *Islamic Mysticism. A Short History* (Leiden: Brill, 2000), 60–63; Annemarie Schimmel, *Mystical Dimensions of Islam* (Chapel Hill: University of North Carolina Press, 1975), 60; and her "Abū'l-Ḥusayn al-Nūrī: Qibla of the Lights," in *The Heritage of Sufism*, ed. Leonard Lewisohn (Oxford: Oneworld, 1999), 1:59–64; Arthur John Arberry, *Sufism. An Account of the Mystics of Islam* (London and New York: Routledge, 2008); cf. also Reynold A. Nicholson, *The Mystics of Islam* (Bloomington: World Wisdom, 2002), 76–77.

8. Cf. Kenneth S. Avery, *A Psychology of Early Sufi Samāʿ* (London and New York: RoutledgeCurzon, 2004), 193–200 and 204–10; expounding upon Nūrī's relation to the so-called mystical concerts, or recitations of poems, and the altered states he displayed on such occasions.

9. Paul Nwyia, "Textes mystiques inédits d'Abū-l-Ḥasan al-Nūrī," *Mélanges de l'Université Saint-Joseph* 46 (1968): 117–54. Nwyia discussed the same treatise in a chapter of his *Exégèse coranique et langage mystique* (Paris: Université de Paris, 1970), 316–48.

10. The source containing that saying (Sīrjānī's *Black and White in the Words of Wisdom)* had not been published yet when Nwyia wrote his works on the *Stations of the Hearts*, and it is only natural that Nwyia was unaware of its existence. However, the fact that Nwyia did not refer to Nūrī's sayings in his treatment of the *Stations of the Hearts* is regrettable since the imageries of the two corpuses are quite distinct.

11. Tirmīdhī, *Bayān al-farq bayna l-ṣadr wa-l-qalb wa-l-fu'ād wa-l-lubb* (Amman: Al-Markaz al-Malakī li-l-Buḥūth wa-l-Dirāsāt al-Islāmiyya, 2012). The authorship of the treatise is questionable, see Bernd Radtke, "Some Recent Research on al-Ḥakīm al-Tirmidhī." *Der Islam* 83 (2006): 40–41.

12. Cf. Kalābādhī, *Kitāb al-taʿarruf li-madhhab ahl al-taṣawwuf.* (Henceforth: Kalābādhī, *Doctrine of the Sufis.*) Edited by Arthur John Arberry (Cairo: al-Khānjī, 1994), 112; and Sīrjānī, *Black and White in the Words of Wisdom*, 251.

13. Richard Gramlich, *Alte Vorbilder des Sufitums* (Wiesbaden: Harrassowitz, 1995), 2:381–46.

14. Kalābādhī, *Doctrine of the Sufis*, 99. Cf. a different version of the story in Sīrjānī, *Black and White in the Words of Wisdom*, 16–17.

15. Arthur John Arberry, *Pages from the Kitāb al-Lumaʿ of Abū Naṣr al-Sarrāj being the Lacuna in the Edition of R. A. Nicholson* (London: Luzac, 1947) 6; and cf. also Sarrāj, *Book of Flashes*, 304–5, where Sarrāj includes Nūrī among those who overtly display ecstasy *(tawājud).*

16. Mojaddedi, "Getting Drunk with Abū Yazīd or Staying Sober with Junayd," 1.

17. The reason for this neglect can only be guessed at. While only one tradition related to Nūrī is quoted in the *Qūt al-qulūb* (an anecdote that does not occur in any of the early sources studied here), Thawrī, whose name is orthographically very similar to Nūrī, is mentioned in the work 110 times (frequently without the first name Sufyān). One might suggest that some of the traditions connected to Thawrī belonged originally to Nūrī since the confusion of these names is well documented in the Sufi sources. (See, for example, several traditions attributed alternatively to Thawrī and Nūrī in Sulamī's *Realities of Interpretation* discussed in the corresponding chapter of this book.) However, none of the 110 traditions is attributed to Nūrī in the early sources.

18. Sarrāj, *Kitāb al-lumaʿ fī l-taṣawwuf.* (Henceforth: *Book of Flashes),* ed. Reynold Alleyne Nicholson (Leiden and London: Brill and Luzac, 1914).

19. Sulamī, *Ṭabaqāt al-ṣūfiyya.* (Henceforth: *Generations of the Sufis)* (Cairo: al-Khānjī, 1997).

20. Kharkūshī, *Tahdhīb al-asrār.* (Henceforth: *Revision of the Secrets*), ed. Bassām Muḥammad Bārūd (Abu Dhabi: al-Majmaʿ al-Thaqāfī, 1999).

21. Qushayrī, *Risāla.* (Henceforth: *Treatise.*), ed. Zurayq (Beirut: Dār al-Jīl, n.d.). Occasionally, another edition was also used: ed. Maḥmūd (Cairo: Dār al-Shaʿb, 1989).

22. Gerhard Böwering and Bilal Orfali, *The Comfort of the Mystics. A Manual and Anthology of Early Sufism.* (Henceforth: Ṭabarī, *Comfort of the Mystics.*) (Leiden and Boston: Brill, 2013).

23. Exact numbers cannot be given, since various traditions occur in more or less divergent versions, and sometimes they are divided into parts in some of the sources while presented as one continuous text in others.

24. Kalābādhī's *Doctrine of the Sufis* and Sulamī's *Generations of the Sufis* have only one tradition shared, while the *Doctrine of the Sufis* and the *Ornament of God's Friends* have no identical tradition quoted in either of them. On the other hand, the overlap between the *Ornament of God's Friends* and the rest of the early sources is greater.

25. Sulamī, *Ḥaqā'iq al-tafsīr* (henceforth: *Realities.*), ed. Sayyid ʿUmrān (Beirut: Dār al-Kutub al-ʿIlmiyya, 2001). For Nūrī's sayings included in Sulamī's commentary, I consulted also Paul Nwyia, "Textes mystiques inédits d'Abū-l-Ḥasan al-Nūrī." *Mélanges de l'Université Saint-Joseph* 46 (1968): 117–54.

26. The text was published by Paul Nwyia, "Textes mystiques inédits d'Abū-l-Ḥasan al-Nūrī." *Mélanges de l'Université Saint-Joseph* 46 (1968): 117–54.

27. Carl W. Ernst, *Words of Ecstasy in Sufism* (Kuala Lumpur: S. Abdul Majeed and Co., 1994), 25.

28. Cf. Qūnawī, *Ḥusn al-taṣarruf fī sharḥ kitāb al-ta'arruf li-madhhab ahl al-taṣawwuf* (Österreichische Nationalbibliothek, MS Cod.N.F.289), fol. 263b, according to which the copy was finished in AH 1246, on "*yawm 'Arafa min shahr ramaḍān*," which probably refers to the second day of the Hajj, *yawm 'Arafa*, when pilgrims visit Mount 'Arafa and stand there praying. That feast is celebrated on the ninth day of the month *dhū l-ḥijja* (and not of the month Ramadan). In any case, both Ramadan and *yawm 'Arafa* in AH 1246 correspond to AD 1831, either in February or May. A printed edition of Qūnawī's commentary was prepared by Ṭāhā al-Dasūqī Ḥubayshī (Cairo, 2016), which was unavailable.

29. Anṣārī, *Iḥkām al-dalāla 'alā taḥrīr al-risāla* 2 vols. (Damascus: Dār an-Nu'mān lil-'Ulūm, 2000); 'Arūsī, *Ḥāshiyat al-'allāma Muṣṭafā al-'Arūsī al-musammā Natā'ij al-afkār al-qudsiyya fī bayān ma'ānī sharḥ al-risāla al-qushayriyya li-shaykh al-islām Zakariyyā ibn Muḥammad al-Anṣārī* 4 vols. (Beirut: Dār al-Kutub al-'Ilmiyya, 2007). The latter contains the commentary by Anṣārī as well.

30. Jawid A. Mojaddedi, *The Biographical Tradition in Sufism* (Richmond, UK: Curzon, 2001), 179–81; Kenneth Avery, *Shiblī. His Life and Thought in the Sufi Tradition* (New York: State University of New York Press, 2014), 82–86.

31. On the *miḥna*, see John A. Nawas, "A Reexamination of Three Current Explanations for al-Ma'mūn's Introduction of the Miḥna," *International Journal of Middle Eastern Studies* 26 (1994), 615–29; John A. Nawas, "The Miḥna of 218 A. H./833 A. D. Revisited: An Empirical Study." *Journal of the American Oriental Society* 116, no. 4 (1996): 698–708; Martin Hinds, "Miḥna," in *The Encyclopaedia of Islam*[2] (Leiden: Brill, 1993, 8:2–6; Nimrod Hurvitz, "Miḥna as Self-Defense," *Studia Islamica* 92 (2001): 93–111.

32. For the date of the final abolition of the inquisition, see Christopher Melchert, "Religious Policies of the Caliphs from al-Mutawakkil to al-Muqtadir, A. H. 232–295/A. D. 847–908," 326–30.

33. Cf. Abū Nu'aym, *Ornament of God's Friends*, 10:249; Dhahabī, *Siyar a'lām an-nubalā'*, ed. by Ḥassān 'Abd al-Mannān (Beirut: Bayt al-Afkār al-Duwaliyya, 2004), 1006.

34. Cf. Abū Nu'aym, *Ornament of God's Friends*, 10:249–50; Dhahabī, *Siyar a'lām an-nubalā'*, 1006.

35. Atif Khalil, "Abū Ṭālib al-Makkī and the Nourishment of Hearts *(Qūt al-qulūb)* in the Context of Early Sufism," *Muslim World* 102, no. 2 (2012): 3.

36. On the conflicts between the Sufis and the religious-political establishment, see Gerhard Böwering, "Early Sufism between Persecution and Heresy," in *Islamic Mysticism Contested*, ed. Frederick de Jong and Bernd Radtke (Leiden: Brill, 1999), 45–67.

37. On the inquisition of Ghulām Ḥalīl, see, for example, Ahmet T. Karamustafa, *Sufism. The Formative Period* (Edinburgh: Edinburgh University Press, 2007), 23; Laury Silvers, *A Soaring Minaret. Abu Bakr al-Wasiti and the Rise of Baghdadi Sufism* (New York: State University of New York Press, 2010), 27.

38. Cf. Sarrāj, *Book of Flashes*, 195.

39. Sulamī, *Generations of Sufis*, 165–66. Cf. also Abū Nuʿaym, *Ornament of God's Friends*, 10:254; Sīrjānī, *Black and White in the Words of Wisdom*, 240.

40. Sīrjānī, *Black and White in the Words of Wisdom*, 239.

41. Cf. Qushayrī, *Treatise*, ed. Zurayq, 439.

42. Cf. Sarrāj, *Book of Flashes*, 193–94; Sīrjānī, *Black and White in the Words of Wisdom*, 24; Avery, *Shiblī*, 91.

43. Cf. Qushayrī, *Treatise*, ed. Maḥmūd, 594.

Chapter 1

1. Arthur John Arberry prepared the edition of the Arabic original based on four manuscripts. It was first published in Cairo in 1934. He also translated the work into English, which appeared under the title *The Doctrine of the Ṣūfīs* (Cambridge: Cambridge University Press, 1935). References to Kalābādhī, *Doctrine of the Sufis*, are to the Arabic text edited by Arberry (although not to the first edition but to Cairo: al-Khānajī, 1994), and all English translations are mine unless otherwise indicated. The *Doctrine of the Sufis* was translated to French by Roger Deladrière, see: Kalābādhī, *Traite de soufisme* (Paris: Sindbad, 1981).

2. On the scarce information about his life and works see Arberry, *Doctrine of the Ṣūfīs*, IX–XV.

3. Abū l-Ḥusayn al-Manṣūr al-Ḥallāj was a Baghdadi Sufi executed in 922 on religious charges. On Ḥallāj see Louis Massignon, *La Passion de Husayn Ibn Mansûr Hallâj* (Paris: Gallimard, 1975).

4. Cf. Arberry, *Doctrine of the Ṣūfīs* XIV–XV, n. 3.

5. Arberry, *Doctrine of the Ṣūfīs*, XV, n. 3.

6. Cf. Arberry, *Doctrine of the Ṣūfīs*, XIII.

7. Subchapter "Some Methodological Observations, the Use of Sufi Commentaries."

8. See the chapter on *taṣawwuf* in any of the basic Sufi manuals, for example, Qushayrī, *Treatise*, ed. Zurayq, 279–88; and also Kalābādhī's other chapter on Sufism, *Doctrine of the Sufis*, 62–64.

9. Kalābādhī, *Doctrine of the Sufis*, 9. Cf. Qushayrī, *Treatise*, ed. Zurayq, 439; Sulamī, *Generations of the Sufis*, 166.

10. On *nafs* see, for example, Schimmel, *Mystical Dimensions,* 112–14; on the relation between *nafs* and *rūḥ,* see Qushayrī, *Treatise,* ed. Zurayq, 86–88.

11. Qūnawī, *Ḥusn al-taṣarruf,* fol. 16a.

12. Kalābādhī, *Doctrine of the Sufis,* 67. Cf. Kharkūshī, *Revision of the Secrets,* 157; and Qushayrī, *Treatise,* ed. Zurayq, 278 (the same saying referring to the poor), and ibid., 281 (as referring to the Sufi). Cf. also Sīrjānī, *Black and White in the Words of Wisdom,* 46–47 (again referring to the Sufi).

13. Cf. Sarrāj, *Book of Flashes,* 26: "The people of Syria call the Sufis poor men *(fuqarā').*"

14. Qūnawī, *Ḥusn al-taṣarruf,* fol. 122b.

15. Ibid.

16. Cited by Qūnawī, ibid.

17. Abū l-Najīb al-Suhrawardī, *Ādāb al-murīdīn.* Edited by Menahem Milson (Jerusalem: Maʿhad al-Dirāsāt al-Āsiyawiyya wa-l-Ifrīqiyya. al-Jāmiʿa al-ʿIbriyya fī Ūrushalīm al-Quds, 1977), 23–24.

18. Cf. Kalābādhī, *Doctrine of the Sufis,* 111.

19. Ibid., 63. Cf. Sīrjānī, *Black and White in the Words of Wisdom,* 41.

20. Saying attributed to Abū Yazīd al-Bisṭāmī, cf. Kalābādhī, *Doctrine of the Sufis,* 63.

21. Kalābādhī, *Doctrine of the Sufis,* 63.

22. Ibid.

23. Ibid.

24. Qūnawī, *Ḥusn al-taṣarruf,* fol. 112b.

25. Ibid., fol. 112b.

26. Ibid., fol. 113a.

27. Especially in the case of the word *al-qawwām.* The original, indefinite prepositional phrase *(ittiṣāl bi-qiwām)* is changed to the phrase *ittiṣāl bi-l-qawwām. Qawwām* means "custodian, caretaker, provider," and with the definite article (which is absent in Nūrī's saying) the word would obviously refer to God. (The doubling of the "w" does not affect the written form of the Arabic word. This word can be read in different ways depending on the vocals and other auxiliary signs that the writing does not indicate.) Qūnawī expounds upon both possible interpretations *(qiwām* or *al-qawwām).* On the one hand, he adds the definite article and juxtaposes God's name *al-ḥaqq* (the Real) to the word *qawwām* (provider), thus making it refer inevitably to God. On the other hand, he explains also the indefinite form meaning "connection with an essence": "Absorption in love and annihilation in the tremendousness of the [divine] substance, in [God's] attributes and acts, when man obtains connection [to God] *(ittiṣāl),* distracting him from turning to the states of others (Qūnawī, *Ḥusn al-taṣarruf,* fol. 113b)." Obviously, the double meaning of Nūrī's saying

is not accidental; concise and ambiguous phrasing is among the main characteristics of Sufi texts. It has to be noted as well that a version of Nūrī's saying preserved in Sīrjānī's *Black and White in the Words of Wisdom* (on p. 41) has *"ittiṣāl bi-dawām,"* meaning "permanent connection."

28. Kalābādhī, *Doctrine of the Sufis*, 63. An interesting peculiarity of the poem is the use of the word *qāl*, which is normally a verb, here has the function of a noun (meaning "speech, utterance"), as evidenced by the preposition and the definite article attached to it *(bi-l-qāl)*. Furthermore, the negation *lā* before the first occurrence of the word *(lā qāla)* is a general negation, which normally stands with nouns. Considering this, and the version in Qūnawī's commentary (fol. 114a), which reads *mā lā qāla bi-l-qāl (=mā lā qawl*[a] *[lahu] bi-l-qawl*[i], "which cannot be uttered") instead of *man lā qāla bi-l-qāl*, the translation "For how could be described that which cannot be uttered?" is possible, too.

29. Qūnawī, *Ḥusn al-taṣarruf*, fol. 114a.

30. Kalābādhī, *Doctrine of the Sufis*, 111. The translation follows the interpretation of Qūnawī, *Ḥusn al-taṣarruf*, fol. 230a.

31. Kalābādhī, *Doctrine of the Sufis*, 112.

32. Qūnawī, *Ḥusn al-taṣarruf*, fol. 233a.

33. Ibid.

34. Kalābādhī, *Doctrine of the Sufis*, 63.

35. Ibid., 37. Cf. Sarrāj, *Book of Flashes*, 37–38, 40; Sīrjānī, *Black and White in the Words of Wisdom*, 69.

36. Kalābādhī, *Doctrine of the Sufis*, 37. The words "proof" and "guide" are identical in Arabic *(dalīl)*, therefore the original phraseology of the two sayings is more closely related than the English translation suggests.

37. Qūnawī, *Ḥusn al-taṣarruf*, fol. 55b–56a.

38. The followers of the Muʿtazilite school of rationalist theology, which flourished in Iraq in the eighth to tenth centuries.

39. *"Inna maʿrifatahu bi-l-dalīl,"* Qūnawī says (*Ḥusn al-taṣarruf*, fol. 55b), but apparently by "proof" he means here textual proofs, that is, the Quran and the *ḥadīth*.

40. Despite that according to medieval views animals do not possess rational faculty. See, for example, William C. Chittick, *The Sufi Path of Knowledge: Ibn Arabi's Metaphysics of Imagination* (Albany: State University of New York, 1989), 159.

41. Qūnawī mentions Quran 28:56 as well: "Surely you won't guide anyone you wish; but God will guide those whom He wants."

42. Kalābādhī, *Doctrine of the Sufis*, 78. Cf. a different version of the same saying in Sarrāj, *Book of Flashes*, 340.

43. For a comprehensive treatment of the concept of union and the variety of terms used for its description, see: Michael Sells, "Bewildered

Tongue: The Semantics of Mystical Union in Islam." In *Mystical Union in Judaism, Christianity and Islam: An Ecumenical Dialogue,* edited by Moshe Idel and Bernard McGinn (London: Bloomsbury Academic, 2016), 87–124.

44. Cf. Qushayrī, *Treatise,* ed. Zurayq, 88 (the chapter on *sirr*).

45. Ibid. The saying is attributed to Ḥallāj by Sarrāj, cf. *Book of Flashes,* 231.

46. Kalābādhī, *Doctrine of the Sufis,* 101. I could not identify the *ḥadīth,* but it appears also in the mystical-magical work of Būnī, *Shams al-maʿārif al-kubrā* (Cairo: Dār al-Kaḥajjā al-Bayḍā', 2011), 11.

47. Qūnawī, *Ḥusn al-taṣarruf,* fols. 150a–b.

48. Kalābādhī, *Doctrine of the Sufis,* 101.

49. Ibid.

50. Qūnawī, *Ḥusn al-taṣarruf,* fol. 150a. Qūnawī attributes this exposition to the "author of *al-ʿAwārif,*" by which he most probably means the *ʿAwārif al-maʿārif* by Suhrawardī. However, I was not able to find the cited passage there. This passage attributed to the author of *al-ʿAwārif* appears in various Sufi works, for example, ʿAbd Allāh ibn Asʿad al-Yāfiʿī: *Nashr al-maḥāsin al-ghāliya fī faḍl al-mashā'ikh al-ṣūfiyya aṣḥāb al-maqāmāt al-ʿāliya* (Beirut: Dār al-Kutub al-ʿIlmiyya, 2000), 22.

51. Kalābādhī, *Doctrine of the Sufis,* 73. Cf. also Sarrāj, *Book of Flashes,* 81; Qushayrī, *Treatise,* ed. Zurayq, 181; Sīrjānī, *Black and White in the Words of Wisdom,* 291.

52. Cf. Qūnawī, *Ḥusn al-taṣarruf,* fols. 137b–138a.

53. Qūnawī, *Ḥusn al-taṣarruf,* fol. 138b.

54. Cf. Qushayrī, *Treatise,* ed. Zurayq, 65–66. For the later development of the concepts of "reunion" *(jamʿ),* "second separation" *(farq thānī* or *farq baʿd al-jamʿ),* and reunion of reunion *(jamʿ al-jamʿ)* in Ibn ʿArabī's school of the unity of existence, its influence on Iranian philosophical thinking in the thirteenth through the seventeenth centuries, parallels in Zen Buddhism, see Toshihiko Izutsu, *Creation and the Timeless Order of Things* (Ashland, OR: White Cloud Press, 1994), especially 11–29.

55. Kalābādhī, *Doctrine of the Sufis,* 78. For an alternative English translation of the poem, and on the concept of proximity in the works of seven early Sufi authors, see Mohammed Rustom, "Approaches to Proximity and Distance in Early Sufism," *Mystics Quarterly* 33, no. 1/2 (2007), 1–25 (Nūrī's poem is on p. 6).

56. Although mystical states are usually supposed to be granted by God *("al-aḥwāl mawāhib,"* cf. Qushayrī, *Treatise,* ed. Zurayq, 57.), sometimes they may originate from one's own consciousness. In the latter case, they are in fact false states that deceive the seeker. Cf. the commentary of Qūnawī (fol. 165b), to be discussed below in connection with Nūrī's saying on ecstasy.

57. Qūnawī, *Ḥusn al-taṣarruf*, fols. 148–49a.

58. Ibid., 149a.

59. The translation follows the version that appears in the manuscript of the commentary (fol. 149a), which is more easily intelligible than that of the printed edition. In the printed edition the first line of the poem is the following: "Oh, You, whom I witness [far?] from me, although I regard to be close to me." The difference between the two versions in the Arabic original is only one letter (*ʿannī* in the printed edition, *ʿandī* in the manuscript). Cf. also the version that appears in Sīrjānī, *Black and White in the Words of Wisdom*, 386: *"Fa-yā man idhā shāhadtuhu khiltu annahu qarīb"* ("Oh, You, whom when I witness, I imagine to be close") corroborating the version of Qūnawī.

60. Kalābādhī, *Doctrine of the Sufis*, 78. Cf. Sīrjānī, *Black and White in the Words of Wisdom*, 386.

61. The idea of contemplation (witnessing) is expressed by words either in the I. stem *(shuhūd)* or in the III. *(ushāhidu*—a verbal form of *mushāhada)* in the poem, suggesting that the terms are interchangeable.

62. Kalābādhī, *Doctrine of the Sufis*, 87.

63. The term denoting God's unseen and unattainable word is usually *ghayb*, while the term denoting the mystic's spiritual withdrawal from mundane matters is *ghayba*. Both forms are grammatically verbal nouns of the verb *ghāba* ("to disappear, to become absent"). Nūrī, however, apparently expresses both meanings with the word *ghayb*. For the definitions of *ghayb* and *ghayba* see ʿAbd al-Munʿim al-Ḥifnī, *al-Mawsūʿa al-ṣūfiyya* (Cairo: Madbūlī, 2006), 1174–75.

64. For a detailed commentary on the poem, see Qūnawī, *Ḥusn al-taṣarruf*, fol. 174a.

65. Kalābādhī, *Doctrine of the Sufis*, 88.

66. For a detailed interpretation of the poem, see Qūnawī, *Ḥusn al-taṣarruf*, fols. 174b–175a.

67. Kalābādhī, *Doctrine of the Sufis*, 73. Cf. Sīrjānī, *Black and White in the Words of Wisdom*, 315.

68. Cf. Qushayrī, *Treatise*, ed. Zurayq, 70 (the chapter on absence and presence, *al-ghayba wa-l-ḥuḍūr)*.

69. Atif Khalil, "Contentment, Satisfaction and Good-Pleasure: *Rida* in Early Sufi Moral Psychology," *Studies in Religion* 43, no. 3 (2014): 371–89, especially 375–77. The quoted phrase is on p. 376.

70. For a detailed interpretation of the poem, see Qūnawī, *Ḥusn al-taṣarruf*, fol. 137b.

71. Kalābādhī, *Doctrine of the Sufis*, 74.

72. Ibid. Anonymous tradition.

73. Kalābādhī, *Doctrine of the Sufis*, 75.

74. Ibid., 109.

75. The same idea appears in the commentary to this Quranic passage by Ibn ʿAṭāʾ: "Recall your Lord when you forget—when you forget yourself and the creatures." Ibn ʿAṭā's Quran commentary was possibly known to Kalābādhī. The commentary did not survive in its entirety but was preserved in the commentary of Sulamī. For the passage see Sulamī, *Ḥaqā'iq al-tafsīr* (Beirut: Dār al-Kutub al-ʿIlmiyya, 2001), 1:408.

76. Kalābādhī, *Doctrine of the Sufis*, 76.

77. On love in Islamic thought, see: Joseph Norment Bell, *Love Theory in Later Hanbalite Islam* (Albany: State University of New York Press, 1979); William Chittick, *The Sufi Path of Love: The Spiritual Teachings of Rumi* (Albany: State University of New York Press, 1983); William Chittick, "The Pivotal Role of Love in Sufism," in *Eranos Jahrbuch 2009–2010–2011: Love on a Fragile Thread*, ed. Fabio Merlini, Lawrence E. Sullivan, Riccardo Bernardini, and Kate Olson, 255–73 (Einsiedeln: Daimon Verlag, 2012); William Chittick, *Divine Love: Islamic Literature and the Path to God* (New Haven, CT: Yale University Press, 2013); William Chittick, "Love in Islamic Thought" *Religion Compass* 8/7 (2014): 229–38; Binyamin Abrahamov, *Divine Love in Islamic Mysticism: The Teachings ofAl-Ghazālī and Al-Dabbāgh* (London: Routledge, 2003); Binyamin Abrahamov, "Ibn ʿArabī on Divine Love," in *Tribute to Michael: Studies in Jewish and Muslim Thought Presented to Professor Michael Schwartz*, ed. Sarah-Klein Braslavy, Binyamin Abrahamov, and Joseph Sadan (Tel Aviv: Tel Aviv University, 2009), 7–36.

78. Sarrāj, *Book of Flashes*, 58. Qūnawī's comment on Nūrī's poem under discussion is probably based on this saying; it corresponds almost verbatim to the words of Sumnūn (without mentioning his name). Cf. Qūnawī, *Ḥusn al-taṣarruf*, fol. 143a.

79. Kalābādhī, *Doctrine of the Sufis*, 76.

80. Cf. Qushayrī, *Treatise*, ed. Zurayq, 321,

81. On the dichotomy of love and passionate love (*ʿishq*) in early Sufism, see Joseph E. B. Lumbard, "From 'Ḥubb' to 'ʿIshq': The Development of Love in Early Sufism," *Journal of Islamic Studies* 18, no. 3 (2007): 345–85.

82. Qūnawī, *Ḥusn al-taṣarruf*, fol. 143a.

83. Kalābādhī, *Doctrine of the Sufis*, 64. Cf. Sarrāj, *Book of Flashes*, 44; Qushayrī, *Treatise*, ed. Zurayq, 95; Sīrjānī, *Black and White in the Words of Wisdom*, 90.

84. For a comprehensive study of the concept in early Sufism, especially in the works of Muḥāsibī and in the *Qūt al-qulūb* by Abū Ṭālib al-Makkī, see Atif Khalil, *Repentance and Return to God* (Albany: State University of New York Press, 2019).

85. Cf. Qūnawī, *Ḥusn al-taṣarruf*, fols. 116a–16b.

86. Kalābādhī, *Doctrine of the Sufis*, 82.

87. Cf. Kalābādhī, *Doctrine of the Sufis*, 88, n. 12. (According to the footnote, the manuscript is preserved in the Dār al-Kutub al-Misriyya, MS Taṣawwuf 170.)

88. Cf. Qushayrī, *Treatise*, ed. Zurayq, 88 (the chapter on *sirr*).

89. Qūnawī, *Ḥusn al-taṣarruf*, fol. 165b.

90. Ibid., fols. 165a–65b.

91. Kalābādhī, *Doctrine of the Sufis*, 99. Cf. a different version of the story in Sīrjānī, *Black and White in the Words of Wisdom*, 16–17.

92. Kalābādhī, *Doctrine of the Sufis*, 85.

93. Cf. Junayd's behavior during an audition ceremony (Qushayrī, *Treatise*, ed. Zurayq, 62.) to be discussed in the chapter on Qushayrī.

94. Kalābādhī, *Doctrine of the Sufis*, 92.

95. Kalābādhī, *Doctrine of the Sufis*, 100. Qūnawī's comments on the story are in line with Kalābādhī's interpretation, cf. *Ḥusn al-taṣarruf*, fol. 198b.

96. Kalābādhī, *Doctrine of the Sufis*, 70.

97. Ibid., 69.

98. Qūnawī, *Ḥusn al-taṣarruf*, fol. 130b.

99. Kalābādhī, *Doctrine of the Sufis*, 71.

100. Qūnawī, *Ḥusn al-taṣarruf*, fols. 122b–23a.

101. Kalābādhī, *Doctrine of the Sufis*, 110.

102. Qūnawī's interpretation of the poem is in line with Kalābādhī's, cf. *Ḥusn al-taṣarruf*, fol. 229a.

103. Kalābādhī, *Doctrine of the Sufis*, 112.

104. Qūnawī, on the other hand, does not strictly differentiate between the two terms, they seem to be interchangeable in his usage. See for example *Ḥusn al-taṣarruf*, fols. 174a–75b).

105. Terms that occur only in one tradition (number of occurrences in parenthesis, if more than one): state *(ḥāl)* (4); gratitude *(shukr)* (4); *jihād* (struggle) (3); intelligence *(ʿaql)* (2); *sitr* (veil, veiling) (2); repentance *(tawba)*; poor *(faqīr)*; preferring others to oneself *(īthār)*; *qunūʿ* (satisfaction); *ḥuḍūr* (presence); *ḥubb* (love); *jamʿ* (reunion); *ṣabr* (patience); *wārid* (oncoming thought); *humūm* (concerns); *ṣāḥin* (sober); *yaqīn* (certainty); *mukāshafa* (unveiling, revelation); station *(maqām)*.

Chapter 2

1. I used the following edition: Sarrāj, *Kitāb al-lumaʿ fī l-taṣawwuf* (henceforth: *Book of Flashes*). Edited by Reynold Alleyne Nicholson (Leiden and London: Brill and Luzac, 1914).

2. Abdel-Kader, *Life, Personality and Writings of al-Junayd*, XIII.

3. On Sarrāj's life see the introduction by Nicholson in Sarrāj, *Book of Flashes*, III–V; see also Alexander Knysh, *Islamic Mysticism*, 118–20. For the German translation of the *Book of Flashes* see Richard Gramlich, *Schlaglichter über das Sufitum* (Stuttgart: Franz Steiner, 1990).

4. Sarrāj, *Book of Flashes*, 408.

5. Arthur John Arberry, *Pages from the Kitāb al-Lumaʿ of Abū Naṣr al-Sarrāj being the Lacuna in the Edition of R. A. Nicholson* (London: Luzac, 1947).

6. Arberry, *Pages*, 6.

7. Sarrāj, *Book of Flashes*, 225.

8. *Wājid* is the active participle of the root WJD, meaning "to find" on the one hand, and "to be in a state of emotional agitation, to be impassioned by, to long ardently after" on the other. *Wajd* is the Sufi technical term for ecstasy.

9. Sarrāj, *Book of Flashes*, 26. Cf. also Qushayrī, *Treatise*, ed. Zurayq, 282, 341; Sīrjānī, *Black and White in the Words of Wisdom*, 47.

10. On *samāʿ*, see Avery, *A Psychology of Early Sufi Samāʿ*, which treats extensively the importance of *samāʿ* and altered states in Nūrī's life. In order to underline the primary role of *samāʿ* in Nūrī's spirituality, Avery cites this utterance of Nūrī, omitting, however, the second half of the sentence and thus shifting its emphasis: modifying its meaning that evidently comprises a certain measure of reservation as well. Cf. Ibid., 194: "One of Nūrī's succinct 'definitions' of what it means to be a Sufi is given as 'one who hears the *samāʿ*.'"

11. On the discussions on the permissibility of *samāʿ* and the reasons for its prohibition, see Schimmel, *Mystical Dimensions*, 179–82.

12. Sarrāj, *Book of Flashes*, 304–5.

13. This poem of Nūrī, for example, is sometimes attributed to the Sufi mystic Abū Bakr al-Shiblī, see for example: Abū Muḥammad ʿAbd Allāh b. Asʿad al-Yāfiʿī, *Nashr al-maḥāsin al-ghāliya fī faḍl al-mashāyikh al-ṣūfiyya aṣḥāb al-maqāmāt al-ʿāliya* (Beirut: Dār al-Kutub al-ʿIlmiyya, 2000), 306. It is ascribed, however, also to Jamīl, see Schimmel, "Abū'l-Ḥusayn al-Nūrī: Qibla of the Lights," 59.

14. As in the poem attributed to Avicenna, beginning: "A dove has alighted to you from the most elevated place" *(Habaṭat ilayka mina l-maḥalli l-arfaʿi / warqā'un dhātu taʿazzuzin wa-tamannuʿi).*

15. Sarrāj, *Book of Flashes*, 302.

16. Ibid., 301.

17. Cf. Ibn Māja, *Sunan*. Edited by Rā'id b. Ṣabrī b. Abī ʿAlfa (Riyād: Dār al-Ḥaḍāra li-n-Nashr wa-l-Tawzīʿ, 2015), 200, no. 1337. Ch. 176; *Kitāb iqāmat al-ṣalāt. Bāb ḥusn al-ṣawt bi-l-Qur'ān*. Cf. also Bukhārī, *Saḥīḥ* (Beirut

and Damascus: Dār ʿIlm Kathīr, 2002), 117, no. 433. Ch. 53, *Kitāb al-ṣalāt, abwāb istiqbāl al-qibla. Bāb al-ṣalāt fī mawāḍiʿ al-khasf wa-l-ʿadhāb.*

18. Ghazālī, *Iḥyā ʿulūm al-dīn* (Beirut: Dār al-Maʿrifa, n.d.), 2:298–99 (in *Kitāb ādāb al-samāʿ wa-l-wajd).*

19. Ghazālī, *Iḥyā ʿulūm al-dīn,* 299.

20. The alternative reading of the Quran passage that is quoted in the name of Ibn ʿAbbās is introduced in his commentary by the formula "it is said" *(yuqāl),* indicating a version, not a mere interpretation, of the Quranic text, cf. Ibn al-ʿAbbās, *Tanwīr al-miqbās min tafsīr Ibn ʿAbbās* (Beirut: Dār al-Kutub al-ʿIlmiyya, 1992), 443. Such a version, however, is not collected in the *Muʿjam al-qirā'āt* enlisting the alternative readings, cf. ʿAbd al-ʿĀl Sālim Mukram and Aḥmad Mukhtār ʿOmar (eds.), *Muʿjam al-qirā'āt al-Qur'āniyya* (Kuwait: Jāmiʿat al-Kuwait, 1988), 6:250.

21. Sarrāj, *Book of Flashes,* 40. Cf. a much shorter version in Kalābādhī, *Doctrine of the Sufis,* 37; Sīrjānī, *Black and White in the Words of Wisdom,* 69.

22. Sarrāj, *Book of Flashes,* 37–38. Cf. Sīrjānī, *Black and White in the Words of Wisdom,* 63.

23. Both passages are cited also in Sīrjānī, *Black and White in the Words of Wisdom,* 63, 69. The passages appear to be unrelated there as well.

24. Sarrāj, *Book of Flashes,* 38.

25. Sarrāj, *Book of Flashes,* 232. For a parallel version, see ibid., 248. Cf. also Kharkūshī, 539, where the poem is quoted in the chapter on the Sufi's correspondence introduced by the words: "Nūrī wrote a letter to Kharrāz, and he wrote in it these verses." Cf. also Sīrjānī, *Black and White in the Words of Wisdom,* 393.

26. ʿAbd al-Raḥmān Ibn Naṣr al Shayzarī, *Rawḍat al qulūb wa-nuzhat al-muḥibb wal-maḥbūb,* ed. David Semah and George J. Kanazi (Wiesbaden: Harrassowitz, 2003), 221. For textual versions of the poem, see n. 74 there.

27. The fourth line quoted in the *Rawḍat al-qulūb* is the following (p. 221):

أكاتم ما في النفس نهيا عن الهوى / مخافة أن يغري بذكراك ذاكر

28. The poem is quoted also on p. 248 of *Rawḍat al-qulūb,* where there are only masculine pronominal suffixes, and the same holds true to Sīrjānī, *Black and White in the Words of Wisdom,* 393.

29. Sarrāj, *Book of Flashes,* 232.

30. Sarrāj, *Book of Flashes,* 248.

31. Ibid., 372.

The form الاولى is also attested in two manuscripts, see Sarrāj, *Book of Flashes,* 372, n. 14.

32. See, for example, the *nasīb* of Imru' al-Qays' Muʿallaqa:

"Stay! let us weep, while memory tries to trace
The long-lost fair one's sand-girt dwelling-place;
Though the rude winds have swept the sandy plain,
Still some faint traces of that spot remain."

William Alexander Clouston, ed., *Arabian Poetry for English Readers* (Glasgow: McLaren and Son, 1881), 373.

33. Quran 7:69, 26:128, 41:15, 89:6–7. See F. Buhl: "ʿĀd," in *The Encyclopaedia of Islam* (Leiden: Brill, 1960), 1:169; W. Montgomery Watt: "Iram," in *The Encyclopaedia of Islam* (Leiden: Brill, (1972) 3:1270.

34. See, for example: Ibn Kathīr, *Al-bidāya wa-l-nihāya.* Edited by ʿAbd Allāh b. ʿAbd al-Muḥsin al-Turkī (Cairo: Dār Hajr, 1998), 14:838; *Sīrjānī, Black and White in the Words of Wisdom,* 258.

35. Sarrāj, *Book of Flashes,* 290. Cf. also Qushayrī, *Treatise,* ed. Zurayq, 306–7; Sīrjānī, *Black and White in the Words of Wisdom,* 358–59, no. 773.

36. Sarrāj, *Book of Flashes,* 288.

37. The behavior of the perfect masters, like Junayd, is described in the subsequent chapter of the *Book of Flashes,* 292–94.

38. The story is related in two slightly different versions in the *Book of Flashes.* The other version of the story, narrated in the chapter on the Sufi masters' way of conduct when they face death, does not contain any reference to audition ceremony, and it shows some insignificant textual variances. That version is quoted also in Qushayrī's *Treatise.* Cf. Sarrāj, *Book of Flashes,* 208. Cf. also Qushayrī, *Treatise,* ed. Zurayq, 306–7.

39. Sarrāj, *Book of Flashes,* 59. Cf. also Qushayrī, *Treatise,* ed. Zurayq.

40. Quran 5:54, 3:31, 2:165.

41. Cf. Qūnawī, *Ḥusn al-taṣarruf,* fol. 149a.

42. Sarrāj, *Book of Flashes,* 58.

43. Ibid., 59.

44. Ibid.

45. Arberry, *Pages,* 5. For a different version of the Ghulām Khalīl incident see Abū Nuʿaym, *Ornament of God's Friends,* 10:250–251; Qushayrī, *Treatise,* ed. Zurayq, 248–49; Sīrjānī, *Black and White in the Words of Wisdom,* 19. On the story about the muezzin and the dog see Qushayrī, *Treatise,* ed. Zurayq, 258–59.

46. Cf. Dhahabī, *Siyar aʿlām an-nubalāʾ,* 1006. For the subsequent "inquisitions" established and abolished by the caliphs in the second half of the ninth century, see for example, Christopher Melchert, "Religious Policies of the Caliphs from al-Mutawakkil to al-Muqtadir, A. H. 232–295/A. D. 847–908," *Islamic Law and Society* 3, no. 3 (1996): 316–42.

47. See, for example, Qushayrī's account, *Treatise,* ed. Zurayq, 248–49.

48. Arberry, *Pages,* 8.

49. Arberry, *Pages*, 8.

50. Sarrāj, *Book of Flashes*, 218–19.

51. Ibid., 421–22.

52. On the audacious manner of talking to God that the friends of God sometimes permit to themselves, including reproaching and threatening Him, or compelling Him to do something for them, see Hellmut Ritter, "Muslim Mystics Strife with God," *Oriens* 5, no. 1 (1952): 1–16.

53. Sarrāj, *Book of Flashes*, 327. Cf. also Abū Nuʿaym, *Ornament of God's Friends*, 10:251; Qushayrī, *Treatise*, ed. Maḥmūd, 575; Sīrjānī, *Black and White in the Words of Wisdom*, 332.

54. Sarrāj, *Book of Flashes*, 325. Cf. also Qushayrī, *Treatise*, ed. Maḥmūd, 575; Sīrjānī, *Black and White in the Words of Wisdom*, 332.

55. Sarrāj, *Book of Flashes*, 325.

56. Both stories are quoted also in Qushayrī's *Treatise*, and similarly to the *Book of Flashes*, they are juxtaposed there as well (cf. Qushayrī, *Treatise*, ed. Maḥmūd, 575). Furthermore, the first story is included in Abū Nuʿaym's *Ornament of God's Friends*, the second, however, is not mentioned there (cf. Abū Nuʿaym, *Ornament of God's Friends*, 10:251).

57. Sarrāj, *Book of Flashes*, 81; cf. also Kalābādhī, *Doctrine of the Sufis*, 73; Qushayrī, *Treatise*, ed. Zurayq, 181; Sīrjānī, *Black and White in the Words of Wisdom*, 291.

58. Sarrāj, *Book of Flashes*, 346. Cf. a different version of the same saying in Kalābādhī, *Doctrine of the Sufis*, 78.

59. Sarrāj, *Book of Flashes*, 346.

60. See for example, Sarrāj, ibid., 117.

61. Sarrāj, *Book of Flashes*, 68.

62. Ibid., 359. Sarrāj quotes the saying in his entry on attribution, ascription *(nisba)*. He includes Nūrī's saying in the entry due to the term "attribution" it contains.

63. Ibid.

64. Ibid.

65. Ibid., 363.

66. Sarrāj, *Book of Flashes*, 212. Cf. also Sulamī, *Generations of the Sufis*, 166; Sīrjānī, *Black and White in the Words of Wisdom*, 370.

67. The term for separation in the Sufi sources may also be *farq* or *tafarruq*, with no difference in the meaning. *Jamʿ* is sometimes translated as "unification" (e.g., by Alexander Knysh, in his English translation of Qushayrī's *Treatise*), "collectedness" (by Annemarie Schimmel, in her *Mystical Dimensions of Islam*), or "concentration" (by Arberry, in his English translation of the *Doctrine of the Sufis*).

68. Sarrāj, *Book of Flashes*, 355. The saying is also preserved in a slightly different version in Sulamī's Quran commentary, the *Realities of*

Interpretation as a comment on Quran 3:152. Cf. Sulamī, *Realities,* 1:123 and Nwyia, "Textes mystiques inédits," 144.

69. Sarrāj, *Book of Flashes,* 355.

70. Sarrāj, *Book of Flashes,* 369. The second line of the poem is quoted also on p. 340. Cf. also Abū Nuʿaym, *Ornament of God's Friends,* 10:250; Sīrjānī, *Black and White in the Words of Wisdom,* 21.

71. Sarrāj, *Book of Flashes,* 369.

72. Cf. Sarrāj, *Book of Flashes,* 369; Qushayrī, *Treatise,* ed. Zurayq, 181.

73. Sarrāj, *Book of Flashes,* 369.

74. Ibid., 340.

75. Ibid.

76. Sarrāj, *Book of Flashes,* 57. Sarrāj includes the last sentence of the story also in the entry on "allusion" *(ishāra)* in his list of Sufi technical terms, without its context. Cf. Sarrāj, *Book of Flashes,* 224.

77. Qushayrī, *Treatise,* ed. Zurayq, 82.

78. Sarrāj, *Book of Flashes,* 57.

79. Arberry, *Pages,* 6.

80. Or, as Rustom summarized the meaning of Nūrī's saying and Sarrāj's interpretation of it: "the knowledge of one's proximity to God is, in reality, distance from God." Rustom, "Approaches to Proximity and Distance in Early Sufism," 11.

81. Sarrāj, *Book of Flashes,* 248.

82. *"Wa-ʿālam al-ḥurūf afṣaḥa l-ʿālam lisānan wa-awḍaḥahu bayānan."* Ibn ʿArabī, *al-Futūḥāt al-makkiyya* (Cairo: Dār al-Kutub al-ʿArabiyya al-Kubrā, no year), 1:58, chapter 1, subchapter *"dhikr baʿḍ marātib al-ḥurūf."*

83. Sarrāj, *Book of Flashes,* 354.

84. On the three stages see, for example, Schimmel, *Mystical Dimensions,* 16, 98–99.

85. Sarrāj, *Book of Flashes,* 353.

86. Ibid., 239.

87. For the full Arabic text of the letters and their English translation, see below, chapter 9.

88. Sarrāj, *Book of Flashes,* 350.

89. Ibid.

90. Ibid.

91. For mystical reflections on divine names, see chapter 45 of the *Book of Flashes* (pp. 88–90).

92. *"Repentance means that you return from everything except from God."* Sarrāj, *Book of Flashes,* 44. Cf. also Kalābādhī, *Doctrine of the Sufis,* 64; Qushayrī, *Treatise,* ed. Zurayq, 95; Sīrjānī, *Black and White in the Words of Wisdom,* 193.

93. Sarrāj, *Book of Flashes,* 209.

94. Sarrāj, *Book of Flashes*, 208–9.

95. Ibid., 108. Cf. also Sulamī, *Generations of the Sufis*, 169; Sīrjānī, *Black and White in the Words of Wisdom*, 141. The word *ḥāl* (state) is probably not used as a Sufi technical term here. Cf. also Kalābādhī, *Doctrine of the Sufis*, 67: "What characterises a poor is that he is calm when he has nothing *(al-sukūn ʿinda l-ʿadam)*, and he spends freely, preferring others [to himself] when he has something."

96. The same verbal root (SKN) appears in both traditions, but unfortunately the divergent meanings of the verbal and the nominal forms cannot be translated using the same English word.

97. Sarrāj, *Book of Flashes*, 195.

98. Cf. Dhahabī, *Siyar aʿlām an-nubalā'*. Edited by Ḥassān ʿAbd al-Mannān (Beirut: Bayt al-Afkār al-Duwaliyya, 2004), 1007.

99. Sarrāj, *Book of Flashes*, 195.

100. Sarrāj, *Book of Flashes*, 193–94. Cf. also Sīrjānī, *Black and White in the Words of Wisdom*, 24.

101. Ibid.

102. Arberry, *Pages*, 6.

103. Cf. Qushayrī's explication of transitory and enduring states, *Treatise*, ed. Zurayq, 57–58 (the chapter on *ḥāl*).

104. Terms that occur only in one tradition (number of occurrences in parenthesis, if more than one): tribulation (*balā'*) (3); absence *(ghayb)* (2); mystical moment *(waqt)* (2); reunion *(jamʿ)* (2); separation *(tafriqa)* (2); attraction *(jadhb)*; true reality *(ḥaqīqa)*; erasure *(maḥw)*; connection *(ittiṣāl)*; adobe *(waṭan)*; running away, straying *(shurūd)*; intimate conversation *(najwā)*; poor *(faqīr)*; sincerity *(ikhlāṣ)*; love *(widād)*; repentance *(tawba)*; heedlessness *(ghafla)*; heart *(lubb)*.

Chapter 3

1. I have used the following edition: Abū ʿAbd al-Raḥmān Muḥammad ibn al-Ḥusayn al-Sulamī, *Ṭabaqāt al-ṣūfiyya* (Cairo: al-Khānjī, 1997). Henceforth: *Generations of the Sufis*. All references with page numbers are to this edition.

2. On the six major Sufi biographical works in general and Sulamī's *Generations of the Sufis* in particular see Jawid A. Mojaddedi, *The Biographical Tradition in Sufism* (Richmond, UK: Curzon, 2001), especially pp. 9–39. See also a detailed introduction by Johannes Pedersen in his edition of Sulamī's work: *Kitāb ṭabaqāt al-ṣūfiyya. Texte arabe avec une introduction et un index par Johannes Pedersen* (Leiden: Brill, 1960), 1–89; and the introduction written by Thibon to his French translation of the *Generations of*

the Sufis, in Sulamī, *Les générations des Soufis.* Translated by Jean-Jacques Thibon (Leiden: Brill, 2019), 1–38.

3. See his introduction to Sulamī, *Les générations des Soufis,* 5.

4. For a survey of Sulamī's published and unpublished works, see: Gerhard Böwering and Bilal Orfali, eds., *Sufi Treatises of Abū ʿAbd al-Raḥmān al-Sulamī* (Beirut: Dar el-Machreq, 2009).

5. Knysh, *Islamic Mysticism,* 125–27.

6. Cf. Mojaddedi, *The Biographical Tradition in Sufism,* 14–15; see also Knysh, *Islamic Mysticism,* 127; Thibon's introduction to Sulamī, *Les générations des Soufis,* 8, 30

7. Sulamī, *Generations of the Sufis,* 164.

8. In Qushayrī's *Treatise* Ḥawārī is mentioned as one of Nūrī's prominent teachers together with Sarī al-Saqaṭī. Muḥammad ibn ʿAlī al-Qaṣṣāb, however, is omitted there. See Qushayrī, *Treatise,* ed. Zurayq, 439.

9. Sulamī, *Generations of the Sufis,* 164.

10. Sulamī, *Generations of the Sufis,* 169. Cf. also Abū Nuʿaym, *Ornament of God's Friends,* 10:251; Sīrjānī, *Black and White in the Words of Wisdom,* 132.

11. Sulamī collected another saying of Nūrī expressing the same view (the saying has been already discussed in the previous chapter): *"Nūrī was asked about the sincere poor, and he said: Who does not accuse God with regard to [the lack of] means, and relies on Him under every circumstances."* Sulamī, *Generations of the Sufis,* 169; cf. also Sarrāj, *Book of Flashes,* 108; Sīrjānī, *Black and White in the Words of Wisdom,* 141.

12. Sulamī, *Generations of the Sufis,* 167–68. Cf. also Abū Nuʿaym, *Ornament of God's Friends,* 10:251; Sīrjānī, *Black and White in the Words of Wisdom,* 226–27.

13. Kharkūshi, *Revision of the Secrets,* 345.

14. Qushayrī, *Treatise,* ed. Zurayq, 195.

15. ʿAṭṭār, *Tadhkirat al-awliyā',* 1:89.

16. Sulamī, *Generations of the Sufis,* 166.

17. Beginning: "Contentment is bitterness swallowed . . ." cf. Kalābādhī, *Doctrine of the Sufis,* 73.

18. Quoted by Schimmel, *Mystical Dimensions,* 136 (in her translation) from Sarrāj, *Book of Flashes,* 50.

19. Cf. the explication of *balā'* in Ḥifnī, *al-Mawsūʿa al-ṣūfiyya,* 846.

20. Sulamī, *Generations of the Sufis,* 166. Cf. also Abū Nuʿaym, *Ornament of God's Friends,* 10:251 and Ṭabarī, *Comfort of the Mystics,* 489, where the verb in the second sentence is *tawaṣṣala* (to reach connection) instead of *tawassala* (to resort to).

21. The definitions of arrival *(waṣl)* and ultimate arrival *(waṣl al-waṣl)* are taken from Ḥifnī, *al-Mawsūʿa al-ṣūfiyya,* 1337–38.

22. The definition of intimacy is taken from Ḥifnī, *al-Mawsūʿa al-ṣūfiyya,* 811–12.

23. Quoted in Kalābādhī, *Doctrine of the Sufis,* 76.

24. The version that appears in the *Ornament of God's Friends* 10:254 slightly differs here: "You are right! [And you,] are you right in [seeking] learning?! *(Aḥsanta. A-tuḥsin al-ʿilm?)"*

25. Sulamī, *Generations of the Sufis,* 166. Cf. also Abū Nuʿaym, *Ornament of God's Friends,* 10:254; Sīrjānī, *Black and White in the Words of Wisdom,* 240.

26. Cf. *s. v.* "Liwāṭ," in *Encyclopaedia of Islam,* 5:776–79. On homoeroticism and companionship with youth, see Salamah-Qudsi, Arin Shawkat. *Sufism and Early Islamic Piety: Personal and Communal Dynamics* (Cambridge: Cambridge University Press, 2019), 215–60; on *naẓar,* see Lloyd Ridgeon, *Awḥad al-Dīn Kirmānī and the Controversy of the Sufi Gaze* (London: Routledge, 2019).

27. ʿAbd al-Wahhāb b. ʿAḥmad al-Shaʿrānī, *Laṭā'if al-minan wa-l-akhlāq* (Cairo: ʿĀlam al-Fikr, n.d.), 490.

28. Abū n-Najīb al-Suhrawardī, *Ādāb al-murīdīn,* ed. Menahem Milson (Jerusalem: Maʿhad al-Dirāsāt al-Āsiyawiyya wa-l-Ifrīqiyya. al-Jāmiʿa al-ʿIbriyya fī Ūrushalīm al-Quds, 1977), 39.

29. *Shakhṣ* ("person") refers usually to a male.

30. Suhrawardī, *Ādāb al-murīdīn,* 42.

31. For example, from the edition of Zurayq. For the chapter, see Qushayrī, *Treatise,* ed. Maḥmūd, 627–28.

32. ʿAbd al-Wahhāb b. ʿAḥmad al-Shaʿrānī, *Al-anwār al-qudsiyya fī maʿrifat qawāʿid al-ṣūfiyya.* Edited by Ṭāhā ʿAbd al-Bāqir Surūr and al-Sayyid Muḥammad ʿĪd al-Shādhilī (Beirut: Maktabat al-Maʿārif, 1988), 1:74.

33. Ibid.

34. *An-niʿāl al-ṣarrāra,* the creaking sandal was a famous product of Cambay in India, which was imported worldwide. It is mentioned by Masʿūdī, (historian and geographer, d. ca. 956) in his *Murūj al-dhahab,* cf. Maçoudi, *Les prairies d'or. Texte et traduction par C. Barbier de Meynard et Pavet de Courteille.* Paris: Impr. Impériale, 1861, 1:253.

35. Cf. the entry "*ʿayn*" in Ḥifnī, *al-Mawsūʿa al-ṣūfiyya,* 1167.

36. Sulamī, *Generations of the Sufis,* 169. Cf. Sīrjānī, *Black and White in the Words of Wisdom,* 236.

37. Chittick, *Sufi Path of Knowledge,* 159.

38. Cf. "Ahl al-Naẓar," *in Encyclopaedia of Islam,* 2:266.

39. See Chittick, *Sufi Path of Knowledge,* 159–60.

40. Sīrjānī, *Black and White in the Words of Wisdom,* 236.

41. Sulamī, *Generations of the Sufis,* 167. Cf. also Ṭabarī, *Comfort of the Mystics,* 490.

42. On "cutting the bonds" see the chapter "Instructions for the seekers" *(al-waṣāya lil-murīdīn)* in Qushayrī, *Treatise*, ed. Zurayq, 380.

43. Sulamī, *Generations of the Sufis*, 169. Cf. also Sīrjānī, *Black and White in the Words of Wisdom*, 290; Ṭabarī, *Comfort of the Mystics*, 489.

44. Qushayrī, *Treatise*, ed. Zurayq, 83–85 (chapter *"al-khawāṭir")*.

45. Ibid., 84.

46. Ibid., 84–85.

47. Sulamī, *Generations of the Sufis*, 169.

48. Sulamī included in his selection of Nūrī's saying another definition of Sufism that has been already discussed: *"Sufism is to renounce what belongs to the self/carnal soul."* Sulamī, *Generations of the Sufis*, 166. Cf. also Kalābādhī, *Doctrine of the Sufis*, 9; Qushayrī, *Treatise*, ed. Zurayq, 439.

49. Sulamī, *Generations of the Sufis*, 167. Cf. also Sīrjānī, *Black and White in the Words of Wisdom*, 45.

50. Farīd al-Dīn al-ʿAṭṭār, *Tadhkirat al-awliyā'*. Arabic translation by Manāl al-Yamanī ʿAbd al-ʿAzīz (Cairo: al-Hay'a al-Miṣriyya li-l-Kitāb, 2009), 2:91.

51. The *ḥadīth* is not included in the normative collections, but it is cited by various authors, see for example, Ibn Taymiyya, *Kitāb al-ṣafadiyya*, ed. Muḥammad Rashād Sālim (Cairo,1986), 2:337.

52. Sulamī, *Generations of the Sufis*, 169. Cf. also Qushayrī, *Treatise*, ed. Zurayq, 439. It is not absolutely clear whether the S/3 masculine personal pronoun in the phrase "speaks about His reality" refers to God or to the mystic, but since a mystic is not supposed to talk about his reality but about that of God, the pronoun "his" is best interpreted as referring to God. In the parallel version in Qushayrī's *Treatise* the pronoun is omitted. According to the commentator of the *Treatise*, Zakariyyā al-Anṣārī, the second part of the saying means that those who repeat what they have heard and understand from their fellows or even from books are numerous; by contrast, those who speak about God's true reality as they have experienced it are scarce. Cf. Anṣārī, *Iḥkām al-dalāla*, 1:156–57.

53. Sulamī, *Generations of the Sufis*, 166. Cf. also Sīrjānī, *Black and White in the Words of Wisdom*, 288.

54. Muslim, *Ṣaḥīḥ*. Edited by Muḥammad Fu'ād ʿAbd al-Bāqī (Beirut: Dār al-Kutub al-ʿIlmiyya, 1991), 4:2167, no. 2814.

55. Cf. Quran 3:84, and the following *ḥadīth:* "Stellet mich nicht über den Jūnus b. Mattā; machet kein tafḍīl unter den propheten und zieht mich nicht dem *Mūsā* vor." Cited in Tor Andrae, *Die person Muḥammads in lehre und glaube seiner gemeinde* (Stockholm: P. A. Vorstedt og söner, 1918), 245, quoting Qadi ʿIyad, *Shifā'* 1:102. In English: "Do not place me above Yūnus ibn Mattā, and do not make any comparisons or preferences

among the prophets, and do not prefer me to Moses." English translation by Annemarie Schimmel, *And Muhammad Is His Messenger* (Chapel Hill and London: University of North Carolina Press, 1985), 61.

56. These ideas were further developed especially by Ibn ʿArabī and ʿAbd al-Karīm al-Jīlī. On the central position of Muḥammad in Sufi mysticism see Schimmel, *And Muḥammad is His Messenger*, especially ch. 7, 122–43; Schimmel, *Mystical Dimensions*, 213–27; Carl W. Ernst, *The Shambala Guide to Sufism* (Boston and London: Shambala, 1997), 45–57. On Ibn ʿArabī's conception of Muḥammad see, for example, Ibn ʿArabī, *The Bezels of Wisdom*, trans. and introduction by R. W. J. Austin (New York: Paulist Press, 1980), 272–84.

57. The *Generations of the Sufis* includes one more saying attributed to Nūrī and has already been discussed: "*Reunion with the Real is separation from everything else, and separation from everything else is reunion with Him.*" Sulamī, *Generations of the Sufis*, 166. Cf. also Sarrāj, *Book of Flashes*, 212; Sīrjānī, *Black and White in the Words of Wisdom*, 370.

58. The narration is included in the rest of the collections studied here, except for Kalābādhī's *Doctrine of the Sufis* (which does not contain biographical entries anyway, and which is not interested in the life of individual mystics).

59. Terms that occur only in one tradition (number of occurrences in parenthesis, if more than one): reunion *(jamʿ)* (2); separation *(tafriqa)* (2); love *(wadd/widād)* (2); intelligence *(ʿaql)* (2); ecstasy *(wajd)*; sudden thought *(khāṭir)*; intimacy *(uns)*; nearness *(qurb)*; contentment *(riḍā)*; detachment *(inqiṭāʿ)*; mystical knower *(ʿārif)*; returning *(rujūʿ)*; contemplation *(mushāhada)*; unveiling *(mukāshafa)*; thanks/gratefulness *(shukr)*; (verbal form of) connection *(WṢL)*; (verbal form of) veiling *(HJB)*; (verbal form of) concealing *(STR)*; (verbal form of) hiding *(KTM)*.

Chapter 4

1. I have used the edition prepared by Sayyid ʿUmrān: Sulamī, *Ḥaqā'iq al-tafsīr* (Beirut: Dār al-Kutub al-ʿIlmiyya, 2001), based on two manuscripts preserved in the Maqtaba Azhariyya. It is not a critical edition obviously, and its text is frequently corrupt. I also consulted Nwyia's collection of Nūrī's sayings in the *Realities*, which he published as an appendix to his article "Textes mystiques inédits d'Abū-l-Ḥasan al-Nūrī." *Mélanges de l'Université Saint-Joseph* 46 (1968): 117–54. Nwyia studied manuscripts Fātih 260, Bashir Aga 36 and Yeni Cami 43 (see his article, p. 126). These represent a different tradition than the manuscripts of the Maqtaba Azhariyya.

2. Goldziher Ignácz, *A Koránmagyarázás különféle irányairól (On the different schools of Quran interpretations)* (Budapest: Magyar Tudományos Akadémia, 1912), 14–17; Ignaz Goldziher, *Introduction to Islamic Theology and Law* (Princeton, NJ: Princeton University Press, 1981), 138. (English translation of Goldziher's *Vorlesungen über den Islam,* 1910.); ibid., *Die Richtungen der Islamischen Koranauslegung* (Leiden: Brill, 1920), 180–262. It has to be noted that Goldziher did not have the opportunity to study the manuscripts of Quran commentaries written by the early mystics (these were not published at that time), and his observations are based mostly on works by al-Ghazālī, Ibn ʿArabī and al-Kāshī, cf. Paul Nwyia, *Exégèse Coranique et Language Mystique* (Beirut: Dar el-Masreq, 1970), 25.

3. Concerning Western scholarship on Sufi Quranic interpretation, including the argumentation of the aforementioned scholars, see Kristin Zahra Sands, *Ṣūfī Commentaries on the Qur'ān in Classical Islam* (London and New York: Routledge, 2006), 1–2.

4. Apparently, he was unaware of the commentary composed by Sahl b. ʿAbd Allāh al-Tustarī (d. 896 in Basra). Tustarī's commentary is considered the earliest mystical running commentary. Böwering analyzed its style and content after studying six manuscripts and described it as an eclectic collection of jottings organized loosely; cf. Böwering, *Mystical Vision of Existence in Classical Islam: The Qur'ānic Hermeneutics of the Ṣūfī Sahl al-Tustarī* (Berlin: Walter De Gruyter, 1980), 128–29.

5. The inclusion of Shiite material in the commentary provoked attacks and charges of heresy against Sulamī, cf. Böwering, "Early Sufism between Persecution and Heresy," 63.

6. The two genres are not *aqwāl* and *āyāt,* as Böwering supposed: "The term *aqwāl* is applied by Sulamī to sayings of Sufi authorities on specific topics of mystical experience, while the term *āyāt* is taken by him as referring to Qur'ānic glosses. Sulamī thus uses the term *āya,* pl. *āyāt,* neither simply in its original meaning of "sign, symbol" nor in its merely restricted, technical meaning of Qur'ānic verse [. . .], but as a term for a Qur'ānic gloss which implies the verse plus its symbolic interpretation." See Böwering: "The Major Sources of Sulamī's Minor Qur'ān Commentary." *Oriens* 35 (1996), 38, n.14. This supposition led to translations like: "The two principal written sources cited by Sulamī were scattered glosses *(āyāt mutafarriqa) . . .*" (ibid., 39). Cf. also Böwering, "The Qur'ān Commentary of al-Sulamī," in *Islamic Studies Presented to Charles J. Adams,* ed. Wael b. Hallaq and Donald P. Little (Leiden: Brill, 1991), 50. Böwering's view was adopted by Kristin Zahra Sands: "In the introduction to his *tafsīr,* al-Sulamī states that he included two types of quotations in his compilation. The first he calls *āyāt,* by which he means interpretations of specific verses,

and the second he calls *aqwāl*." See Sands, *Ṣūfī Commentaries*, 69. In my opinion, however, it is clear that the word *āyāt* does not mean "glosses" or "interpretative comments," but Quranic verses (as is common). The erroneous translation of the term resulted from the misunderstanding of the Arabic text, in which the governing noun *(fahm,* "interpretation") is omitted from the construction *fahm āyāt* ("interpretation of verses") since it already appeared in the preceding, parallel construction *fahm ḫiṭābihi,* "interpretation of His discourse." In the case of such defective genitive constructions, verbal agreement may follow the determining noun instead of the governing noun. For more details, see the second paragraph of my translation of Sulamī's introduction below, where the sentence structure is clearly indicated.

7. On the manuscripts, see Böwering, "Major Sources," 38, ibid., "The Qur'ān Commentary of al-Sulamī," 45–48; Sulamī, *Ziyādāt ḥaqā'iq al-tafsīr*, ed. Gerhard Böwering (Beirut: Dār al-Mashriq, 1995), 17 (of the English introduction by Böwering).

8. Entitled *Kitāb ahl al-ṣafwa fī l-fahm wa-l-ittibāʿ li-kitāb Allāh,* in his *Book of Flashes*, 72. On the Sufi terms of exegesis and their relation to *tafsīr,* see Sands, *Sufi Commentaries*, 67–68.

9. Sulamī, *Ziyādāt ḥaqā'iq al-tafsīr*, 1 (Arabic text).

10. Cf. Sulamī, *Ziyādāt ḥaqā'iq al-tafsīr*, 17, note 9 (English introduction by Böwering).

11. Ibid., 20. The single mention is by Raḍī al-Dīn ʿAlī Ibn Ṭāwūs (d. 1266) in his *Saʿd al-suʿūd,* cf. Böwering, "The Qur'ān Commentary of al-Sulamī," in *Islamic Studies Presented to Charles J. Adams*, ed. Wael b. Hallaq and Donald P. Little (Leiden: Brill, 1991), 48.

12. Sulamī, *Ziyādāt ḥaqā'iq al-tafsīr*, 20 (English introduction).

13. Sulamī, *Realities*, 1:19–20. The text seems to be corrupt in this edition, and therefore I also consulted a short excerption of Sulamī's introduction transcribed from a supposedly better manuscript, which is published in Muḥammad Ḥusayn al-Dhahabī, *al-Tafsīr wa-l-mufassirūn* (Cairo: Maktabat Wahba, 1995), 2:285. Deviations from the text edited by Sayyid ʿUmrān follow the version published by Dhahabī.

14. Gerhard Böwering, "Qur'ān Commentary of al-Sulamī," 52.

15. Nwyia, "Textes mystiques inédits," 144. Cf. also Sulamī, *Realities*, 1:54 (where the first word of the saying is mistyped).

16. Abū Nuʿaym, *Decoration of the Saints*, 10:253.

17. Sulamī, *Realities*, 1:53.

18. In one of the manuscripts studied by Nwyia, and also in the printed text edited by Sayyid ʿUmrān, the text reads as "realm of my love" *(dār maḥabbatī).*

19. Nwyia, "Textes mystiques inédits," 144. Cf. also Sulamī, *Realities,* 1:57. The comment is quoted anonymously in Kharkūshi, *Revision of the Secrets,* 204.

20. Ṭabarī, *Comfort of the Mystics,* 302. Cf. Sīrjānī, *Black and White in the Words of Wisdom,* 116.

21. Sulamī, *Realities,* 1:57.

22. Sulamī, *Realities,* 1:57. The saying is attributed to "one of the Baghdadians" without further specification.

23. Ibid., 1:57–58. Anonymous saying.

24. Sulamī, *Realities,* 1:58.

25. Ibid., 1:74. In the version Nwyia published, the pronouns "you" are omitted, and the text reads as follows: "'*For God constrains and extends—Abū l-Ḥusayn an-Nūrī said: Constrains by Himself and extends to Himself.*" Cf. Nwyia, "Textes mystiques inédits," 144.

26. Sulamī, *Realities,* 1:74.

27. Ibid.

28. Ṭabarī, *Comfort of the Mystics,* 242.

29. For an elaborate explication of the terms, see: Schimmel, *Mystical Dimensions,* 128–29; Iványi Tamás, "Qabḍ and basṭ: On the History of Two Ṣūfī Terms," *Arabist* 30 (2012): 67–83; Qushayrī, *Treatise,* ed. Zurayq, 58–60.

30. Sulamī, *Realities,* 1:74.

31. Sulamī, *Realities,* 1:83 and Nwyia, "Textes mystiques inédits," 144.

32. Sulamī, *Realities,* 1:98.

33. Ibid.

34. Ibid.

35. Ibid.

36. Nwyia, "Textes mystiques inédits," 144.

37. Qushayrī, *Treatise,* ed. Zurayq, 220.

38. Ibid.

39. Cf. Schimmel, *Mystical Dimensions,* 16–17; Qushayrī, *Treatise,* ed. Zurayq, 279.

40. Sulamī, *Realities,* 1:109 and Nwyia, "Textes mystiques inédits," 144.

41. Sulamī, *Realities,* 1:109.

42. Qushayrī, *Treatise,* ed. Zurayq, 88.

43. Bukhārī, *Ṣaḥīḥ* (Beirut and Damascus: Dār Ibn Kathīr, 2002), 796, no. 3219.

44. Abū Ṭālib Muḥammad al-Makkī, *Qūt al-qulūb* (Cairo, 1991), 9–10. For an alternative translation and interpretation of the *ḥadīth,* see Sviri, *Perspectives on Early Islamic Mysticism,* 311–14.

45. Sulamī, *Realities,* 1:119 and Nwyia, "Textes mystiques inédits," 144. In Nwyia's publication the comment attributed to Nūrī is longer.

46. Ibid.

47. Sulamī, *Realities*, 1:123 and Nwyia, "Textes mystiques inédits," 144. The reading *ḥadda bihim* (in the edition of Sayyid ʿUmrān) instead of *jadhabahum* (in Nwyia's publication and in Sarrāj's parallel place) is apparently erroneous.

48. Sarrāj, *Book of Flashes*, 355.

49. *Aḥwāl*, the plural of *ḥāl* (state) is translated as "circumstances" since it is not used as a Sufi term here.

50. Sulamī, *Realities*, 1:163 and Nwyia, "Textes mystiques inédits," 145.

51. Cf. Rafīq al-ʿAjam, *Mawsūʿat muṣṭalaḥāt al-ṣūfiyya fī l-islām* (Beirut: Maktabat Lubnān, 1999), 489.

52. Sulamī, *Realities*, 1:163 and Nwyia, "Textes mystiques inédits," 145.

53. Sulamī, *Realities*, 1:197 and Nwyia, "Textes mystiques inédits," 145.

54. Sulamī, *Realities*, 1:197.

55. Sulamī, *Realities*, 1:207 and Nwyia, "Textes mystiques inédits," 145.

56. Sulamī, *Realities*, 1:207.

57. Sulamī, *Realities*, 1:220 and Nwyia, "Textes mystiques inédits," 145.

58. Cf. Qushayrī, *Treatise*, ed. Zurayq, 88.

59. Nwyia, "Textes mystiques inédits," 145.

60. Ḥifnī, *al-Mawsūʿa al-ṣūfiyya*, 763, *s.v. abad.*

61. Sulamī, *Realities*, 1:299 and Nwyia, "Textes mystiques inédits," 145.

62. Sarrāj, *Book of Flashes*, 218–19.

63. Anonymous saying cited in Ḥifnī, *al-Mawsūʿa al-ṣūfiyya*, 1002, *s.v. "Ru'ya."*

64. Sulamī, *Realities*, 1:316 and Nwyia, "Textes mystiques inédits," 145.

65. Sulamī, *Realities*, 1:316.

66. Ibid., 1:315.

67. Nwyia, "Textes mystiques inédits," 145. cf. also Sulamī, *Realities*, 1:342, where the saying is attributed to Sufyān al-Thawrī. Note that al-Thawrī (الثوري) and an-Nūrī (النوري) are easily confoundable forms in manuscripts.

68. Nwyia, "Textes mystiques inédits," 145. cf. also Sulamī, *Realities*, 1:356, where the reading is corrupt: it has حببوا and حببت instead of حييوا and حييت. The version of Nwyia is confirmed by its parallel in Rūzbihān Baqlī, ʿArāʾis al-bayān fī ḥaqāʾiq al-Qurʾān. Ed. Aḥmad Farīd al-Mazīdī (Beirut: Dār al-Kutub al-ʿIlmiyya, 2008), 2:298–99.

69. Nwyia, "Textes mystiques inédits," 146 and Sulamī, *Realities*, 1:410.

70. Sulamī, *Realities*, 1:410.

71. Ibid.

72. Ibid., 1:409.

73. Ibid.

74. Ibid., 1:410.

75. Nwyia, "Textes mystiques inédits," 146 and Sulamī, *Realities*, 2:29

76. *Iʿtiṣām* is a Sufi technical term, which means "persisting in obedience and observing the command [of God]." It has three levels: performance of the concept (1) by the body, that is, observing the religious laws; (2) by cutting the attachments to the world *(inqiṭāʿ)*; (3) by connection to God *(ittiṣāl)*, which equals "witnessing the Real solely, and that is the meaning of holding fast to God *(al-iʿtiṣām bi-llāh)*." Cf. Ḥifnī, *al-Mawsūʿa al-ṣūfiyya*, 792, *s.v.* "*Iʿtiṣām.*"

77. Nwyia, "Textes mystiques inédits," 146 and Sulamī, *Realities*, 2:57, which reads "God" instead of "the Real."

78. Sulamī, *Realities*, 2:57.

79. This conception of *fitna* is not the general Sufi approach: according to a saying Sulamī attributes to Kharrāz, *fitna* is originated by God (cf. Sulamī, *Realities*, 2:57). For a definition of the term, see for example: ʿAjam, *Mawsūʿat muṣṭalaḥāt al-ṣūfiyya fī l-islām*, 704, where *fitna* is defined as God's test aimed at putting one's faithfulness to the proof. The Quranic incident that illustrates this is the golden calf, which is ". . . nothing else than Your *fitna*, You make err by it whom You wish, and guide by it whom You wish" (Q 7:155).

80. Translation of Muḥammad Marmaduke Pickthall. *The Meaning of the Glorious Koran* (Tripoli: Islamic Call Society, 1973), 499.

81. Nwyia, "Textes mystiques inédits," 146. Cf. also Sulamī, *Realities*, 2:92, where the saying is attributed to Thawrī.

82. Sīrjānī, *Black and White in the Words of Wisdom*, 337.

83. Cf. "*Makr*" in Ḥifnī, *al-Mawsūʿa al-ṣūfiyya*, 1283–84.

84. Nwyia, "Textes mystiques inédits," 146. Cf. also Sulamī, *Realities*, 2:161, where the saying is attributed to Thawrī.

85. Nwyia, "Textes mystiques inédits," 146. Cf. also Sulamī, *Realities*, 2:173 (attributed to Thawrī).

86. Nwyia, "Textes mystiques inédits," 146. Cf. also Sulamī, *Realities*, 2:202 (attributed to Thawrī); and Kharkūshī, *Revision of the Secrets*,186 (attributed to Nūrī).

87. Nwyia, "Textes mystiques inédits," 146. Cf. also Sulamī, *Realities*, 2:303, where the saying is attributed to Abū l-Ḥusayn al-Thawrī, which is evidently a misspelling for Nūrī. The version in the edition of *Realities* by Sayyid ʿUmrān has "they allude" instead of "we allude."

88. Sarrāj, *Book of Flashes*, 57; Qushayrī, *Treatise*, ed. Zurayq, 82.

89. Nwyia, "Textes mystiques inédits," 146–47.

90. For comments on the verse, see Sulamī, *Realities*, 2:305–308. The saying attributed to Nūrī, however, does not appear among these.

91. Sarrāj, *Book of Flashes*, 37–38.

92. Nwyia, "Textes mystiques inédits," 147. Cf. also Sulamī, *Realities*, 2:353.

93. Kalābādhī, *Doctrine of the Sufis*, 37.

94. Nwyia, "Textes mystiques inédits," 147 and Sulamī, *Realities*, 2:413.

95. Sīrjānī, *Black and White in the Words of Wisdom*, 313. Variations of the saying (with significant textual divergence) can be found in Kharkūshī, *Revision of the Secrets*, 130 and Qushayrī, *Treatise*, ed. Zurayq, 196.

96. The sayings cited with reference to Quranic verses 2:29, 3:152, 4:128, 7:2, 7:29, 10:22, 11:17, 18:28, 24:63, 36:61, 56:85, 57:3, 72:3, 98:8—that is, fourteen sayings altogether.

97. The comments on Q 2:40, 2:245, 2:273, 3:35, 3:97, 3:128, 6:9, 6:36, 6:83. 14:10, 15:72, 22:78, 35:32, 39:60—again fourteen sayings.

98. The comments on Q 2:29, 3:152, 39:60, 56:85, 57:3, 98:8. Cf. also Nūrī's comment on Q 2:245, which is attributed to him in Ṭabarī's *Comfort of the Mystics*, as well.

99. Terms that occur only in one tradition (number of occurrences in parenthesis, if more than one): holding fast *(iʿtiṣām)* (6); subsistence *(baqā')* (3); farness *(buʿd)* (2); station *(maqām)*; detachment *(inqiṭā')*; love *(maḥabba)*; constraint *(qabd)*; expansion *(basṭ)*; poverty *(faqr)*; state *(ḥāl)*; tribulation *(balā')*; audition *(samāʿ)*; overseeing *(iṭṭilāʿ)*; attraction *(jazb)*; erasure *(maḥw)*; sincerity *(ikhlāṣ)*; (verbal form of) unveiling *(kashf)*; connection *(ittiṣāl)*; heedlessness *(ghafla)*; observance *(murāqaba)*; heart *(qalb)*; (verbal form of) allusion *(ishāra)*; contentment *(riḍā)*.

Chapter 5

1. The work has two printed editions. I have used the edition prepared by Bassām Muḥammad Bārūd (Kharkūshī, *Tahdhīb al-asrār*. Abu Dhabi: al-Majmaʿ al-Thaqāfī, 1999. Henceforth: *Revision of the Secrets*. Another edition was prepared by Sayyid Muḥammad ʿAlī (Beirut: Dār al-Kutub al-ʿIlmiyya, 2006). None of these is a critical edition, nor contains an index of names.

2. See for example, Kharkūshī, *Revision of the Secrets*, 479–88.

3. A. J. Arberry, "Khargūshī's Manual of Sufism," Bulletin of the School of Oriental Studies 9, no. 2 (1938): 345–49.

4. Sara Sviri, "The Early Mystical Schools of Baghdad and Nīshāpūr," *Jerusalem Studies in Arabic and Islam* 30 (2005): 450–82.

5. Christopher Melchert, "Khargūshī, Tahdhīb al-asrār," *Bulletin of the School of Oriental and African Studies* 73, no. 1 (2010): 29–44.

6. The overlap with later collections is greater: seven with Qushayrī's *Treatise*, three with Sīrjānī's *Black and White in the Words of Wisdom* and seven with Ṭabarī's *Comfort of the Mystics*.

7. Melchert, "Khargūshī, Tahdhīb al-asrār," 30–32.

8. Ibid. For biographical and bibliographical details, see the articles by Arberry, Melchert, and Sviri, and the sources enumerated in these.

9. Melchert, "Khargūshī, Tahdhīb al-asrār," 31.

10. Ibid.

11. Jacqueline Chabbi, "Remarques sur le développement historique des mouvements ascétiques et mystiques au Khurasan," *Studia Islamica* 46 (1977): 5–72; Chrisopher Melchert, "Sufis and Competing Movements in Nishapur," *Iran* 39 (2001): 237–47.

12. Kharkūshī, *Revision of the Secrets,* 39.

13. Arberry, "Khargūshī's Manual of Sufism," 346.

14. Kharkūshī, *Revision of the Secrets,* 23.

15. Ibid., 23–24.

16. "There is a certain ineluctable anachronism in Khargūshī's habit of beginning sections with quotations of the Prophet." Melchert, "Khargūshī, Tahdhīb al-asrār," 41.

17. Sviri, "The Early Mystical Schools of Baghdad and Nīshāpūr," 457–62; Melchert, "Khargūshī, Tahdhīb al-asrār," 33–34.

18. Kharkūshī, *Revision of the Secrets,* 28.

19. Ibid. Cf. Kalābādhī, *Doctrine of the Sufis,* 9; Qushayrī, *Treatise,* ed. Zurayq, 439; Sulamī, *Generations of the Sufis,* 166; For the second saying, cf. Kalābādhī, *Doctrine of the Sufis,* 67; Qushayrī, *Treatise,* ed. Zurayq, 278 the same saying referring to the poor, and ibid., 281 as referring to the Sufi. Cf. also Sīrjānī, *Black and White in the Words of Wisdom,* 46–47 (referring to the Sufi).

20. Kharkūshī, *Revision of the Secrets,* 28.

21. Quoted for example by Qushayrī, *Treatise,* ed. Zurayq, 55.

22. Qushayrī, *Treatise,* ed. Zurayq, 55.

23. Kharkūshī, *Revision of the Secrets,* 216. Cf. also Qushayrī, *Treatise,* ed. Zurayq, 287.

24. Kharkūshī, *Revision of the Secrets,* 215.

25. Ibid., 28.

26. Ibid., 345.

27. Sulamī, *Generations of the Sufis,* 167–68. Cf. also Abū Nuʿaym, *Ornament of God's Friends,* 10:252; Sīrjānī, *Black and White in the Words of Wisdom,* 226–27.

28. Kharkūshī, *Revision of the Secrets,* 54.

29. Ibid.,177.

30. Cf. Qushayrī, *Treatise,* ed. Zurayq, 88.

31. Kharkūshī, *Revision of the Secrets,* 501–2.

32. Cf. Ibn Manẓūr, *Lisān al-ʿarab.* Edited by ʿAbdallah ʿAlī al-Kabīr et al., Cairo: Dār al-Maʿārif, no date, 3366–367.

33. Kharkūshī, *Revision of the Secrets,* 500.

34. Quoted in the name of Jaʿfar b. Muḥammad al-Ṣādiq, cf. Kharkūshī, 322.

35. Kharkūshī, *Revision of the Secrets,* 322.

36. Ibid., 322. The translation follows the reading in Ibn Khamīs, *Manāqib al-abrār wa-maḥāsin al-akhyār* (Abu Dhabi: Markaz Zayed li-l-turāth wa-l-tārīkh, 2006), 1:404. The version in the *Revision of the Secrets* reads *tuʿabbir ʿan al-ʿibāra* ("expresses the expression") instead of *tughnī ʿan al-ʿibāra* ("makes expression superfluous"), and *wajal al-ishāra* ("dread of allusion") instead of *wijdān al-ishāra* (ecstasy of allusion), which is most probably corrupt.

37. Quoted in Abū Sulaymān's name by Kharkūshī, *Revision of the Secrets,* 185.

38. Kharkūshī, *Revision of the Secrets,* 82.

39. Ibid., 92.

40. Cf. Qushayrī, *Treatise,* ed. Zurayq, 88.

41. Kharkūshī, *Revision of the Secrets,* 506. The translation takes into consideration an alternative version preserved in Abū Nuʿaym's *Ornament of God's Friends,* 10:253. The most significant difference between the two versions is the last line. Abū Nuʿaym's text reads as follows: *"So my inner heart began to make superfluous my attribute to each and every thing / and the Real began to suffice me and to suffice it."*

42. Beginning "By my life! I have never entrusted my secret . . ." Kharkūshī, *Revision of the Secrets,* 539. The poem is also quoted in Sarrāj, *Book of Flashes,* 232; it has been already discussed.

43. Kharkūshī, *Revision of the Secrets,* 85.

44. Ibid., 135.

45. On the concept of *tawakkul* in the Quran, the *ḥadīth,* early and later Sufism, see Leonard Lewisohn, "Tawakkul." In: *The Encyclopaedia of Islam*[2] (Leiden: Brill, 2000), 10:376–378; and his "The Way of *Tawakkul:* The Ideal of 'Trust in God' in Classical Persian Sufism," *Islamic Culture* 53, no. 2 (1992): 27–62.

46. Kharkūshī, *Revision of the Secrets,* 385. The translation follows the grammatically more correct version in Ṭabarī, *Comfort of the Mystics,* 236.

47. Kharkūshī, *Revision of the Secrets,* 506. A similar poem is attributed to Ḥallāj, cf. *Dīwān al-Ḥallāj.* Edited by Muḥammad Bāsil ʿUyūn al-Sūd (Beirut: Dār al-Kutub al-ʿIlmiyya, 2007), 168.

48. Qushayrī, *Treatise,* ed. Zurayq, 69.

49. Ibid., 70.

50. Kharkūshī, *Revision of the Secrets,* 499.

51. Ḥifnī, *al-Mawsūʿa al-ṣūfiyya,* 828, *s. v. "al-bādī."*

52. Kharkūshī, *Revision of the Secrets,* 510. Cf. also Abū Nuʿaym, *Ornament of God's Friends,* 10:253.

53. Kharkūshī, *Revision of the Secrets,* 352.

54. Ibid., 356; cf. Arberry, Khargūshī's Manual of Sufism, 348–49.

55. Kharkūshī, *Revision of the Secrets,* 356.

56. Qushayrī, *Treatise,* ed. Zurayq, 57–58.

57. "*What characterizes the poor* (faqīr) *is calmness when he has nothing, and spending freely, preferring others [to himself] when he has something.*" Kharkūshī, *Revision of the Secrets,* 157. Cf. also Kalābādhī, *Doctrine of the Sufis,* 67; Qushayrī, *Treatise,* ed. Zurayq, 278, 281; Sīrjānī, *Black and White in the Words of Wisdom,* 46–47.

58. Kharkūshī, *Revision of the Secrets,* 154.

59. Ibid., 130. Variations of the saying can be found in Qushayrī, *Treatise,* ed. Zurayq, 196; and Sīrjānī, *Black and White in the Words of Wisdom,* 313. The version quoted by Sīrjānī is also attested in Sulamī's *Realities of Interpretation* as a comment on Q 98:8, cf. Nwyia, "Textes mystiques inédits, 147; and Sulamī, *Realities,* 2:413.

60. Kharkūshī, *Revision of the Secrets,* 186. Cf. Nwyia, "Textes mystiques inédits," 146; Sulamī, *Realities,* 2:202 (attributed to Thawrī).

61. Kharkūshī, *Revision of the Secrets,* 204. Cf. Nwyia, "Textes mystiques inédits," 144. Cf. also Sulamī, *Realities,* 1:57.

62. Kharkūshī, *Revision of the Secrets,* 203.

63. Ibid., 523.

64. Zamakhsharī, *Rabīʿ al-abrār wa-nuṣūṣ al-akhbār,* 2 vols. (Beirut: Mu'assasa al-Aʿlamī li-l-Maṭbūʿāt, 1992).

65. Kharkūshī, *Revision of the Secrets,* 412. Cf. also Qushayrī, *Treatise,* ed. Maḥmūd, 599; Abū Nuʿaym, *Ornament of God's Friends,* 10:251.

66. Kharkūshī, *Revision of the Secrets,* 286–87. Cf. also Qushayrī, *Treatise,* ed. Zurayq, 248–49; Abū Nuʿaym, *Ornament of God's Friends,* 10:250–251; Sīrjānī, *Black and White in the Words of Wisdom,* 19; Ṭabarī, *Comfort of the Mystics,* 124.

67. Arberry, *Pages,* 5.

68. Qushayrī, *Treatise,* ed. Zurayq, 248–49. Cf. also Abū Nuʿaym, *Ornament of God's Friends,* 10:250–51 where the name of the investigating judge is mentioned (Ismāʿīl b. Isḥāq); Sīrjānī, *Black and White in the Words of Wisdom,* 19; Ṭabarī, *Comfort of the Mystics,* 124.

69. Cf. Sarrāj, *Book of Flashes,* 210, 290; Qushayrī, *Treatise,* ed. Zurayq, 306–7; Sīrjānī, *Black and White in the Words of Wisdom,* 358–59; Ṭabarī, *Comfort of the Mystics,* 450.

70. Kharkūshī, *Revision of the Secrets,* 549. Cf. also Qushayrī, *Treatise,* ed. Zurayq, 306–7; Ṭabarī, *Comfort of the Mystics,* 450, both also giving account of Nūrī's fatal ecstasy caused by a poem.

71. Anṣārī, *Sharḥ,* 4:98–99. Cf. also p. 97 on the agony of Shiblī and Yaḥyā al-Iṣṭakhrī, who were also requested to recite the Muslim creed; see their reaction and Anṣārī's explication there.

Chapter 6

1. On the *Ornament of God's Friends* see Mojaddedi, *The Biographical Tradition in Sufism,* 41–67; Knysh, *Islamic Mysticism,* 128–29; Christopher Melchert, "Abū Nuʿaym's Sources for Ḥilyat al-awliyā', Sufi and Traditionist," in *Les Maîtres soufis et leurs disciples,* ed. G. Gobillot and J.-J. Thibon (Beirut: Presses de l'Ifpo, 2012), 145–59.

2. Mojaddedi, *Biographical Tradition is Sufism,* 42.

3. The modern editions of the *Ornament of God's Friends* are divided into paragraphs; each tradition introduced by a chain of transmitters constitutes a separate (and numbered) paragraph. If a tradition, which seems to be independent (for example, due to its introductory formula) lacks *isnād,* it is presented as pertaining to the previous tradition. I used the following edition: Abū Nuʿaym al-Iṣfahānī. *Ḥilyat al-awliyā' wa-ṭabaqāt al-aṣfiyā'* (Beirut: Dār al-Kutub al-ʿIlmiyya, 1988).

4. Cf. Sulamī, *Generations of the Sufis,* 169 on *sabab* (secondary means); 167–68 on a disease afflicting both Nūrī and Junayd; 165–66 on Nūrī looking at a handsome youth in Baghdad; see 166 on love.

5. Cf. Kharkūshī, *Revision of the Secrets,* 286–87 on the Sufis' detention; 412 on the story about Nūrī and the thief; 506 (a poem beginning "The secrets of my inner heart . . ."); 510 (a poem beginning "How sad it is that I call out for You . . .").

6. On Nūrī demanding a miracle from God, seeSarrāj, *Book of Flashes,* 327.

7. Cf. Qushayrī, *Treatise,* ed. Zurayq, 439 criticizing contemporary Sufism; ibid., 248–49 on the Ghulām Khalīl incident; and Qushayrī, *Treatise,* ed. Maḥmūd, 599 on Nūrī and the thief; ibid., 575 on Nūrī demanding a miracle from God.

8. Abū Nuʿaym, *Ornament of God's Friends,* 10:249.

9. Ibid.

10. Abū Nuʿaym, *Ornament of God's Friends,* 10:251; Kharkūshī, *Revision of the Secrets,* 412; Qushayrī, *Treatise,* ed. Maḥmūd, 599.

11. Abū Nuʿaym, *Ornament of God's Friends,* 10:254; Sulamī, *Generations of the Sufis,* 165–66; Sīrjānī, *Black and White in the Words of Wisdom,* 240.

12. Abū Nuʿaym, *Ornament of God's Friends,* 10:251.

13. Abū Nuʿaym, *Ornament of God's Friends,* 10:252; Sulamī, *Generations of the Sufis,* 167–68, Sīrjānī, *Black and White in the Words of Wisdom,* 226–27.

14. Abū Nuʿaym, *Ornament of God's Friends,* 10:251; Sarrāj, *Book of Flashes,* 327; Qushayrī, *Treatise,* ed. Maḥmūd, 575; Sīrjānī, *Black and White in the Words of Wisdom,* 332.

15. Ibid., 10:250. Cf. Kharkūshī, *Revision of the Secrets,* 286–87; Qushayrī, *Treatise,* ed. Zurayq, 248–49; Sīrjānī, *Black and White in the Words*

of Wisdom, 19. For the remarkably divergent version of the *Book of Flashes,* see Arberry, *Pages,* 5.

16. Abū Nuʿaym, *Ornament of God's Friends,* 10:249–50.

17. Beginning "The secrets of my inner heart. . . ." Abū Nuʿaym, *Ornament of God's Friends,* 10:253; cf. Kharkūshī, *Revision of the Secrets,* 506.

18. It is not clear which noun the pronoun is substituting for.

19. This refers probably to an earlier letter of Junayd, apparently Nūrī and Junayd exchanged various letters.

20. The pronoun "it" seems to refer to the "crown of the Glorious." The sentence should be understood in a figural sense, meaning that God is the ultimate source of mystical states.

21. The dual employed in the sentence should not be understood literally (as if Junayd had two possible choices instead of three) but as a grammatical peculiarity reflecting that a choice is finally made between two things only.

22. Abū Nuʿaym, *Ornament of God's Friends,* 10:254.

23. Beginning "By my life! I've never entrusted my secret. . . ."; Sarrāj, *Book of Flashes,* 232, 248; Kharkūshī, *Revision of the Secrets,* 539. Cf. also Sīrjānī, *Black and White in the Words of Wisdom,* 393.

24. Beginning "How said it is that I call out for You. . . ." Abū Nuʿaym, *Ornament of God's Friends,* 10:253; Kharkūshī, *Revision of the Secrets,* 510.

25. *Mutakallim.* This term is usually translated as "theologian," but in the context of Nūrī, it is probably not intended as a technical term and not used in its strict sense.

26. Abū Nuʿaym, *Ornament of God's Friends,* 10:250, the parallel version is on p. 251. Lines 1, 3, and 5 of the poem (with slight modifications) are quoted in Sarrāj, *Book of Flashes,* 369, and line 3 on p. 340, too. Cf. also Sīrjānī, *Black and White in the Words of Wisdom,* 21. The short poem might be an abbreviated variant of a more complete version or, conversely, its original nucleus. The second possibility seems to be more plausible since the language in lines 3 and 5 is almost identical to that of the verses in the *Book of Flashes,* and the divergent versions of line 1 also show a clear connection. It seems that a poem composed originally of three lines was extended with lines inserted between lines 1–3 and 3–5.

27. Abū Nuʿaym, *Ornament of God's Friends,* 10:251.

28. Abū Nuʿaym, *Ornament of God's Friends,* 10:253. The first sentence is quoted as a comment on the Quran (2:29) by Sulamī, cf. Nwyia, "Textes mystiques inédits"; Sulamī, *Realities,* 1:54.

29. Abū Nuʿaym, *Ornament of God's Friends,* 10:253–54.

30. Qushayrī, *Treatise,* ed. Zurayq, 439.

31. Qushayrī, *Treatise,* ed. Zurayq, 378–85; ibid., ed. Maḥmūd, 618–32; Sīrjānī, *Black and White in the Words of Wisdom,* 409–10.

32. Abū Nuʿaym, *Ornament of God's Friends,* 10:252–53.

33. On the controversy concerning *samāʿ*, see for example the corresponding chapters of Suhrawardī's (d. 1234) *ʿAwārif al-maʿārif* (Cairo: Dār al-Muqaṭṭam, 2017), 187–219.

34. Abū Nuʿaym, *Ornament of God's Friends,* 10:251; Qushayrī, *Treatise,* ed. Zurayq, 439; Sīrjānī, *Black and White in the Words of Wisdom,* 110.

35. On the imitators and followers of Sufis, who accompany and join them without being full-fledged members of the communities or brotherhoods, see Arin Shawkat Salamah-Qudsi, "The Idea of Tashabbuh in Sufi Communities and Literature of the Late 6th/12th and early 7th/13th Century in Baghdad," *Al-Qanṭara* 32, no. 1 (2011): 175–97.

36. Suhrawardī, *Ādāb al-murīdīn,* 19–20.

37. Ibid., 80–98.

38. Ibid., 98.

39. Besides the traditions discussed and translated in this chapter, see also Nūrī's saying on finding intimacy in the Beloved's closeness quoted also in Sulamī, *Generations of the Sufis,* 166; and Abū Nuʿaym, *Ornament of God's Friends,* 10:251.

Chapter 7

1. On Qushayrī and especially on his *Treatise,* see Alexander D. Knysh's introduction to his English translation: Abu 'l-Qasim al-Qushayri, *Al-Qushayri's Epistle on Sufism* (Reading: Garnet, 2007), xix–xxvii; Knysh, *Islamic Mysticism,* 60–63; Mojaddedi, *Biographical Tradition in Sufism,* 99–124; Michael A. Sells, *Early Islamic Mysticism* (New York and Mahwah, NJ: Paulist Press, 1996), 97–150; Hamid Algar, "Introduction to Qushayri's Principles," in al-Qushayri. *Principles of Sufism.* [English translation of selected parts from Qushayrī's *Treatise* by B. R. Schlegell] (Berkeley: Mizan, 1992), I–XVII; Jawid A. Mojaddedi, "Legitimizing Sufism in al-Qushayri's Risala," *Studia Islamica* 90 (2000): 37–50; Francesco Chiabotti and Martin Nguyen, "The Textual Legacy of Abū l-Qāsim al-Qushayrī: A Bibliographic Record," *Arabica* 61 (2014): 339–95; Martin Nguyen, *Sufi Master and Qur'an Scholar: Abū l-Qāsim al-Qushayrī and the Laṭā'if al-Ishārāt* (Oxford: Oxford University Press and Institute of Ismaili Studies, 2012); and the entire *Journal of Sufi Studies* vol. 2, no. 1 (2013) dedicated to Qushayrī. For a list of Qushayrī's published works see Richard Gramlich, *Das Sebdschreiben al-Qushayri's über das Sufitum* (Wiesbaden: Franz Steiner Verlag, 1989), 17.

2. I have used the text edited by Maʿrūf Zurayq and ʿAlī ʿAbd al-Ḥamīd Balṭajī (Beirut: Dār al-Jīl, n.d.), which, however, omits most of the chapter on miracles performed by Sufi masters. These are supplemented from the edition of ʿAbd al-Ḥalīm Maḥmūd and Maḥmūd ibn al-Sharīf (Cairo: Dār al-Shaʿb, 1989). Unlike the edition of Zurayq-Balṭajī, Knysh's translation and the edition of ʿAbd al-Ḥakīm-Muḥammad ibn al-Sharīf contains chains of tradition.

3. I have used an edition that contains both works under the title *Ḥāshiyat al-ʿallāma Muṣṭafā al-ʿArūsī al-musammā Natāʾij al-afkār al-qudsiyya fī bayān maʿānī Sharḥ al-risāla al-qushayriyya li-shaykh al-islām Zakariyyā ibn Muḥammad al-Anṣārī* (Beirut: Dār al-Kutub al-ʿIlmiyya, 2007), 4 vols. (Henceforth: ʿArūsī, *Natāʾij* and Anṣārī, *Sharḥ).* Anṣārī's commentary has been printed separately as well, see Abū Yaḥyā Zakariyyā al-Anṣārī, *Iḥkām al-dalāla ʿalā taḥrīr al-risāla* (Damascus: Dār an-Nuʿmān lil-ʿUlūm, 2000), 2 vols.

4. Algar, "Introduction to Qushayri's Principles" XVII, n. 23 referring to Kātib Çelebi, *Kashf al-ẓunūn,* eds. Yaltkaya and Bilge (Istanbul, 1971), 1:883.

5. In the *Generations of the Sufis* by Sulamī the list of Nūrī's teachers is slightly different. Aḥmad ibn Abī l-Ḥawārī is not regarded by Sulamī as Nūrī's teacher (he mentions only Sarī al-Saqatī and Muḥammad ibn ʿAlī al-Qaṣṣāb), although he remarks that Nūrī "saw Aḥmad ibn Abī l-Ḥawārī," without explaining what that actually meant. Since Aḥmad ibn Abī l-Ḥawārī was the foremost Syrian Sufi master of his time, probably in the later tradition, concerning Nūrī, he took the place of the lesser-known Muḥammad ibn ʿAlī al-Qaṣṣāb.

6. Qushayrī, *Treatise,* ed. Zurayq, 438–39.

7. Anṣārī, *Sharḥ,* 1:230.

8. Qushayrī, *Treatise,* ed. Zurayq, 439.

9. Qushayrī, *Treatise,* ed. Zurayq, 439. Cf. Kalābādhī, *Doctrine of the Sufis,* 9; Sulamī, *Generations of the Sufis,* 166; Kharkūshī, *Revision of the Secrets,* 28.

10. *"The greatest things in our days are two: a learned person who practices what he has learned, and a knower, who speaks about reality."* Qushayrī, *Treatise,* ed. Zurayq, 439.

11. *"Tattered rugs were coverings for pearls; nowadays they have become dunghills upon corpses."* Qushayrī, *Treatise,* ed. Zurayq, 439. Cf. also Abū Nuʿaym, *Ornament of God's Friends,* 10:251; Sīrjānī, *Black and White in the Words of Wisdom,* 110. Qushayrī's fifteenth-century commentator, Anṣārī understands the saying as referring to imitators. While commenting on Nūrī's saying, he reproaches hypocrites of his own age, who transform the Sufis' modest and even meek garment into a piece of luxury: "Wearing

tattered rugs [. . .] used to be the mark of humbleness and indifference to the world. [. . .] Now, tattered rugs became dunghills upon corpses, or more disgusting than that, since they became ornaments made from exquisite clothes! That is wasting the money and [false] imitation of the righteous, seeking to attain high rank in the eyes of the people—since the hearts are devoid of abstinence and do not wish to shun the world." Anṣārī, *Sharḥ,* 1:230–231.

12. *"If you see someone who claims that a state granted by God may make him violate religious law, do not approach him!"* Qushayrī, *Treatise,* ed. Zurayq, 439. Cf. also Abū Nuʿaym, *Ḥilyat al-awliyā,* 10:252–53 where this saying is included among the spiritual advice Nūrī gave to his companions.

13. Qushayrī, *Treatise,* ed. Zurayq, 439.

14. The concept of *ṣidq* is expounded in a relatively long chapter of the *Treatise* bearing the same title, cf. Qushayrī, *Treatise,* ed. Zurayq, 210–14.

15. Qushayrī, *Treatise,* ed. Zurayq, 211.

16. Cf. Ibid., 212–13.

17. Ibid., 439.

18. Ibid., 71.

19. Ibid.

20. ʿAbd Allāh al-Harawī, *Manāzil al-sā'irīn* (Beirut: Dār al-Kutub al-ʿIlmiyya, 1988), 120.

21. Qushayrī, *Treatise,* ed. Zurayq,72.

22. ʿAlí b. ʿUthmán Hujwírí. *The Kashf al-Maḥjúb. The Oldest Persian Treatise on Sufism,* trans. Reynold A. Nicholson (London: Luzac and Co., 1911), 186.

23. Harawī, *Manāzil al-sā'irīn,* 121.

24. Qushayrī, *Treatise,* ed. Zurayq, 258–59; Arberry, *Pages,* 5.

25. Nūrī's utterances regarding the muezzin and the dog are also quoted in Ṭabarī, *Comfort of the Mystics,* 156, again independently from his trial (which is narrated on p. 124 in a version identical with Qushayrī's).

26. Qushayrī, *Treatise,* ed. Maḥmūd, 575; Kharkūshī, *Revision of the Secrets,* 286–87; Abū Nuʿaym, *Ornament of God's Friends,*10:251; Sarrāj, *Book of Flashes,* 327; Sīrjānī, *Black and White in the Words of Wisdom,* 332.

27. Qushayrī, *Treatise,* ed. Zurayq, 306–7. Cf. also Sarrāj, *Book of Flashes,* 210, 290; Kharkūshī, *Revision of the Secrets,* 549; Sīrjānī, *Black and White in the Words of Wisdom,* 358–359; Ṭabarī, *Comfort of the Mystics,* 450. The *Book of Flashes* and the *Black and White in the Words of Wisdom* do not contain the part referring to the recitation of the Muslim creed, while Kharkūshī does not report the story of the fatal love poem.

28. Ṭabarī, *Comfort of the Mystics,* 450.

29. Qushayrī, *Treatise,* ed. Maḥmūd, 599. Cf. also Kharkūshī, *Revision of the Secrets,* 412; Abū Nuʿaym, *Ornament of God's Friends,* 10:251.

30. Qushayrī, *Treatise,* ed. Maḥmūd, 575. Cf. also Abū Nuʿaym, *Ornament of God's Friends,* 10:251; Sarrāj, *Book of Flashes,* 327; Sīrjānī, *Black and White in the Words of Wisdom,* 332.

31. Qushayrī, *Treatise,* ed. Maḥmūd, 575. Cf. also Sarrāj, *Book of Flashes,* 325; Sīrjānī, *Black and White in the Words of Wisdom,* 332.

32. Qushayrī, *Treatise,* ed. Zurayq, 232.

33. Qushayrī, *Treatise,* ed. Zurayq, 234. Cf. also Ṭabarī, *Comfort of the Mystics,* 309.

34. Qushayrī, *Treatise,* ed. Zurayq, 234.

35. Ibid.

36. Ibid.

37. Quoted in ibid., 232. Cf. Abū ʿĪsā Muḥammad al-Tirmidhī, *al-Jāmiʿ al-kabīr*. Edited by Bashshār ʿAwwād Maʿrūf (Beirut: Dār al-Gharb al-Islāmī, 1996), 5:200, no. 3127.

38. Qushayrī, *Treatise,* ed. Zurayq, 231.

39. Qushayrī, *Treatise,* ed. Zurayq, 235.

40. Ibid.

41. Ibid., 236.

42. Ibid., 233.

43. Ibid.

44. Ibid., 235.

45. Qushayrī, *Treatise,* ed. Zurayq, 233–34.

46. Ibid., 234.

47. Anṣārī, *Sharḥ,* 3:316–17.

48. ʿArūsī, *Natā'ij,* 3:317.

49. Qushayrī, *Treatise,* ed. Maḥmūd, 594. Cf. also Ṭabarī, *Comfort of the Mystics,* 339–40.

50. Qushayrī, *Treatise,* ed. Zurayq, 282, 341. Cf. also Sarrāj, *Book of Flashes,* 26; Sīrjānī, *Black and White in the Words of Wisdom,* 47.

51. Anṣārī, *Sharḥ,* 4:225.

52. ʿArūsī, *Natā'ij,* 4:225. This view contrasts with Nūrī's opinion on the *samāʿ* (different in the case of advanced Sufis and beginners) collected among his spiritual advice by Abū Nuʿaym.

53. ʿArūsī, *Natā'ij,* 4:16.

54. Qushayrī, *Treatise,* ed. Zurayq, 62.

55. Ibid., 61–62.

56. Ibid., 306–7.

57. Qushayrī, *Treatise,* ed. Zurayq, 62.

58. Qushayrī, *Treatise,* ed. Zurayq, 324. Cf. also ibid., 287.

59. Qushayrī, *Treatise,* ed. Zurayq, 319.

60. Anṣārī, *Sharḥ,* 4:166.

61. ʿArūsī, *Natāʾij*, 4:166.
62. Qushayrī, *Treatise*, ed. Zurayq, 181. Cf. also Kalābādhī, *Doctrine of the Sufis*, 73; Sarrāj, *Book of Flashes*, 81; Sīrjānī, *Black and White in the Words of Wisdom*, 291.
63. Qushayrī, *Treatise*, ed. Maḥmūd, 160.
64. Qushayrī, *Treatise*, ed. Zurayq, 76.
65. Anṣārī, *Sharḥ*, 2:124.
66. ʿArūsī, *Natāʾij*, 2:124.
67. Qushayrī, *Treatise*, ed. Zurayq, 169.
68. Ḥifnī, *al-Mawsūʿa al-ṣūfiyya*, 1024.
69. Qushayrī, *Treatise*, ed. Maḥmūd, 578, in the chapter on the miracles *(karāmāt)* performed by the friends of God.
70. Anṣārī, *Sharḥ*, 3:102.
71. Qushayrī, *Treatise*, ed. Zurayq, 196. Variations of the saying can be found in Kharkūshī, *Revision of the Secrets*, 130; and Sīrjānī, *Black and White in the Words of Wisdom*, 313. The version quoted by Sīrjānī also appears in Sulamī's *Realities of Interpretation* as a comment on Q 98:8, cf. Nwyia, "Textes mystiques inédits, 147 and Sulamī, *Realities*, 2:413.
72. Kalābādhī, *Doctrine of the Sufis*, 73.
73. Sulamī, *Generations of the Sufis*, 166.
74. Anṣārī, *Sharḥ*, 3:187; ʿArūsī, *Natāʾij*, 3:187.
75. Qushayrī, *Treatise*, ed. Zurayq, 127.
76. Ibid., 126.
77. ʿArūsī, *Natāʾij*, 2:310.
78. Anṣārī, *Sharḥ*, 2:310.
79. Attributed to Wāsiṭī. Qushayrī, *Treatise*, ed. Zurayq, 128. On the pair of concepts, fear and hope, and on the coexistence of opposite concepts in Sufi mysticism in general, see Sara Sviri, *Perspectives on Early Islamic Mysticism* (London and New York: Routledge, 2020), 139–69 (chap. 7, entitled "Between Fear and Hope").
80. Qushayrī, *Treatise*, ed. Maḥmūd, 239. The version that appears in the edition of Maḥmūd seems to be more correct than that of the Zurayq edition.
81. Qushayrī, *Treatise*, ed. Zurayq, 45.
82. Anṣārī, *Sharḥ*, 1:81; ʿArūsī, *Natāʾij*, 1:81–82.
83. Qushayrī, *Treatise*, ed. Zurayq, 43.
84. ʿArūsī, *Natāʿij*, 1:75. Cf. Jīlānī, *al-Maqālāt al-dhawqiyya lil-imām al-Kīlānī*, ed. Mīʿād Sharaf al-Dīn al-Kīlānī (Beirut: Dār al-Kutub al-ʿIlmiyya, 2011), 159–60.
85. Traditions that are quoted in the earlier collection and are not discussed in this chapter include the following: a saying on the poor pre-

ferring others to himself (Qushayrī, *Treatise,* ed. Zurayq, 278, 281; Kalābādhī, *Doctrine of the Sufis,* 67; Kharkūshī, *Revision of the Secrets* 157; Sīrjānī, *Black and White in the Words of Wisdom,* 46–47; *"He who does not discipline himself according to the moment, [makes] his moment loathsome."* (Qushayrī, *Treatise,* ed. Zurayq, 287; Kharkūshī, *Revision of the Secrets,* 216); a story of speaking allusively on the closeness to God (Qushayrī, *Treatise,* ed. Zurayq, 82; Sarrāj, *Book of Flashes,* 57, 224); *"Repentance means that you return from everything except from God"* (Qushayrī, *Treatise,* ed. Zurayq, 95. Cf. Kalābādhī, *Doctrine of the Sufis,* 64; Sīrjānī, *Black and White in the Words of Wisdom,* 90).

86. These include: practice *(ʿamal);* self-discipline *(ta'addub);* poor *(faqīr);* recollection *(dhikr);* negligence *(ghafla);* hearts *(albāb);* audition *(samāʿ);* share of the carnal soul *(ḥaẓẓ an-nafs);* state *(ḥāla);* love *(widād);* love *(maḥabba);* veils *(astār);* unveiling *(kashf);* secrets *(asrār);* trustworthiness *(ṣidq);* contentment (riḍā); mystical knower *(ʿārif);* certainty *(yaqīn).*

Chapter 8

1. Bilal Orfali and Nada Saab, eds., *Sufism, Black and White. A Critical Edition of Kitāb al-Bayāḍ wa-l-Sawād by Abū l-Ḥasan al-Sīrjānī* (Leiden and Boston: Brill, 2012). Henceforth: Sīrjānī, *Black and White in the Words of Wisdom.* The editors' translation of the title disregards the chapter of the book entitled *bāb al-murīd wa-l-murād* (ch. 55, pp. 308–11), which clearly explains that the *murīd* is the Sufi disciple who seeks God by his own initiative, while the *murād* is the person God attracts to Himself irrespectively of his actions. The *murād,* thus, is a synonym of the most common term *majdhūb,* and it does not correspond to "mystic quest" translated in the title. The terms *murīd* and *murād* mentioned in the title denote the Sufis' two basic types: those who seek God and those who are sought after by God.

2. For more details about his life and work, see the introduction by Bilal Orfali and Nada Saab to Sīrjānī, *Black and White in the Words of Wisdom,* 1–5.

3. Sīrjānī, *Black and White in the Words of Wisdom,* 251.

4. Ibid., 16–17.

5. On *istinbāṭ* cf. also Sarrāj, *Book of Flashes,* 105–6.

6. Sīrjānī, *Black and White in the Words of Wisdom,* 25.

7. Ibid.

8. Ibid.

9. Sīrjānī, *Black and White in the Words of Wisdom,* 31: *"ʿAlimnā dhālika ishāratan fa-idhā ṣāra ʿibāratan khafa'a."* The verb خفئا seems to be a mistake for خفى.

10. Sīrjānī, *Black and White in the Words of Wisdom*, 33.
11. Ibid.
12. Sīrjānī, *Black and White in the Words of Wisdom*, 33.
13. Ibid., 44.
14. Kharkūshī, *Revision of the Secrets*, 322. For a more accurate reading, see Ibn Khamīs, *Manāqib al-abrār wa-maḥāsin al-akhyār* (Abu Dhabi: Markaz Zayed li-l-Turāth wa-l-Tārīkh, 2006), 1:404.
15. Sīrjānī, *Black and White in the Words of Wisdom*, 402.
16. Cf. Ibid., note 2.
17. Ibid., 104.
18. Ibid., 100.
19. Ibid., 102.
20. Ibid.
21. Ibid., 104.
22. In the context of the saying the word "secret" *(sirr,* plural: *asrār)* obviously alludes to the inner heart *(sirr, plural: sarā'ir).*
23. Sīrjānī, *Black and White in the Words of Wisdom*, 104.
24. Ibid., 308.
25. Ibid.
26. Ibid.
27. Sīrjānī, *Black and White in the Words of Wisdom*, 309.
28. Ibid., 308.
29. Sīrjānī, *Black and White in the Words of Wisdom*, 287.
30. Qushayrī, *Treatise*, ed. Zurayq, 88.
31. al-Ḥakīm al-Tirmīdhī, *Bayān al-farq bayna l-ṣadr wa-l-qalb wa-l-fu'ād wa-l-lubb* (Amman: Al-Markaz al-Malakī li-l-Buḥūth wa-l-Dirāsāt al-Islāmiyya, 2012).
32. Cf. Lane, *Arabic-English Lexicon*. 1:2323–2324, *s.v. fu'ād*.
33. Such speculations concerning the structure of the heart can be found in magical-mystical texts also, cf. Būnī, *Shams al-ma'ārif al-kubrā* (Cairo: Dār al-Maḥajjāt al-Bayḍā', 2011), 11–12.
34. Published by Paul Nwyia, "Textes mystiques inédits d'Abū-l-Ḥasan al-Nūrī." *Mélanges de l'Université Saint-Joseph* 46 (1968): 117–54.
35. The description is quoted by Nwyia, *Exégèse coranique*, 321. Nwyia wrote his book before the publication of Sīrjānī's collection and therefore was unaware of the parallel version it includes.
36. Cf. Junayd's words on *naẓar* quoted by Sīrjānī, *Black and White in the Words of Wisdom*, 236.
37. Ibid., 240.
38. Ibid., 236.
39. Sulamī, *Generations of the Sufis*, 165–66, 169.
40. Sīrjānī, *Black and White in the Words of Wisdom*, 237–38.

41. Ibid., 239.
42. Ibid., 156.
43. Ibid., 97.
44. Ibid., 96.
45. Ibid., 116.
46. Cf. Qushayrī, *Treatise*, ed. Zurayq, 196.
47. Sīrjānī, *Black and White in the Words of Wisdom*, 114.
48. Ibid.
49. Ibid., 116.
50. Ibid., 313, quoted also in Sulamī's *Realities of Interpretation* as a comment on Q 98:8, cf. Nwyia, "Textes mystiques inédits, 147 and Sulamī, *Realities*, 2:413. Variations of the saying can be found in Kharkūshī, *Revision of the Secrets*, 130 and Qushayrī, *Treatise*, ed. Zurayq, 196.
51. Sīrjānī, *Black and White in the Words of Wisdom*, 368.
52. Ibid., 307.
53. Ibid., 305.
54. Ibid., 304.
55. Ibid., 307.
56. Ibid., 337.
57. Ibid.
58. Translation of Muḥammad Marmaduke Pickthall. *The Meaning of the Glorious Koran* (Tripoli: Islamic Call Society, 1973), 499.
59. Sīrjānī, *Black and White in the Words of Wisdom*, 338.
60. Ibid., 337.
61. Ibid., 338.
62. Ibid., 158.
63. Ibid.
64. Ibid., 158.
65. Ibid., 161.
66. Sīrjānī, *Black and White in the Words of Wisdom*, 16–17, 19, 21, 24, 41, 45–47, 63, 69, 90, 132, 141, 226–27, 236, 240, 288, 290, 291, 315, 332, 358–59, 370, 386, 393.

Chapter 9

1. I published an article about this Genizah fragment putting it in the context of Jewish pietists in medieval Egypt who were strongly attracted by Sufism. Cf. Dora Zsom, "Sobriety and Intoxication in Mystical Sayings from the Cairo Genizah," in *Contacts and Interactions*, ed. Jaakko Hämeen-Anttila et al. (Leuven: Peeters, 2017), 493–504. The article contains

some passages of Nūrī's and Junayd's letters in my translation. The first complete translation, however, is published here.

2. I am grateful to Efraim Wust who was so kind as to examine the fragment from a palaeographical point of view.

3. On the genre of *shaṭaḥāt*, see Ernst, *Words of Ecstasy in Sufism*.

4. ʿAbd al-Raḥmān Badawī, *Shaṭaḥāt al-ṣūfiyya* (Kuwait: Wikālat al-Maṭbūʿāt, 1978).

5. Abū Yazīd al-Bisṭāmī, *al-Majmūʿa al-ṣūfiyya al-kāmila*, ed. Qāsim Muḥammad ʿAbbās (Damascus: al-Madā, 2004).

6. I have published the Arabic transcription and the English translation of fols. 4b, line 12–7a, line 18. Cf. Dora Zsom, "Sufi Stories from the Cairo Genizah," *Arabist* 36 (2015): 89–104.

7. Abdel-Kader, *The Life, Personality and Writings of al-Junayd*. For the French translation of Junayd's writings, see Roger Deladrière, *Junayd, Enseignement spirituel, traités, lettres, oraisons et sentences* (Paris: Sindbad, 1983).

8. Junayd, *Rasā'il*, ed. Jamāl Rajab Saydabī (Damascus, Beirut: Dār Iqra', 2005).

9. Junayd, *Tāj al-ʿārifīn*, ed. Suʿād al-Ḥakīm (Cairo: Dār al-Shurūq, 2007).

10. Sarrāj, *Book of Flashes*, 239.

11. Ibid., 353.

12. Cf. Sells, *Early Islamic Mysticism*, 281.

13. Cf. Muḥammad ibn ʿAbd al-Jabbār an-Niffarī. *Kitāb al-mawāqif*, ed. Arthur John Arberry (London: Messrs and Luzac, 1935), 7. For the English translation of the "standing of the sea" see ibid., 31; and Sells, *Early Islamic Mysticism*, 285–86.

14. Cf. Sarrāj, *Book of Flashes*, 353; Sulamī, *Generations of the Sufis*, 166–68, Abū Nuʿaym, *Ornament of God's Friends*, 10:251, Sīrjānī, *Black and White in the Words of Wisdom*, 226–27, 302.

15. Kalābādhī, *Doctrine of the Sufis*, 63, 111, 112; Sarrāj, *Book of Flashes*, 248, 353, Sulamī, *Realities*, 1:316 and Nwyia, "Textes mystiques inédits," 145, 146; Kharkūshī, *Revision of the Secrets*, 500; Abū Nuʿaym, *Ornament of God's Friends*, 10:253–54; Qushayrī, *Treatise*, ed. Zurayq, 82; Sīrjānī, *Black and White in the Words of Wisdom*, 33, 41, 57.

16. Cf. Sarrāj's words on Nūrī in Arberry, *Pages*, 6; Sulamī, *Generations of the Sufis*, 164; Abū Nuʿaym, *Ornament of God's Friends*, 10:250; Qushayrī, *Treatise*, ed. Zurayq, 438–39; Sīrjānī, *Black and White in the Words of Wisdom*, 251.

17. Fol. 8a, lines 3–4.

18. Fol. 10a. lines 1–3.

19. Fol. 9b, line 11.

20. *Intiṣāb:* standing uprightly, raising one's head, that is, proudly.

21. The reading is dubious; some letters of the word have disappeared completely. It is clear, however, that the word is an infinitive in stem VII, VIII, or X, and the last two root letters are "r" and "d."

22. By proof probably the perfect man *(al-insān al-kāmil)* is meant, see the explication of the term in Ḥifnī, *al-Mawsūʿa al-ṣūfiyya,* 909. *s.v. ḥujja.*

23. The last line is barely legible.

24. The reading is dubious.

25. *Am jaʿalta fatḥahā ghalqan.* It is not clear which word the S/3 fem. pronominal suffix refers to. Perhaps it is a mistake for *fatḥahu,* in which case the suffix would refer to the preceding *bāb* (door).

26. One word is missing.

27. Literally: "You remained alone with yourself towards yourself."

28. Reading أبد instead of ابدى.

29. The reading is dubious.

30. The pronominal suffix attached to the Arabic verb most probably refers to *baqā',* "subsistence [in/with God]."

31. The P/3 masculine pronominal suffix refers to "those selected by God" (see fol. 9a line 22–fol. 9b, line 6).

32. Reading *masālik* instead of *maslak* (*wa-huwa tarīq ʿuwwirat al-masālik dūnahu).*

33. Decree *(ḥukm)* apparently refers to the mystics' state *(ḥāl)* here.

34. The reading is dubious.

35. Literally, "If there appears to you an appearance originating from Him, which refers to your state." The term "appearance" *(al-bādī)* denotes the impression one's heart *(qalb)* gains regarding a certain state. Cf. Ḥifnī, *al-Mawsūʿa al-ṣūfiyya,* 828, *s. v. "al-bādī"*: "When the appearance of the Real appears, every appearance will perish, save the Real."

Chapter 10

1. MS Haci Mahmud 2415, fols. 53a–55a; MS Nafiz Pasha 457, fols. 1a–6b; MS Shehid Ali 2826, fols. 1a–4b; MS Bagdadli Vehbi 2150, fols. 17b–22b. For a more detailed description of the manuscripts, see Nwyia, "Textes mystiques inédits," 124–25.

2. "The *Stations of the Hearts* by Abū l-Ḥusayn an-Nūrī Aḥmad ibn Muḥammad, the Sufi, who died in 295 AH [907/8 A.D.]." Kātib Çelebi, Mustafā ibn ʿAdallah Hājjī Khalīfa, *Kashf al-ẓunūn ʿan asmā' l-kutub wa-l-funūn* (Der-i Saʿādet: Maṭbaʿat al-ʿAlam, 1893) 2 vols. 2:496. It has to be

noted that in the edition of *Kashf al-ẓunūn* that Nwyia used, the treatise is attributed to a certain Abū l-Ḥasan an-Nawawī, who died in the same year as Nūrī, cf. Nwyia, "Textes mystiques inédits," 123. On the confusion between the names Nūrī and Nawawī see below.

3. Kalābādhī, *Doctrine of the Sufis,* 11. Nūrī did refer to allusive discourse in his sayings collected in the earliest sources, cf. Sarrāj, *Book of Flashes,* 57. A verbal form of the term *ishāra* occurs also in the *Stations of the Hearts* once, but that passage can be found also in the *Revision of the Secrets* by Kharkūshī, where it is attributed to Shiblī. Cf. Kharkūshī, *Revision of the Secrets,* 200.

4. For the exact references, see Nwyia, "Textes mystiques inédits," 123.

5. Besides the passages Nwyia mentioned there are also others that can be found in early Sufi works, for example in Kharkūshī's *Revision of the Secrets,* see below, in chapter VI of the *Stations of the Hearts.*

6. Sīrjānī, *Black and White in the Words of Wisdom,* 287.

7. Cf. chapters III, IV, IX, XIV, XVII, XIX of the *Stations of the Hearts.*

8. The attribution of the treatise to Tirmīdhī is questionable, see Bernd Radtke, "Some Recent Research on al-Ḥakīm al-Tirmidhī," *Der Islam* 83 (2006): 40–41; cf. also Bernd Radtke, *Al-Ḥakīm al-Tirmiḏī. Ein islamischer Theosoph des 3./9. Jahrhunderts* (Freiburg: K. Schwarz, 1980), 59.

9. Cf. Bernd Radtke and John O'Kane, *The Concept of Sainthood in Early Islamic Mysticism. Two Works by Al-Ḥakīm Al-Tirmidhī* (Richmond, UK: Curzon Press, 1996), 5. For the date of Tirmīdhī's death, see Radtke, *Al-Ḥakīm al-Tirmiḏī,* 38.

10. Būnī, *Shams al-maʿārif al-kubrā* (Cairo: Dār al-Maḥajjāt al-Bayḍā', 2011), 11–12.

11. Saeko Yazaki, *Islamic Mysticsm and Abū Ṭālib al-Makkī. The Role of the Heart* (London and New York: Routledge, 2013), 36–38.

12. It has to be noted that in the *Kitāb al-riyāḍa* ("The Training of the Self"), also attributed to Tirmīdhī, the sequence of the organs is reversed; there the outer part is called *fu'ād,* while the inner part is the *qalb,* cf. Sviri, *Perspectives on Early Islamic Mysticism,* 279.

13. Cf. especially Qushayrī, *Treatise,* ed. Zurayq, 86–88.

14. Cf. Schimmel, "Abū' l-Ḥusayn al-Nūrī, Qibla of the Lights," 63.

15. Lúce López-Baralt, *Islam in Spanish Literature: from the Middle Ages to the Present* (Leiden: Brill, 1992), 91–142. Originally published as *Huella del Islam en la literature Española* (Madrid, 1985).

16. Miguel Asín Palacios, "El símil de los castillos y moradas del alma en la mística islámica y en Santa Teresa." *Al-Andalus* 2 (1946): 263–74. The note regarding the date of the redaction of the *Nawādir* is on p. 266.

The passage in question was translated by Miguel Asín Palacios, see. pp. 267–68. The translation is quoted by López-Baralt as well, *Islam in Spanish Literature*, 108.

17. López-Baralt, *Islam in Spanish Literature*, 110.

18. The word *ḥaqq* means both "rightness, right" and "duty." Evidently, in this context it refers to man's duties and to God's rights.

19. The image is borrowed *(iqtibās)* from the Quran (14:24).

20. The verb *(ʿarafa,* "to know") refers here to inspired knowledge *(maʿrifa).*

21. Allusion to Quran 33:27 "We offered trust *(amāna)* to the heavens, earth and mountains but they refused to bear it, since they feared from it, so man bore it—he is tyrannical and ignorant."

22. The expression "sound heart" *(qalb salīm)* that appears in the title of the chapter is taken from the Quran (26:89), from Abraham's preaching against idol worship. In Sufi tradition Abraham is regarded as the possessor of sound heart, and this passage of the *Stations of the Hearts* is quoted by Kharkūshī in his *Revision of the Secrets* (on p. 200), where it is attributed to Shiblī: "Shiblī was asked about the sound heart, and he said: That is the heart of Abraham, and he used to indicate with his heart from its lower part to faithfulness *(wafā'),* from its upper part to contentment *(riḍā'),* from its right to donations *(ʿaṭā'),* from its left to destiny *(manan),* from its frontal part to encounter *(liqā'),* and from its rear part to devoutness *(tuqan).*" The sole difference between this saying and the one quoted in the *Stations of the Hearts* is the last word, which is devoutness (تقى) in the *Revision of the Secrets* and subsistence (بقاء) in the *Stations of the Hearts.* This might be a scribal error given the orthographic similarity of the words.

23. Sulamī attributes the following saying to Abū ʿUthmān, a disciple of Shāh Kirmānī. Cf. Nwyia, "Textes mystiques inédits," 123.

24. The epithet "beloved" *(ḥabīb)* usually refers to the Prophet Muhammad, here, however, God addresses Moses as His beloved. Intimate conversation with God *(munājāt)* is a frequent Sufi topic, to which the precedent is God's confidential talk with Moses mentioned in the Quran (19:52).

25. The fire of loving God destructs every kind of dependence, including enjoying the sweetness of obedience to God.

26. Allusion to *maʿrifa,* inspired knowledge.

27. This means, that man acquires the quality of humility and fear of God by virtue of experiencing divine might, splendor, and knowledge.

28. Admonition urges one to ponder upon his deeds, which results in correcting his manners, that is, in obedience to God.

29. The differentiation between *tafsīr* and *ta'wīl* might point toward the possibility that the treatise was written by a later author than Nūrī,

since in the first three Islamic centuries these concepts were not clearly distinguished. In later terminology *tafsīr* referred to the interpretation of the literal and manifest *(ẓāhir)* meaning of the Quran, while *ta'wīl* to the hidden, allegorical-mystical *(bāṭin)* level. See A. Rippin: "Tafsīr," in *The Encyclopaedia of Islam* (Leiden: Brill, 2000), 10:83–88.

30. That is, he inquires about the meaning of mystical interpretation those familiar with it.

31. The mental image of the edifice with a throne in it is parallel to chapter I's description of a house with a couch in it; it might be suggested also that chapter XVI unfolds chapter I. The words used in both parables are identical *(bayt* and *sarīr,* meaning "house" and "couch / throne" respectively, but in chapter I nothing indicates that the dwelling and the divan-like couch in it is in fact a royal throne.

32. Majesty causing reverence: the manifestation of divine majesty inspires reverence in man, cf. Ibn ʿArabī, *al-Futūḥāt al-makkiyya,* 2:540 (chapter 239): "Reverence is a state of the heart caused by the effect of the manifestation of divine splendour *(jalāl)* and benevolence *(jamāl)."*

33. That is, obedience resulting from man's humility.

34. The quality of man's last acts before his death.

35. *Zīna:* apparent, superficial embellishment that does not correspond to inner reality.

36. Nwyia's edition of the Arabic text indicates that the reading of the word "path" is dubious.

Chapter 11

1. The percentages refer to the number of traditions, not to their length. The estimates are rough and serve only as an illustration since a complier may opt for combining several traditions into one, or conversely, to divide one tradition into separate parts.

2. Cf. Kalābādhī, *Doctrine of the Sufis,* 9.

3. For example: *Kayfa yakūnu mukayyafan man kayyafa al-kayf am kayfa yakūnu muḥayyathan man ḥayyatha al-ḥayth fa-sammāhu ḥaythan* ("How could be described by 'how' Him who made 'how-ness', and how could be described by 'where' Him who made where-ness and named it 'where' "?); Sarrāj, *Book of Flashes,* 37–38 (also quoted in Sīrjānī, *Black and White in the Words of Wisdom,* 63).

4. Cf. for example one of the definitions of Sufism in Kalābādhī, *Doctrine of the Sufis,* 9; Qushayrī, *Treatise,* ed. Zurayq, 439; Sulamī, *Generations of the Sufis,* 166.

5. Sarrāj, *Book of Flashes,* 57; Qushayrī, *Treatise,* ed. Zurayq, 82.

6. Kalābādhī, *Doctrine of the Sufis,* 112.

7. For example, Sarrāj quotes the same saying with a narrative context in *Book of Flashes*, 57, and without it on p. 224; while Qushayrī records the context with most details, see *Treatise*, ed. Zurayq, 82.

8. Abū Nuʿaym, *Ornament of God's Friends*, 10:250, 251.

9. Cf. a variant of the same poem in Sarrāj, *Book of Flashes*, 369, and a sole verse of it on p. 340.

10. Cf. Sarrāj, *Book of Flashes*, 81: *al-yaqīn al-mushāhada* ("Certainty is witnessing"), also quoted in Qushayrī, *Treatise*, ed. Zurayq, 181.

11. Abū Nuʿaym, *Ornament of God's Friends*, 10:252–53.

12. Cf. Abū Nuʿaym, *Ornament of God's Friends*, 10:253–54; Sarrāj, *Book of Flashes*, 239, 353.

13. These are the poems mentioned above; that which he repeated in his mortal ecstasy (he heard it at a *samāʿ* session, but it was not composed by him), and the poem that the young man recited to Nūrī in Baghdad.

Appendix A

1. The reading is very doubtful, some letters of the word have disappeared completely. It is clear, however, that the word is an infinitive in stem VII, VIII or X, and the last two radicals are „r" ad „d."

2. The last line is barely legible.

3. The reading of the word is dubious.

4. The word is not clearly legible.

5. *Sic*, instead of ينجو.

6. *Sic*, instead of استأثر.

7. *Sic*, instead of تعابير.

8. The reading of the first three words is dubious.

9. The reading is dubious.

10. The reading is dubious, the diacritical signs of the word appearing in the manuscript (يرايحاله) do not make sense. I suggest correcting the word to بارتحاله which fits the context.

11. *Sic*, instead of يرى.

12. The verb in the manuscript is inflected in S/3 masc. (يعرفه), which seems to be erroneous; therefore, I corrected it to S/2 masc. (تعرفه).

13. Two dots can be seen below the second letter, but reading „b" instead of „y" seems to be more fitting to the syntax of the sentence.

14. Correction in the margin. The word كله was added later by another hand.

Bibliography

Abdel-Kader, Ali Hassan. *The Life, Personality and Writings of al-Junayd.* London: Luzac, 1976.

Abrahamov, Binyamin. *Divine Love in Islamic Mysticism: The Teachings of Al-Ghazālī and Al-Dabbāgh.* London: Routledge, 2003.

Abrahamov, Binyamin. "Ibn ʿArabī on Divine Love." In *Tribute to Michael: Studies in Jewish and Muslim Thought Presented to Professor Michael Schwartz,* edited by Sarah-Klein Braslavy, Binyamin Abrahamov, and Joseph Sadan, 7–36. Tel Aviv: Tel Aviv University, 2009.

Abū Nuʿaym, *Ornament of God's Friends* = Abū Nuʿaym, Aḥmad ibn ʿAbd Allāh al-Iṣfahānī. *Ḥilyat al-awliyāʾ wa-ṭabaqāt al-aṣfiyāʾ.* 10 vols. Beirut: Dār al-Kutub al-ʿIlmiyya, 1988.

ʿAjam, Rafīq. *Mawsūʿat muṣṭalaḥāt al-ṣūfiyya fī l-islām.* Beirut: Maktabat Lubnān, 1999.

Algar, Hamid. "Introduction to Qushayri's Principles." In *Principles of Sufism* by al-Qushayri, I–XVII. English translation of selected parts from Qushayrī's *Treatise* by B. R. Schlegell. Berkeley: Mizan, 1992.

Andrae, Tor. *Die person Muḥammads in lehre und glaube seiner gemeinde.* Stockholm: P. A. Vorstedt og Söner, 1918.

Anṣārī, Abū Yaḥyā Zakariyya ibn Muḥammad al-. *Iḥkām al-dalāla ʿalā taḥrīr al-Risāla.* 2 vols. Damascus: Dār al-Nuʿmān lil-ʿUlūm, 2000.

Anṣārī, *Sharḥ* = Abū Yaḥyā Zakariyyā ibn Muḥammad al-Anṣārī. *Ḥāshiyat al-ʿallāma Muṣṭafā al-ʿArūsī al-musammā Natāʾij al-afkār al-qudsiyya fī bayān maʿānī sharḥ al-risāla al-qushayriyya li-shaykh al-islām Zakariyya ibn Muḥammad al-Anṣārī.* 4 vols. Beirut: Dār al-Kutub al-ʿIlmiyya, 2007.

Arberry, Arthur John. *The Doctrine of the Ṣūfīs.* Cambridge: Cambridge University Press, 1935.

Arberry, Arthur John. "Khargūshī's Manual of Ṣūfism." *Bulletin of the School of Oriental Studies* 9, no. 2 (1938): 345–49.

Arberry, *Pages* = Arberry, Arthur John. *Pages from the Kitāb al-Lumaʿ of Abū Naṣr al-Sarrāj being the Lacuna in the Edition of R. A. Nicholson.* London: Luzac, 1947.

Arberry, Arthur John. *Sufism. An Account of the Mystics of Islam.* London and New York: Routledge, 2008. First published in 1950.

ʿArūsī, *Natāʾij* = ʿArūsī, ʿMuṣṭafā, al-. *Ḥāshiyat al-ʿallāma Muṣṭafā al-ʿArūsī al-musammā Natāʾij al-afkār al-qudsiyya fī bayān maʿānī sharḥ al-risāla al-qushayriyya li-shaykh al-islām Zakariyya ibn Muḥammad al-Anṣārī.* 4 vols. Beirut: Dār al-Kutub al-ʿIlmiyya, 2007.

Asín Palacios, Miguel. "El símil de los castillos y moradas del alma en la mística islámica y en Santa Teresa." *Al-Andalus* 2 (1946): 263–74.

Attar, Farid ud-Din. *The Conference of the Birds.* Translated by Afkham Darbandi and Dick Davis. London: Penguin, 1984.

ʿAṭṭār, Farīd al-Dīn al-. *Tadhkirat al-awliyāʾ.* Arabic translation by Manāl al-Yamanī ʿAbd al-ʿAzīz. 2 vols. Cairo: al-Hayʾa al-Miṣriyya li-l-Kitāb, 2009.

Avery, Kenneth S. *A Psychology of Early Sufi Samāʿ. Listening and Altered States.* London and New York: RoutledgeCurzon, 2004.

Avery, Kenneth S. *Shiblī. His Life and Thought in the Sufi Tradition.* New York: State University of New York Press, 2014.

Badawī, ʿAbd al-Raḥmān al-. *Shaṭaḥāt al-ṣūfiyya.* Kuwait: Wikālat al-Maṭbūʿāt, 1978.

Bell, Joseph Norment. *Love Theory in Later Hanbalite Islam.* Albany: State University of New York Press, 1979.

Bisṭāmī, Abū Yazīḍ al-. *al-Majmūʿa al-ṣūfiyya al-kāmila.* Edited by Qāsim Muḥammad ʿAbbās-Damascus: al-Madā, 2004.

Böwering, Gerhard. "Early Sufism between Persecution and Heresy." In *Islamic Mysticism Contested,* edited by Frederick de Jong and Bernd Radtke, 45–67. Leiden: Brill, 1999.

Böwering, Gerhard, and Bilal Orfali, eds. *Sufi Treatises of Abū ʿAbd al-Raḥmān al-Sulamī.* Beirut: Dar el-Machreq, 2009.

Bukhārī, Muḥammad al-. *Saḥīḥ.* Beirut and Damascus: Dār Ibn Kathīr, 2002.

Bukhārī, Muḥammad al-. *Ṣaḥīḥ.* Edited by L. Krehl and Th. W. Juynboll. 4 vols. Leiden: Brill, 1862–1908.

Buhl, F. "ʿĀd." In *Encyclopedia of Islam*[2,] 1:169. Leiden: Brill, 1960.

Būnī, Aḥmad ibn ʿAlī al-. *Shams al-maʿārif al-kubrā.* Cairo: Dār al-Maḥajjāt al-Bayḍāʾ, 2011.

Chabbi, Jacqueline. "Remarques sur le développement historique des mouvements ascétiques et mystiques au Khurasan." *Studia Islamica* 46 (1977): 5–72.

Chiabotti, Francesco, and Martin Nguyen. "The Textual Legacy of Abū l-Qāsim al-Qušayrī: A Bibliographic Record." *Arabica* 61 (2014): 339–95.

Chittick, William C. *The Sufi Path of Love: The Spiritual Teachings of Rumi.* Albany: State University of New York Press, 1983.

Chittick, William C. *The Sufi Path of Knowledge: Ibn Arabi's Metaphysics of Imagination.* New York: State University of New York, 1989.

Chittick, William C. "The Pivotal Role of Love in Sufism." In *Eranos Jahrbuch 2009–2010–2011: Love on a Fragile Thread,* edited by Fabio Merlini, Lawrence E. Sullivan, Riccardo Bernardini, and Kate Olson, 255–73. Einsiedeln: Daimon Verlag, 2012.

Chittick, William C. *Divine Love: Islamic Literature and the Path to God.* New Haven, CT: Yale University Press, 2013.

Chittick, William C. "Love in Islamic Thought." *Religion Compass* 8/7 (2014): 229–38.

Clouston, William Alexander, ed. *Arabian Poetry for English Readers.* Glasgow: McLaren and Son, 1881.

Dhahabī, Abū ʿAbd Allāh al-. *Siyar aʿlām al-nubalāʾ.* Edited by Ḥassān ʿAbd al-Mannān. Beirut: Bayt al-Afkār al-Duwaliyya, 2004.

Deladrière, Roger. *Junayd, Enseignement spirituel, traités, lettres, oraisons et sentences.* Paris: Sindbad, 1983.

Encyclopaedia of Islam.[2] 11 vols. Leiden: Brill, 1960–2002.

Ernst, Carl W. *Words of Ecstasy in Sufism.* Kuala Lumpur: S. Abdul Majeed and Co., 1994.

Ernst, Carl W. *The Shambala Guide to Sufism.* Boston and London: Shambala, 1997.

Franke, Patrick. *Begegnung mit Khiḍr: Quellenstudien zum Imaginären im traditionellen Islam.* Beirut and Stuttgart: Franz Steiner, 2000.

Ghazālī, Abū Ḥāmid al-. *Iḥyāʾ ʿulūm al-dīn.* 5 vols. Beirut: Dār al-Maʿrifa, n.d.

Jīlāni, ʿAbd al-Qādir al-. *al-Maqālāt al-dhawqiyya lil-imām al-Kīlānī.* Edited by Mīʿād Sharaf al-Dīn al-Kīlānī. Beirut: Dār al-Kutub al-ʿIlmiyya, 2011.

Gramlich, Richard. *Das Sendschreiben al-Qušayri's über das Sufitum.* Wiesbaden: Franz Steiner Verlag, 1989.

Gramlich, Richard. *Schlaglichter über das Sufitum. Abū Naṣr al-Sarrāǧs Kitāb al-lumaʿ.* Stuttgart: Franz Steiner, 1990.

Gramlich, Richard. *Alte Vorbilder des Sufitums.* 2 vols. Wiesbaden: Harrassowitz, 1995.

Ḥallāj, Ḥusayn b. Manṣūr al-. *Dīwān al-Ḥallāj.* Edited by Muḥammad Bāsil ʿUyūn al-Sūd. Beirut: Dār al-Kutub al-ʿIlmiyya, 2007.

Harawī, ʿAbd Allāh al-. *Manāzil al-sāʾirīn.* Beirut: Dār al-Kutub al-ʿIlmiyya, 1988.

Ḥifnī, ʿAbd al-Munʿim al-. *al-Mawsūʿa al-ṣūfiyya.* Cairo: Madbūlī, 2006.

Hinds, Martin. "Miḥna." In *The Encyclopaedia of Islam*[2], 8:2–6. Leiden: Brill, 1993.

Hujwírí, ʿAlí b. ʿUthmán. *The Kashf al-Maḥjúb. The Oldest Persian Treatise on Sufism.* Translated by Reynold A. Nicholson. London: Luzac, 1911.

Hurvitz, Nimrod. "Miḥna as Self-Defense," *Studia Islamica* 92 (2001): 93–111.

Ibn al-ʿAbbās, Abd Allāh. *Tanwīr al-miqbās min tafsīr Ibn ʿAbbās.* Beirut: Dār al-Kutub al-ʿIlmiyya, 1992.

Ibn ʿArabī, Abū ʿAbd Allāh Muḥammad. *al-Futūḥāt al-makkiyya.* 4 vols. Cairo: Dār al-Kutub al-ʿArabiyya al-Kubrā, n.d.

Ibn ʿArabī, Abū ʿAbd Allāh Muḥammad. *The Bezels of Wisdom.* Translation and introduction by R. W. J. Austin. Toronto: Paulist Press, 1980.

Ibn Khamīs, *Manāqib al-abrār wa-maḥāsin al-akhyār.* Edited by Muḥammad Adīb al-Jādir. Abu Dhabi: Markaz Zayed li-l-turāth wa-l-tārīkh, 2006.

Ibn Kathīr, ʿImād al-Dīn Abū l-Fidāʾ Ismāʿīl. *al-Bidāya wa-l-nihāya.* Edited by ʿAbd Allāh b. ʿAbd al-Muḥsin al-Turkī. 14 vols. Cairo: Dār Hajr, 1998.

Ibn Māja, Abū ʿAbd Allāh Muḥammad. *Sunan.* Edited by Rāʾid b. Ṣabrī b. Abī ʿAlfa. Riyād: Dār al-Ḥaḍāra, 2015.

Ibn Manẓūr, Muḥammad ibn Mukarram. *Lisān al-ʿarab.* Edited by ʿAbdallah ʿAlī al-Kabīr, Cairo: Dār al-Maʿārif, no date.

Ibn Taymiyya, Taqī l-Dīn Aḥmad. *Kitāb al-ṣafadiyya.* Edited by Muḥammad Rashād Sālim. 2 vols. [Cairo], 1986.

Iványi, Tamás. "Qabḍ and basṭ: On the History of Two Ṣūfī Terms." *Arabist* 30 (2012): 67–83.

Izutsu, Toshihiko. *Creation and the Timeless Order of Things.* Ashland, OR: White Cloud Press, 1994.

Junayd, Abū l-Qāsim al-. *Rasāʾil.* Edited by Jamāl Rajab al-Saydabī. Damascus and Beirut: Dār Iqraʾ, 2005.

Junayd, Abū l-Qāsim al-. *Tāj al-ʿārifīn. Aʿmāl kāmila li-l-Junayd al-Baghdādī.* Edited by Suʿād Ḥakīm. 3rd ed. Cairo: Dār al-Shurūq, 2007.

Kalābādhī, Abū Bakr Muḥammad ibn Isḥāq al-. *Traite de soufisme.* Translated by Roger Deladrière. Paris: Sindbad, 1981.

Kalābādhī, *Doctrine of the Sufis* = Kalābādhī, Abū Bakr Muḥammad ibn Isḥāq al-. *Kitāb al-taʿarruf li-madhhab ahl al-taṣawwuf.* Edited by Arthur John Arberry. Cairo: al-Khānjī, 1994.

Karamustafa, Ahmet T. *Sufism. The Formative Period.* Edinburgh: Edinburgh University Press, 2007.

Khalil, Atif. "Abū Ṭālib al-Makkī and the Nourishment of Hearts *(Qūt al-qulūb)* in the Context of Early Sufism," *Muslim World* 102, no. 2 (2012): 1–22.

Khalil, Atif. "Contentment, Satisfaction and Good-Pleasure: *Rida* in Early Sufi Moral Psychology." *Studies in Religion* 43, no. 3 (2014): 371–89.

Khalil, Atif. *Repentance and Return to God.* Albany: State University of New York Press, 2019.

Kharkūshī, *Revision of the Secrets* = Kharkūshī, Abū Saʿīd ʿAbd al-Malik al-. *Tahdhīb al-asrār fī uṣūl al-taṣawwuf.* Edited by Bassām Muḥammad Bārūd. Abu Dhabi: al-Majmaʿ al-Thaqāfī, 1999.

Knysh, Alexander. *Islamic Mysticism. A Short History.* Leiden: Brill, 2000.
Lane, Edward William. *Arabic-English Lexicon.* 2 vols. Cambridge, UK: Islamic Texts Society, 1992.
Lewisohn, Leonard. "The Way of *Tawakkul:* The Ideal of 'Trust in God' in Classical Persian Sufism." *Islamic Culture* 53, no. 2 (1992): 27–62.
Lewisohn, Leonard. "Tawakkul." In *The Encyclopaedia of Islam*[2]. Leiden: Brill, 2000, 10:376–78.
López-Baralt, Luce. *Islam in Spanish Literature: From the Middle Ages to the Present.* Leiden: Brill, 1992.
Lumbard, Joseph E. B. "From 'Ḥubb' to ''Ishq': The Development of Love in Early Sufism." *Journal of Islamic Studies* 18, no. 3 (2007): 345–85.
Maçoudi. *Les prairies d'or. Texte et traduction par C. Barbier de Meynard et Pavet de Courteille.* Paris: Impr. Impériale, 1861.
Makkī, Abū Ṭālib al-. *Qūt al-qulūb fī muʿāmalat al-maḥbūb wa-waṣf ṭarīq al-murīd ilā maqam al-tawḥīd.* Edited by Maḥmūd b. Ibrāhīm al-Raḍwānī. 3 vols. Cairo: Dār al-Turāth, 2001.
Massignon, Louis. *La Passion de Husayn Ibn Mansûr Hallâj.* 4 vols. Paris: Gallimard, 1975.
Melchert, Christopher. "Religious Policies of the Caliphs from al-Mutawakkil to al-Muqtadir, A. H. 232–295/A. D. 847–908." *Islamic Law and Society* 3, no. 3 (1996): 316–42.
Melchert, Christopher. "Sufis and Competing Movements in Nishapur." *Iran* 39 (2001): 237–47.
Melchert, Christopher. "Abū Nuʿaym's Sources for Ḥilyat al-awliyā', Sufi and Traditionist." In *Les Maîtres soufis et leurs disciples,* edited by G. Gobillot and J.-J. Thibon, 145–59. Beirut: Presses de l'Ifpo, 2012.
Mojaddedi, Jawid A. "Legitimizing Sufism in al-Qushayri's Risala." *Studia Islamica* 90 (2000): 37–50.
Mojaddedi, Jawid A. *The Biographical Tradition in Sufism.* Richmond, UK: Curzon, 2001.
Mojaddedi, Jawid A. "Getting Drunk with Abū Yazīd or Staying Sober with Junayd: The Creation of a Popular Typology of Sufism." *Bulletin of the School of Oriental and African Studies* 66, no. 1 (2003): 1–13.
Mukram, ʿAbd al-ʿĀl Sālim and Aḥmad Mukhtār ʿOmar, eds. *Muʿjam al-qirā'āt al-qur'āniyya.* 8 vols. Kuwait: Jāmiʿat al-Kuwayt, 1988.
Muslim, Ibn al-Ḥajjāj. *Ṣaḥīḥ.* Edited by Muḥammad Fu'ād ʿAbd al-Bāqī. 5 vols. Beirut: Dār al-Kutub al-ʿIlmiyya, 1991.
Nawas, John A. "A Reexamination of Three Current Explanations for al-Ma'mūn's Introduction of the Miḥna." *International Journal of Middle Eastern Studies* 26 (1994): 615–29.
Nawas, John A. "The Miḥna of 218 A. H./833 A. D. Revisited: An Empirical Study." *Journal of the American Oriental Society* 116, no. 4 (1996): 698–708.

Nguyen, Martin. *Sufi Master and Qur'an Scholar: Abū l-Qāsim al-Qushayrī and the Laṭā'if al-Ishārāt.* Oxford: Oxford University Press and Institute of Ismaili Studies, 2012.

Nicholson, Reynold A. *The Mystics of Islam.* Bloomington: World Wisdom, 2002. Originally published in London: G. Bell and Sons, 1914.

Niffarī, Muḥammad ibn ʿAbd al-Jabbār al-. *Kitāb al-mawāqif.* Edited by Arthur John Arberry. London: Messrs and Luzac, 1935.

Nwyia, Paul. "Textes mystiques inédits d'Abū-l-Ḥasan al-Nūrī." *Mélanges de l'Université Saint-Joseph* 46 (1968): 117–54.

Nwyia, Paul. *Exégèse coranique et langage mystique.* Paris: Université de Paris, 1970.

Pickthall, Muḥammad Marmaduke. *The Meaning of the Glorious Koran.* Tripoli: Islamic Call Society, 1973.

Rustom, Mohammed. "Approaches to Proximity and Distance in Early Sufism." *Mystics Quarterly* 33, no. 1/2 (2007): 1–25.

Qūnawī, ʿAlā al-Dīn ʿAlī ibn Ismāʿīl al-. *Ḥusn al-taṣarruf fī sharḥ kitāb al-taʿarruf li-madhhab ahl al-taṣawwuf.* Österreichische Nationalbibliothek, MS Cod.N.F.289.

Qushayrī, *Treatise,* ed. Zurayq = Abū l-Qāsim al-Qushayrī. *al-Risāla al-qushayriyya fī ʿilm al-taṣawwuf.* Edited by Maʿrūf Zurayq and ʿAlīʿAbd al-Ḥamīd Balṭajī. Beirut: Dār al-Jīl, n.d.

Qushayrī, *Treatise,* ed. Maḥmūd = Abū l-Qāsim al-Qushayrī. *al-Risāla al-qushayriyya fī ʿilm al-taṣawwuf.* Edited by ʿAbd al-Ḥalīm Maḥmūd and Maḥmūd ibn al-Sharīf. Cairo: Dār al-Shaʿb, 1989.

Qushayri, Abu 'l-Qasim al-. *Al-Qushayri's Epistle on Sufism.* English translation by Alexander D. Knysh. Reading: Garnet, 2007.

Bernd Radtke, *Al-Ḥakīm al-Tirmiḏī. Ein islamischer Theosoph des 3./9. Jahrhunderts.* Freiburg: K. Schwarz, 1980.

Radtke, Bernd, and John O'Kane. *The Concept of Sainthood in Early Islamic Mysticism. Two works by Al-Ḥakīm Al-Tirmidhī.* Richmond, UK: Curzon Press. 1996.

Radtke, Bernd. "Some Recent Research on al-Ḥakīm al-Tirmidhī." *Der Islam* 83 (2006): 39–89.

Ridgeon, Lloyd. *Awḥad al-Dīn Kirmānī and the Controversy of the Sufi Gaze.* London: Routledge, 2019.

Rippin, A. "Tafsīr." In *The Encyclopaedia of Islam²*, edited by Peri J. Bearman, 10:83–88. Leiden: Brill, 2000.

Ritter, Hellmut. "Muslim Mystics Strife with God." *Oriens* 5, no. 1 (1952): 1–16.

Salamah-Qudsi, Arin Shawkat. "The Idea of Tashabbuh in Sufi Communities and Literature of the Late 6th/12th and early 7th/13th Century in Baghdad." *Al-Qanṭara* 32, no. 1 (2011): 175–97.

Salamah-Qudsi, Arin Shawkat. *Sufism and Early Islamic Piety. Personal and Communal Dynamics.* Cambridge: Cambridge University Press, 2019.

Shaʿrānī, ʿAbd al-Wahhāb b. ʿAḥmad al-. *Laṭā'if al-minan wa-l-akhlāq.* Cairo: ʿĀlam al-Fikr, n.d.

Shaʿrānī, ʿAbd al-Wahhāb b. ʿAḥmad al-. *al-Anwār al-qudsiyya fī maʿrifat qawāʿid al-ṣūfiyya.* Edited by Ṭāhā ʿAbd al-Bāqir Surūr and al-Sayyid Muḥammad ʿĪd al-Shādhilī. 2 vols. Beirut: Maktabat al-Maʿārif, 1988.

Sarrāj, *Book of Flashes* = Abū Naṣr ʿAbd Allāh ibn ʿAlī al-Sarrāj. *The Kitab al-Luma fi 'l-Taṣawwuf of Abú Naṣr ʿAbdallah b. ʿAlí al-Sarráj al-Ṭúsí.* Edited by Reynold Alleyne Nicholson. Leiden and London: Brill and Luzac, 1914.

Shayzarī, ʿAbd al-Raḥmān Ibn Naṣr al-. *Rawḍat al qulūb wa-nuzhat al-muḥibb wal-maḥbūb.* Edited by David Semah and George J. Kanazi. Wiesbaden: Harrassowitz, 2003.

Schimmel, Annemarie. *Mystical Dimensions of Islam.* Chapel Hill: University of North Carolina Press, 1975.

Schimmel, Annemarie. *And Muhammad is His messenger. The Veneration of the Prophet in Islamic Piety.* Chapel Hill: University of North Carolina Press, 1985.

Schimmel, Annemarie. "Abū'l Ḥusayn al-Nūrī: Qibla of the Lights." In *The Heritage of Sufism. Classical Persian Sufism from its Origins to Rumi (700–1300),* edited by Leonard Lewisohn, 1:59–64. 2 vols. Oxford: Oneworld, 1999.

Sells, Michael. *Early Islamic Mysticm.* New York and Mahwah, NJ: Paulist Press, 1996.

Sells, Michael. "Bewildered Tongue: The Semantics of Mystical Union in Islam." In *Mystical Union in Judaism, Christianity and Islam: An Ecumenical Dialogue,* edited by Moshe Idel and Bernard McGinn, 87–124. London: Bloomsbury Academic, 2016.

Silvers, Laury. *A Soaring Minaret. Abu Bakr al-Wasiti and the Rise of Baghdadi Sufism.* New York: State University of New York Press, 2010.

Sīrjānī, *Black and White in the Words of Wisdom* = Bilal Orfali and Nada Saav, eds. *Sufism, Black and White. A Critical Edition of Kitāb al-Bayāḍ wa-l-Sawād by Abū l-Ḥasan al-Sīrjānī (d. ca. 470/1077).* Leiden and Boston: Brill, 2012.

Smith, Margaret. *Readings from the Mystics of Islam.* London: Luzac, 1950.

Suhrawardī, Abū l-Najīb al-. *Ādāb al-murīdīn.* Edited by Menahem Milson. Jerusalem: Maʿhad al-Dirāsāt al-Āsiyawiyya wa-l-Ifrīqiyya. al-Jāmiʿa al-ʿIbriyya fī Ūrushalīm al-Quds, 1977.

Suhrawardī, Shihāb al-Dīn. *ʿAwārif al-maʿārif.* Cairo: Dār al-Muqaṭṭam, 2017.

Sulamī, *Generations of the Sufis* = Sulamī, Abū ʿAbd al-Raḥmān Muḥammad al-. *Ṭabaqāt al-ṣūfiyya.* Cairo: al-Khānjī, 1997.

Sulamī, Abū ʿAbd al-Raḥmān Muḥammad al-. *Kitāb ṭabaqāt al-ṣūfiyya. Texte arabe avec une introduction et un index par Johannes Pedersen.* Leiden: Brill, 1960.

Sulamī, Abū ʿAbd al-Raḥmān Muḥammad al-. *Ziyādāt ḥaqā'iq al-tafsīr.* Edited by Gerhard Böwering. Beirut: Dār al-Mashriq. 1995.

Sulamī, *Realities* = Sulamī, Abū ʿAbd al-Raḥmān Muḥammad al-. *Ḥaqā'iq al-tafsīr.* Edited by Sayyid ʿUmrān. 2 vols. Beirut: Dār al-Kutub al-ʿIlmiyya, 2001.

Sulamī, Abū ʿAbd al-Raḥmān Muḥammad al-. *Les générations des Soufis.* Translated by Jean-Jacques Thibon. Leiden: Brill, 2019.

Sviri, Sara. "Hakim Tirmidhi and the Malamati movement in Early Sufism." In *The Heritage of Sufism. Classical Persian Sufism from its Origins to Rumi (700–1300),* edited by Leonard Lewisohn, 1:583–613. 2 vols. Oxford: Oneworld, 1999.

Sviri, Sara. "The Early Mystical Schools of Baghdad and Nīshāpūr or: In Search of Ibn Munāzil." *Jerusalem Studies in Arabic and Islam* 30 (2005): 450–82.

Sviri, Sara. *Perspectives on Early Islamic Mysticism.* London and New York: Routledge, 2020.

Ṭabarī, *Comfort of the Mystics* = Gerhard Böwering and Bilal Orfali, eds. *The Comfort of the Mystics. A Manual and Anthology of Early Sufism.* Leiden and Boston: Brill, 2013.

Tirmidhī, Abū ʿĪsā Muḥammad b. ʿĪsā al-. *al-Jāmiʿ al-kabīr.* Edited by Bashshār ʿAwwād Maʿrūf. 6 vols. Beirut: Dār al-Gharb al-Islāmī, 1996.

Tirmīdhī, Muḥammad ibn ʿAlī al-Ḥakīm al-. *Bayān al-farq bayna l-ṣadr wa-l-qalb wa-l-fu'ād wa-l-lubb.* Amman: Al-Markaz al-Malakī li-l-Buḥūth wa-l-Dirāsāt al-Islāmiyya, 2012.

Watt, W. Montgomery. "Iram." In *Encyclopedia of Islam*², 3:1270. Leiden: Brill, 1972.

Yāfiʿī, ʿAbd Allāh ibn Asʿad al-. *Nashr al-maḥāsin al-ghāliya fī faḍl al-mashā'ikh al-ṣūfiyya aṣḥāb al-maqāmāt al-ʿāliya.* Beirut: Dār al-Kutub al-ʿIlmiyya, 2000.

Yazaki, Saeko. *Islamic Mysticsm and Abū Ṭālib al-Makkī. The Role of the Heart.* London and New York: Routledge, 2013.

Zamakhsharī, Abū l-Qāsim Maḥmūd b. ʿOmar al-. *Rabīʿ al-abrār wa-nuṣūṣ al-akhbār.* Vol. 3. Beirut: Mu'assasa al-aʿlamī li-l-maṭbūʿāt, 1992.

Zsom, Dora. "Sufi Stories from the Cairo Genizah." *Arabist* 36 (2015): 89–104.

Zsom, Dora. "Sobriety and Intoxication in Mystical Sayings from the Cairo Genizah." In *Contacts and Interactions,* edited by Jaakko Hämeen-Anttila, Petteri Koskikallio, Illkka Lindstedt, 450–93. Leuven: Peeters, 2017.

Index

Abbasid society, 14–16, 88
Abū Ḥamza, 17, 64, 72, 126, 149, 174, 256, 269, 283, 286
Aḥmad al-Ṣūfī, Abū Ismāʿīl, 186
ʿaql (intellect), 30, 79, 221, 235, 253, 256, 261, 282, 283, 285, 287

balā' (trial, tribulation), 123; Nūrī's letter on, 73–74, 203, 205–217, 259; Nūrī's poems on, 85–86, 260, 285; Nūrī's sayings on, 197, 273, 289
Basrī, al-Ḥasan al-, 223
Bisṭāmī, Abū Yazīd al-, 1, 64, 66, 185, 203–205

Cairo Genizah, 10, 14, 74, 203–204, 209, 246, 251, 334n1

Daqqāq, Abū ʿAlī al-Ḥasan al-, 40, 41, 165, 173
dhawq (tasting), 34
dhikr (recollection), 39–42; Nūrī's sayings on, 140, 198, 233, 236, 262, 274, 287, 290; Nūrī's poems on, 39, 41, 45, 144, 254, 264; in the Quran, 40, 106, 116, 147

ecstasy *(wajd, tawājud, wijdān),* 39–43, 46–48, 51–52; 78–79, 140, 142, 160, 176, 184, 198, 244, 249, 254–255, 264, 269, 274, 282–284, 289–290, 306n8; as a sign of intoxication, 1, 7, 169, 204; compared to illness, 84, 98, 137; exhibiting or hiding ecstasy, 3, 42, 54–55, 84–85, 137, 151, 177, 247; love poem inducing ecstasy, 53, 60, 170, 248, 258
ecstatic utterances *(shaṭaḥāt),* 3, 7, 24, 51, 170, 203–204, 243, 246

Fāris al-Dīnawarī, 19
firāsa (intuition), 119, 171–175, 270, 272, 289

Ghazālī, Abū Ḥāmid al-, 55, 165
Ghulām Khalīl 4, 15, 16, 62, 64–65, 76, 83, 98, 148–149, 155, 170, 184, 244, 249, 259, 263, 266, 270, 284, 288

Ḥallāj, Manṣūr al-, 1, 3, 19, 23, 60, 110, 191, 223
Ḥīrī, Abū ʿUthmān al-, 82, 133, 220
homosexuality, 15–16, 87–90, 194–195

Ibn Ḥanbal, Aḥmad, 15–16

Ibn Isḥāq, Ismāʿīl, 155
Ibn Nujayd, Abū ʿAmr Ismāʿīl, 81, 82, 132, 133
immoderate love (*ʿishq, farṭ al-ḥubb*), 7, 40, 43–44, 46, 254
inner heart (*sirr*), 32, 192, 224–226, 230; Nūrī's poems on, 44, 57–58, 139, 141, 156–157, 257, 265, 268, 269; Nūrī's sayings on, 116, 121, 140, 142, 254, 255, 256, 262, 264, 271
ishāra (allusion), 50, 79, 104, 139–140, 151, 188, 189, 207, 219–220, 264, 287
Ismāʿīlites, 15
ittiḥād, 32, 33, 35

Jaʿfar al-Khuldī, 49, 194
Jaʿfar al-Ṣādiq, 102, 104, 110, 193
jamʿ (reunion), 34–35, 69–70, 254, 257, 260
Junayd, Abū Qāsim al-, 17, 24, 39, 43, 49, 62, 64, 87, 93, 95, 117, 119, 123, 136, 149, 167, 170, 174, 177, 200; as counterpart of Nūrī, 2–3, 44, 169, 261, 267, 271; his opinion on Nūrī, 5, 7, 42, 66, 168, 171, 183–184, 194–196, 255, 271, 273; letters exchanged between him and Nūrī, 10, 14, 73–74, 156–157, 203, 205–217, 259, 269, 274–279; relationship between him and Nūrī, 28–29, 46–47, 78, 84, 85, 98, 155, 163, 251–252, 255

Khawwāṣ, Ibrāhīm al-, 185, 195–196
Khorasan, 3, 49, 82, 133, 143, 295n4
Kirmānī, Shāh Shujāʿ al-Dīn al-, 185, 220, 233

love, 4, 36, 51–55, 57–64, 67, 78, 79, 86, 126, 136, 138, 159, 163, 169, 177–178, 184, 191, 198, 208, 210, 215, 222, 224, 230, 237, 238, 244, 247–248; *maḥabba*, 21, 40, 61, 142, 182, 234, 235; *ḥubb*, 39–40, 222, 233; *wudd*, 40, 222; *widād*, 60, 86; *hayamān* 182. *See also* immoderate love

magic, 65, 75, 115, 173, 222
Ma'mūn, 15
miracles, 65–67, 148, 155, 171, 258, 267, 272, 284
moderateness, 1–7, 51, 67, 75, 77–79, 163, 183, 196, 107, 243–244, 250, 252. *See also* soberness
Muḥāsibī, Ḥārith al-, 168, 223
murīd (seeker, disciple), 72, 89, 113, 160, 161, 185, 189–191, 273, 274, 289, 290, 332n1
Mustamlī, Ismāʿīl al-, 20
Muʿtaḍid, 7
Muʿtamid, 15, 64, 76
Muʿtazila, 15, 30, 91, 92, 174
Muwaffaq, Abū Aḥmad al-, 15, 62–64

Nībājī, Abū ʿAbd Allah al-, 25
Niffarī, Muḥammad ibn ʿAbd al-Jabbār al-, 206
Nishapur, 3, 81, 82, 132, 133, 153, 165

Qarmaṭians, 15
Qūt al-qulūb, 8, 112, 222–223, 297n17

Rābiʿa al-ʿAdawiyya, 223
Raqqa, 15, 155
riḍā (contentment) 38, 45, 94, 147, 151, 180, 230, 233, 234, 254, 263, 270, 287

repentance *(tawba)* 41, 143, 184, 253, 256, 270, 305, 311

samāʿ (audition, mystical concert), 7, 50, 55, 60–61; Junayd on *samāʿ*, 177; Nūrī's sayings on *samāʿ*, 52, 115, 161–162, 175, 256, 271, 283
Samarra, 15
school of Baghdad, 3
Shiblī, Abū Bakr al-, 17, 24, 64, 73–75, 77, 81, 150, 199
Shīʿites, 15, 135, 316n5
soberness, 24, 39, 42–43, 46, 98, 129, 151, 178, 184; sober-drunken dichotomy, 1–3, 6–7, 134, 169–170, 243–247, 251–252. *See also* moderateness
spirit *(rūḥ)*, 21, 87, 95, 120
spiritual struggle *(jihād, mujāhada)*, 45, 95, 143, 196, 255, 283
Suhrawardī, Abū l-Najīb al- (d. 1168), 24, 88–89, 162
sukr (drunkenness), 1, 134, 169
Sumnūn, 40, 64, 199

Tirmīdhī, al-Ḥakīm al-, 4, 192, 193, 221–225
Tustarī, Sahl al-, 97, 107, 162, 223, 316n4

yaqīn (certainty) 34, 68, 79, 140, 151, 193, 221, 254, 256, 259, 262, 270, 287

Zanj slaves, 15
zuhd (asceticism, abstinence), 132, 143, 145, 196, 240, 241, 273, 289

www.ingramcontent.com/pod-product-compliance
Ingram Content Group UK Ltd.
Pitfield, Milton Keynes, MK11 3LW, UK
UKHW041922140426
5217IPUK00014B/267

9 781438 498423